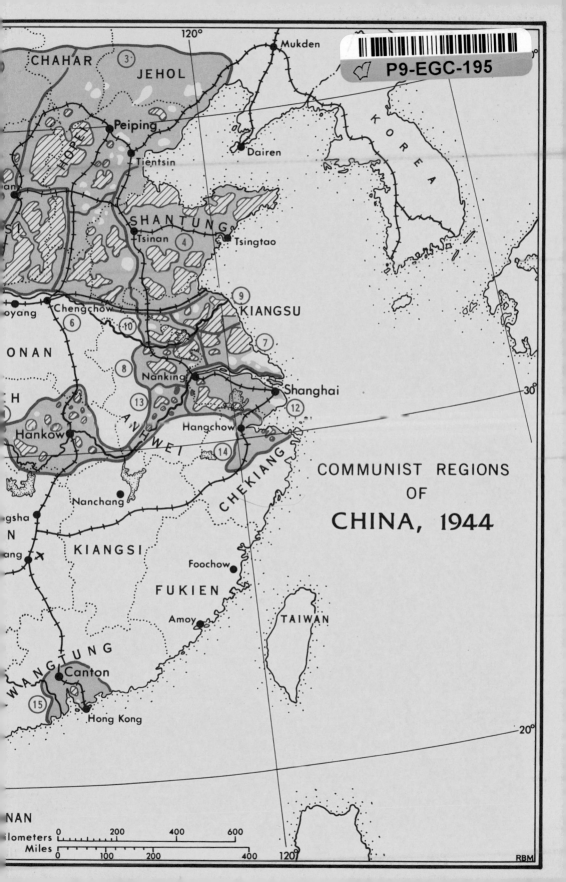

CHAHAR

JEHOL

Peiping

Tientsin

HOPEI

Mukden

Dairen

KOREA

SHANTUNG

Tsinan

Tsingtao

④

③

KIANGSU

⑨

oyang

Chengchow

⑥

⑩

⑦

ONAN

⑧

Nanking

⑬

Shanghai

⑫

Hankow

ANHWEI

Hangchow

⑭

CHEKIANG

Nanchang

COMMUNIST REGIONS
OF
CHINA, 1944

gsha

ang

KIANGSI

Foochow

FUKIEN

Amoy

TAIWAN

ANGTUNG

Canton

⑮

Hong Kong

NAN

| Kilometers | 0 | 200 | 400 | 600 |

| Miles | 0 | 100 | 200 | 400 |

RBM

120°

30°

20°

120°

Lost Chance in China

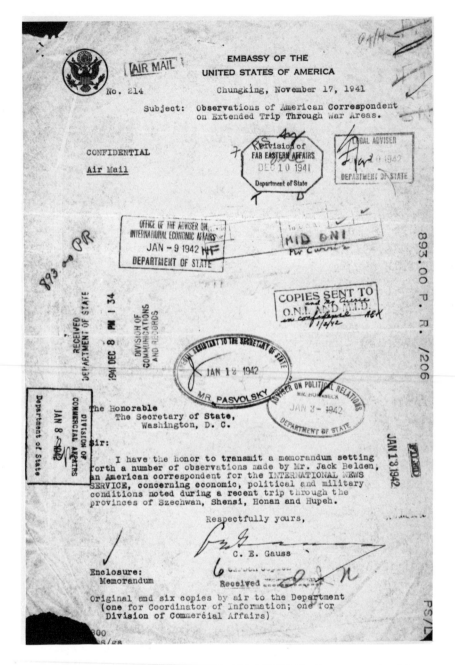

EMBASSY OF THE
UNITED STATES OF AMERICA

No. 214   Chungking, November 17, 1941

Subject: Observations of American Correspondent
on Extended Trip Through War Areas.

CONFIDENTIAL

Air Mail

The Honorable
    The Secretary of State,
        Washington, D. C.

Sir:

        I have the honor to transmit a memorandum setting
forth a number of observations made by Mr. Jack Belden,
an American correspondent for the INTERNATIONAL NEWS
SERVICE, concerning economic, political and military
conditions noted during a recent trip through the
provinces of Szechwan, Shensi, Honan and Hupeh.

                        Respectfully yours,

                        C. E. Gauss

Enclosure:
    Memorandum   Received

Original and six copies by air to the Department
    (one for Coordinator of Information; one for
    Division of Commercial Affairs)

Ambassador Gauss's covering despatch for the first report in this
volume: Service's interview with Jack Belden. Note that the despatch
reached Washington the day after Pearl Harbor and was sent to
Lauchlin Currie in the White House.

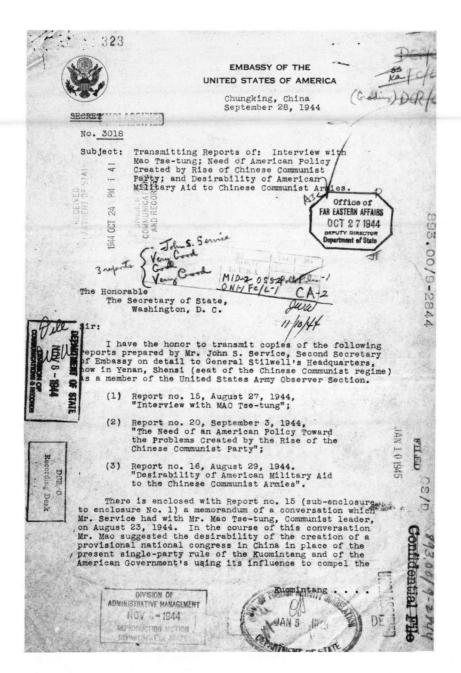

323

**EMBASSY OF THE
UNITED STATES OF AMERICA**

Chungking, China
September 28, 1944

No. 3018

Subject: Transmitting Reports of: Interview with
            Mao Tse-tung; Need of American Policy
            Created by Rise of Chinese Communist
            Party; and Desirability of American
            Military Aid to Chinese Communist Armies.

Office of
FAR EASTERN AFFAIRS
OCT 27 1944
DEPUTY DIRECTOR
Department of State

The Honorable
    The Secretary of State,
    Washington, D. C.

Sir:

I have the honor to transmit copies of the following
reports prepared by Mr. John S. Service, Second Secretary
of Embassy on detail to General Stilwell's Headquarters,
now in Yenan, Shensi (seat of the Chinese Communist regime)
as a member of the United States Army Observer Section.

   (1) Report no. 15, August 27, 1944,
        "Interview with MAO Tse-tung";

   (2) Report no. 20, September 3, 1944,
        "The Need of an American Policy Toward
        the Problems Created by the Rise of the
        Chinese Communist Party";

   (3) Report no. 16, August 29, 1944.
        "Desirability of American Military Aid
        to the Chinese Communist Armies".

There is enclosed with Report no. 15 (sub-enclosure
to enclosure No. 1) a memorandum of a conversation which
Mr. Service had with Mr. Mao Tse-tung, Communist leader,
on August 23, 1944. In the course of this conversation
Mr. Mao suggested the desirability of the creation of a
provisional national congress in China in place of the
present single-party rule of the Kuomintang and of the
American Government's using its influence to compel the

Kuomintang . . . .

*Gauss's despatch transmitting Service's August 27, 1944, interview
with Mao and his two recommendations on policy.*

Lost Chance in China

The World War II Despatches of John S. Service

Edited by Joseph W. Esherick

RANDOM HOUSE / NEW YORK

Library of Congress Cataloging in Publication Data

Service, John S   1909–
Lost chance in China.
"Note on sources": p. xxv.
1. China—Politics and government—1937–1949—Sources.
2. China—Foreign relations—United States—Sources.
3. United States—Foreign relations—China—Sources.
I. Esherick, Joseph W., ed.
II. Title.
DS777.55.S443   320.9'51'042   73–17316
ISBN 0–394–48436–3

To those who chose honesty

Veritas odium parit

No legacy is so rich as honesty.
—Shakespeare,
All's Well That Ends Well

Contents

The Kuomintang Dictatorship

Chiang Kai-shek and the "Royal Family"

Miscellaneous News Items

Critics of the Kuomintang Regime

Introduction

Although politicians have often justified their wars as "the war to end all wars" or the war to bring about "a generation of peace," the fact is that war has a nasty habit of breeding more war. Either the factors which produced war in the first place remain to ensure its future repetition, or in the chaos and bloodshed of battle, new seeds are sown and new forces born which develop into new kinds of wars. In Asia in the middle of the twentieth century, the second pattern would occur. World War II ended the century of struggle between the Great Powers for the domination or division of the Asian continent. Japan was militarily crushed and psychologically scarred by atomic dust, the British quickly beat a diplomatic retreat from Empire, the French spent their blood and treasure and honor to no avail in the jungles of Vietnam, and both Russia and the United States slowly discovered that Asia was too much for either of them. Meanwhile, on the Asian mainland, revolutionary forces of nationalism and Communism rose phoenix-like from the ashes of war—emboldened by the hard-won support of the peasant masses and strengthened by the setbacks of imperialism and its domestic allies during the course of the world war. When the United States decided to commit its economic and military resources to the containment of these popular revolutions, the stage was set for the Cold War in Asia and its hotter by-products—Korea and Vietnam.

Nowhere was this process more evident than in China. The Nationalist Government of Chiang Kai-shek's Kuomintang (KMT) grew weaker with every passing month. Driven by the Japanese attacks of 1937–1938 from its political base in the Westernized treaty ports of the coast, the KMT was forced to rely on the most reactionary groups of inland China.

This made it impossible for the KMT to generate popular support from the impoverished peasantry and caused a growing disillusionment of the small but influential educated groups. The Communists, on the other hand, steadily expanded their base of support in the villages of their Shensi-Kansu-Ninghsia Border Region in the North and the far-spread guerrilla bases in the Japanese rear. Responding creatively to the task of popular resistance to Japan, and capitalizing on the breakdown of the traditional institutions of elite power and authority, the Communists had become, by the war's end, the certain inheritors of China's future.

There were any number of Americans observing and chronicling this transfer of heaven's mandate in China, but none were better trained or better informed than that mandarinate of the U.S. Department of State—the China Service. They were an elite group: skilled in language and knowledgeable in the history and the ways of China. For many of them, China was both a birthplace and a profession. The names of several are well known, especially the names of those who were to endure vilification at the hands of Joe McCarthy and his cohorts in the 1950s. There were John Carter Vincent, O. Edmund Clubb, John Paton Davies, George Atcheson, Raymond P. Ludden, Edward Rice and John Stewart Service. All of these men contributed greatly to the fund of American expertise on China, but it was John S. Service whose reports best spanned the length and breadth of Kuomintang and Communist areas of China in the 1940s.

Jack Service, as he is known to friends, was born in Chengtu, the capital of the West China province of Szechwan on August 3, 1909. His mother and father were missionaries, sent to this distant outpost to establish a branch of the Y.M.C.A. As a boy, young Jack learned to speak the local Szechwanese dialect, but his schooling was at home with his mother, who preferred the Calvert correspondence method to the Canadian-run school that most missionary children attended. He read voraciously and by the age of eleven was packed off to the Shanghai American School for his high school education. There he remained until his parents went back to the United States on furlough. Jack returned with them to his father's home in Berkeley, California, and at the age of fifteen graduated from Berkeley High School. Then, after a year as an architectural draftsman for the Y.M.C.A. in Shanghai and another year traveling back to the United States via Southeast Asia, India and Europe, he entered Oberlin College in the fall of 1927.

At this small Midwestern liberal arts school with its long background of contacts with China, Service majored in economics and the history of art, waited on tables to help support himself, and captained the cross-country and track teams in his senior year. After earning his B.A., he did an extra year of graduate work and then made his decision to enter the Foreign Service. He passed the examinations in 1933, but the Depression meant a long delay in any hope for a career appointment. He decided to sail to China, save the State Department the travel expense, and try to gain an earlier entry into the Foreign Service through the avenue of a clerkship.

Back in China, Service was posted to a clerkship in the American Consulate at Kunming, the capital of Yunnan, in the extreme southwest of China. There he learned the nitty-gritty of Foreign Service work and came in contact with one of the more complex, warlord-ridden provinces of China. He married Caroline Schulz, whom he had met at Oberlin, and the first of their three children was born during these years. In 1935 the Chinese Communists passed almost beneath the walls of Kunming on the Long March, then dashed on north to beat the KMT troops to the Yangtze River. On this occasion Service had no contact with the Communist leaders he later came to know so well. His task was to supervise the safe evacuation of American women and children.

In the fall of 1935 Service was commissioned as a Foreign Service officer and sent to Peking as a language attaché. There he perfected his command of the written language, converted his Szechwanese accent into the more prestigious Pekingese, and studied Chinese history, law and economics. These were exciting years in Peking. Shortly after his arrival Service witnessed the massive student movement of December 9, 1935, in which patriotic youths urged the KMT to a more active resistance to Japanese aggression in Manchuria and North China. Before he left in January 1938, full-scale war had broken out between China and Japan after the Marco Polo

Bridge Incident just a few miles outside the city. Between those two events Service began to know a large number of newspapermen, scholars and military officers who were to play such a vital role in American-Chinese relations and who were ultimately, with Service, to suffer as a result. Among these were Owen Lattimore, Edgar Snow, Joseph W. Stilwell (then military attaché to the U.S. Embassy) and David D. Barrett (Stilwell's assistant and later head of the Dixie Mission to Yenan).

From 1938 to 1941, Service worked in the Shanghai Consulate General, most of the time under Clarence E. Gauss. Then, with the situation in the Far East looking ever more ominous, he was transferred to the Nationalist Chinese capital of Chungking as Third Secretary. Within a month, Gauss was appointed Ambassador and became Service's superior once again. The two worked well together, and Gauss had the greatest regard for his younger colleague (Service was then in his early thirties). On August 1, 1942, at the conclusion of an efficiency report which listed virtually every positive quality a Foreign Service officer could possibly have (". . . tolerant, just, well balanced . . . devoted . . . industrious, cooperative . . . ambitious . . . thorough . . . painstaking . . . good political sense . . . keen in his analysis . . ."), Gauss wrote that "He is the outstanding younger officer who has served me in over 36 years of service."*

Gauss later made this statement of Service's duties:

In Chungking, Mr. Service was a political officer of the Embassy. His job was to cover the waterfront. His job was to get every bit of information that he possibly could, and he went over to the Chungking side of the river every day and he saw everybody that he could. Now it was difficult to get information in those days. We had censorship. They had all these wonderful stories about Chinese victories which never proved to be true . . . Jack Service's job was

---

* This report was read by Gauss during his testimony before the State Department Loyalty Security Board in May 1950. It is printed in *State Department Employee Loyalty Investigation,* Hearings before a Subcommittee of the Committee on Foreign Relations, United States Senate, 81st Congress, 2nd Session, pursuant to S. Res. 231 (Washington, 1950), pp. 2067–68. This Senate subcommittee was the Tydings Committee and this volume is hereafter cited as *Tydings.*

to go to the other side of the river and to see everybody that he could. He would see the foreign press people. He saw the Chinese press people. He saw anybody in any of the embassies or legations that were over there that were supposed to know anything. He saw any people in the foreign office or any of the other ministries. He went to the Kuomintang headquarters and talked with whomever he could see there. He went to the *Ta Kung Pao* . . . which was the independent newspaper. . . . He went to the Communist head-quarters. He associated with everybody and anybody in Chungking that could give him information, and he pieced together this puzzle that we had constantly before us as to what was going on in China, and he did a magnificent job at it.*

Naturally, Service's wide-ranging contacts did not endear him to the KMT, and Gauss once heard to his annoyance that Generalissimo Chiang Kai-shek had complained about Foreign Service officers visiting the Chinese Communists. The Ambassador urged Service to continue, and as a result Service became, in Gauss's words, "our governmental authority on Chinese communism."†

Not all of Service's work was in Chungking. In fact, he spent almost half of his time traveling in the field. There were trips through Burma, to central Szechwan, to the Northwest, to a "listening post" in Kansu, along the Indochina border and finally to the Communist capital of Yenan. Some of these trips were made while Service was still attached to the Embassy. Others were made after August 1943 when Gauss was in a hospital in California and (in the Ambassador's words) ". . . the Army grabbed him and attached him to military headquarters."‡ It was this attachment to the military which, in July 1944, allowed Service to accompany the United States Army Observer Section—the Dixie Mission—to Yenan. As the Foreign Service's expert on the Chinese Communist Party (CCP) he was the natural choice for the job.

As the documents printed in this volume show, Service became, in 1944–1945, the advocate of a distinct policy position. He was, of course, not alone in this: the most critical policy recommendation drafted by him was signed, in Febru-

---

* *Tydings*, pp. 2064–65.
† *Ibid.*, p. 2067.
‡ *Ibid.*, p. 2063.

ary 1945, by every political officer of the Embassy in Chungking. What Service and the others were suggesting was above all a need for *realism* in our relations with China. Their observations of both the KMT and the CCP convinced them that China was rushing toward a civil war in which the Communists would be the certain victor. They urged the necessity of freeing the United States from a position of exclusive support of the KMT. Such support both increased KMT intransigence and disinclination to either reform itself or compromise with the Communists, and ensured that the Communists, when they ultimately triumphed, would have every reason for unremitting hostility toward the United States. The Foreign Service officers recommended that we instead follow a policy similar to Allied policy toward Yugoslavia: aid those, including the Communists, who were actively fighting the enemy. Thus, while the war tipped the internal Chinese political balance in favor of the Communists, it also provided a rationale for a flexible American policy. Those final years of war were perhaps the last best hope for friendly U.S. relations with the Chinese Communists.

The policy of Service and the others was rejected. President Franklin D. Roosevelt gave the nod in the last months of his life to the policy of Major General Patrick J. Hurley. Hurley had succeeded Gauss as Ambassador to China in November 1944 and adhered to a policy of unilateral support for Generalissimo Chiang Kai-shek. In the spring of 1945, Hurley was in Washington for consultations. When he learned of the February recommendation of his Embassy staff, Hurley had Service and the others recalled from China. Then, in November 1945, Hurley announced his resignation and explained his failure to prevent civil war in China with the claim that "The professional foreign service men sided with the Chinese Communist armed party and the imperialist bloc of nations whose policy it was to keep China divided against itself."* Despite the implausibility of the Communist-imperialist alliance which

---

* From Hurley's letter of resignation to the President, November 26, 1945, in *Foreign Relations of the United States, 1945,* Vol. VII, *The Far East, China* (Washington: Government Printing Office, 1969), p. 723. Volumes in this series are hereafter cited as *Foreign Relations,* followed by the appropriate year.

the Foreign Service officers had allegedly supported, Hurley's charge of pro-Communist sympathies was to dog these men for the rest of their careers. Subsequent elaborations on the theme were to provide McCarthy with all the ammunition he needed. Their policy was held to have caused the "loss of China," yet few paused to consider the fact that their policy was never adopted.

The charges against Service were complicated by the so-called *"Amerasia* affair." Upon his return to Washington in April 1945, Service was introduced to Philip Jaffe, editor of *Amerasia,* a left-leaning fortnightly magazine on contemporary Asia. Nobody warned Service that both Jaffe and the Navy lieutenant who had introduced Service to him were under F.B.I. surveillance on the suspicion of pilfering government documents. It had been a common practice in Chungking to exchange information with and brief journalists on various matters, but when Service, in an admitted indiscretion, loaned Jaffe his personal copies of eight or ten factual memoranda from Yenan he was immediately implicated in the whole affair. Consequently, on June 6, 1945, Service, Jaffe and four others were arrested by the F.B.I. Two months later a grand jury unanimously voted not to indict Service, and a subsequent State Department hearing found him innocent of any wrongdoing. Three others were ultimately indicted and two induced to plead guilty, though the government's case against them was severely tainted by a total of thirteen illegal entries and searches by the F.B.I. and the C.I.A.'s predecessor, the O.S.S. The *Amerasia* case was, in fact, an early example of the sort of "national security" breaking-and-entering operation which the F.B.I. and the O.S.S. began and which culminated in Nixon's "plumbers" and the Watergate and Ellsberg's psychiatrist operations. And, as in the Ellsberg case, the principal fear of the government was that leaked official documents might support the arguments of journalistic critics on the left.

From 1945, loyalty and security hearings became almost an annual event for Service. He was cleared in 1946, 1947, 1949, 1950 and 1951, but then, with McCarthy and the congressional China lobby clamoring for some State Department blood, the Civil Service Loyalty Review Board took up Service's case (on which the State Department board had just rendered its sixth favorable ruling) and offered its own verdict, on December 13, 1951, with this bit of tortured logic:

We are not required to find Service guilty of disloyalty, and we do not do so, but for an experienced and trusted representative of our State Department to so far forget his duty to his trust as his conduct with Jaffe so clearly indicates, forces us with great regret to conclude that there is reasonable doubt as to his loyalty. The favorable finding of the Loyalty Security Board is accordingly reversed.*

That same day, Secretary of State Dean Acheson dismissed Service. Both the Loyalty Review Board's action in taking up the case and Acheson's action in firing Service after a *favorable* decision by the Department board were, however, contrary to existing regulations, and in 1957 the Supreme Court in *Service* v. *Dulles* unanimously ruled in Service's favor.

That the ostensible reason for Service's dismissal was his behavior in the *Amerasia* affair was in fact irrelevant. Sooner or later McCarthy and the China lobby would have forced the State Department to dispense with him, just as they eventually caused the dismissal of John Carter Vincent and John Paton Davies and induced the retirement of O. Edmund Clubb, none of whom had anything to do with the *Amerasia* affair. The fact is, these were the men who had predicted the defeat of Chiang Kai-shek, had counseled against tying the United States to Chiang and the KMT, and had advocated a policy which would allow the United States to live at peace with the Chinese Communists. Ever since the publication of some of these views in the China White Paper of 1949, the China lobby had dedicated itself to ridding the State Department of such dangerous opinions. It was, in fact, for the perceptive and prophetic analyses shown in the reports published here that Service was dismissed from the Foreign Service, and not for any indiscretion committed with Jaffe in 1945.

There are at least two reasons for publishing these despatches at this time. In the first place, they provide a vivid

* Quoted in Ross Koen, *The China Lobby in American Politics* (New York: Macmillan, 1960), p. 210.

picture of China at war as seen through the eyes of one exceedingly astute and literate observer. Their range is fantastic: from the hardships of peasant life to the gossip of Chungking, to the politics and economy of the Communist Border Region and the most clear and explicit statements by Mao Tse-tung on Communist policy, and Mao's hopes for the future of Sino-American relations. Here is a vivid, firsthand view of China at the very moment when the East was turning Red. It is, furthermore, a view which the best recent scholarship has confirmed as essentially correct. Books by scholars of all political persuasions, from Chalmers Johnson's *Peasant Nationalism and Communist Power* to Mark Selden's *The Yenan Way,* have shown Service's analyses to be capable of standing the test of time.

Second, and even more important, these reports and these policy recommendations suggest that World War II in Asia need *not* have led directly to a Sino-American Cold War. Here, indeed, was an alternative policy which might have been able to avert many of the subsequent catastrophes that have beset the United States in her relations with Asia. Had policy makers in Washington only been able to recognize the fatal weaknesses of the KMT, the burgeoning strength of the CCP and the clear desire of the latter to avoid any postwar conflict with the United States, then decades of Sino-American hostility might have been avoided. Instead of Nixon in Peking in 1972, we might even have had Eisenhower going there (and not to Korea) two decades earlier. Such, at least, was the suggestion of any number of historians, journalists and editorialists, once Nixon's visit to China popularized the notion that accommodation with Peking was not a naïve hope but a realistic policy.*

One can, of course, play with such "ifs" ad infinitum.

---

* See, for example, Barbara W. Tuchman, "If Mao Had Come to Washington: An Essay in Alternatives," *Foreign Affairs* (October 1972); E. J. Kahn's "Foresight, Nightmare, and Hindsight," a Profile of Jack Service in *The New Yorker* (April 8, 1972); Service's own *The Amerasia Papers: Some Problems in the History of US–China Relations;* and the *New York Times* article (January 31, 1973) and editorial (February 4) on the occasion of a luncheon in honor of Service and the other "old China hands" at the Foreign Service Association in Washington.

But that is hardly the point. Rather, the point is that the sort of policy Service and the others were recommending was soundly based on a clear understanding of the political realities of China in 1944–1945. That understanding was in turn based on an appreciation of the fact that despite any KMT superiority in military hardware, the political strength of the CCP in the countryside of China made it an indomitable revolutionary force. This book shows that if the United States, or any other power, ignores again the popular strength and appeal of Asian peasant revolutions, it will do so at its own peril.

In this volume are published all or portions of seventy-one despatches and memoranda written by Service. Even this substantial total represents less than one half of the signed despatches which I have been able to locate. The best are printed here. They cover the years 1941–1945 and include factual reports on both the KMT and CCP areas, analytical assessments of the strengths and weaknesses of the two parties, and recommendations for U.S. policy. Of these despatches, twenty-six have never before been published. I am particularly indebted to Dr. Milton O. Gustafson of the National Archives and Donald J. Simon of the State Department Records Services Division for their assistance in obtaining copies of many of these unpublished reports.

The despatches printed here were not, of course, written with any expectation that they would ever be collected into a book. Service himself would be the first to admit that they were often composed in great haste and inevitably contain both minor inaccuracies and undigested information. More important, each despatch was designed to be coherent in and of itself and might, therefore, repeat information included in separate despatches. Others were summary despatches, obviously written with the hope that they might reach higher policy makers who would not have read the day-to-day descriptive and analytical despatches. Consequently, considerable redundancies appear when all the despatches are bound together in a single volume. In order to keep the size of this volume within reasonable limits, such redundancies and some details of less enduring historical significance have been eliminated. Still, despatches have been printed in their entirety wherever practicable, and thirty-five of them are complete.

Though the arrangement of the despatches in this volume generally reflects the progress of Service's career in China, no attempt has been made to adhere to a strict chronological arrangement of the reports. Instead, despatches are grouped under broad topical headings, with some attempt to preserve chronological order within any given heading. There is also a tendency to place summary despatches at the end of a particular section. Consequently, some readers particularly interested in Chinese Communism and Sino-American relations might want to skip portions of Part I, which deals with the KMT, and start with the long summary despatch of June 20, 1944, entitled "The Situation in China and Suggestions Regarding American Policy."

Needless to say, I, as editor, am fully responsible for any statements or misstatements in this Introduction, in the Epilogue or in the introductions to the individual reports which follow. I would be most remiss, however, if I did not thank Jack Service himself for allowing me to pester him during and after his work at the University of California's Center for Chinese Studies, and for long hours of interviews in September and December 1972 which provided much of the background for my introductions to his reports. In some cases, I have quoted directly from Service's comments in these interviews and incorporated his words in the introductory passages. With the exception of those direct quotations, however, all save the despatches themselves is the work and the responsibility of the editor.

J. W. E.

Note on Sources

The despatches and memoranda printed in this volume have been collected from a variety of sources. Wherever possible, they have been checked for authenticity against other available copies, and the most complete and accurate version has been printed. It should be noted, however, that in no cases do other printed versions of the documents appear to have been deliberately distorted. In particular, the two volumes of *The Amerasia Papers,* published by the Senate Committee on the Judiciary from motives quite hostile to Mr. Service, seem to have been set in type directly from photostatic copies of the original documents. Such errors as exist are purely typographical. In this volume, the documents have been altered only in order to correct spelling, grammar and typographical errors.

In identifying the source of individual documents, the following abbreviated titles are used:

AMERASIA PAPERS   Subcommittee to Investigate the Administration of the Internal Security Act and Other Internal Security Laws of the Committee on the Judiciary, United States Senate: *The Amerasia Papers: A Clue to the Catastrophe of China,* 2 vols. paginated consecutively (Washington: Government Printing Office, 1970).

FOREIGN RELATIONS, *1942   Foreign Relations of the United States, Diplomatic Papers: 1942, China* (Washington: Government Printing Office, 1956).

FOREIGN RELATIONS, *1943   Foreign Relations of the United States, Diplomatic Papers: 1943, China* (Washington: Government Printing Office, 1957).

FOREIGN RELATIONS, *1944*   *Foreign Relations of the United States, Diplomatic Papers: 1944,* Vol. IV, *China* (Washington: Government Printing Office, 1967).

FOREIGN RELATIONS, *1945*   *Foreign Relations of the United States, Diplomatic Papers: 1945,* Vol. VII, *The Far East, China* (Washington: Government Printing Office, 1969).

SERVICE   John S. Service, *The Amerasia Papers: Some Problems in the History of US-China Relations* (Berkeley: Center for Chinese Studies, 1971).

TYDINGS   *State Department Employee Loyalty Investigation,* Hearings before a Subcommittee of the Committee on Foreign Relations of the United States Senate, 81st Congress, 2nd Session, pursuant to S. Res. 231, Part 2: Appendix (Washington: Government Printing Office, 1950).

ARCHIVES COPY   from the files of the State Department housed in the National Archives in Washington. (The number following these references is the State Department file number.)

STATE SECURITY COPY   from the file of Service's despatches compiled for Service's hearing before the State Department's Loyalty Security Board, and kept in the Security Office of the State Department.

PERSONAL COPY   from duplicate copies in the possession of John S. Service.

Note on Romanization

Chinese proper names appearing in this volume have generally been transcribed according to the modified Wade-Giles system of romanizing Mandarin Chinese, which has become standard in publications on China. With the exception of certain conventional spellings of prominent figures (Sun Yat-sen, Chiang Kai-shek, T. V. Soong and H. H. Kung), the editor has adhered strictly to this Wade-Giles system, and, where appropriate, Service's spellings of proper names have been altered to conform to the Wade-Giles system.

As a brief guide to the reader interested in pronouncing Chinese names correctly, the following rough English equivalents are given for some of the most commonly mispronounced Chinese sounds and names appearing in this book.

VOWELS:

a (of W*a*ng, etc.) as in f*a*ther
ai (of P*ai* Ch'ung-hsi) as in b*y*
ao (of M*ao* Tse-tung) as in h*ow*
e (of P'*e*ng T*e*h-huai) as the *u* in *u*p.
i (of Liu Sha*o*-ch'*i*) as the *ee* in ch*ee*se
o (of P*o* Ku) as in *awe*
ou (of Ch*ou* En-lai) as in sl*ow*
uo (of K*uo*mintang) as in sq*ua*wk

CONSONANTS: Here the primary difficulty is created by the aspirated and unaspirated sounds, indicated by the presence or absence of the apostrophe (').

ch' (of *Ch'*en Yi) as in *ch*ar   *ch* (of *Ch*ou) as in *j*ar
k' (of Ch'en Chia-*k'*ang) as in *k*ill   *k* (of *K*uomintang) as in *g*ill

p' (of *P*'eng) as in *p*ie   *p* (of *P*ai) as in *b*uy
t' (of Yeh *T*'ing) as in *t*ell   *t* (of Mao Tse-*t*ung) as in *d*ell
ts (of Mao *T*se-tung) as in be*ds*
j (of Li Tsung-*j*en) resembles the English *r* of *r*un
hs (of Pai Ch'ung-*h*si) resembles the English *sh* of *sh*e

PART I

Kuomintang China

Yet the first bringer of unwelcome news
Hath but a losing office, and his tongue
Sounds ever after as a sullen bell
Remember'd knolling a departing friend.

              —Shakespeare,
              Henry IV, Part II

AN EARLY MEMO

It was the spring of 1941 when John S. Service arrived in Chungking, the wartime capital of China's Kuomintang Government. Pearl Harbor was still seven months away, yet China had already been fighting a full-scale war against Japan for four years. The toll that war was to take from the Chinese people was evident to all, and was a major focus of political reporting from the U.S. Embassy in Chungking. As Third Secretary of Embassy, Service normally drafted despatches for the Ambassador's signature. For the years 1941–1942 there are very few memoranda or despatches actually signed by him. The first on record, and the only one from 1941, is an account of a conversation with the American journalist Jack Belden.* While the observations and views expressed are those of Belden, the topics covered are an indication of Service's own interests: the plight of the peasantry, morale in the army and Kuomintang-Communist relations. Service's subsequent observations on these matters tended to confirm much of what he heard from Belden.

Memorandum for the Ambassador

October 30, 1941
Archives copy: 893.00 P.R./206

During the afternoon and evening of October 29, I had a long talk with Mr. Jack Belden, the International News Service correspondent, who has just returned to Chungking after about six months of travel through the provinces of Szechwan,

---

* Belden subsequently wrote a classic account of the Chinese civil war of 1946–1949, *China Shakes the World* (New York: Harper & Brothers, 1949; reprinted by Monthly Review Press in 1970).

Shensi, Honan and Hupeh. Belden is a friend of some years standing and talked freely. Having his journal with him, he referred to it continually for the actual details of incidents and conditions which he mentioned. He traveled very simply, without official auspices, and, as he speaks Chinese fluently, made a practice of talking to farmers and villagers along the road and in towns where he stayed. These conversations, covering such points as grain requisition, food prices, local conscription practice, and so on, he took pains to record. Although under some suspicion by the Chinese authorities for sympathy with the Chinese Communists, I believe that he is a good observer and has made the most of the rather unusual opportunity which his trip gave him. The following points may be of interest.

Economic Problems

The outstanding problem through most of the areas traveled (in actual occupation by Chinese troops) was food. He felt that there was and would be a definite shortage, the importance of which had not been sufficiently realized.

[The causes Belden listed for the grain shortages are covered in far greater detail in the following despatch, and are thus deleted here.]

He was surprised at the volume of importations from the Japanese-occupied territory. The main center of this trade was a small town on the Hupeh-Anhwei border. He was told that imports to the amount of $30 million* a month passed through there and the traffic on the road, mainly small carts, was the heaviest he had seen on any road in China. One flour miller had even succeeded in bringing German milling machinery in from Tientsin. The Japanese exact "squeeze" but permit this traffic. In the instance just cited the miller admitted having paid $90,000. Some of the trade is in articles needed by the Chinese, such as the machinery just mentioned. But most of

---

* All figures are given in Chinese dollars. At the time, the official value of the Chinese dollar was about 5 U.S. cents, its black-market value about 1 cent. Though the official exchange rate remained substantially unchanged throughout the war, rampant inflation caused the free-market value of the Chinese dollar to fall to 0.06 U.S. cent by the end of the war. (This and all subsequent footnotes have been added by the editor unless explicitly noted otherwise.)

the importation is of cigarettes, with large quantities of luxuries such as toilet articles, cloth, mirrors, etc. also coming in. No evident effort is made to stop this. Prices in this area are much cheaper than in Szechwan, as might be expected.

Land Tax in Kind

He saw no indication of this tax having been put into effect in the districts through which he passed. These districts were already suffering from military requisitions and he did not believe that they could give any more grain as tax. . . .

Military Morale

Morale among the troops seemed, on the whole, to be good. The fighting spirit at Ichang was especially high and he remarked on the cheerfulness of the wounded men on the ship which brought him up river from the Ichang front. However, he found among junior officers, up to the grade of battalion and regimental commanders, some resentment of the widespread spying on them. He was told that every Group Army Headquarters had another separate spying organization which operated independently and made its reports direct to Chungking, and that there were in addition other secret police and political spying organizations. One effect of this pressure was to deny the junior officers privileges and pleasures enjoyed by higher officers. Resentment against spies was so great that they were apt to be shot if they became known. Some high commanders (Li Tsung-jen* was especially mentioned) indicated to him their dislike of and scorn for these secret police activities. Toward the prosecution of the war itself, the morale of the officers was good.

Civilian Morale

Most of Belden's actual investigation—in the form of conversations—was among farmers and villagers along his route. Morale and attitude toward the war varied according to

* Li Tsung-jen was a leader of the Kwangsi Clique, discussed in the despatch on pp. 42–48. After Chiang Kai-shek's resignation as President in 1949, Li served briefly as Acting President of China until the Communist victory was complete. He then moved to the United States, where he lived until 1965, when he returned to the People's Republic of China to die in 1969.

the burden of military food requisitions (comparatively small requisitions in rather poor mountainous country usually held by the Chinese troops being sufficient to bring real hardship to the people) and according to whether or not the people had had the experience of actual invasion by Japanese forces. In parts of Honan where the Japanese had not been the people were outspokenly bitter in their complaints and frankly hoped that the Chinese troops would move on. On the other hand, around Ichang, the peasant morale was high and they cooperated willingly and well in such work as carrying the wounded back from the front.

There was widespread resentment of conscripting, which hit the poorer farm families the hardest. The price of conscripts varied and in some districts was as high as $900.* One village, stated to have "150 families," had been required to give 39 men in 1939, 40 in 1940 and 20 during the first six months of 1941. Sons of the well-to-do escape by payment, by going to school, or by getting minor official posts in the *hsien* [district or "county"] government.

Kuomintang-Communist Relations

He saw no signs of any improvement in Kuomintang-Communist relations. The Communist representative in Loyang appeared to be allowed little freedom. About fifty persons going to Yenan had to wait in Loyang for a long time, some of them for months, before they were allowed to proceed. He talked to officers connected with a military "tribunal" who told him that their work was to suppress and punish members of the "traitor party." They agreed that this included Communists. The three prisoners in their charge at the time were members of the New Fourth Army. One of these was a Japanese Communist who had deserted to and served with the Fourth Army and had been sent by his division commander in an effort to establish liaison with the Kuomintang troops in his area. The man's only crime was apparently his professed belief in Communism (which had led him to desert the Japanese forces and join the Chinese). Another was a young boy

* When the son of a wealthy family was conscripted, the family could purchase a poor peasant to stand in his place. Thus there was a regular market for conscripts, with a definite price structure.

of seventeen who had joined the Fourth Army rather than be conscripted into it.

[Belden] confirmed that medical supplies for the Eighteenth Group (Communist) Army were not being permitted to go through to their destination. He doubted the truth of a recent rumor, which I mentioned, that some supplies from Russia were being delivered by plane directly to the Communist area. (In this connection a recent statement made to me by Mr. A. V. Ravenholt of the International Red Cross may be of interest. When asked whether it was true, as recently said by another relief worker, that the Chinese had been so afraid of medical supplies trickling through to the Communists that for most of the summer there had been practically no movement of supplies north of Kweichow and Yunnan, Ravenholt replied that this was approximately correct. He added that just the evening before, he had been told by the "head of the Chinese Army Medical Service" that in future it would probably be very difficult to move medical supplies north of Szechwan.)

THE PLIGHT OF THE PEASANTRY

Shortly after Service arrived in Chungking, Clarence E. Gauss replaced Nelson T. Johnson as Ambassador to China. With a background of thirty years of consular work in China, Gauss was a meticulous, hard-nosed treaty-port American, often unjustly accused of anti-Chinese attitudes. He was a skeptic by nature, less inclined to accept the propagandistic communiqués and press briefings of the Kuomintang Government. Furthermore, by the spring of 1941 it was becoming increasingly apparent that the American role in China was likely to change from mere observation of Japanese aggression to more active involvement in countering aggression. The Embassy, under Gauss, began to put a new emphasis in independent, firsthand reports from the field so as to develop its own, reliable picture of what was happening in China.

Service, who "hated the monotonous desk work in the Embassy,"* enjoyed getting out into the field. Because of his fluency in Chinese and the local Szechwanese dialect in particular, he was a logical candidate to make such field trips.

Service's experiences in the field were to have a significant impact on his reporting from China. He saw for himself the miseries inflicted on the Chinese people in the Kuomintang-controlled areas of China at war. He saw the starving and haggard refugees from famine. He had young conscripts leap in front of his jeep in hopes of escaping a slow but near-certain death in the Chinese armies. He witnessed the ominous signs of popular discontent and even open rebellion against the Chungking Government. As the son of a missionary, Service often turned to missionaries for information. Many were Catholics or members of the China Inland Mission, whose converts tended to be the poorer members of society. These apolitical C.I.M. fundamentalists had little sense of the import of

* This and all subsequent unattributed direct quotations are statements made by John S. Service in interviews with the editor in September and December 1972.

their own observations, but to Service their tales of rising taxes, forced conscription and corruption in local government had profound political significance. Here in the countryside of China, he witnessed the failure of the Kuomintang and the loss of its mandate to rule.

The next three reports all deal with some aspect of rural distress under the Kuomintang. They cover the years 1942, 1943 and 1944, and the provinces of Honan, Kansu and Szechwan. The first, on "The Famine in Honan Province," was written after Service returned from his first extensive trip to North China in the fall of 1942. He had accompanied a party of engineers and press representatives to inspect oil fields in Northwest China. On his way back to Chungking, Service left the rest of the group to make a side trip to Honan to investigate the reports of famine. There his detailed and precise observations formed the basis for a chilling and prophetic report on the causes and impact of the famine and the inadequacy of the Government's relief efforts.

The Famine in Honan Province*

November 5, 1942
Archives copy: 893.48/3069

Sources of Information

I visited Honan province from October 14 to 17, proceeding from Sian to Loyang by train, spending the 15th and 16th at that city, and then returning to Sian. Conditions in the area traveled through are not good but actual famine except for high prices and crowds of refugees—is not seen. I discussed the situation, however, with many informed persons in Sian and Loyang and was permitted by them to study reports in their possession. These persons include: Mr. Ch'i Ta-p'eng, representative at Sian of the National Relief Commission; members of locally organized Chinese and international relief committees

---

* Service's original memorandum is replete with detailed footnotes. Many of these have been eliminated here, or incorporated into the body of the text.

at Sian; the head of the Chinese Industrial Cooperatives'* organization in Honan; members of an American relief committee at Loyang, including Bishop Megan of the Catholic Church and Mr. Elmer Wampler of the American Brethren Mission; and of course the occasional man in the street and refugee.

Locality

The famine-stricken area is to the west and south of Loyang. Linju, Chengchow, Hsuchang and Yencheng are important centers. This is the "front line" region along the west bank of the new Yellow River. In some places, particularly around Fukou and Weishih, the situation has been made worse by flood after a new opening of the dikes by the Chinese army in an attempt (reportedly unsuccessful) to divert the Yellow River so as to cut off the Japanese foothold established last fall on the west bank of the river at Chungmou. There is also famine on the east bank of the Yellow River but the extent of the area affected is not clearly known.

Numbers Affected

There are various estimates of the population involved. Mr. Ch'i claims that 18 million will suffer to some degree, that 6 million will need help, and that 2 million may starve. The American Committee, whose information is probably more reliable, reports that at least 10 million will be affected, but agrees that about 2 million will be in desperate straits. Some addition to these numbers may be made by migration, as yet small, of famine refugees from the east, Japanese-occupied bank of the Yellow River, where no relief work is being done. Mr. Wampler, who has had considerable experience of famine relief work in China, made the statement that in his opinion the famine would be "less widespread than that of 1921–22 but worse than that of 1928–29."

---

* The Chinese Industrial Cooperatives (also known as Indusco) were organized in support of wartime production by a Sino-foreign group which included missionaries, educators and such liberal journalists as Edgar and Helen Foster Snow. They operated in both Kuomintang and Communist areas, and the Kuomintang tended to regard the organizers of these cooperatives as pro-Communists.

Severity

In the affected areas the 1942 spring wheat harvest was only about 20 percent of what is rated a "normal" crop. The summer crops of kaoliang, millet and barley were a complete failure in some districts but were generally also about 20 percent. Some other crops such as sweet potatoes and peanuts did slightly better, being estimated at 50 percent. And the rains, which broke the long drought about the first of October, helped late crops such as buckwheat and some green vegetables, and permitted the planting of what promises to be a good crop of wheat.

Relief workers state that conditions have not yet reached their worst and believe that food stocks in the province will, generally speaking, last until about the end of the year. The greatest suffering will come in the first four months of 1943 before the wheat can be harvested. Already, however, one hears many reports of districts where the inhabitants are eating grass, bark and roots. And the relief workers are seeing corpses of starved refugees along the roads. The price of a woman (common index in China of hard times) has fallen from about $3,000 to one tenth of that, but that of a conscript, interestingly enough, from $3,000 only to about $2,000.*

Immediate Cause

The immediate cause of the famine is protracted drought during most of 1942 which held the spring and summer crops to about 20 percent. But this statistic is misleading: 100 percent to a Chinese farmer is an unusually good crop, 70–80 percent is normal, and in Honan he can "get along" on 40 percent. Even crops as small as this year's would not cause great hardship in

---

* To the very common saying, alluding to the terrible treatment of conscripts, "It is better to die under the bombs at the front than to endure training in the rear," the Honan farmer has apparently added: "It is also better to starve at home." But to a family in a famine area, there is also a shift in the relative importance of men and women. [Women and especially young girls were often, in hard times, sold to become servants, slaves or prostitutes.] The woman may be one more mouth to feed; the man will be needed to plant and harvest the new crop, he may earn something by selling his strength as a coolie on the labor market, or he may lead the family out of the famine area, pushing the few essential possessions on a wheelbarrow. [Footnote in original.]

normal times because in a rich agricultural area such as Honan there is enough carry-over to enable the farmer to weather one and even two bad seasons.

Background Causes

There would be hunger but no real famine if it were not for the war and its background in Honan of brutal and oppressive treatment of the farmers by their own government and army. This is so obvious that it was mentioned to me by every relief worker, American or Chinese, with whom I talked. Some went so far as to call this "a man-made famine."

As the Embassy has previously reported (accounts of trips by Jack Belden and Graham Peck,* forwarded to the Department by despatch), the condition of the farmers in Honan has been deteriorating for the past several years.

Due to the difficulty in free China of transporting grain (the Japanese hold nearly all important transportation lines), it is the practice to require each area to feed the troops stationed in it. Thus the closer to the front, generally speaking, the larger the number of troops and the greater the impositions on the farmer.

This has been especially true in Honan, which faces the Japanese on three sides, north, south and east. Since the Chinese defeats at Chungtiaoshan (May 1941) and Chengchow (October 1941), the already large numbers of troops in the province have been further increased and are variously estimated by relief workers as now totaling between 500,000 and 1,000,000. They are stationed in the largest numbers in the western section of the province, which is now famine-stricken and which has already suffered in various ways as a result of the war. Sections were flooded by the opening of the Yellow River dikes in 1938 and this spring. Many areas have been devastated by hostilities. Military conscription in Honan has been especially heavy and—despite the famine—is still going on. Labor conscription has been even more widespread. Military transport requires an immense number of coolies. Roads have been built and torn up,

---

* An American writer and artist who traveled through China on his own, Peck worked for the Chinese Industrial Cooperatives and later joined the U.S. Office of War Information. In 1950 he published a book on his years in China, *Two Kinds of Time.*

thousands of fortifications constructed, a 30-foot moat dug around the city of Loyang, channels dug for the diversion of the Yellow River, and great trenches* dug to check the advance of the Japanese from the bridgehead which they still hold at the Yellow River crossing north of Chengchow. Sometimes the farmer is paid for this work; more often, apparently, not. When he is paid, it is at a rate only one-third to one-fourth regular wages and hence insufficient to pay even for his food. (Labor for the moat at Loyang was paid $8 a day; labor rates in the city at the time were $22–$26).

The greatest burden on the Honan farmer, however, has been steadily increasing taxation in kind and requisitioning of military grain. This burden has been made heavier by the requirement that the province help to feed the armies in south Shansi (before the loss of the Chungtiaoshan) and in the relatively poor province of Shensi, where the main task of some 400,000 troops is to "guard" the Communists.

From numerous sources I was given estimates that total imposts are from 30–50 percent of a farmer's crop. These include a local government tax, the national land tax in kind (collected through the provincial government), and military demands which are varying and unpredictable. The taxation rates are based on the normal crop, rather than the actual yield for the year. Therefore, the poorer the crop, the larger the proportion which is taken from the farmer. And as the farmer does not devote all of his land to wheat, which is demanded for the tax, the percentage of this crop which he must turn over is much higher.

There is considerable evidence that the amount of military grain taken from the people is unnecessarily large. The time-honored custom of Chinese military officers, of reporting a larger strength than their units actually have, still holds good. By drawing full rations for his supposed strength the commander has a surplus to be disposed of for his profit. A large part of the grain on the open market in Loyang comes from this source. . . .

There is a common complaint, also, that the impositions are not evenly and fairly distributed. Collections are made

---

* A Canadian missionary from Chengchow believes that more than 100,000 coolies were working at one time on these ditches. [Footnote in original.]

through the local *pao-chia*** officials, who are themselves the
gentry and landlords, and who often see that they, and their
friends, do not suffer too heavily. Influence is still based on
wealth and property: the poorer farmer sees a larger proportion
of his grain taken—just as he sees his sons, rather than those of
the *chia-chang* and landlord, taken for the army.

Conditions in Honan have been so bad that for several
years there has been a flow of population into Shensi, Kansu
and north Szechwan. . . . The result is a partial depopulation
[of Honan] and relatively greater imposition on those who remain behind. This movement has been heaviest from the "front-
line area," where life for the farmer was hardest and which is
now hardest hit by famine. A missionary from Chengchow says
that many farms in that district had already been abandoned last
year—before the present famine.

The culmination of these conditions has come this year.
That there would be a serious grain shortage was known to the
blindest government official in the early spring after the failure
of the wheat crop. As early as July, refugees estimated at 1,000
a day were leaving the province. But the grain-collection program remained unchanged. In many districts the entire crop
was insufficient to meet the demands of the collectors. There
were gestures of agrarian protest: all weak, scattered and in-
effectual.† Apparently, in a few places, troops were used against
the people. But generally the people, failing in their peaceful
protests, watched their grain being taken and then, with no hope
of surviving the coming winter, killed their animals, sold their
tools and few effects (at greatly reduced prices) and took to the

---

* The *pao-chia* was the traditional Chinese system of local public
security, revived by Chiang Kai-shek's Kuomintang in the 1930s as
part of its campaign against the Communists. Theoretically, a *pao* was
a unit of one hundred families headed by a *pao-chang,* and a *chia* was
a unit of ten families, headed by a *chia-chang.* In wartime China, the
primary functions of the *pao-chia* were tax and grain collection and
the conscription of soldiers for the army.

† In some *hsien* the farmers carried their farming implements to
the *yamen* [local government office] and laid them on the magistrate's
"doorstep." In others the old women were sent to plead with the officials the impossibility of living if their men were forced to give up
all their grain. There is a report that a peasant delegation tried unsuccessfully to see the governor. Banditry became rife, requiring the
stationing of troops at intervals of about a mile along the main roads.
[Footnote in original.]

road. The American Committee estimates that 100,000 have left their homes in one district, Mihsien. 460,000 are reported to have left seven badly affected *hsien*.

The tax collection months are the late summer and early autumn. It was not until September 10 that the tax was canceled and attempts to collect it given up. But by that time probably one half of the tax had already been taken in.* This cancellation, furthermore, did not include delinquent taxes which the farmers were in many cases owing from previous seasons.

The Problem of Relief

The chief factor limiting the possibility of direct relief by the importation of grain into the province is the cutting off and crippling of transportation by the war. Honan is crossed by the Lunghai railway from east to west and the Pinghan railway from north to south. In normal times, food could be brought into the province from all four directions. Three of these lines are now in the hands of the Japanese: the capacity of the fourth (from Shensi) is seriously limited by being within the range of Japanese artillery fire for the 80 kilometers between Tungkuan and Linpao. Truck and other transport from Shensi cannot be mustered in significant volume; nor does Shensi itself have a surplus of grain.

Military considerations also prevent the distribution of grain stocks in granaries. The one line of rail communications with the rest of free China is precariously held and in the case of its being cut, this grain will be needed for the army.

The problem therefore becomes one of an insufficiency of grain—with no means of shipping in large enough quantities to effectively relieve the situation. It follows accordingly that little can be accomplished by straight cash relief.

Steps Taken by the Government

The most important action taken by the Government has been discontinuance—late as it was—of further attempts to collect grain.

* The original goal for the collection of military grain was 6 million bags (of 110 pounds). This was later reduced to 4.7 million. It is reported (unofficially) that 2.5 million bags were actually collected before the cancellation date. This figure does not include the local and provincial tax in kind. [Footnote in original.]

Grain is also now being shipped into the province but in relatively small quantities and for the army only.*

A government grant of $5 million for cash relief was quickly exhausted with, according to American relief workers, little actually reaching the farmers. What happened in many districts was that the plight of the local petty officials (through whom distribution was made) was so desperate that they received most of the funds. In any case the amount involved was ridiculously inadequate.

A proposed loan of $4 million for seed grain to assist in the planting of the wheat crop was not acted upon in time by the National Government and at the time of my visit had not yet been passed. Meanwhile farmers who had not left their land had managed to find enough grain to plant a crop which, aided by the timely rains, had already sprouted and was showing good promise.

For many people in the seriously affected districts the only hope seemed to be to leave their land and move out of the famine area. The only way open was westward. The Government is giving them free transportation on the railway from Loyang to Sian and Paoki.† About three thousand a day were traveling into Shensi by this route. In addition, an unknown but probably smaller number were moving west by road. To assist these people, the local authorities commenced giving each person

* The railway section chief at Tungkuan claimed that he had no tonnage figures but told me that usually two trains were moving east every night. These appeared to average about ten cars which, varying in capacity from 15 to 40 tons, may be assumed to carry about 25 tons each. The eastbound cargo is almost entirely, as far as I could see, grain. I therefore estimated that at least 15,000 tons a month is moving into Honan. Rail operation is extremely difficult and hazardous. Trains run the gauntlet at night under Japanese artillery fire. Almost all bridges have been destroyed, requiring the construction of makeshift detours. The railway men have shown great heroism and ingenuity in keeping the line open. [Footnote in original.]

† The railway stations at Loyang and along the line are filled with large numbers of those refugees who may have to wait for days before they can get on a train. They ride in the open, on flat cars or the top of boxcars, and once on refuse to leave the train, even when passing the dangerous section along the Yellow River. Numbers have been killed. They were the principal victims of the Japanese air raid on Loyang on the day that Mr. [Wendell] Willkie [in China as President Roosevelt's personal representative] was at Tungkuan. [Footnote in original.]

$5 or $10 (the amount varied in different localities) as "traveling money." The appropriation was quickly exhausted and payment even of this small amount stopped. Nothing is done by the authorities to care for or feed these refugees along the route. Some of the refugees, estimated by one worker at 10 percent, become discouraged with the difficulties met with and try to return home. Many of the rest are reduced to begging and stealing.

The provincial government of Shensi has agreed to accept 100,000 refugees to be placed in three new cultivation areas. Actually, far more than 100,000 have already entered Shensi. Their numbers are creating a serious problem. There are large colonies living in mat huts and in caves around cities such as Sian and Paoki. I saw refugees moving along the roads as far away as Pinhsien on the road into Kansu. A Chinese source said that efforts were now being made to discourage refugees from entering Shensi. . . .

The representative in Sian of the National Relief Commission outlined a comprehensive but rather vague program calling for the expenditure of $150 million. His plan included:

Opening the granaries in Honan.
Purchasing and shipping into the province for distribution quantities of mixed grains (*tsa liang*).
Undertaking on a relief basis public works such as roads, canals and much needed construction of Yellow River dikes.
Use of refugee labor on the new extension of the Lunghai railway from Paoki to Tienshui.
The settling of refugees on new land in Shensi and Szechwan and their assistance through loans.
The setting up of homes for infants and orphans.
Soup kitchens for the refugees and the provision of winter clothes.

The amount involved only represents a pre-war purchasing power of $3 million (about US $1 million) and is of course inadequate to meet the need. The proposals, furthermore, are apparently Mr. Ch'i's own and have not received official approval. He was obviously not sanguine of the funds being granted.

[Here a brief section on private, and largely American-sponsored, relief efforts is omitted.]

Effects of the Famine

Militarily, the conditions in Honan have the effect of spreading disorganization and demoralization in a vitally strategic region immediately behind a front which protects the Chinese north flank.* An American described conditions as "chaos—and getting worse."

Economically, the effects must include temporary loss and long-term impairment of an important Chinese economic base. Other immediate effects are local restrictions on normal trade— because of the fear of increasing local shortage†—and the stimulation of hoarding. The economic effects, also, are spreading rapidly to the neighboring provinces. Honan has become the focus of an accelerated price rise throughout the Northwest.‡ At the same time the large influx of refugees into Shensi is causing a glut on the labor market and in places an actual reduction of wages, while the necessity of shipping military grain into Honan from Shensi has increased the burden on farmers there and provoked signs of agrarian unrest.

---

* Evidences of these tendencies are numerous. The plight of petty civil officials is desperate and in some districts local government is described as being near a state of collapse. Military morale in this area was notoriously poor even before the famine and is now admitted by Chinese to be worse. Smuggling and trade across the lines, with great profit to the local military commanders is still on a large scale. A recent development is the import of drugs in quantity, also by the military or with their connivance. Morphine is now about $4 (US $0.20) a "shot" in Loyang and easily obtainable. In the general breakdown of government, restrictions such as those on opium tend to be relaxed. [Footnote in original.]

† This was reportedly the primary cause of the rise in the price of flour at Loyang from $2 a catty [about 1½ pounds] in early July to $11 in September. Many districts refused to allow the shipment of wheat. After the cancellation of the taxes, the price dropped to about $6. . . . [Footnote in original.]

‡ When I went north in July, Chungking was still the focus of high prices; they gradually diminished as one went north. The price of rice was about $3.50 in Chungking; flour was $2.50 in Sian, $2 in Loyang and $1.80 in Lanchow. Other commodities generally followed this proportion. By October, prices in Loyang had tripled (ignoring the temporary panic in September), had doubled in Sian, had risen 50 percent in Lanchow and about 30 percent in Chungking. Loyang was by then the most expensive place in China, and Sian was about the same as Chungking. An interesting price phenomenon observed was that prices of imported goods followed those of basic local commodities; thus cigarettes, soap and other goods from Tientsin were cheaper as one went west. [Footnote in original.]

Agriculturally, the famine is resulting in serious loss for the future through the wholesale slaughter of farm animals and the destruction of good farm land by erosion.

Socially, there are immediate effects in the uprooting and infliction of hardships on a large part of the population. But the more important effects are the changes in the attitudes and state of mind of the people which these sufferings may produce. The farmers in Honan already have no interest in the war; there is the possibility that their suffering may breed discontent which can develop into open dissatisfaction with their condition.*

There is as yet no indication that an upheaval is near, nor any indication of the form that it may take.† It is possible that the farmers will continue to suffer in silence in hopes of better times. But the atmosphere of longing for peace and of dislike of the government and army which are supposed to protect them is unmistakable.

Service's prognostication that peasant discontent could ultimately take a more active form was quite correct. In the spring of 1944, the Japanese launched a major offensive in Honan. The local inhabitants' antipathy toward the Chinese army was by then so great that they assisted the Japanese in disarming the Kuomintang soldiers.

From June to August 1943, Service was detailed to a "listening post" in Lanchow, the capital of Kansu—a sensitive area adjacent to the Communists' Shensi-Kansu-Ninghsia Border Region. At the time, Kansu was the locus of considerable rural unrest and even

---

* Bishop Megan remarked that "No other people in the world would stand for the treatment the Honan peasant has received." This idea was interestingly enough confirmed by a Cantonese who on a different occasion said: "You could never treat the Kwangtung people the way these people (the Honanese) have been governed." [Footnote in original.]

† Most Americans who discussed the subject did not think that many of the farmers had any knowledge of Communism. Communist influence, wherever found, is rigorously suppressed. [Footnote in original.]

outright rebellion against the Chungking Government. Here, not only poor peasants but landlords, gentry and the ever-powerful Chinese secret societies united in opposition to Kuomintang rule. KMT fears that the Chinese Communists might capitalize on these disturbances to expand their control made the Kuomintang's repressive measures doubly harsh.

The Political Situation in Kansu

July 18, 1943
Archives copy: 893.00/15112

I have the honor to transmit to the Embassy a memorandum discussing the political situation in Kansu, with particular attention to the apparent fear of local unrest.

The following is a *brief summary* of the memorandum. Agrarian unrest in the south and central parts of the province was chiefly caused by resentment of taxation and dislike of the Government. There was no sign of Communist participation and the situation is now much quieter, probably because of the harvest. But there is obvious fear on the part of the Government of further unrest. Additional troops are being brought into the province and defensive measures such as the building of gates and blockhouses around Lanchow undertaken. There are some indications that what the local government fears most is not local unrest but a Communist move to occupy the province. This fear is confirmed by the expectation of persons having Communist contacts.

NOTES ON THE POLITICAL SITUATION IN KANSU

Reliable and comprehensive reports of the strength and numbers involved in the agrarian unrest—or "banditry"— which was prevalent through most of the central and southern parts of Kansu in the spring of this year are difficult to obtain.

A certain small share in the trouble was caused by ordinary professional bandits. These probably number several thousand men, are chiefly Mohammedans, and pillage from time to time in the southwest part of the province. In times of unrest like the present, their numbers grow and activity increases.

But this does not explain the very large groups of men which were operating this spring. These groups were organized under a semblance of military discipline, with "generals" and officers of other ranks. The different groups were also linked together in some form of loose organization.

A difference from ordinary banditry is the fact that these bands had their own propaganda. In this the chief emphasis was laid on the relief of the sufferings and burdens of the people. Slogans (seen by American missionaries) attacked conscription, promised reduction of taxes and collections in kind, and demanded local self-government. I saw the remnants of a few of these slogans in the town of Ma-ying, Kansu. But generally they are completely destroyed as soon as the Central Government troops reoccupy a town evacuated by the rebels.

At one time the rebels held most of the southern part of the province, with the exception of the larger towns of Minhsien and Lintao. The movement spread north and they took the towns along the highway from Tienshui to Lanchow. A force of several thousand was reported at one time in the hills only a few miles from Lanchow itself. Airplanes were used to bomb Yüchung, the next *hsien* city to the southeast of Lanchow, and for a period bombing and reconnaissance planes flew out daily from Lanchow, reportedly on missions against the rebels. It is believed that Russian planes were used, at least for the bombing.

Most foreigners credit reports that these rebels totaled at least 50,000 fighting men. But some Chinese mention figures as high as 200,000. And the head of the Kansu Livestock Improvement Bureau, whose stations have all been closed because they are in the area affected, scoffs at attempts to give exact figures. He claims that all the population of the rural areas are either actual or potential supporters of the movement.

The Government took vigorous military measures to cope with the disturbances. Two divisions of the Thirty-sixth Army were brought into the province, in addition to sizable forces already here. Large reinforcements of recruits were also marched in from Szechwan and Honan. Other forces were brought in from the Sian or Pingliang area. These included cavalry and some heavy equipment.

The effectiveness of these forces was apparently not always high. In conversations with foreigners some of them freely expressed their dislike of fighting poor and heavily burdened *lao-pai-hsing*.* Local and provincial forces such as the *pao-an-tui* (Peace Preservation Corps) proved almost useless because of the consistent regularity with which they went over to the side of the rebels.

However, this large addition to the troops in the province made possible the heavy garrisoning of all the main towns and the gradual confinement of the rebels to one or two areas. The chief of these at present is the district south of Lungsi and Kanku, and between Minhsien and Chenghsien. Small-scale sporadic action, apparently more of the orthodox bandit type, still goes on and travel in much of the province is not safe. For instance, a small village only about 10 miles from Lanchow was attacked as recently as three weeks ago.

As summer came on, the movement subsided, presumably because of the occupation of the rural population in the harvest. At present there are few reports of any large-scale activity. The Government forces recently captured one of the "generals" of the movement, a former *chuan-yuan* (supervisory magistrate) of Minhsien. According to rumor he has been tortured to death —by such means as the breaking of his legs—in efforts to have him name confederates.

Government officials generally dismiss the whole matter as "ordinary banditry" and claim that the situation is completely under control. Both official preparations for further trouble, and the general opinion of foreign residents of the province and of private Chinese, disprove this optimism.

There are ample indications that the disturbances are at least in large part an indication of popular dislike of the Government and resentment of conscription, heavy grain collections, labor service and general misgovernment. This resentment is shared by almost the entire population of the province, rather than by any one particular group. Thus there is difficulty in picking one group as the instigating or organizing force.

* Common people. Literally "old hundred names."

The provincial government is regarded as "foreign." The Commissioner of Reconstruction is almost the only native member of it. The governor [Ku Cheng-lun] a former gendarmerie commander, is disliked and considered ruthless and harsh.

The age-old feud in the Northwest between Mohammedans and Chinese is never far in the background. The present government is entirely Chinese and there is Mohammedan dissatisfaction. General Ma Pu-fang, the governor of Chinghai, is perhaps willing, under cover, to assist because he may thus at the same time help his fellow Mohammedans and, by embarrassing the Central Government in Kansu, strengthen his own position in Chinghai.

The provincial government has apparently been trying to carry out a policy of opium suppression. But the opium trade is largely in the hands of the very widespread and influential secret societies. Incidentally, Governor Ku has the reputation of having been a bitter enemy of the *Ch'ing-hung Pang* (important secret societies of East China) when he was commander of gendarmerie in Nanking. If he has continued this attempt to curb the power of the societies, this may be a partial cause of the trouble.

The landlords and gentry of the province have been strongly opposed to the present government because they are excluded from it, and because they are being forced to pay higher taxes in kind.

The grievances of the farmer need no description.

There are thus several large groups which might be expected to furnish opposition to the Government. But the farmer is unorganized and without leadership. The secret societies are closely linked to the landlord-gentry class.

It is probable that the instigation, leadership, and what organization there is, have come chiefly from the discontented local landlords and gentry. The secret societies already had close ties and a common cause with them. It was a simple matter with propaganda to capitalize on latent discontent of the peasants. There were a large number of former soldiers of General Teng Pao-san, once governor of Kansu, in the southern part of the province. They were disbanded after General Teng lost his position. Not being paid, most of these men kept their arms. Under their former officers, also of the gentry class, many of these men were reorganized and apparently furnished the back-bone of some of the larger and better units. Some of these men were peasants. But the chance of plunder and the desire to escape conscription were enough to win most. The provincial forces, such as the *pao-an-tui,* were discontented because of their generally poorer treatment than the Central Government troops. They also had natural ties with the people and with these former troops of General Teng. It was therefore easy for them to join up.

One interesting factor is the apparently negligible part that the Communists have had in these disturbances. Government propaganda only occasionally and half-heartedly makes the claim of Communist instigation. Most Chinese agree that primary instigation has come from landlords and gentry—in party phraseology: corrupt and backward provincial interests.

In spite of the present subsidence, it is the general opinion of foreigners and Chinese that there will be a recurrence of the trouble, and probably on a larger scale, in the autumn. This is the season for collection of taxes in kind. Although the crops in the Lanchow area are good, they are not uniformly favorable all over the province. The southern part of the province, the section already most affected by the agrarian unrest, has suffered from too little rain and from the effects of the fighting and disturbances in the spring. In eastern Kansu the crops in three *hsien* were almost ruined by late frosts. At the same time, because of the greatly increased number of troops in the province, the impositions on the people will be even heavier than usual.

But quite apart from the question of whether the grain collections are, in proportion to what the farmer has, heavier than normal, most observers believe that the movement has attained sufficient momentum, and the dislike of the farmers for their present condition is so deep-rooted that further disturbances are unavoidable. This will certainly be true if the Government continues to employ the measures so far used: military suppression carried out by troops from other provinces; bombing of towns held by the rebels; and, coincidentally, failure to do anything to remedy the conditions which are the root of the trouble.

Despite official statements, it seems obvious that the Government expects and fears further trouble. Troops and recruits are steadily being brought into the province. During the past two months the outer city gates of Lanchow, which were torn down about two years ago for a city-modernization and street-widening program, have been hurriedly rebuilt. They are now guarded by gendarmerie, whereas last year the spaces where the gates had been were guarded by members of the local *pao-an-tui*. A large number of small brick blockhouses are being built in the countryside and on the hills around Lanchow. This work is being rushed to such an extent that it is almost impossible to buy bricks or hire masons in Lanchow for private work. There are reports that large forces are still being kept as garrisons for towns in or near the rebel area.

These preparations seem too elaborate for ordinary banditry. Some informed persons believe that what the Government really fears, even more than a recurrence of these agrarian disturbances, is a Communist attempt to capitalize on these disturbances to make a westward drive into central Kansu and thence perhaps move northwest toward Sinkiang.

Such a fear on the part of the Government may well be true. They must consider that the Communists are fully aware that the great impetus for the emphasis on the "development of the Northwest" is a political one—aimed at the eventual encirclement and elimination of the Communists. There are many obvious indications of strong anti-Communist sentiment of the Party and authorities in this area. I hope to make these the subject of a separate report.

Interestingly, this Government fear of a Communist move into Kansu tends to be confirmed by news reaching people with Communist contacts from their friends across the line in the Communist area. These people appear to expect this Communist move within a year.

The Communist move into Kansu never materialized. Nevertheless, the summer of 1943 marked a new height of Kuomintang-Communist tensions, and for a time both sides seemed headed toward open civil war. Though the details remain obscure, it appears that the Communists felt threatened by the tremendous build-up of Central Government forces in Kansu—many of which were undoubtedly the troops mentioned in the suppression of the disturbances here. When the Communists responded with a build-up of their own, tensions and mutual recriminations increased. The situation did not begin to cool off until the fall of 1943, when Chiang Kai-shek made a major speech favoring a "political solution" to the Communist problem.

By 1944 the situation had changed, but not improved, for the Chinese peasant. In many areas, his life was complicated by the influx of large numbers of American troops and airmen who had come to carry the air war to Japan. Nowhere was this truer than in Chengtu, where early in 1944 construction began on several huge airfields to accommodate the new B-29 Superfortress. When this new disruption of peasant life produced predictable signs of unrest and reports of anti-American sentiment, Service—by then attached to General Joseph Stilwell's headquarters—was sent to investigate. Chengtu, the capital of Szechwan province, was Service's birthplace. He knew the area. He knew the local dialect. He knew the facts of peasant life. His report from Chengtu showed a sensitivity to all the particular details of the local situation—yet his findings would no doubt find parallels in any other peasant society which has been forced to play host to the U.S. Army.

The Impact of the American Army on the Chengtu Area

February 26, 1944
Archives copy: 893.248/291

The following is a brief general report on what I consider the situation in Chengtu, and a suggestion of measures which might be taken to cope with it. . . .

A number of incidents when the projects were started in the Chengtu area gave the impression of opposition to the projects and unfriendliness toward the American Army. After payment for most of the land taken for the projects, this violent opposition ceased and it appears that the most likely immediate cause of incidents has been removed.

This does not mean that the American Army, or the projects, are welcomed. The general attitude, among all classes, while not quite openly hostile, is one of apprehension. With the lack of interest in the war, the strong provincialism, and the latent antiforeign feeling in the Chengtu area, there is always the possibility that these fears, if realized, may turn to more active resentment. . . .

1. Land Problems

The landowners feared that they would not be paid for their land. Tenant farmers, who work most of the land in the Chengtu plain, were afraid that they would not be compensated for crops and homes destroyed.

These fears could be considered justified because owners and tenants *did not* receive compensation for previous Chinese airfield construction in this area—including many of the fields now being improved.

The haste with which the present projects were started resulted in engineers arriving on the sites and work commencing before the landowners had been notified and negotiations for purchase undertaken. Immediate violent opposition forced the withdrawal of the engineers from several fields and delay for periods up to about ten days until arrangements could be made to pay for the land required.

Payment for practically all land was completed about February 8. The highest price I learned of having been paid to landowners was CN$16,000 per *mou* [one *mou* equals ⅙ acre]. While this is close to official valuation, it is probably only one third or one fourth of actual land values. And there is good evidence that not all of the sums allotted reached the owners. It is reported, for instance, that on one project the magistrate concerned has paid out only $10 million of the $16 million agreed upon, the balance being held pending completion of formalities such as clarification of land titles. It is obvious that under present conditions of rapid inflation, these money payments become rapidly less valuable the longer they are delayed.

Arrangements were also made for compensation to tenants. Reports differ as to whether this compensation was made by the landlord or the Government direct. Tenants to whom I talked had received $800 a *mou* for destroyed wheat and $2,000 for their home. Both figures are very inadequate: an agricultural expert of the West China University estimated that $800 per *mou* would not even pay for fertilizer at present prices.

Neither owners nor tenants are satisfied. But despite the facts that no one likes to lose land during inflation and that the tenants may be rendered homeless and will not be able to find other land in the already overcrowded Chengtu plain, it is significant that payment so reversed past experience and satisfied fears that opposition ceased.

It may be possible for us to show an interest in having any outstanding payments fully and promptly made.

2. The Labor Problem

The fear of the conscript laborers is that they will not be able to return home in time to harvest the winter crop and plant the summer rice. . . .

The present attitude of the conscripts differs from project to project. On several fields they appeared rather sullen. At most, however, they were normally friendly. That this is true is a tribute to the good nature and long-suffering attitude of the Chinese peasant. One *pao* (theoretically about one hundred families), concerning which I learned a good deal from a Chinese concerned in the recruiting, may be considered as typical. The number of men demanded was greater than the number of households. Thus some households (which, however, may contain more than one branch of a family) had to send several men. There was no warning. The men were notified one day that they were to leave the next. They had to provide themselves with food for a week, with straw for bedding and poles for a shelter, and take with them their own baskets, hoes and wheelbarrows. This happened only ten days before the great holiday of the year, Chinese New Year, which meant separation at the time all Chinese families try to be together. Finally, they were told that this was because the Americans demanded the airfields.

Actual conditions of work are probably no worse than usual for conscript labor, and may be better. Conscripts agree that after they have arrived on the site and have been organized, they are fairly well fed—on rice, meager vegetables and a little salt. They complain of lack of money to buy necessary articles such as straw sandals, and small luxuries such as tobacco.

There were also complaints, heard in Chengtu, of the almost total lack of medical attention, poor sanitary facilities and absence of means for writing to their families.

It is probable, on projects of this size and short-term nature, that little can be done, either by us or the Chinese Government, regarding these last complaints. But the unanimous and stubborn insistence of every worker with whom I talked (certainly over a hundred individuals) that he had received no money whatsoever raises a question. There are varying reports of the cash payment that the conscripts are supposed to receive. But officials connected with the projects agreed that wages had been specified and they generally stated that this was to be CN$20 a day in addition to food. It is obvious that the workers are not now receiving this. The officials responsible appear to be the district magistrate and the *pao* officials under them.

Our primary concern in regard to these conscripts is to get them back to their farms before their own agricultural "target dates. . . ."

We should also—especially if we are eventually to pay for the projects—try to see that money promised actually reaches the workers. . . .

3. Fear of Increased Central Government Influence

There is undoubtedly fear on the part of the Szechwanese ruling groups that the Central Government, which has charge of the construction of the projects, will through them be able to increase its power in this part of Szechwan. . . .

This is, of course, a purely domestic Chinese political problem which we may note but can do nothing about.

4. Fear of Friction with American Troops

Some of the officials and gentry in Chengtu fear that there will be friction and possibly incidents arising from the presence of large numbers of American troops.

One background to this fear is undoubtedly the exaggerated reports which are widely current of the rowdiness of the AVG,* and subsequently American troops, in Kunming and other cities. Our reputation, unfortunately, is not good.

* The AVG was General Claire Lee Chennault's American Volunteer Group, otherwise known as the "Flying Tigers."

Another part of the background is the strong Szechwan provincialism already mentioned, which has had at times in the past a strong tinge of antiforeignism. Chengtu is an important educational center, with a large number of students, nationalistically inclined and under the influence of the Kuomintang. It is also a city of wealth and the wartime refuge of the families of large numbers of officials and rich Chinese. So far the local experience, since the city is not a port or site of concessions, has been almost entirely with missionaries.

There is need in Chengtu at once of capable and enterprising Public Relations and O.W.I. [Office of War Information] representatives. There might also be assigned a special officer for liaison with the Chinese authorities. Or close contact might be maintained with the American Embassy representative [in Chengtu] for this purpose.

One objective of these several officers should be to try to improve local good will toward America, create interest in the American Air Force, and stimulate local appreciation of its part in the war. They may be able by quiet efforts to allay some of the alarm now being caused by the fantastic rumors of the number of Americans (in rumor, as high as 200,000) who are going to descend on the city.

These officers and the Special Services or other divisions concerned should proceed as soon as possible to make definite plans for the reception and recreation of American troops in the city. . . .

5. Fear of Japanese Bombing

Among all classes there is some fear that these projects will attract Japanese bombing, both of the fields themselves and of Chengtu.

Recent Japanese radio threats to do just this have not yet reached general knowledge—since I heard no mention of them. And there is no evidence of direct Japanese propaganda by such means as the leaflets they have air dropped in other parts of China. But this fear is a natural one to Chinese psychology and is justified by local experience. The Chengtu area has been bombed in the past by the Japanese primarily because it was an aviation center. And public opinion knows that there was no effective protection against those attacks.

It is appropriate to mention again that the provincially-minded average Szechwanese has little war-consciousness or interest in the war. His province has never been invaded and is far from actual hostilities.

Propaganda, both by ourselves and the Chinese, may be of some help, although there is little time. The best propaganda and morale booster, of course, will be the news of the successful accomplishment and importance of the missions for which the projects are designed.

But the most important thing that can be done is to get adequate fighter protection into the area as soon as possible. Early provision of this protection should have the highest priority. If military considerations permit, the arrival of this fighter strength should be widely publicized, perhaps by aerial demonstration.

6. Fear of Inflation

All sections of the population, but probably more especially the urban, fear that the large materials requirements of the projects and the problem of feeding large numbers of Americans will cause prices to skyrocket. The prevalence and effect of these fears cannot be overemphasized. The general state of mind is close to panic.

Prices in the Chengtu area have already risen considerably. Basic cost of living items have risen 70 percent to 100 percent in the past sixty days. Flour, a special case, has tripled. Building materials have approximately quadrupled. Unfortunately the blame for this is laid, in the popular mind, entirely on the American Army.

The inflationary effect of these construction projects, involving the expenditure of immense sums of currency in a restricted and self-sufficient economic area, cannot be denied. Likewise the feeding of any considerable number of American troops may cause drains on the limited local supply of certain food items, particularly potatoes, high-grade flour, beef and eggs.* But it is incorrect to attribute price rises entirely to the projects and the American Army.

---

* At Stilwell's insistence, the United States flew no food into China whatsoever. Tonnage over the "Hump" was too valuable. Consequently, G.I.s ate off the local market.

a. There is a steady inflationary process going on in China. . . .

b. There is an actual shortage in the Chengtu area of some commodities. For instance, the last wheat crop was a poor one.

c. The rise in prices has been accelerated by the flagrant hoarding and manipulation of the Szechwanese interests . . .

d. The rise in food prices has also been boosted by the fantastically exaggerated rumors, which are universally current, of the numbers and demands of the American troops. Common reasoning is as follows:

200,000 Americans will each need 5 eggs a day. This means 1 million eggs a day. Chinese freely predict that eggs, now risen from $3 to $6 each, will soon reach a price of $70 or $80. Large-scale and widespread hoarding is a natural result and helps to push prices up even faster.

Possibilities for alleviating action on our part are limited. The most important need is for effective price-control measures by the Chinese Government to prevent prices from getting completely out of hand. . . .

A second important need is to push the projects to completion as soon as possible. This requires the prompt provision by the Chinese Government of adequate amounts of currency. . . .

One minor action which we might consider, not connected with the costs of the projects themselves but the problem of feeding the troops, is the adjustment of diet to local supply. . . . Substitution of rice or sweet potatoes, at least once a day, will work no hardship. There is little beef in the Chengtu plain. It might partially be replaced by pork, beans of various kinds, and bean curd. There appears to be no substitute for eggs, unless it be more hot cakes, but the number of eggs consumed may have to be restricted more than Americans in China have been used to.

THE STATE OF THE ARMY

In his role as a political reporter, Jack Service found it necessary to pay considerable attention to the state of the Chinese armies. These armies were often subservient to particular political interests, and the general condition of China's armies was of obvious interest to her American allies in the war against Japan. Service's assessments of the Kuomintang armies became particularly important when he visited the Communist areas and compared the CCP armies to those of the KMT. They allowed him to make the crucial judgment that Kuomintang expectations of victory in a civil war with the Communists were illusory.

One of Service's most telling reports on the KMT armies was a description of troop and conscript movements along the route he traveled from Chungking to Lanchow in the summer of 1943. Some of these movements were related to the political conflict between the Central Government and the local Szechwan warlords. Both sides seemed to be concentrating forces in the provincial capital of Chengtu.* The troops moving north were mostly new conscripts. "It was standard practice to take new recruits away from their local area, so that it would be more difficult for them to desert. When, as in this case, they had new recruits from Szechwan, the first thing they would do was haul them over the Ch'in-ling Pass into Shensi, so that if they would run away they would have no place to go. They were half starved, there were bodies lying in the ditch; and the poor beggars were having to carry the officers."

---

* Service had written a report on this subject on May 24, 1943, entitled "Friction between Central Government and Szechwan Warlord-Gentry" (not printed here; in State Department file 893.165/95).

Military Movements Noted Along
Road from Chungking to Lanchow

July 2, 1943
State Security copy: 893.22/49

I have the honor to enclose general notes regarding movements and general condition of military forces noted along the road from Chungking to Lanchow. These may be briefly summarized as follows:

There were indications of some concentration of troops around Chengtu and of apparently normal movement of conscripts northward out of Szechwan, but the only important recent movement of troops in this area appears to have been the entry of several divisions into Kansu to deal with local disturbances. The condition of conscripts and troops generally can only be described as miserable.

A. Movements

Between Chungking and Chengtu (June 5–7) about thirty Air Force trucks were observed transporting baggage, household effects and families southward. Military personnel were a minority among the passengers. . . .

At Chengtu there were reports current that some time before (perhaps early in May), General Liu Wen-hui, governor of Sikang and one of the Szechwan "warlords," had commenced a movement of part of his troops from Yaan toward Chengtu. At about the same time there had been local disturbances in the city of Chengtu between the police and forces of the garrison commander; and Central Government forces had been concentrated around the city of Chengtu. There had been an encampment of Central Government troops just outside the city walls and across the river from the campus of the West China Union University. These troops were reported by foreigners to have been well equipped and very businesslike. They had been withdrawn about two weeks before my arrival (June 7).

The town of Hsintu, about 25 kilometers north of Chengtu, appeared to be filled (June 10) with Szechwan provincial forces. Temples and inns were being used as barracks with unit pennants—vermilion with black characters—displayed at the entrances. General appearance was good. . . .

On June 13, about 2,000 men were moving south near Lokiang (95 km. north of Chengtu). They were dressed in tuck-in shirts, shorts and straw sandals. Equipment was light, consisting of small packs in bamboo baskets carried on the back, and large Szechwanese rainhats. Only about one in ten carried rifles. Each unit carried cooking utensils. They were moving down the road in close order and at a very good speed. Officers walked. Dialect was Szechwanese but appearance of men was good, their bare legs being noticeably free from the usual sores. They obviously had had some training and might be partially trained recruits or reserves.

There were a large number of troops of the "New 9th Division" in garrison in and around Kwangyuan (June 15). There was no opportunity to judge equipment, but a large proportion of the troops were boys.

On June 18, three groups of about 100 each of Szechwanese conscripts were marching north into Shensi in the vicinity of Miaotaitze (Liupa). Each group had an armed guard of about ten men armed with rifles and was under the charge of an officer, in most cases carried by the conscripts in an improvised chair. With one group there was also a woman being carried by conscripts. The conscripts had no individual equipment; group cooking utensils and rice were divided among them. I was told that there is a steady movement of Szechwanese conscripts northward over this road. In October 1942 I observed many groups on the same road roped together with their hands tied behind their backs. . . .

Two divisions of the Thirty-sixth Army were reported to have moved westward through Tienshui in May in a drive against the bandits then active in central Kansu. These troops are now said to have the bandits surrounded in the south-central part of the province. In addition there has been a steady westward movement of conscripts through Tienshui.

All the towns between Tienshui and Lanchow appear to be garrisoned, presumably because of the disturbed local conditions.

B. *Condition of Troops*

The physical condition of troops observed in Szechwan, especially in the Chengtu area, was generally fair. The condition of the conscripts and troops in Shensi and Kansu was very poor—so poor at times as to almost beggar description.

This miserable condition of the conscripts, especially, is so general in the Northwest that it is a universal subject of comment by both foreigners and Chinese. Almost everyone has several "horror stories" to tell.

In the 6 kilometers just below the Miaotaitze pass (an easy pass of about 5,000 feet elevation on the motor road south of Shuangshihpu) one group of about a hundred conscripts lost two men by exhaustion. One was already dead and was being dragged to the side of the road (by his feet) as my truck passed. Another was breathing his last, lying head down in [a] ditch. Two men, themselves walking skeletons and apparently detailed to carry him, were watching impassively.

One foreigner has actually seen men near death from exhaustion or disease being beaten to death to save the trouble of carrying them.

Sixty men are reported to have died in Shuangshihpu in one night. Most of the bodies were unburied. It is common to see bodies along the roads. Some are thrown in the river.

All along this route there have been epidemics of typhus and relapsing fever. At Tienshui the conscripts were quartered on the populace; houses where they had stayed became centers of infection. Paoki and Shuangshihpu have had a great deal of typhus. Malaria, brought up from Szechwan, is becoming common in Shensi.

Chinese themselves freely state that the conscripts are starved because their officers squeeze on the grain. When I have watched them eat, they have had nothing but rice. It is usually a question of the strongest and fittest getting the most. The weak and sick get little. In Kwangyuan I saw a group of conscripts attack a crippled candy peddler. He was pushed over and all of his wares plundered in a matter of seconds. The guards paid no attention until after it was over. They then kicked several in the stomach and hit others with the butts of their rifles. The men seemed obviously starved.

Groups of sick soldiers being led to hospitals or dispensaries are a common daily sight in Lanchow. Most of the men are barely able to walk. But each group is guarded by one or two men with rifles.

Every missionary has had experiences with runaway soldiers appealing for protection and help, requests which the missionaries are forced to refuse. One group of Honan refugees impressed into service told a foreigner that more than one half of their number had died on the march to Kansu. The compound of the China Inland Mission at Lanchow backs up to the city wall. Several soldiers managed to desert by clambering down from the wall onto the roofs of the Mission and thus escaping. Finally the authorities built a wall along the inside edge of the city wall to prevent such escapes. The chief reason for the nocturnal searches of inns and lodging houses is to find men without proper identification papers, who are thereby assumed to be deserters. Some missionaries have had experience with deserters of rank as high as lieutenant.

Service's field reports made it quite clear that the Kuomintang armies were in a sorry state: inadequately armed, underfed, disease-ridden, ill trained and poorly led. With the size of the army inflated by the incorporation of personal armies of local warlords and political generals, the military also represented a tremendous drain on the resources of the nation, absorbing some 80 percent of the Chungking Government's revenues. Both American officers like General Stilwell and a few progressive Kuomintang military thinkers like Ch'en Ch'eng (later Vice President of the Nationalist Chinese Government of Taiwan) suggested a reduction in the size of the Chinese army as a way of enhancing its quality and lessening the burden on the population which supported it. In the report below, Service explains why such an action would be desirable, and why it would not come about. In making his argument, he gives an excellent summary of the incurable ills which beset the Kuomintang and its military forces.

Unlikely Acceptance of Plan
to Reduce the Chinese Army

March 19, 1944
Archives copy: 893.20/802

Item 2 of the reference memorandum* reported that Chinese circles are talking of a plan to reduce the Chinese army to about one-half its present size.

Discussion of such a plan goes back at least to the fall of 1942, when General Ch'en Ch'eng was understood to be actively advocating it. It has also been suggested by foreign writers on China and tacitly by foreign officials in informal discussions with Chinese friends.

Reduction of the Chinese army could be supported by a number of arguments:

1. Standards of equipment, training, medical care and rationing could be more easily improved. Present standards in most of these respects, for at least the greater part of the army, are shockingly low. A smaller but better fed, trained and equipped army should be more effective than the present undernourished, half-armed mob.

2. There would be a lessening of the present wasteful drain on productive Chinese manpower. During seven years of war, millions of men have been taken from the farms. These millions have not been and are not being effectively used. While they remain in idleness, their ranks are decimated by disease, malnutrition and desertion. And their numbers are a scourge to the people of the districts in which they are stationed. In some areas farm production has been seriously interfered with. A large part of the army would be of more use to the country if sent back to the farms.

3. In addition to this economic value of helping to increase, or at least maintain, production, the drastic reduction of the

---

* The reference memorandum, entitled "Miscellaneous News Items," March 16, 1944, has not been located and is therefore not printed.

army might assist in slowing inflation by making possible budgetary savings.

4. Politically, the advantages of army reduction might be very important. The two principal causes of the general rural unrest are ruthless conscription and grain collections. Both of these complaints could be lessened.

5. Another advantage would be the opportunity presented to get rid of commanders and units whose loyalty or ability are questionable.

Despite these arguments there are a number of reasons, perhaps peculiar to China, which make it unlikely that any very drastic reduction in the size of the Chinese army will take place.

1. There are tremendous vested interests in recruiting. These include: the lowly *pao-chia-chang* who habitually takes bribes for not conscripting (sometimes from the same man year after year); the unit commander who shares the price of the hired conscript making a living by deserting to sell himself again; the conscripting officer who receives a bounty for each recruit; and the officer who squeezes on the allotments for food and care of the conscripts—and in the process starves the men to death. These malpractices are common, and everywhere complained of. They are probably inevitable under the Chinese system. In the Northwest in 1943 the price of a conscript was CN$9,000. Even in famine-stricken Honan in the fall of 1942 it was CN$4,000.* The desperation of the farmers and their willingness to sell even their land to avoid conscription, which because of the terrible treatment is regarded as certain death, has led to important changes in landholding. This perhaps creates still another class interested in the perpetuation of conscription: the gentry or merchant with capital and a desire to hedge against inflation by buying land.

2. Another obstacle is the problem of *whose* armies are to be reduced. The Central Government would presumably be most

---

* This figure is apparently in error. In his report on the Honan famine (above), Service gives the price of a conscript as $2,000.

interested in cutting down the older provincial armies. But the main source of power of these warlords lies in their armies. The Central Government has been trying all through the war to reduce their strength, but by reorganizations, physical separation and attrition through using them in the front lines has achieved only modified success. The allegiance of these warlords to the Central Government is only tenuous. If drastic action is taken, they may resort to independent recruiting. The same may be true to a lesser extent of the major Central Government field commanders, who keep an eye toward the future when the Generalissimo may leave the scene, and who in their own separate areas are building themselves up as semi-independent and self-sufficient satraps—commonly referred to by Chinese as the "new warlords." The same is likewise true of the Chinese Communists, who have at least the argument that they have been holding large guerrilla territories and fighting the Japanese.

3. Finally, it goes without saying that if the Central Government cannot succeed in reducing these potentially opposition forces, it will not consider a reduction of its own forces. In the last analysis the power of the Central Government rests on its military might. This all boils down to the facts of the uncompleted unity of China, the continuing struggle for power, and the universally accepted inevitability of civil war.

China remains a country where life is valued very little, where corruption is deep-rooted and prevalent, where economics have been consistently ignored or not understood, where power derives from military strength and that strength is measured in numbers, where the interests and welfare of the people have not (except perhaps in Communist North China) been a concern of their rulers, and where the basic, overriding consideration is the struggle for power.

There does not appear to be any hope for the reduction of "China's scourge"—its armies—until China becomes a unified, modern state. That time is still far off.

WARLORDS AND PUPPETS

As the preceding report indicates, the Kuomintang armies were made critically weak by the presence of a large number of old warlord armies of dubitable loyalty to Chiang Kai-shek. Chiang's treatment of such armies was fairly typical: they would be sent to the front, far from their home base, to fight the Japanese and deplete their strength vis-à-vis the Central Government forces. Some fought quite valiantly, none more so than the Kwangsi troops under Li Tsung-jen and Pai Ch'ung-hsi; but in the end they found themselves isolated, alone and unaided by the Central Government, which hoarded American military aid for its own armies. Other warlords took an easier route: surrender to the Japanese to become puppets, or local accommodation with opposing Japanese forces. Service wrote a number of reports describing these various warlord strategies. In doing so, he was making some of the earliest attempts to analyze systematically the nature and behavior of warlord armies. His reports were as much works of scholarly research and analysis as they were examples of straightforward political reporting.

Of the various warlord armies, none was better known than the Kwangsi Clique of Li Tsung-jen and Pai Ch'ung-hsi. In March 1945, when the Clique seemed to be at the nadir of its power, Service sat down to write its history. He drew upon material from the earliest years of the war, and from his own trip through Kwangsi in 1943, when he accompanied a U.S. Army engineer on reconnaissance of highways linking China and Vietnam. He was able to show that while Chiang might enhance his own power, he did so at the expense of popular support and support from one of the more capable and patriotic of the warlord armies.

Chiang Kai-shek's Treatment
of the Kwangsi Clique

March 21, 1945
Amerasia Papers, pp. 1434–39

Summary: The break-up of the Kwangsi Clique, in which adroit political separation of the leaders, dissipation of the provincial troops in front-line fighting without adequate supply and far from home, and Japanese action have all had a part, is a mirror of Chiang's methods, by which he seeks to further his power—which he calls unity—through weakening all other groups, but which actually increases disunity and loses the possibility of the most effective war effort. *End of Summary.*

When the Japanese attacked China in 1937, the whole country rallied around Chiang and the Central Government in a burst of nationalistic fervor unprecedented in China's modern history. All rival groups buried their hatchets. For a year or more there was a real United Front.

Among those who hurried to offer their services—and their armies—to Chiang and the country were the Kwangsi Clique under Li Tsung-jen and Pai Ch'ung-hsi. Having been old enemies of Chiang, they were congratulated the country over for thus forgetting their long-standing grievances.

It is interesting, therefore, to see what the Kwangsi Clique got for its patriotic gesture. And whether Chiang forgot *his* grievances against these old—and potential future—rivals.

*   *   *

Of the two Kwangsi military leaders, Li Tsung-jen was the senior. He was sent to the field with troops. But Pai Ch'ung-hsi, the junior, was given a higher job as Deputy Chief of Staff and Minister of Military Training.

This is a job without direct command of troops. But it is close to the "center." So Pai was encouraged that it might lead to something really big. Thus he became a participant, though a weak one, in General Staff politics—one of the men, like

Ho Ying-ch'in, Ch'en Ch'eng, Hu Tsung-nan,* who have thought that they might be the lucky one "if something should happen to the Leader."

Thus the two leaders who were the backbone of the Kwangsi Clique were separated and friction between them created. Li and Pai have not since been considered partners.

Among Chinese armies, the Kwangsi troops were relatively well trained and equipped. They had proved in earlier days that they were good fighters—against the Northern warlords, against Chiang and against the Communists. So they were given the honor of an important place in the front lines—but north of the Yangtze and far from their home province. They fought well—and lost heavily—at Taierchuang and Hsuchow.

This rounded out the picture of the typical handling of provincial armies—removed from their base, mixed with other forces, placed among a population with whom they cannot establish solidarity because they are "foreign," and dissipated as shock troops against the enemy.

But the history of the Kwangsi Clique was not yet finished.

In the fall of 1938 it was apparent that Hankow was doomed. Foreseeing that they would be cut off from their home province, the Kwangsi military men asked the Generalissimo to allow them to withdraw to the south bank of the Yangtze. Here they could have been in contact with their home through Hunan. They could also have protected Kwangsi against Japanese attack from north or south. But their request was refused.

Instead they were ordered to stay behind and to establish a base on the Hupeh-Honan-Anhwei borders in the Tapieh Mountains. Ostensibly they would be in a position here to threaten the rear of Hankow. Actually the area was to be held because it was an important Communist center in the civil-war days of the early 1930s—and the Communists were already showing signs of resurgence leading to control of all Japanese-occupied areas. . . .

The generals had no choice but to stay with their troops

---

* Ho Ying-ch'in was Chiang's Chief of Staff and, until November 1944, Minister of War. Hu Tsung-nan and Ch'en Ch'eng were leaders of the Whampoa Clique and the two most powerful field commanders in the KMT armies.

and try to hold them together. But when possible they engaged in—or through "squeeze" took a part of the profits of—trade with the occupied areas. The effect of this is inevitably demoralizing.

Forced to live almost entirely off the people in a relatively poor area, the army's relations with the people were not good. They could not be expected to be. Heavily taxed and conscripted, the people tended to reduce production and to regard the troops as their enemies.

Left in poor condition, with few supplies and no new equipment, and lacking effective political indoctrination—impossible under these conditions—the morale and fighting ability of the soldiers fell continuously. Desertions increased steadily, complicating the problem of keeping the units up to anything like fighting strength.

When they were able to, junior officers got away. There has been a slow trickling back of these men to the south. Their stories and attitude did nothing to improve feeling back home. The several junior officers I traveled and became well acquainted with while in Kwangsi in 1943 were all strongly anti-Chiang and critical of the Central Government.

The Central Government, meanwhile, had gotten control in Kwangsi. It lost no time in abolishing the very effective system of peasant militia, which had been intended to give every able-bodied man military training and which had been an important source of strength of the Kwangsi Group in the early pre-war days of opposition to Chiang. The Government collected their arms. . . .

For the next few years the Kwangsi forces both in the north (where Li Tsung-jen had become the commander of the 5th War Zone) and in Kwangsi became notorious "poor relations" as far as reinforcements and a share of Central Government supplies were concerned. At the end of 1943 it was obvious that Kwangsi was open to attack.

It is not surprising, therefore, that dissatisfaction developed into the formation of a sort of "Southwest bloc" under the leadership of Li Chi-sen at Kweilin [the provincial capital of Kwangsi]. Chiang's reaction was to remove Li from his position as commander of the Generalissimo's field headquarters in Kweilin and "promote" him to chairman of the Military

Advisory Council, a high-ranking but nonfunctioning sinecure organization in Chungking. Li found reasons to delay taking up his new post and sat tight in Kweilin. The opposition movement in the Southwest prospered.

The Japanese threat to Hunan and Kwangsi began to develop early in 1944. But Chiang was suspicious of Li Chi-sen and Chang Fa-k'uei, one of China's best fighting generals and in command of the 4th War Zone [which included Kwangsi] but on intimate terms with Li. Chiang was even a little dubious about Hsueh Yueh's* growing power and reputation.

Pai Ch'ung-hsi, superficially a suitable man because he was a native of Kwangsi but actually "safe" because he was now tied into the Chungking camp, was sent into the breach to accomplish the impossible job of saving Kwangsi. The onus of losing his own province would not help Pai's prestige or position. His job was hopeless. But little was done to help him. His command was never clarified. Reinforcements were too few and too late.

American commanders were alarmed. But the Central Government said that it had enough forces and supplies. Efforts to turn over equipment to Hsueh Yueh while there still was time were blocked. When the Japanese drive finally threatened the railhead at Tushan, tens of thousands of tons of unused equipment had to be destroyed.

Whether or not it is true, it is important—as a factor in Chinese morale—that most Chinese believe that Chiang was not sorry to have the Japanese clean up his opposition in the Southwest. . . .

Li Chi-sen and a part of his group carried out their already completed plan of withdrawing southward to the Kwangsi-Kwangtung border and setting up a guerrilla area. Under the military leadership of Ts'ai T'ing-k'ai, of Nineteenth Route Army fame, this area is now busy building up a new army and is seeking to establish a working agreement with the Chinese Communists, whose methods of stimulating popular mobilization it seems to be following. Its relation to Chungking is one of practical independence.

* The governor of Hunan and commander of the 9th War Zone, with headquarters in the provincial capital, Changsha.

This new group now wants to receive American supplies. Strategically situated close to the coast, behind the Japanese and close to communication lines, it would be justifiable on military grounds for us to aid them. Chiang is refusing to permit us. We can expect that he will continue to. . . .

Meanwhile Li Tsung-jen's position in the North was not happy. His 5th War Zone had suffered losses and been cut in two by the Japanese drive in the spring of 1944 along the Peiping–Hankow railway. It was not surprising that his troops —ill supplied, demoralized and without the support of the people—were routed. That part of them in the Tapieh Mountains, east of the railway, was now completely cut off.

Despite these "watchdog" forces, the Communists had reestablished themselves and expanded steadily around Hankow during the past five years. Now the situation became even worse from the viewpoint of the Central Government. The whole area east of the Peiping–Hankow railway, being behind the new Japanese lines, had now, according to the Communist definition, become legitimate ground for their activities. Li's forces in the Tapieh Mountains were ordered to stop this expansion. They made at least a half-hearted attempt. There has been sporadic fighting and an American officer was with Communists in this area when they were attacked by Li's troops. . . .

The Japanese drive into Kwangsi, which broke the Southwest clique and sent a part of it into independent guerrilla opposition to Chiang, made it easier for Chiang to take his next step. Robbed of his political base, Li was weaker and hence less necessary to appease. Chinese said that it would not be long before Li would be in trouble.

They were right. In February 1945, Li was superseded as commander of the 5th War Zone and "promoted," in accordance with the familiar pattern, to head of the Generalissimo's field headquarters at Hanchung, South Shensi. Nominally, this is a big job because it is supposed to mean control of several war areas. Actually, it means nothing because it is without direct command of any troops. The forces in the field get their orders from Chungking. . . .

*   *   *

Chiang now may be able to rest easier: the Kwangsi Clique seems to be finished. But is it? A province has been lost and its people and soldiers embittered. And the liberal group under Li Chi-sen, taking a leaf from the Communist book by organizing popular resistance behind the Japanese, where Chiang cannot reach them, may yet have to be reckoned with.*

Chiang can congratulate himself that "unity" has been furthered by the clever disruption—in which the Japanese had an important part—of a strong provincial group. But is the result really unity?

*   *   *

This example of Chiang's methods is of interest, not because it is so clear-cut and so devastatingly complete in result, but because it is typical. The pattern can be applied in varying degrees to his handling of the Szechwan warlords, the Northeastern armies, the Feng Yü-hsiang† group, and many others.

This general policy has been consistently followed by Chiang since at least 1927. . . . The attempt has been to maintain a balance of power, hence lack of power, among and within these groups outside the Central Government. Once a leader has been divested of his army, or political strength, he is elevated to a meaningless position of high rank but no power.

This thorough and viciously Machiavellian application of "Divide and Rule" may have seemed to Chiang to be his only alternative. Being itself weak, the only hope of the Central Government, by this limited view, was in weakening—and keeping weak and disunited—all the opposition groups. "Unity," to Chiang, obviously means domination.

---

* Li Chi-sen's plans to organize guerrilla actions against the Japanese never amounted to much, but they moved him toward his final break with Chiang Kai-shek. In 1947 he fled to Hong Kong and urged an end to the civil war between the Kuomintang and the Communists. That led to his expulsion from the Kuomintang and to his founding, in January 1948, of the Revolutionary Kuomintang Committee, of which he was chairman and Madame Sun Yat-sen honorary chairman. After the Communists completed their conquest of the mainland, Li served as a Revolutionary Kuomintang member of the National People's Congress and other United Front organizations of the People's Republic of China until his death in 1959.

† On Feng, see Service's report on pp. 113–16.

Unfortunately the price of such a policy is heavy. The country cannot be honestly unified on such a basis. No people are more sophisticated than the Chinese in this game. The effect for the war is to convince the provincial groups that they are fools to waste their armies and sole base of power in fighting the Japanese.

Actually the result of Chiang's policy is to increase disunity and weaken the war effort. Through his inability to progress beyond his early days of civil-war intrigue, Chiang has lost much of the confidence of the people of China and is faced today with the problems of a country far less unified than when it rallied to his support in the early months of the war against Japan.

For the American government, fighting a long and bloody war against Japan, the China Theater was an unending source of frustrations. Not the least of these frustrations was the tendency for officers of the Chinese armies to defect with their units and fight for the Japanese. It was not a subject which the Chungking Government liked to discuss, but both the Communists and the Japanese made repeated mention of the phenomenon and were willing to cite facts and name names to support their contentions. The Japanese, of course, saw such defections as indicators of growing Chinese allegiance to their Greater East Asia Co-Prosperity Sphere. The Communists had a more involved explanation: they were apt to claim that the KMT was deliberately instructing its front-line generals to defect. The CCP saw a KMT grand plan to get anti-Communist forces in place in occupied China. These forces would then prevent the area from falling into Communist hands after Japan's surrender. To the Communists it was just another example of the KMT looking more to a future civil war with the CCP than to the present war with Japan. Service, while admitting that the results might conform to the Communist prediction, was more subtle in his search for causes. He wrote this fascinating study of the puppetization of the KMT and warlord armies.

Willingness of Chinese Military
Leaders to Become "Puppets"

November 3, 1943
State Security copy

According to the Chinese Communists, there are now more than 600,000 puppet troops in China, mostly in the Northeastern provinces. Other reliable Chinese sources agree that there are at least 500,000. The number is constantly growing—partly by recruiting in the occupied territory, but chiefly by the defection of whole units, up to divisions and armies, of Central Government forces. Domei* has recently reported several such cases.

Nominally these forces turn over to Chinese, i.e., the "National Government of China" at Nanking (Wang Ching-wei), or the North China Political Council (Wang K'o-min).† Actually, of course, they are under Japanese control. There are Japanese officers with them; they cooperate with the Japanese in military operations; and they assist the Japanese by guarding communication lines and doing garrison duty. Many of them are organized into units bearing the name "Emperor Assisting Army" (*huang hsieh chün*). Their service undoubtedly assists the Japanese by reducing somewhat the number of Japanese troops necessary to garrison and hold the occupied areas. This usefulness is, however, limited: the Japanese also need to watch the puppets.

This willingness of Chinese to serve the enemy is naturally embarrassing to the Central Government's propaganda—which wants the rest of the world to see China as a country fighting desperately and heroically, in the Russian style, against the foreign invader. Chinese propaganda therefore has constantly minimized these puppet forces, disguising their nature by calling them "Manchurians," "Koreans" or "Formosans." For instance, the non-Japanese forces participating in the west Hupeh drive in June 1943, although so described, were actually

* The official Japanese news agency.
† These were the Japanese-established puppet governments of East and North China.

Chinese. By now so many large groups have gone over to the Japanese that it is obvious that by far the greater number of these puppet forces are native Chinese. The Chinese themselves have helped to break down the myth by their frequent reports of puppet troops who have supposedly turned "traitor" to their masters by joining the Chinese side.

As this situation has become better known to the world, Chinese propaganda has had to take some cognizance of it. The usual line—which I have heard, for instance, in English programs over XGOY*—is somewhat as follows: The Chinese force was isolated (usually in North China) and strongly attacked by the Japanese. They made many determined counterattacks to break out of the encirclement. But the Central Government was unable to send them reinforcements or supplies in time. Therefore, after they had expended their last bullet, the beleaguered force had no alternative but to "surrender" to the Japanese. A common embellishment is that they had to surrender because they were attacked in the rear by the Communists. And in one program I have heard—lauding the "heroic" struggle of General P'ang Ping-hsun, who led the whole Group Army under him to service under the Japanese—the blame was by clear implication laid on China's allies for failure to give her sufficient planes.

This story, however, fails to explain the unpleasant fact, difficult for Westerners to understand, that the Chinese force not only surrendered but turned traitor. The Communists, whose views on traitorism are more Western than those of most Chinese, have published a list of fifty-eight Central Government commanders of general rank who have turned over to the Japanese and are now in command of puppet troops. The defection of most of these is admitted and well known.

Actually there would seem to be several alternatives to becoming puppet. The Communists claim—and there is no evidence to refute them—that none of their units, operating in the same general region, have turned puppet.

The first alternative, if the Central Government forces are hard-pressed, would be to cooperate with or join the Com-

* The radio station of the Chungking government's Ministry of Information.

munists. The Communists claim that they would welcome this and have never refused such cooperation. They cite many instances where they have actually saved Central Government forces by such cooperation.

The second alternative would be to adopt Communist methods of warfare—extreme mobility, guerrilla tactics by small units, and close cooperation with the local inhabitants. These methods have enabled the Communists to exist and to maintain some form of resistance in the same areas for more than six years.

The third alternative, if it becomes literally impossible to continue fighting, would be simply to surrender and become prisoners of war of the Japanese.

The question thus arises: Why are none of these alternatives taken? Why do whole large units go over, apparently so readily, to the Japanese?

The usual Chinese explanation—believed by many Chinese, and which the Chinese would like the foreigners to believe—is that these puppets are still loyal, that they are simply being fed and armed by the Japanese, and that they will rise against their masters and rejoin China at the right moment. This line appeals to the Chinese dislike of needless sacrifice ("no use in continuing a hopeless struggle if you can live to gain your victory in the end"), and to the deep-seated Chinese failing for intrigue ("we are really fooling the Japanese"). But this is only a partial explanation and is far too simple.

The usual Communist explanation is that these large complete units turn over to the Japanese as part of a Central Government plan to regain control after the war of the Communist-dominated guerrilla areas of North China. The Communists point out: (1) The Central Government is at present unable to maintain forces in the areas behind the Japanese lines in North China. Therefore, when the Japanese withdraw, the whole of North China may be left in the occupation of the Communists. By becoming puppets, Central Government forces are able to enter this area. When the Japanese withdraw, these Central Government forces will hence be left in occupation of the cities and communication lines—the same stranglehold that the Japanese now have on North China. (2) By turning puppet, these Central Government forces are no longer worn down by Japanese attrition. Instead they have an opportunity to strengthen themselves for the civil war—not only by whatever supplies the Japanese allow them, but also by being able to live off the richer occupied areas. This "mass puppetry" is therefore, in Communist eyes, an *ad hoc* collaboration between the Kuomintang and the Japanese against the Communists. The Communists accordingly attack the puppets when they are in a position to do so.

There is some basis for the Communist fears. Central Government officials have openly stated that the puppets will cooperate with Central Government forces after the war to eradicate the Communists. They admit present contact with the puppets and infer that such collaboration already exists. There is no doubt that most Chinese expect some postwar compromise involving forgiveness for most of the present puppets, and that they do in fact hope to be able to use the puppets against the Communists.*

It might also be argued—though as yet on a purely theoretical basis—that the Japanese are willing to fall in with these arrangements. The reasoning would be as follows: The Japanese now foresee eventual defeat in China. Their greatest fear is Communism. They would much prefer to have a Kuomintang Government in China because it would probably be weaker and more inclined to be cooperative than a strictly Communist one. There is danger that the Communists may become strong enough to overthrow the Kuomintang, or to establish a separate Communist North China—the area in which Japan is naturally most interested. This development would be especially unfavorable to Japan if—as would be likely—the Chinese Communists were supported by or closely linked to Russia. Therefore the Japanese have everything to gain by helping the Kuomintang to be in a position to deal successfully with the Communists. Such assistance may also be expected to obtain better peace terms from the Central Government, and to lay the basis for the postwar collaboration—necessary from the Japanese standpoint—with China. Certainly anti-Communism, rather than attacks on Chungking, is now the main theme of

* These hopes and expectations did, of course, prove to be well founded: most of the puppet troops did in fact join the Kuomintang in its postwar civil war with the Communists.

Japanese—and hence puppet—propaganda in North China. And the puppet troops are more [active] against Communist than Central Government forces.

This explanation of "puppetry" is not, however, entirely satisfactory. It is a little too slick, too deep. It fits some of the circumstances, but not all of them. The creation of an anti-Communist army in North China, eventually to be used by the Kuomintang, is probably more of a fortuitous development, as far as the Kuomintang is concerned, than a deep-laid Kuomintang plot with Japanese connivance. This explanation, therefore, is more a description of results than an analysis of causes.

Non-Communist Chinese, who are experienced political observers, and who are willing to discuss such questions frankly, have pointed out a number of background factors in the situation which seem to be pertinent. These may be summarized briefly as follows.

Generally speaking, it has been the regular policy of the Central Government to place in the front and in isolated forward areas the remnants of the old provincial, "warlord" armies. This policy has two objectives: (1) to conserve the Central Government's own troops—usually better trained and equipped; and (2) to dissipate these other armies—which have been, and may in the future again be, threats to the Kuomintang's power. It is true that most of these commanders, and most of the armies which have turned puppet, particularly in North China, are such relics of the warlord era. Many are remnants of the Manchurian "Tung-pei" Army (under Yü Hsueh-chung) who have been kicked around China for more than ten years. A large number belonged to the Kuominchün (once under General Feng Yü-hsiang)—for instance, Generals P'ang Ping-hsun and Sun Lien-chung. Others, such as Ch'i Hsieh-yuan and Shih Yu-san, belong to the old provincial warlord class, whose typical record was "up from banditry."

Viewed against this background, the willingness to turn puppet becomes more understandable.

In the first place, these military commanders, and the men under them, have no desire to continue what is—for them personally—a hopeless fight. They are no match for the Japanese forces against them. The leaders may in recent years have owed nominal allegiance to the Central Government. But they have never been real Kuomintang men. Rather, they have had a background of fighting against the Kuomintang. The lower ranks have never been strongly indoctrinated politically. If they are holdovers from the warlord days, they were recruited from the riffraff and dregs of the population. If they are recent recruits, they have been impressed into service. If they are volunteers, they signed up because they could not make a living any other way, or are of the bandit type. In any case they are without much national feeling and without enthusiasm for hard fighting. And in the background consciousness of both leaders and men there is a distrust of the Kuomintang and the suspicion that they are being sacrificed by the Central Government for its own ends.

In the second place, there is no cooperation with the Communists because the leaders, by background, are bitterly anti-Communist. The provincial warlords, to whom these men belong, sought individual power and great wealth. They usually had close connections with the local landlord-gentry class. Because of these reasons, they were consistently fought by the Communists. Warlords and Communists don't mix—even in the face of an enemy.

Thirdly, they do not adopt Communist methods because they are unable to. The leaders, generally of low military caliber, have not been trained and do not think along guerrilla lines. And their armies are not hardy or vigorous enough. Furthermore, they are unable, because of their treatment of the people, to gain the support which is necessary to successful guerrilla warfare. They are mercenaries who, in the old days, were used to leading a largely sedentary life of garrisoning towns and living off the people. They see no attraction in taking to the poor and thinly populated mountains and marshes as closely pursued and hard-pressed guerrillas.

Finally, they are willing to turn puppet and work, if necessary, for the Japanese for these reasons and because, fundamentally, they are mercenaries. Under the Central Government they are miserably paid, fed and equipped. This was particularly true of these armies, who were distant or physically isolated from the main Chinese rear. From the Japanese the leaders get promises of high rewards and rank. The men are offered better pay, better food and more arms. Furthermore, by going over to the Japanese, they have an opportunity to live better by garrisoning the larger cities and richer areas—all under Japanese control. And by assisting and following the Japanese, they have a better chance at plunder. A Chinese writer, describing the fighting in west Hupeh has reported, for instance, that the depredations of the puppets were worse than those of the Japanese. Similar stories are told by missionaries who went through several years of the bitter fighting in Shansi. There is no question of the men being willing to follow their leaders in turning puppet because, in addition to these mercenary attractions, these warlord forces are "personal" armies. They owe allegiance to their leader only.

These are also, of course, reasons why the army does not surrender and become prisoners. . . . In the first place, surrender would not be acceptable to the Japanese. They have no use for a lot of idle prisoners when the men can be made to work for them. But actually surrender is probably never even considered—by either side. It was not done in warlord China. If a leader decided that he was on the losing side, or found that he could profit sufficiently, he went over to the other side —and took his personal army with him. Things do not change quickly in China. It is common for these commanders to have contact—through trade or more direct channels—with the Japanese or Chinese puppets under them. When a satisfactory arrangement—probably backed up by a threat of military annihilation—is reached, the change in allegiance is made.

If this is the chief explanation of puppetry, it is logical to query the probable usefulness of these forces—either, as the Chinese hope, in a rising against the Japanese or as a force to break the Communist hold on North China.

The answer probably is that the factors which make them willing to turn puppet will also reduce their value to the Central Government. They are mercenaries, with little national consciousness, and without devotion to the cause of the Kuomintang.

As a force against the Japanese, it must be realized that the Japanese are not so foolish as to permit them great strength. Hence they are still poorly armed and are kept scattered in relatively small units. They can be expected to try to rejoin the Chinese side. But only at a very late period when the defeat of the Japanese has already substantially been achieved.

As a force against the Communists, it must be borne in mind that their leadership is poor and the quality of the troops is low. Their leaders may be ideologically willing to fight the Communists. But they will first be concerned with the promotion of their own selfish interests and ambitions. Their armies will be the basis of their claim for power: they will have no desire to see those armies dissipated by the Kuomintang in anti-Communist civil war. As for the men, they will have as little enthusiasm then as now for hard fighting. They will be no match for a Communist army which is well trained, politically indoctrinated, supported by the population, and fighting for its life.

In general, therefore, we may reach the conclusion that, except for the added complication which they inject into the situation in China, the relatively minor assistance they render the Japanese by garrison duty, and the depredation they carry out as jackals of the Japanese, the Chinese puppet armies may be largely discounted. The figure 600,000 is not as formidable as it looks.

Short of becoming outright puppets, several Chinese military leaders made local accommodations with the Japanese forces facing them. The most notable of these was Yen Hsi-shan, long the master of Shansi province. His wartime dealings with the Japanese were of particular concern to the Chinese Communists, for he controlled the area just to the east of the Border Region. In the spring of 1945, while Service was in Yenan, he was able to establish definitely that Yen Hsi-shan had indeed been collaborating with the Japanese, even while maintaining his position within the Kuomintang's military structure.

Yen Hsi-shan's Dealings with the Japanese

March 20, 1945
Amerasia Papers, pp. 1427–30

Summary: Captured documents in the hands of the Communists and free statements to a foreign observer by a captured general of Yen Hsi-shan's army are conclusive proof that Yen has relations with the Japanese which are undoubtedly known to the Central Government. *End of Summary.*

Reference is made to a report* which I wrote about August 1944 reporting conflicts between the military forces of General Yen Hsi-shan, chairman of Shansi province and commander of the 2nd War Zone (both under the Central Government) and Communist troops. In that report I mentioned Communist charges that Yen had close relations with the Japanese.

Documents which the Communists claimed to have in their possession proving their assertions of Yen's dealings with the Japanese did not actually arrive in Yenan until after my departure. They were loaned to Captain Stelle for photographing and it is understood that copies have been sent to Theater Headquarters. I am told that these documents included originals of captured messages between Yen's officers and Japanese commanders. These concerned minor frictions and misunderstandings and clearly indicated the existence of an agreement between Yen and the Japanese permitting Yen's forces to operate in certain areas, including the expansion east of the Tung-pu railway which brought them into conflict with the Communist forces already occupying that zone. There was also an alleged copy of the full agreement written on official Japanese army stationery but lacking other evidences of authenticity.

Additional to these documentary evidences are the statements of a major general (one star) of Yen's Sixty-first Army captured by the Communists in the fighting which took place when that army moved across the Japanese-held Tung-pu rail-

---

* This report, dated August 19, 1944, and entitled "Communist Charges against General Yen Hsi-shan" may be found in *Amerasia Papers,* pp. 767–76.

way in the spring of 1944. This officer was eventually brought to Yenan, where he was kept for several months but allowed what seemed to be almost complete freedom—presumably because he was willing to admit his wrongs. During his sojourn (he was later permitted to return to Yen because of threats to his family) he met Mrs. Michael Lindsay. Learning that her father was formerly an important political and military figure in Shansi province, he called on her and her husband (an English ex-professor of Yenching University who escaped from Peiping on December 7, 1941). The call turned into an evening meal and long evening of discussion in which the officer became mildly intoxicated and "let down his hair." There were no other persons present, and Mr. Lindsay, who describes the general as an intelligent, open and genuinely patriotic man in his thirties, believes that he talked with candor and honesty. The following are the highlights of his talk.

In the summer and fall of 1941 the Japanese tried to persuade Yen to become the head of the government of North China. This was after the disastrous rout of the Chinese armies in the Chungtiao Mountains (South Shansi) and the German attack on Russia. The situation for China was dark. Yen considered the Japanese proposal very seriously because he expected a Japanese attack on Russia and an early Axis victory. (I remember that in Chungking there were many rumors at about this period that Yen's allegiance was doubtful.) However, Yen hung on the fence for a while. Meanwhile, Pearl Harbor changed the outlook in China's eventual favor.

The Japanese then staged a minor campaign against Yen —not serious but enough to frighten him and cause fairly heavy losses to his meager military forces. This fighting in the spring of 1942 is the last real fight between the Japanese and Yen.

After the military admonishment, which was not pressed too vigorously, the Japanese tried new tactics. They concluded that the time was not propitious for Yen to turn over openly. They therefore proposed undercover cooperation. Their calculations were right. An agreement was reached which is still the basis for present relations. By this agreement both sides avoid hostilities against the other and operate within specified areas; Yen resists any Communist encroachment on his zone; he maintains liaison with the Japanese through a representative in Taiyuan; and Yen's subordinates participate in the puppet organizations in Shansi. At present twenty-three puppet *hsien* magistrates in Shansi are actually Yen men appointed under this agreement. (When AGAS* sent a representative to visit Yen in the spring of 1944, he claimed authority and ability to rescue American airmen in areas of Shansi far beyond his actual zone of military control and including many districts divided between the Japanese and Communists.)

On this basis, relations between Yen and the Japanese became quite cordial. Trade became open and Yen was able to get some needed supplies from Taiyuan. The Japanese commander in Shansi actually visited Yen. (Yen admitted this meeting to the foreign correspondents who visited him in June 1944, but explained it on the ground that he and the Japanese commander were graduates of the same military school in Japan.) During the visit the Japanese, looking for publicity for the day when Yen would become an open puppet, took photographs. Yen, who is leary of certain types of publicity, took the precaution of wearing civilian clothes. Somehow a copy of this photograph reached Chungking. When Chiang asked for an explanation, Yen replied that the picture could not be of him because he had worn nothing but his military uniform since the outbreak of the "war of resistance."

In January 1944, General Hsu Yung-ch'ang, chief of the Board of Military Operations in Chungking and an old Shansi military man, made a trip to Yen's headquarters. (The fact of this trip was well known in Chungking at the time.) Hsu's proposal was that Yen move into southcentral Shansi. The Central Government would then send troops across the Yellow River from east of Tungkuan, and the two forces would then operate a pincer movement to reoccupy the Chungtiao Mountains.

Yen agreed. But to try this by force was impossible because it involved crossing the Japanese-held Tung-pu railway. And it would violate his understanding with the Japanese and cause retaliations—which made it unthinkable. He therefore put the matter up to the Japanese on the basis of being able to recover territory then under the control of the Communists. He could at the same time make the pretense of complying with the Central Government plan.

* Air Ground Aid Service of the U.S. forces in China.

The Japanese, who apparently did not fear the Central Government drive northward from Honan, since they themselves were already planning their Honan offensive, were agreeable, and details of the new area to be occupied by Yen were arranged.

Yen then called a conference of his military officers which lasted January 16–20, 1944. (In this the captured general took part personally.) The plan was explained and preparations started for the "offensive."

Yen's Sixty-first Army, the one selected for the task, did not actually get under way until March. The "campaign" soon took on comic-opera aspects. For the sake of appearances, in order to give the impression of having to "force" the Tung-pu railway, the army planned to cross the zone at night with sham battle effects. The Japanese, however, had other ideas and insisted that the crossing be by day. In broad daylight, therefore, it was, with Japanese officers welcoming their Chinese brothers and serving refreshments to them as they passed through the Japanese zone. They did not omit having photographers on hand to record this glowing instance of Sino-Japanese cooperation.

The taking over of the new area also involved relieving several Japanese-garrisoned strongpoints. Here again the Chinese were denied "face." They had wanted the staging of mock hostilities and a Japanese withdrawal. But the Japanese insisted on the same polite formalities—with the same serving of refreshments and taking of photographs.

Once across the railway in the Linfen area, Yen's troops had some stiff fighting with the Communists. Eighth Route forces, however, were relatively few and not concentrated and were forced to withdraw before the more numerous Sixty-first Army. In that fighting the informant was captured while commanding a regiment.

(An American officer who recently spent some time in Yen's area reports that he was not permitted to visit these forces east of the Tung-pu railway. Noting other evidences of collusion between Yen and the Japanese, he concluded that Yen wished to conceal the fact that maintenance and suppy of these troops across the Japanese-held railway could not be accomplished without Japanese agreement.)

The officer claimed that there is a great deal of dissatisfaction among Yen's younger and more patriotic officers because of this situation in which Yen is dealing traitorously with the Japanese. They are, however, helpless. Yen rules autocratically and requires every man to take a personal oath of allegiance, a part of which is to commit suicide (by eating opium) if he disobeys orders. In addition Yen relies on rigorous secret-police methods and the widespread use of spies. For instance, the officers' servants must be supplied by Yen. They are trained in a special school and report on their masters. The whole Yen organization is so riddled with this sort of thing that no one trusts anybody else. Yen keeps a further hold on his subordinates by the time-honored scheme of making practical hostages of their families.

An ironic note in the whole situation is that the [Communist] Eighth Route (18th Group) Army, which Yen has been fighting rather than the Japanese, is under his command as head of the 2nd War Zone, with Chu Teh as Vice War Zone Commander. Although the only sign on Chu Teh's headquarters in Yenan is "Headquarters of the Vice Commander of the 2nd War Zone," there is now no direct liaison between him and his "commander."

It may be considered that I have given undue attention to a sideshow of the situation in China. The incidents described are indeed minor. But they are typical and the aspect of the situation which they reflect is fundamental. In the particular instance, they are so well documented that they cannot be ignored. And Yen Hsi-shan's position is so obvious that even the most charitable-minded cannot assume that Chungking does not know of the situation.

It is by knowledge of this type of attitude shown by Yen, and of Chungking's complicity in it, that we can better understand the basic issues in China and the fact that the internal struggle for power has precedence over the defeat of the foreign enemy.

THE KUOMINTANG DICTATORSHIP

It was an embarrassing fact that our Chinese ally in the war against the Axis was a one-party proto-fascist dictatorship, a fact not all Americans chose to face. The Kuomintang, founded by Sun Yat-sen in 1911 and dominated by Chiang Kai-shek since Sun's death in 1925, controlled the government, the army, the secret police, the press, the schools and many of the leading economic institutions of China. Sun Yat-sen's United Front policy of alliance with the Chinese Communist Party was abruptly ended by Chiang's bloody suppression of the Communists in 1927. For the next ten years Chiang, with his German advisers, waged a relentless war to eradicate the CCP. Then Chiang's own generals kidnapped him in Sian and forced him to re-establish the United Front and concentrate on the war against Japan. The United Front against Japan functioned relatively well for the next two years, with the Communists concentrating on guerrilla warfare from their bases in North China, and Chiang Kai-shek "trading space for time" in the South and slowly retreating toward his wartime capital of Chungking. Then, in January 1941, after a series of minor clashes between Kuomintang forces and the Communist New Fourth Army, Chiang's forces attacked and decimated the headquarters detachment of the New Fourth Army, killing some two thousand and capturing an equal number, including the commander, Yeh T'ing. Though the Communists continued to maintain a small office and operate a heavily censored newspaper in Chungking, this incident marked the end of any genuine United Front.

The end of the United Front affected far more than the relations between the KMT and the CCP. The presence of the Communists as rivals of the Kuomintang had allowed a great variety of liberals, intellectuals and dissident elements to make themselves heard. In the years after 1941, dissent became far more difficult, and the fascist tendencies of the KMT became increasingly obvious. These tendencies were visible in any number of areas, but one of the most obvious was the realm of propaganda. This section is a brief "Background" to a long untitled despatch on propaganda agencies in Kuomintang China, written while Service was a Third Secretary in the Chungking Embassy.

Memorandum on Propaganda, Psychological Warfare and Morale Agencies in Free China

July 10, 1942
Foreign Relations, 1942, pp. 203–5

II. BACKGROUND

A description of Chinese propaganda and related work requires as background a brief consideration of recent political history and the present political, social and economic situation in China.

The first of these is the Kuomintang dictatorship. This has given the Party a monopoly of all propaganda, even within the army. Education is frankly identified with propaganda.* The press is controlled. All propaganda takes on a political character, and the strengthening and perpetuation of the Kuomintang's position becomes one of its primary objectives.

A second, but related, factor is the situation growing out of the breakdown of the "united front." The truce with the Chinese Communists and other left-wing elements, made after the Sian incident at the end of 1936, became genuine and apparently wholehearted cooperation in the early stage of the war with Japan. That conflict provided a powerful rallying force. There was real effort to arouse and unite the people, and great activity in propagandizing and organizing guerrilla operations in the

---

* The Ministry of Education might with justification be called the most important and extensive propaganda agency. This is borne out in numerous public statements such as the recent broadcast by the Ministry of Education, Ch'en Li-fu, to the occupied territory emphasizing the importance of "San Min Chu I education" of children and youth. The Ministry does not seem to be directly within the field of this survey but its own concept of its mission, its strong political and nationalistic character, and its influence, through selection of textbooks and control of primary, secondary and to a slightly lesser extent of higher education, should be noted. [Footnote in original.]

areas close to and under Japanese occupation. In this spontaneous outburst of enthusiastic war work, the country's leading
writers and artists (most of them left-wing) and the Communists
took a major part. Many people—even within the present Government—look back on this period as that of the Government's
greatest efficiency and effectiveness.

For reasons which need not be discussed in detail here,
there was a reaction which dates roughly from the moving of
the Government away from Hankow in the fall of 1938. The
Kuomintang apparently became jealous of the growing influence of the Communists and subjected them and the left wing
to a growing repression which, culminating in the clash with
the New Fourth Army, has led to the present situation of suspicion and near hostilities. The effect was to kill much of the
active, creative propaganda work which was being done and to
give Kuomintang propaganda a strong anti-Communist bias. To
certain sections of the [Kuomintang] Party, combating Communism became an important, if not the most important, part of
propaganda work. The vitality and vigor of anti-Japanese propaganda and psychological warfare activity has declined since this
time.

A third factor is the effect of general war-weariness and
economic difficulties. After five years of war there has come
an inevitable letdown of morale and enthusiasm. The capital is
now located far from the almost inactive fighting fronts. Communication and transportation are extremely difficult. Supplies
are difficult to obtain—even paper and printing present great
problems. Inflation has brought a tremendous increase in costs.
The result is that many organizations, which for a time did more
or less effective work, have greatly reduced their activity or become moribund.

A recent development greatly affecting propaganda work
among Chinese in the occupied areas and abroad was the
seizure by the Japanese in December 1941 of the foreign settle-
ments at Shanghai and Tientsin and the capture of Hong
Kong and "south sea" cities. In all of these places there was a
Kuomintang-subsidized press and extensive propaganda and
secret-service activity, some of which might be considered a
psychological warfare against the Japanese and their puppets.
Immediately after occupation by the Japanese, the persons en-

gaged in this work were arrested or forced to flee. As a result, work in the occupied areas is admittedly at an almost complete standstill.

A fifth factor, mentioned because it adds to the difficulty of a clear survey, is the Chinese tendency to multiply organizations without limiting their functions or unifying their control. We find that almost every department in the Government and major Party organization has its own propaganda or publicity branch. And despite the original complexity of the Government-Party structure, there has been a tendency, as the war progressed and new situations arose, to superimpose on the existing framework new and often vaguely defined organizations. For instance, the recently established National General Mobilization Council has a "Culture Branch," presumably to initiate and coordinate propaganda in support of the national mobilization effort. The steady bureaucratic growth seems, in many cases, to have increased confusion, divided responsibility and reduced initiative and effectiveness.

In June 1943, while traveling by truck from Chungking to Lanchow, Service passed the time most profitably by noting and recording propaganda slogans written on houses and walls along the route. The result was a report which, while lengthy, was precise, sophisticated and fascinating. It was really a work of political science—of content analysis. The State Department commended Service for this report with one of its rare ratings of "EXCELLENT."

Chinese Propaganda as Shown by
Wall Slogans in the Northwest

July 5, 1943
Archives copy: 800.20293/6

. . . [*Summary*] The first section discusses the importance in China of wall slogans and the reasons therefor. The second section is a list of some 150 slogans classified by subject. The third section discusses the relative frequency of the various types of slogans, both as to subject and locality, and points out that propaganda activity of this type, except in Kansu, seems to have slackened during the past two or three years. The fourth section gives attention to the multiplicity of organizations engaged in slogan propaganda, mentioning the increasing share being taken by the San Min Chu I Youth Corps.* The fifth section is a tentative attempt to evaluate and analyze the slogan material collected. It points out: (1) that all propaganda is monopolized by Kuomintang Party organizations, but an opposition is implicit in many of the slogans; (2) that the slogans used generally seem to lack popular appeal; (3) that there is a noticeable emphasis on political subjects, with important classes of slogans advocating the leadership principle, racism, and the primacy of the Party; (4) that the war is given relatively less emphasis, slogans dealing with it omitting mention of the world conflict and failing to utilize several logical propaganda appeals; (5) that the slogans are sometimes contradictory and obscure; (6) that the constant use of old and often unimaginative slogans seems to indicate a tendency toward sterility and deterioration in the Party's propaganda; and (7) that the subjects and frequency of certain types of slogans are an indication of the gravity and continuance of problems confronting the Kuomintang such as: provincialism, local unrest, opium growing and hoarding, Mohammedan dissidence, and resistance to grain collections and conscription.

A. INTRODUCTION

1. Reasons for Study of Slogans

The Kuomintang, which developed its propaganda technique during the period of Russian collaboration, has always laid great emphasis on wall slogans.

In addition to its generally accepted merits of simplicity, visual presentation and constant reiteration, this method seems

---

* The San Min Chu I were the "Three People's Principles" of Sun Yat-sen: nationalism, people's rights and people's livelihood. The San Min Chu I Youth Corps was the Kuomintang's party organization for young people, similar to the Nazi's Hitler Youth or the Soviet's Young Pioneers.

to have particular adaptability to China. The language lends itself to the making of epigrammatic phrases suitable for slogans. Chinese have, to our minds, a great tolerance for pat expressions, and this method is widely used in primary education (comparable in a way to propaganda for the masses) where subject matter is simplified and condensed into brief sentences which are repeated in unison until memorized by the pupils. This technique is used even in adult institutions such as the Central Training Corps at Chungking for Party workers and Government officials. Another example is the fondness of the Chinese for adages and proverbs. Finally, newspapers are comparatively few in number and their circulation limited. Especially in the country districts there are few newspapers, no theaters, and very poor distribution of new books or other printed material.

Since most of the rural population, and a very large proportion of the people in the cities cannot read, it might be considered more appropriate to stress pictorial posters. But this method has limitations in China, particularly under present war conditions. Many propaganda ideas are difficult to express pictorially. Chinese paper is of poor quality and posters would be impermanent. There are no adequate printing facilities, and hand-drawn posters would be expensive and generally of poor quality. On the other hand, the Chinese have a great respect for the written character—for its form and beauty, as well as for its meaning. And it may be assumed that even if a person cannot read, his natural curiosity will lead him to inquire the meaning of characters painted on the side of his home or posted prominently along the roads so that he must pass them daily.

The result is that China is literally plastered with slogans, while pictures are a rarity and generally nothing more than a simplified drawing of the Generalissimo or a soldier. These slogans occupy almost every blank wall facing the road in some sections of the country. They are painted on city walls, on rocks along the highways, and on the sides of farmhouses. In the Northwest, they are sometimes written on the red paper slips pasted over and at the sides of front doors (these used to be quotations from the classics or phrases meant to bring good luck and prosperity to the occupants). In many places builders of new walls or houses are required to incorporate preparations, such as inset plaster panels, for the painting of slogans. . . .

2. Territory Covered

All slogans listed are from Szechwan, Shensi and Kansu.
A few notes were taken during my travel through this area in
the summer and fall of 1942. Most of the slogans, however,
were observed during my travel from Chungking to Lanchow
between June 5 and 25, 1943, my route passing through
Chengtu, Kwangyuan, Paocheng, Shuangshihpu and Tienshui.
A very few slogans, not more than two or three, were not personally observed but were given me by foreigners whose knowledge of Chinese is dependable. . . .

B. CLASSIFICATION LISTS OF SLOGANS

[Here follows a list of 150 different slogans observed by
Service, with indications of their frequency of appearance. Their
subject matter ranged from such "Follow the Leader" slogans
as "Follow the Supreme Leader Chiang" to the anti-Communist
slogan "Wipe out Traitors," to blunt warnings that "Planters of
Opium Will Be Shot" or polite advice to "Take a Bath At Least
Once a Week."]

C. DISTRIBUTION, FREQUENCY AND DATES

Generally, slogans are found along the main motor highways, on the main streets of towns, and in the immediate
vicinity of the larger cities. In the smaller villages, away from
the roads, and in the country, they are fewer in number, and in
some districts hardly found.

[Service then goes on to discuss specific regional variations in
the types of slogans which appear and the dates of their posting.]

A large number of the slogans are found all through the
provinces covered. Although in some localized areas these may
be outnumbered by specialized slogans such as those dealing
with opium or conscription, these are, considering the whole
field, the commonest and most frequent. This universal class
includes the following:

> Follow the Leader: Support the Government
> Follow the Supreme Leader, Chairman Chiang
> The Race Above All: The Nation Above All
> Be Loyal to the Party: Love the Country

Join Ideas and Determination: Unite Strength
Build a New San Min Chu I China
Fight Back: Build the Country
Military Affairs First: Victory First
Good Sons Become Soldiers
Good Chinese Become Soldiers
Those Who Have Money, Give Money: Those Who Have
    Strength, Give Strength

D. SLOGAN-POSTING ORGANIZATIONS

The oldest slogans generally have no indication of the organization responsible for their posting. However, this practice has become increasingly general and is now almost universal.

These "signatures" indicate that a bewildering number of organizations are engaged in slogan propaganda work. Local "*tang-pu*" (Party headquarters) appear to be the originators of most of the slogans in the towns. But along the highways, and in cities where troops are or have been garrisoned, a large proportion of the slogans are posted by the military *tang-pu* or Political Affairs Department of the units concerned. In villages, slogans are often put up by the local village government or the *pao-chia* organization. An interesting development is the very large proportion of the newer slogans, especially in *hsien* cities, which have been posted by the San Min Chu I Youth Corps. These always carry such prominent indication of their origin that they seem to be a form of advertising for the corps itself. Their numbers would seem to indicate growth and activity of the corps. . . .

E. GENERAL COMMENT AND ANALYSIS

The examination of this number of slogans and data relevant to them permits the making of several observations and an attempt to analyze them and appraise their effectiveness.

1. Kuomintang Monopoly but Implication of Opposition

One notes the fact that all slogans are posted by agencies of the Kuomintang, either civilian or military. No slogans by any other party are permitted. Even if an apparently nonpolitical organization, as for instance the Northwest Highway Bureau, which posts slogans urging promotion of transportation, goes in for this type of propaganda, it is carried out by the special Party branch for the organization. The Rural Cooperative Administration of the Ministry of Social Affairs may post slogans urging the organization of cooperative societies, but the Chinese Industrial Cooperatives are not permitted to do so.

Under special circumstances opposition slogans do appear. For instance, when the "bandits" recently active in Kansu captured a town, they put up slogans attacking the policies of the Central Government. I saw remnants of a few of these in Maying along the line of: "Welcome to the Lightener of the People's Sufferings" and "Drive Out the Central Troops." But such slogans are destroyed as quickly as the Central forces regain control.

There are therefore no opposition slogans, no slogans advocating any policy other than "follow the leader" and "carry out the San Min Chu I."

Hence it is interesting to find in many slogans an implication of opposition or of doctrines other than those advocated by the Party. For instance: "Chairman Chiang is China's Only Leader" implies that there are actually, in the minds of the public, other leaders. The same is true of slogans such as: "Only the San Min Chu I Can Save China," and "The San Min Chu I Are the Only Principles for Saving China."

However, this opposition is never named. The Kuomintang is the only party mentioned. The Communists are never, one might say, dignified by being named. The only exception to this rule is in the area of north Szechwan, between Kwangyuan and Paocheng, where old anti-Communist slogans may still be seen.* That these old slogans should have been allowed to remain is, in itself, rather interesting. That the failure to remove them is not an oversight appears to be proved by one or two instances of new political slogans—of the post–"united front" era—being painted just beside old anti-Communist slogans which have not been touched.

---

*This area was occupied by the Communists in 1934–1935. The old anti-Communist slogans undoubtedly dated from the subsequent Kuomintang reoccupation of the area.

2. Lack of Popular Appeal

This complete monopoly of propaganda may not have worked to improve the quality of Kuomintang work in this line. Technically, and aside from the fact that the majority of the population of China does not read, it may be questioned whether the slogans now being used by the Kuomintang are a very effective means of reaching and persuading the mass of the people.

The great mass of the slogans is in literary style and language, and almost universally dogmatic and assertive in tone. In view of the provincialism, slight education and lack of political sense or national feeling of the average Chinese, it is surprising that there is so little attempt at explanation, persuasion or individual appeal. . . . Numerous are such slogans as: "Complete the National Defense Scientific Reconstruction Movement" (which example, incidentally, was painted on the wall of a farmhouse at the outskirts of a small country village in which probably not more than one or two persons would have any knowledge or understanding of what it meant). The ultimate of unreality was a slogan in large English letters— "Army Needs You"—found on the walls of a house in a small mountain hamlet in north Szechwan.

An attempt at a rational appeal seems to be made in some of the conscription slogans, an important and numerous type. For instance: "To Build the Country, First Build an Army: To Protect the Home, First Protect the Country." But the greater number of these slogans hardly seem calculated to make an appeal to the average person faced with the probability of being forced into military service with all the hardships which that entails in China. On several occasions Chinese in the coolie class have in my hearing indicated an active resentment of the idea expressed in the common slogan: "Those Who Have Money, Give Money: Those Who Have Strength, Give Strength" (which, of course, is a direct contradiction of the democratic idea of universal military service).

Another important type are the anti-opium slogans. But their tone is threatening and the lack of any attempt at popular education is obvious. The commonest of these slogans is: "Planters of Opium Will Be Shot."

A foreigner may notice absence of a popular touch in the failure to use catchy phrases, rhymes or puns. Examples of what is meant are the current American slogans: "Bonds or Bondage" and "Pay Your Taxes: Beat the Axis." The failure is the more surprising since puns are common in Chinese humor, and the small number of sounds makes alliteration and rhyming easy.

Another evidence of the lack of touch with the average reader is the fondness of some slogan-posting organizations for modernistic or monogram styles of characters. This is a recent fad of some of the more Westernized students, comparable to modernistic styles of Western lettering. Often there is great distortion of the character to fit prescribed shapes, and being merely the fanciful design of the slogan painter, they have puzzled educated Chinese in my company who have admitted deciphering some of them by their context. This tendency toward bizarre lettering was most marked in Szechwan but rare in Kansu.

Having thus discounted the effectiveness of Chinese slogans, there might appear to be little use of further comment. However, several points are of interest.

3. Emphasis on Political Subjects

. . . Noteworthy are the diversity and frequency of slogans of the following classes:

1. "Follow the Leader"
2. "The Race Above All"
3. "The Supremacy of the Party"
4. "Support the (Central) Government"
7. "Anti-traitor" (in the Kuomintang vocabulary
   a member of any other party is a traitor)

In the list on pages [68–69] of common "universal" slogans (i.e., appearing all through the territory) it will be noted that six out of eleven slogans are primarily political.

The relative precedence of different parts of some of these slogans may be significant. For instance: "Follow," a strong term, is almost always used with "Leader"; while "Support," a weaker phrase, is coupled with "Government." Furthermore, the phrase "Follow the Leader" is always placed ahead of "Support the Government," thus apparently giving it greater importance.

Examples of the same rigid rule of precedence are:

The *Race* Above All: The *Nation* Above All
Complete Loyalty to *Party* and *Country*
Be Loyal to the *Party:* Love the *Country*

The last example is of particular interest because of its very common—almost unfailing—use in military barracks and headquarters. It is commonly found, for instance, on the large wall usually facing the front entrance of such official establishments. It has even "graduated," one might say, from the ordinary rank of slogans, since it is often found on the "*pien,*" or horizontal wooden tablets, which are carved with personally written characters and given as rewards to deserving subordinates by men of very high rank such as the Generalissimo. This general use of the slogan "Be Loyal to the Party: Love the Country" on military establishments implies, of course, that the army is a "Party army," rather than a national one, and that the soldier owes his first duty, loyalty, to the Party.

The resemblance, intended or accidental, of some of the slogans to foreign models is obvious. For instance: "One Race, One Party, One Leader" (i.e., *Ein Volk, Ein Reich, Ein Führer*).

[A brief section, "*4. Secondary Emphasis on War,*" is omitted.]

5. Contradictions and Obscurities

I asked a third-year college student what race was meant in the slogan "Race Above All: Nation Above All." He replied that it was the Chinese race. But when I raised the question of the five races—Han, Manchu, Mongol, Tibetan and Mohammedan mentioned in Dr. Sun's Three Principles—he grew confused. . . .

6. Apparent Sterility and Deterioration in Kuomintang Propaganda

. . . The failure of the Party to devise new and original slogans to keep up the interest of the people and to meet the changing conditions of the war, and these other facts just mentioned, would seem to justify the conclusion that there is a growing sterility and deterioration of the Kuomintang's propaganda.

7. *Slogans as Evidence of Internal Problems*

Quite apart from the question of the effectiveness of the Kuomintang's slogans as mass propaganda, they have interest as an evidence of internal problems confronting the Government. From them one gets a very different picture from that drawn by China's writers of propaganda for foreign consumption. Some of the problems with which these slogans deal are unmentioned by China's foreign propagandists; others are denied to exist.

Most important of these problem slogans are those dealing with conscription and opium. Their great numbers are evidence of the continuance of these problems.

Slogans such as "Support the Central Government" and "Obey All the Laws and Edicts of the Central Government" are apparently aimed at persistent provincialism. . . .

The slogans dealing with grain collection would tend to confirm reports of opposition to the grain collection program. . . .

The popular idea of soldiery is hinted at in the slogan "Central Government Troops Do Not Disturb the People."

As the war dragged on, the sterility of Kuomintang propaganda and the undemocratic nature of its ideology became more pronounced than ever. One small indication of this was a speech by Tai Chi-t'ao to the Central Executive Committee of the Kuomintang, which in the spring of 1944 was preparing for an important plenary session. Tai was a leader of the right wing of the Kuomintang. His earlier political career had run the gamut from founding member of the Chinese Communist Party in 1921 to virulent anti-Communist and defender of China's Confucian and Buddhist traditions from the mid-twenties on. Throughout his career he remained personally close to Chiang Kai-shek and an influential adviser of the Generalissimo.

Buddhist State Philosophy of Tai Chi-t'ao

May 15, 1944
Personal copy

There have been several informal preparatory meetings of Central Executive Committee members in Chungking to discuss problems relative to the forthcoming plenary session of the committee.

The first two of these are reported to have discussed Party and Government affairs. Nothing of special interest is known to have happened except that Sun Fo* used the occasions freely to express his views on the need of reform.

The third meeting about the beginning of May has been widely discussed because of some remarks made by Tai Chi-t'ao, president of the Examination Yuan.† Tai has acquired the status of a Party Elder, although it is hardly his by right. He is conservative and has turned increasingly toward the study of the classics and other pursuits of the traditional Chinese elder statesman. He is known to have great influence with the Generalissimo and is generally regarded as Chiang's philosophical mentor. (On a slightly different plane, it might be mentioned that he is also universally believed to be the father of the Generalissimo's eldest son, who was borne by a Japanese maid shared by the two men while students in Japan and later married by the Generalissimo when Tai preceded him back to China.)

The influence of Tai with the Generalissimo and conservative sections of the Party is apparently the reason for the interest attached to his remarks (I have heard the story from five sources). The gist of his remarks, as reported, was:

"Democracy is after all only a form of government. Any form of government to be successful must have inspiration and guiding principles. In these respects we can learn much from a study of Buddhism and its principle of Trinity. This Trinity is the Buddha, the Sacred Canons, and the Monks. The Buddha is symbolized by our Leader, the Sacred Canon is symbolized by our San Min Chu I (Sun Yat-sen's Three Principles). The

* On Sun Fo, see pp. 111–12.
† For an explanation of *Yuan,* see p. 99n.

Monks are symbolized by our Party organization. The Leader is the highest ideal. He must be obeyed by the Party and followed and respected by the people."

*   *   *

If this is any reflection of the ideas of the Generalissimo, the outlook for speedy progress toward democracy is not bright. The reaction of Chinese liberals to this sort of line is despair. But perhaps it may serve some use in showing up the reaction of certain sections of the Party, and in forcing the drawing of political lines. Madame Sun's comment was that "Tai died years ago."

The one-party dictatorship of the Kuomintang did not mean that Chiang Kai-shek's China was devoid of political conflict. It only meant that controversy would take place *within* the confines of the Party. In wartime Chungking there was no lack of factions and cliques willing to engage in bitter political infighting. The most prominent and powerful of these was the "C-C Clique," headed by the brothers Ch'en Li-fu and Ch'en Kuo-fu, who were natives of Chiang Kai-shek's home province of Chekiang, close personal associates of the Generalissimo, and the nephews of Chiang's political mentor, Ch'en Ch'i-mei. The power of this clique derived primarily from its control of the Kuomintang party bureaucracy, the schools (Ch'en Li-fu was Minister of Education) and propaganda. While the content of its ideological pronouncements stressed the preservation and restoration of Chinese culture, its tactics of party dictatorship could quite accurately be described as fascist.

Several other groups were able to challenge the C-C Clique in particular areas, as the Generalissimo sought to preserve a rough balance of power among the contending factions. The Political Science Clique, which included some of the more experienced bureaucrats, controlled the Ministry of Economics and most of the critical provincial governorships. Though conservative and strongly anti-Communist, they did not have the reactionary reputation of the C-C Clique. However, with a power base more in the Government than in the Party, they often found themselves too weak and divided to influence significantly party policy. In the military, one of the most potent cliques was the Whampoa Clique, composed of former cadets of Chiang Kai-shek's Whampoa Military Academy. These younger and sometimes very capable military men, like Ch'en Ch'eng, often found themselves at odds with Chiang Kai-shek's Minister of War and Chief of Staff, Ho Ying-ch'in. (See Service's report on the "Young Generals Group," pp. 116–18.)

Finally, there were factions surrounding individuals personally related to Chiang, and of these individuals none were more important than T. V. Soong and H. H. Kung. Soong was the Harvard-educated son of the Shanghai businessman Charles Jones Soong. His three sisters were Madame Sun Yat-sen (Soong Ch'ing-ling), Madame Chiang Kai-shek (Soong Mei-ling) and Madame H. H. Kung (Soong Ai-ling). T. V. Soong's expertise on matters of finance made him one of the more valuable members of the Kuomintang leadership, but his independent and headstrong nature frequently got him into trouble with Chiang Kai-shek, as the following despatch reveals. From 1940, Soong was involved primarily in foreign affairs, first as Chiang Kai-shek's personal representative in the United States, then as Minister of Foreign Affairs. Meanwhile, control of financial matters passed to H. H. Kung.

H. H. Kung, another brother-in-law of the Generalissimo and a lineal descendant of Confucius, was until his downfall in the last year of the war one of the most powerful and least popular men in the Chungking Government. Regarded by many Western-trained financial experts as incompetent, he nonetheless brought more and more economic institutions under his sway.

Service was in a good position to keep tabs on Kung's operations. He shared a house with the U.S. Treasury Department representative Solomon Adler, and H. H. Kung's confidential secretary, Chi Ch'ao-ting, was living upstairs. The report which follows is as much about Kung as it is about T. V. Soong. It succeeds beautifully in describing the manner in which Chiang Kai-shek, acting through Kung, sought to control the economy and monopolize the institutions of finance, trade and development.

The Fall of T. V. Soong

March 7, 1944
Archives copy: 893.00/15330

One of the major recent changes in the Chinese political scene, certainly as concerns relations with the United States, is the dramatic eclipse of T. V. Soong. As in most of these sudden, unpredictable political shifts in China, the explanation has been kept "in the family." But the importance of the event and its possible consequences have given rise, in the absence of definite knowledge of causes, to widespread conjecture and rumor.

Taken together, the various rumors build up a fairly circumstantial explanation of a supposed break between the Generalissimo and Soong. These stories (the list is probably far from complete) may be pieced together as follows:

1. Chiang and Soong have always had difficulty in getting along with each other: Chiang is dictatorial, Soong outspoken and strong-willed. They have quarreled on several previous occasions. For instance, Soong quit the finance-ministership in 1933 after a violent argument in which Chiang blamed the failure of the current anti-Communist campaign on lack of funds and ended by slapping Soong's face (this is rumor but commonly believed).

2. Soong got his present job as Foreign Minister because he was supposed to be tough enough to get recognition, money and supplies from the United States. In these tasks he has not been particularly successful—at least not successful enough to please Chiang. In addition there are reports that his tactics made him unpopular in Washington; he has had the unpleasant task of warning the Generalissimo, at least twice, of unfavorable American reaction to any threat of action against the Chinese Communists; and he is blamed for the escape of American informed opinion from its spell of rosy illusionment regarding China in the early stage of the Pacific War.

3. As Foreign Minister, Soong was too independent to please the Chiangs (both Mr. and Mrs.), who prefer to manage their own foreign relations and hence like "weak" men for the job. . . . The story is also told that after Soong returned to

Chungking he was upbraided by Chiang for having failed to have China included in the armistice with Italy. Soong replied that he had neither received instructions nor authority. To which Chiang retorted: "You've always been able to take initiative on other matters."

4. Furthermore, as Foreign Minister and particularly in the field of relations with the United States, Soong took a dog-in-the-manger attitude which made him influential enemies. First, he opposed the Hsiung Shih-hui Military Mission to the United States (which is regarded by the political dopesters as an attempt of the Political Science Group to get into the foreign relations field) and by undercover sabotage helped to bring about its failure.* Second—and probably more important in its effect on family relationships—he advised against Madame Chiang's visit, failed to assist it while in the United States, and repeatedly told the Madame that she had outstayed her welcome and should go home.

5. Finally, Soong enraged Chiang and alarmed H. H. and Madame Kung (commonly spoken of as the "most powerful person in China") by caustic criticism of Chinese mishandling of economic problems and by suggestions (possibly inferential) that he should be made economic "czar." The story is widely told that after the initial break, which apparently was in November [1943], the family arranged a meeting late in December at which it was hoped that a reconciliation could take place. Unfortunately Chiang asked Soong for his ideas on how to deal with the economic situation. Soong replied that one reason for lack of effective control was that there were too many agencies, each without power and sometimes working at cross purposes. What was therefore needed was a single organization with adequate power to cope with all economic problems. Chiang countered that the setting up of such an agency (it has actually been talked of for a year or more, with Soong as the reported likely head) would upset the whole government structure and would be unconstitutional. To which Soong retorted: "You've always been able to change the Constitution (Organic

* In 1942, Hsiung was sent at the head of a military mission to the United States, whose task was to obtain greater U.S. aid for the Chinese army and to try to deflect the United States from its "Europe first" policy. He failed and was recalled in December 1942.

Law) whenever you wished, as for instance when you decided to be President." This interview is supposed to have ended with Chiang throwing a teacup at Soong's head, and, of course, the abandonment of hope for any immediate reconciliation.

*   *   *

I do not feel, however, that any of these stories, or even all of them taken together, are a sufficient explanation of the developments that have occurred.

In the first place, although most of them are concerned with Soong as Foreign Minister, that is the only job he has been allowed to keep—even though he has been reduced to a position of apparent impotence and inactivity.

In the second place, most of the repercussions which are known to have taken place since the break have been in the economic sphere, especially in organizations concerned with China's economic foreign relations. And they have invariably worked to reduce Soong control over those organizations and to place them in the hands of Kung—which means Chiang, because Kung is little more than his front or yes man.

This centralization of domestic and international economic control in the hands of Kung is clearly shown by a summary of recent changes.

1. The Bank of China passed from Soong's control to Kung's at the recent meeting of its board of directors (the first held for several years) when a number of directors were added and Kung made chairman. Tsuyee Pei, nominally a Soong man, remains but he is regarded as a weak man who will accommodate himself to the prevailing wind. Already there is taking place a shift of personnel to the Bank of China from other older Kung organizations such as the Central Bank and Central Trust. Especially important is the resignation of Ho Yao-ming, one of Soong's close associates, who was head of personnel for the Bank of China, and through whom Soong sent many of his confidential telegrams to the Generalissimo when he was acting in Washington as Foreign Minister.

The Bank of China is the oldest and strongest of the Chinese Government banks, the designated foreign exchange bank and agent for the financing of foreign trade, and the largest investor in modern Chinese industry. It was the main basis for Soong's power in China.

2. China Defense Supplies, now demoralized and apparently becoming a political football, is expected to be reorganized. It is rumored that it may be placed under the Central Bank or a new Ministry of Supply. P. W. Kuo, a Kung man, is generally expected to be its new head. R. C. Chen, a Soong man who has been in charge of operations in Chungking, is rumored to be on his way out. He denies that he is resigning but the uncertainty regarding his future is reflected by the current inability of our Lend-Lease delegation in Chungking to transact any business with him.

China Defense Supplies is strategically important because as the funnel for Lend-Lease to China it gave Soong control over all American war-matériel aid. The important question of whether it might have a share in the control of American aid after the war has not, so far as I know, ever been settled.

3. All foreign cash purchasing of the Chinese Government has recently been placed under the Central Trust, a wholly Kung organization. . . .

4. Kung likewise has gained control of the Chinese interest in UNRRA*—through T. F. Tsiang and P. W. Kuo. . . .

5. Carrying the theme of postwar economic collaboration a little further—Kung (together with the C-C Clique) controlled the Chinese delegation to the International Labor Conference, and Kung controlled the Chinese delegation to the Food Conference.

6. In the domestic sphere, one of Soong's major remaining interests is his Bank of Canton. But even here he is having trouble. The manager of the important Hong Kong office, named Teng, was arrested by Tai Li† sometime ago and there is considerable mystery over his fate—he was reportedly shot.

The Bank of Canton is one of the main handlers of Chinese emigrant remittances.

To show the completeness of Kung's blanket control of the Chinese economic structure it may be noted that he already had direct or predominant control of:

* United Nations Relief and Rehabilitation Administration.
† Tai Li was head of the Chinese secret police, and one of the most unsavory characters in the Kuomintang hierarchy.

Banking

The Central Bank
  The bank of issue and Government fiscal agent
The Central Trust
  The business agent of the Central Bank
The Bank of Communications
  (dominant Kung control)
The Farmers Bank
  (Chiang is the nominal but Kung the actual head.)
The Joint Head Office of the four Government banks
  (The actual head, K. Y. Liu, is nominally a Political Science
  man. But he is not a political figure and his being placed in the
  position was regarded as a victory for Kung.)
The Manufacturers Bank
In addition Kung controls a number of smaller private banks

Government Foreign Trading Companies

The Wah Chang Trading Company
  (K. C. Li is regarded as a Kung man.)
The Universal Trading Company
The Fu Hsing Trading Company
  (which absorbed the Fu Hwa Trading Company in 1942 and
  now has a monopoly of the export of China's main raw material
  commodities)

Industrial Concerns (list probably incomplete)

The National Agricultural Engineering Corporation
  (newly organized, with Kung and the Ministry of Finance having
  dominant control, to monopolize business in dehydrated fruits
  and vegetables, to monopolize the manufacturing in China of
  modern agricultural machinery, to act as sole agents for American manufacturers of such equipment, and to acquire American
  patent rights)
The Hunan Industrial Development Corporation
North West Industries
The China Industrial Company
  (steel plants and rolling mills)
Kung is reputed to have important holdings in numerous other industrial enterprises and, through the Ministry of Finance, to have
  a large measure of control of the various provincial development
  companies which are now an almost universal feature of Chinese
  economic development. (The similarity of these holding companies [in which the government, holding a major share, goes
  into partnership with important private capital] to the develop-

ment companies set up by the Japanese in Manchuria and Occupied China would be an interesting subject for study.)

Government Monopolies (all established in 1942 under the Ministry
of Finance)

Salt
Tobacco
Sugar
Matches
In this class may also be included:
  The China Tea Corporation (monopoly of exports)
  The China Vegetable Oil Corporation (intended to have export
  monopoly)

Taxation

Finally, it must be acknowledged that in a country where taxation
is not based on normal constitutional procedure and is usually so
loosely enforced that the rate and even payment may depend on
negotiation, Kung has great punitive and discriminatory power
over all private business.

*   *   *

Basing my conclusions on these surveys of the recent tendencies in economic control, I suggest two hypotheses, admittedly based on chiefly circumstantial evidence:

(1)   That Soong's downfall was brought about primarily be-
       cause Chiang and Kung wished to wrest from him all
       voice in or control over the most important economic
       stake on China's horizon—American, and to a lesser ex-
       tent British, collaboration and aid in the postwar re-
       habilitation and industrialization of China.

       With the financial machinery, government purchasing
       agencies, trading companies (basic materials for barter
       agreements), UNRRA and CDS (Lend-Lease) all in
       Kung's hands, his control over the character and disposi-
       tion of this foreign economic aid would seem to be abso-
       lute.

(2)   That the basic reason for this determination to oust
       Soong from any share in postwar economic aid may be
       a fundamental difference of opinion between Soong on

one side and Chiang and Kung on the other as to the type of economic development China should have.

Soong, and the Bank of China, are reputed to be in favor of economic development somewhat along the lines it has had in the United States: large-scale private capitalistic enterprise, with encouragement of the profit motive and freedom as far as possible from government control.

On the other hand, the type of economic planning sketchily described in Chiang's book *China's Destiny* points to government direction of economic development which, while it may be argued whether it is Fascist or Communist, is certainly not to be free. The Party economists find a similar gospel in the writings of Sun Yat-sen: heavy industries and those enterprises "naturally monopolistic in nature" to be carried on by the government; light industries to be left to private capital. (Heavy industries and communications are generally those in which foreign capital is most needed.) Finally, Kung in his persistent creation of monopolies and government industrial and trading concerns shows a similar trend. Although present monopolies, such as tobacco, were set up as "war measures," the Party's propaganda extols them as proper permanent institutions, and there is no expectation that they will be abolished when the war ends. Recent organization of such government monopolistic enterprises as the National Agricultural Engineering Corporation (referred to above) must be taken as an indication of the type of development which Kung will seek to promote. Uneasiness of private foreign capital interested in China can be readily understood. The general conclusion, for instance, is that recent proposals for an insurance monopoly (which would have been Kung-controlled) were given up for fear of unfavorable foreign reaction and perhaps because the Chinese were not sure that they were yet able to swing it themselves—not because the idea of such a monopoly has been permanently given up. . . .

[Here Service examines a few possible secondary reasons for Soong's ouster.]

*   *   *

Connected with these problems, and depending in part on the validity of the suggested hypotheses, it would be appropriate to make careful study of the effects that can be expected to follow from the downfall of Soong and the increasing ascendancy of Kung. I tentatively suggest that among these effects may be the following:

1. By dropping Soong, Chiang may hurt his own interests because Kung does not enjoy to so great a degree the confidence of either Chinese or foreign business and financial interests.

2. Greater emphasis in the obtaining of foreign economic aid may be shifted toward government loans. Private capital may be scared away.

3. The efficiency of the Bank of China and CDS will suffer from "bureaucratization." This is already becoming apparent. Under Soong these organizations had a reputation for businesslike effectiveness. Soong was hard-boiled but he attracted good men and paid them well. Kung's organizations, even the Central Bank, are *"chi-kuan"* (loosely translated as government bureaus). Kung's many connections with such institutions as Yenching, Oberlin, the Y.M.C.A., and so forth, make him China's number-one target for job hunters. Like a good politician he never fails to oblige, and the staffs of the organizations he controls are padded and stuffed with this type of person.

4. Soong, in opposition to Chiang and Kung may find that his political potency, in these days of increasing dissatisfaction with the *status quo,* is increased. All these disgruntled elements may now try to seek in him a leader. At present Soong does not appear to be trying to take advantage of this situation, but that he may be aware of it is shown by the following story from a possibly well-informed source. After Soong's first break with Chiang, his private "brain trust" suggested to him three alternate lines of action: (1) To publicly renounce all his posts

and withdraw from the government, thus making clear his lack of sympathy with the present government and drawing to him the liberal forces; (2) to try to hang on to his chairmanship of the Bank of China, his most important post for his own personal economic interests; (3) to sit tight and do or say nothing. Soong has apparently taken the last course, the one which his advisers thought the poorest.

CHIANG KAI-SHEK AND THE "ROYAL FAMILY"

In 1937, as China battled bravely through the first months of full-scale war against Japan, Chiang Kai-shek and his attractive Wellesley-educated wife were selected as *Time* magazine's "Man and Wife of the Year." From November 1942 to May 1943, Madame Chiang made a triumphant visit to the United States, staying for a while in the White House and captivating the U.S. Congress with a speech which brought the members to their feet for a four-minute standing ovation. The press was overwhelming in its praise of this charming First Lady of China and her austere, determined husband.

At the very time that Madame Chiang was making her dramatic appeal for support from the American President, Congress and people, her husband was losing support in China. Reverence and respect for Chiang as the symbol of resistance against Japan was replaced by skepticism and ridicule of a man whose early career as a stockbroker and gangster was suddenly recalled. For Service, this shift in public opinion was significant. In a dictatorship, any piece of information or any rumor about the dictator becomes an important datum for the political reporter. Furthermore, it was clearly necessary for the United States to understand the mind of the Generalissimo, whom Roosevelt, at the November 1943 Cairo Conference, welcomed into the fold of the Big Four. Consequently, many of Service's reports of this period are concerned with the person and the family of Chiang Kai-shek. In September 1943, in a personal memorandum to General Stilwell analyzing the causes for the removal of a particular pro-American official, he made one of his first attempts to interpret the workings of Chiang's mind:

Rumored Reasons for Removal of
Tseng Yang-fu, Minister of Communications

September 14, 1943
Personal copy

An attempt to "psychoanalyse" Chiang would probably have to note the conflict between his fundamental nationalism (of the narrow Fascist type) and his consciousness of dependence on American help (with its political, economic and cultural implications). The effects of this inner conflict are heightened by the fact that in his relations with the even more conservative and Fascist-minded men around him (both the C-C and military leaders such as Ho Ying-ch'in), Chiang is on the defensive against accusations that he is "pro-American" and too dependent on America.

One event which diminished the reputation of the General-issimo in both American and liberal Chinese circles was the pub-lication of Chiang's book *China's Destiny* in March 1943. Its strong attacks on "liberalism" and Communism, and its corresponding lack of criticism of the Fascism against which the Allies were then fighting a world war, were not well received. Yet the book became required reading matter for all Kuomintang Party mem-bers, officials and students. To Service, *China's Destiny* and a sec-ond book attributed to Chiang, *Chinese Economic Theory*, were "an authoritative expression of the mixed Fascism, chauvinism, feudalism and paternalism which characterize the Generalissimo and the conservative leaders around him who now control China."* In response to criticism from Chinese intellectuals, the Americans and the Chinese Communists, a revised edition of *China's Destiny* appeared in January 1944. Service prepared a translated digest of the new edition, with the following introductory summary:

* From "Generalissimo's Book—*Chinese Economic Theory*," June 26, 1944 (personal copy).

[China's Destiny—Revised Edition]*

March 1944

Amerasia Papers, pp. 409–10

The changes that have been made in the new edition are relatively small and unimportant. Certain obvious factual errors have been corrected. There has been apparently only slight attempt to meet the strong and well-founded Communist criticism. A term "assimilation" referring to the Chinese process of extending control over other peoples has been changed to "fusion." "Liberalism" has been changed in a few derogatory passages to "individualism." But on his racial line that all the various peoples of China (Tibetans, Mongols, Chinese, etc.) are really one—a point on which the Communists attacked him strongly—the Generalissimo not only has not given ground but has tried to nail down his argument by fantastic references to classical sources stating, for instance, that the Hsiung-nu (Huns) were descended from the purely legendary Huang-ti, who is also one of the supposed ancestors of the Chinese. There remains unchanged a bitter anti-Communist bias and the flat assertion that only the Kuomintang can lead China to salvation.

A number of changes are obvious efforts to remove some of the most offensive references to foreign aggression in China. Most of these changes, however, are merely the elimination or alteration of one or two particularly objectionable words and do not alter the meaning or emphasis of the passages in which they occur. There has also been added the text of Chiang's fairly moderate speech after the signing of the treaties abolishing extraterritoriality.

The map which accompanies the book has been changed to show Chinese claims to North Burma, including the Hukawng Valley. Both editions show Hong Kong, and of course all of Mongolia (including Tannu Tuva) and Tibet, as Chinese.

The new edition includes the Liu Chiu Islands† as territory belonging to China and necessary for her existence.

* Service's memo is printed without a title or date of its own. The covering despatch of Major V. F. Meisling is dated March 25, 1944.

† The Liu Chiu Islands, now usually known by their Japanese name, Ryukyu, are the chain of small islands between Japan and Taiwan, including Okinawa.

The surprising thing, in the face of the universal criticism that it received, is that the book has been changed so little. It remains a bigoted, narrow, strongly nationalistic effort at a special interpretation of history—that foreign aggression is to blame for all of China's troubles and failure to go ahead during the past one hundred years. In its scientifically untenable racialism, its lauding of the "ancient virtues" and old philosophy, its glorification of conservatives like Tseng Kuo-fan (regarded by liberal Chinese as a traitor for his service to the Manchu suppression of the Taipings), and his refusal of modern democracy, the book is still a revealing *Mein Kampf* of China's present leader.

The question perennially comes up of translation and publication abroad. The small extent of the changes made indicates that the Generalissimo remains convinced of the rightness of his own views. They also probably mean that the authorities in charge of Chinese propaganda will continue to consider (rightly from their own standpoint) that the book is still unsuitable for foreign consumption.

For these very reasons foreign opinion, and those concerned in dealings with China, should have a chance to read the book.

————————————

In the spring of 1944, Americans from General Stilwell to President Roosevelt became increasingly distressed over Chiang's lack of cooperation in the campaign to retake Burma and open up an easier supply route to China. In this context, Service returned again to the subject of the Generalissimo. He concluded a despatch reporting a speech by Chiang with the following interpretation and suggestions for U.S. policy:

Reported Views of the Generalissimo

March 20, 1944
Amerasia Papers, pp. 406–7

China is in a mess. No military action on a significant scale is in sight. The economic crisis continues to drift and worsen. Internal unrest is active and growing. Relations with all her allies are estranged.

China is still Chiang Kai-shek. Although we may have to deal with others—H. H. Kung or Ho Ying-ch'in—we must recognize them as substantially only yes men.

We are, it is true, partially to blame for adding to China's economic problems. But for the sorry situation as a whole, Chiang, and only Chiang, is responsible.

That under these serious circumstances Chiang should be acting as he is seems incredible. Instead of all-out cooperation to win the war, we meet with "active noncooperation." Military commitments are not being fulfilled. Construction projects are delayed. Vital financial negotiations make little progress. The simple request for observers to obtain military intelligence from Communist North China is refused.

Yet Chiang knows that we are going to win this war, and that his destiny is linked to us. He is completely dependent on the United States—in foreign relations, militarily and economically. Even his internal position would be endangered if American support were withdrawn.

The answer to the apparent enigma lies in Chiang's background and limitations, and in our failings in dealing with him.

Chiang's experience as a young man in Shanghai is important to an understanding of his methods. As a broker he learned to push his luck when things seemed to be going his way. From his contact with the gangster underworld he learned the usefulness of threats and blackmail. To these he adds the traditional Chinese habits of bargaining and of playing off one opponent against another.

Chiang shows these traits in everything he does. He has achieved and maintained his position in China by his supreme skill in balancing man against man and group against group, by his adroitness as a military politician rather than a military commander, and by reliance on a gangster secret police.

Chiang expects America to defeat Japan for him. And in the process to strengthen his external position by diplomatic support, and his internal position by financial aid and by improving and supplying his armies. The fundamental consideration today of Chiang and the Kuomintang is not the war against Japan but the continuing struggle for internal power, the desire to liquidate the Communists and the almost certain inevitability of civil war.

Chiang believes that by bluff and by taking advantage of our weakness and lack of unity in dealing with him, he can evade American efforts to jolt him out of this course. He believes that we are so committed to him that he can "have his cake and eat it too."

Thus the recurrent alarms of new Japanese threats, the cries of imminent economic collapse (unfortunately with a foundation of truth, but about which he does nothing constructive), and the repeated demands for loans and other aid on an unreasonable scale.*

Thus also the difficulty in dealing with Chiang and in getting delivery on promises. The words of the Ambassador carry little weight—because the State Department has not taken a strong policy and because it does not, in any event, speak for the White House. He does not fear General Stilwell—because the General cannot demonstrate the unqualified backing of the War Department, or the White House.

Chiang *will* cooperate if the United States, upon which he is dependent, makes up its mind exactly what it wants from him and then gets hard-boiled about it. Until the President determines our policy, decides our requirements, and makes these clearly and unmistakably known to Chiang, Chiang will continue in his present ways.

The President can do this directly or through fully authorized and completely supported representatives. These might be the Ambassador and General Stilwell acting in close concert.

This may mean taking an active part in Chinese affairs. But

---

* In 1944 Chiang was demanding a US $1 billion loan as his price for joining the Burma campaign and assisting in the construction of the airfields at Chengtu.

unless we do it, China will not be of much use as an ally. And, in doing it, we may save China.

As breeding grounds for rumors, nothing can equal small towns and national capitals. And among the national capitals, Chungking had just the right combination of Byzantine politics and executive secrecy to produce an interminable flood of rumors. In the absence of a free press, such rumors became an important index of public opinion. This was doubly true when the subject of the rumor was the Generalissimo or his family. Thus when, in the spring of 1944, a spate of rumors began to circulate about the private life of Chiang Kai-shek and his relations with his wife and in-laws, it was Service's duty as a political observer to report the existence and analyze the significance of the various sordid stories.

Domestic Troubles in the Chiang Household

May 10, 1944
Personal copy

Chungking is literally seething with stories of the domestic troubles of the Chiang household. Almost everyone has new details and versions to add to the now generally accepted story that the Generalissimo has taken a mistress and as a result his relations with the Madame are—to say the least—strained. There is so much smoke, it would seem that there must be some fire.

Normally such gossip about the private lives of government leaders would not be considered as within the scope of political reporting. This is hardly the case, however, in China where the person concerned is a dictator and where the relationship between him and his wife's family is so all-important. That relationship is already weakened by the strained relations between the Generalissimo and T. V. Soong. If the Madame, whose nature is both proud and puritanical, should openly break with her husband, the dynasty would be split and the effects both in China and abroad might be serious. Even if the present situation becomes generally known abroad, as it almost certainly and eventually will, there will be a great loss of prestige to both the Generalissimo and the Madame.

*   *   *

The stories generally agree that the Generalissimo (whose sexual life was not particularly monogamous—there is argument as to whether the Madame is his third or fourth wife, and he is supposed to have been a gay blade in his Shanghai broker days) took up with his present attachment while the Madame was in the United States.

Stories of the lady's identity differ. The chief are:

that she is Miss Ch'en Chieh-ju, the Generalissimo's concubine just before his marriage to the Madame, who was supposedly pensioned off and put out of sight;

that she is a cousin of Ch'en Li-fu, of considerable youth and beauty, introduced by him during the Madame's absence in America as a not-very-original effort to solidify his own and C-C Clique's position;

that she (or by some accounts a second girl) is a beautiful Fukienese who found her way to the Generalissimo's favor by introduction of the *cheng hsueh hsi* (Political Science Group) as their attempt to play petticoat politics.

There is, however, fairly general agreement that the lady is pregnant and that the Generalissimo will be a father in about two months.

Reports as to her present whereabouts again differ. Some say categorically that she has been sent "far away" to have the child; others that she is living at the Generalissimo's house on the South Bank. Another story, which seems circumstantial, is that she is living in a house near the Chiu Lungpoo airfield, about six miles outside of Chungking.

One explanation of the story that there were two women is that the second—a Miss T'ao, Jao or Yao—is a friend of the Generalissimo's eldest son, Ching-kuo, and has been at the "palace" a number of times at his invitation.

The prevalence and belief of these stories, and the humorous elaborations which are passed around, are at least indications of the unpopularity of the Madame (it is generally regarded by Chinese as a joke at her expense) and the decline in respect for both her and the Generalissimo (I have never heard anyone try to deny the stories, or refuse to be a party to such scandal mongering).

Typical of these anecdotal stories are:

The Madame now refers to the Generalissimo only as "That Man."

The Madame complains that the Generalissimo now only puts his teeth in when he is going to see "that woman."

The Madame went into the Generalissimo's bedroom one day, found a pair of high-heeled shoes under the bed, threw them out of the window and hit a guard on the head. (The guard's supposed remark on the troublesomeness of women does not translate well into English.)

The Generalissimo at one time did not receive callers for four days because he had been bruised on the side of the head with a flower vase in a spat with the Madame.

*   *   *

All these stories may be nothing more than malicious gossip. But a number of surface indications might be interpreted as indicating at least serious tension between the Generalissimo and the Madame.

The Madame has spent much of the time since her return from the United States living with her elder sister, Madame Kung.

She has avoided social life and public appearances. She has been seen rarely with the Generalissimo, and when together, they have seemed to observers to be very cool.

The Madame is not well: her complaint, a skin irritation, is regarded medically as being a result of nervous strain. She avoids photographers. And people who have seen her at close range have remarked on the hardening of lines in her face and that she seems irritable.

*   *   *

If the situation as reported is true, it has undoubtedly been a great strain on the Madame—because of her pride as a woman, her puritanical Methodism (there are generally accepted stories of several government officials in the past who have suddenly lost their positions because their wives were able to call the attention of the Madame to their husband's peccadilloes), and her knowledge of the effect it will have on her prestige.

Nonetheless, most observers believe that the stakes of power are so important to the Soong family that they (with the exception of Madame Sun but the important addition of H. H. Kung) will do everything possible to prevent an open break and that she will swallow her pride and put up with the situation.

Critics of the Generalissimo regard it all as evidence of the hollowness of his Christian and New Life moralizing, and another indication that he is after all not far from being an old-fashioned "warlord."

MISCELLANEOUS NEWS ITEMS

While detailed to General Stilwell's headquarters and stationed in Chungking, Service was normally without specific duties or assignments and functioned instead as a roving reporter on all types of political news. On a typical day, he would spend the morning in his office composing and filing reports and memoranda, and then use his afternoons, evenings and mealtimes to meet with Chinese newspapermen; such members of the foreign press corps as Theodore H. White, Guenther Stein or Brooks Atkinson; or Chinese officials like T. F. Tsiang (with whom Service sometimes played bridge), later Nationalist Chinese Ambassador to the United Nations and the United States. Service's rank was not high enough to permit direct access to senior officials, though while attached to the Embassy he had frequently accompanied the Ambassador to take notes and write memoranda of conversations with the Foreign Minister. Occasionally he would have important interviews with people like Feng Yü-hsiang or Madame Sun Yatsen, both critics of the Generalissimo. And since he had become somewhat of a specialist in Chinese Communist affairs, he was often in contact with members of the Communist office in Chungking.

Most of the time, however, Service got his information from Chinese newspapermen and minor officials. From the rather extensive network of contacts which he had built up, he would gather tidbits of gossip and information on all aspects of life in Chungking. Many of these were reported in a series of memoranda which he called "Miscellaneous News Items." Extracts from these Miscellaneous News Items and from one other brief report on factional squabbling in the Kuomintang are collected below to suggest something of the flavor of wartime Chungking.

April 4, 1944
Personal copy

From many sources come reports that the Generalissimo has been under great strain during the past few weeks, some even saying that he has been "half crazy." There is general agreement that the problems worrying the Generalissimo are: increasing foreign criticism (Chinese are desperately curious to learn the contents of recent articles in the foreign press which are known to have been published but which of course are not released in China); relations with the American Army, including Army expenditures, negotiations over exchange rate, and problems brought up by General Stilwell (the story is around that the Generalissimo hit the roof after his talk with the General); and the Sinkiang situation* (the Generalissimo is credited with daily tantrums at the slow progress of the Central Government military reinforcements moving toward Sinkiang by truck, and the jittery attitude of Chinese officials regarding publicity is explained by the Generalissimo's order that nothing be released except after his approval).

May 12, 1944
Personal copy

Possible Personnel Changes
Rumors of this type are so numerous and varied that it is difficult to sort out and evaluate them. Many represent wishful thinking or hypothetical conjecture. Others are trial balloons put out by a man's supporters; others may be put out by his enemies to kill his chances. Actually, because of the domination of the Party by the Generalissimo, they mean little. Personnel changes are usually not voted on—and may not even be announced by the Generalissimo until after the meetings have ended.

These rumors have interest, therefore, primarily as showing intra-Party trends and rivalries.

The most obvious fact at present is that Dr. H. H. Kung,

* See "The Situation in Sinkiang," pp. 121–29.

the Minister of Finance, is under attack from almost all factions. Joined with him as the targets of the attack are his wife and sister-in-law, Madame Chiang; it can be expected that the prevalence of malicious gossip about the Madame's having been pushed from the Generalissimo's favor by a rival must have some political motivation. Complaints against Kung stem from the fact that he has become too powerful. Even the C-C Clique, which supported him in the CEC session of December 1942, has turned against him. Rumors in this connection are that Kung will give up the ministership of finance, that he will go abroad, and that the four Yuan* presidents have threatened to resign if he does not. Kung has actually asked to resign (a favorite gesture in the face of criticism), but it is unlikely that his resignation will be accepted. He is too valuable to the Generalissimo. Rumors that Hsu Kan, at present Minister of Food, will become Minister of Finance can therefore be discounted. The Madame seems to be becoming a less active factor in internal politics and may leave the country for a long summer vacation.

May 15, 1944
Personal copy

A rumor is reportedly circulating in "Szechwanese circles" that the Generalissimo will resign at the forthcoming CEC meeting. There have been fairly persistent reports that the Generalissimo is not in good health. It is also possible—but only barely—that he might make a gesture on the ground that the government has been subjected to criticism both at home and abroad and that this is a reflection of lack of confidence in him. It is inconceivable that this would be more than a gesture. Such a rumor of intended resignation would have been impossible earlier in the war and is interesting as an indication of the decline in the Generalissimo's prestige.

* The Five *Yuan* were the divisions of the Nationalist Government, modeled after Sun Yat-sen's Five-Power Constitution. Kung himself was acting president of the Executive Yuan (Chiang Kai-shek was nominal president). The other four Yuan were the Legislative, Judicial, Control and Examination Yuan.

May 26, 1944
Personal copy

A current joke around town is a special issue of matches put out by the Match Monopoly and the Central Trust to commemorate the tenth anniversary of Kung's ministership of finance. The box and matches are much better than usual quality. On the top is a very complimentary picture of Kung; on the back, quotations from his speeches. The universal name for these matches (which were distributed to government organizations but are not for sale) is "horse-hide brand." The allusion is to the Chinese colloquial expression "beating the horse's hide"—meaning "shameless flattery." The boxes have become a collector's item.

June 28, 1944
Personal copy

The appointment of Lai Lien, formerly Dean of the Northwest Engineering College, as Administrative Vice Minister of Education is significant. Lai is regarded by liberals and educators as one of the worst of the C-C political hacks. He has absolutely no reputation as an educator or academic leader, and his administration of the Northwest University resulted in the discharge of a number of liberal professors, the disruption of the institution, and the tragic lowering of its academic standards. His appointment indicates that the C-C Clique is riding high, and along the same lines—only more so.

May 23, 1944
Personal copy

Preparations for [U.S. Vice President] Wallace's arrival are apparently proceeding with a large-scale beggar, street-urchin roundup. I have seen police chasing and collaring these miserable children, and the last two mornings I have seen long lines of them, tied together with ropes, being driven down the streets.

CRITICS OF THE KUOMINTANG REGIME

If Service's reporting seems to have become unusually critical of the Kuomintang, it was not without cause. His frequent trips to the field made him very much aware of the suffering of the Chinese people under the Kuomintang. In addition, while in Chungking, he was conscious of a substantial amount of dissatisfaction and criticism of Chiang Kai-shek's regime. He was definitely not alone in his negative appraisal of the Kuomintang. In fact, to a large degree his assessment mirrored that of a host of Chinese critics.

Such criticism was very much in evidence when Service returned to China in the spring of 1943, after four and a half months of leave in California and consultations in Washington. Shortly after his return he had two long conversations with his friend Kao Chi. Kao was a reporter for the *Ta Kung Pao*, the best of the Chungking newspapers (sometimes called the *New York Times* of China) and in Chungking politics, an organ of the Political Science Clique. Kao was particularly concerned about the defeatism and demoralization in Chungking, and the fact that Chiang Kai-shek and the conservative groups in the Kuomintang continued to manifest interest in Japanese overtures to make a separate peace—overtures which were particularly notable in early 1943.

Chinese Newspaperman's Concern Regarding Present Situation in China

May 25, 1943
Archives copy: 893.00/15048

A staff member of the *Ta Kung Pao* in a long private conversation on May 15 expressed the view that the National Government was approaching a crisis in regard to its future part in the war. At considerable length, he advanced the following arguments.

The early Chinese hopes of a speedy Allied victory over Japan have been replaced by a demoralizing and discouraging belief, generally held, that it will probably be four years before Japan can be defeated and the war in China brought to an end. Whether justified or not, the Chinese feel that they have been left out of the overall planning of the war. They no longer have hopes of being able to change the basic strategy, as apparently decided upon, that Germany must be defeated first.

This encourages the idea that China must look out for herself.

It is generally believed in government circles that China cannot possibly go on fighting, even in the present way, for any such period as four years.

The economic situation is rapidly going to pieces. Inflation is getting out of hand and price control is an unmitigated failure. Famine affects at least three provinces.

Agrarian unrest, which is a protest against conscription, labor service, heavy taxation, grain collections and official corruption—but also a reflection of the economic situation and general warweariness—has reached the stage of armed uprisings at places in almost every province.

The quality and morale of the army has deteriorated greatly. The army is now ineffective either for resistance to Japanese attack or for quelling these agrarian disturbances. Many troops are half starved. Increasing numbers are deserting. More and more are turning over to the Japanese and Wang Ching-wei. (Generals he mentioned as having recently gone over with their troops are: Sun Tien-ying, Sun Lien-chung and P'ang Ping-hsun. Generals who have lost all their troops and are now in Chungking are Yü Hsueh-chung and Lu Chung-lin.)

The morale of the salaried government officials and teachers is at a low ebb. Many, finding it impossible to live on their incomes, are either joining in the general corruption or leaving their official employment for private business. An increasing number are heeding Wang Ching-wei propaganda and inducements of better pay and higher position to go back to the occupied areas—which for most of them means the home from which they have been long separated.

The failure to receive much American material help has been a bitter disappointment, and there is disillusionment regarding the possibility of getting enough to help significantly in the effort to keep up the fight on even the present limited scale. General

Arnold's* statement of the tonnage (75,000 a month?) needed to keep as small a number as five hundred planes operating in China brought home the realization that even the distant and still problematical (in view of distrust of the British and the general situation in India) reopening of the Burma Road will not appreciably help out China's military difficulties.

The hope of help from Russia, either in the form of an attack on Japan or substantial supplies over the Northwest Road, has also died.

Everyone knows that the whole economic structure depends on the continuance of reasonably good crops in Szechwan—but the indications for this year are at present below average.

This is what might be called the internal situation. Against it, the government leaders must consider the external situation.

Wang Ching-wei is being given more power and prestige. Apparently all of occupied China is now to be under at least his nominal control. He is being permitted to build up a larger army.

The Japanese army, which cannot now be effectively opposed, is winning at China's own game of attrition. Its campaigns, even when with limited objectives, cause great loss to Chinese forces by dispersion, scorch the earth and capture food supplies. But now with the drives in western Hupeh and Hunan, Japan directly threatens Chungking. No place of retreat, from which the government could operate effectively, seems safe if Chungking falls.

At this time—goading by a military threat, enticing by better treatment of Wang Ching-wei, and trading on the discouragement and desperate plight of Chungking—the Japanese offer favorable peace terms. The manner of Wu K'ai-hsien's release by the Japanese and the fact of his acceptance by Chungking made it certain that he brought these terms.† Statements that he knew the terms (Tojo is said to have interviewed him) but refused to present them is meaningless, as is also the claim that he has been in retirement in Chung-

---

* General Henry H. Arnold, commander of the U.S. Army Air Forces, visited China in February 1943 and gave the Chungking Government a sobering estimate of the difficulties which would plague any attempt to defeat the Japanese in China through air power, as General Chennault and others were urging.

† Wu K'ai-hsien was a KMT underground agent in Shanghai who, following his arrest by the Japanese secret police, became a courier for messages between the Chungking Government and the Japanese.

king and has had no conferences (he is staying in the home of Chu Chia-hua*). These terms are reported to include seven points but their content is not known. It may be taken for granted that they are designed to appeal to the Chinese Government at this particular time.

In this situation the government faces two alternatives: to compromise with Japan; or to carry out internal reforms which can improve the government, check present retrograde tendencies and make possible continued resistance.

The government as at present constituted is not capable of reform. It represents hidebound conservatism. The Generalissimo has no understanding of economic matters. The Soong family and Kung are concerned with their own interests. The government itself rests upon and has its roots in the landlord-militarist-speculator class. Its conception of the method for dealing with the present situation is shown by the sending of bombing planes and troops without good, and only harmful, effect against the peasant uprisings. A first essential of a real effort to continue the struggle against Japan and improve conditions in the country is resurrection of the United Front, co-operation with the Communists and utilization of Communist methods of mass mobilization coupled with better economic controls. But this is a hurdle which the unrelenting anti-Communist leaders of the present government can never get over. Rather than undertake the necessary reforms, the present leaders of the government, the men around Chiang, most of them potentially capitulationist and anti-Western, are more likely to compromise with Japan. The Generalissimo may reach a point where he can no longer stand out and may be forced into such action, or to retire.

In a second long talk with the same man on May 22, he returned to the subject. He reported that the sweeping and sudden Allied victory in Tunisia had so strengthened the Generalissimo's position that Wu K'ai-hsien and the peace talks had been put aside. But he felt that the general situation was

* The Director of the Organization Department of the Kuomintang and a leading conservative in the Party. Educated in Germany, Chu was strongly suspected of pro-Nazi sentiments.

unchanged. In Chinese eyes it remained to be seen what the Allies could do to save China soon enough. Meanwhile Japanese actions in Hupeh were more menacing. The peace terms could still be considered—or the threat of them used as a bargaining point by Chiang for the Allies to come to his support. . . .

[The remainder of this despatch describes Kao's belief that the Political Science Clique was the only hope for reform of the Kuomintang, and his admission that there was little chance that this particular clique would be able to gain control of the government.]

During the course of the war, Chinese intellectuals grew increasingly disenchanted with the Kuomintang. This disenchantment was particularly striking to Service when he returned to Chungking in April 1943. Intellectuals were bothered by Kuomintang censorship, by the leadership's shallow ideology and by the tendency of Chiang and his supporters to look to China's Confucian past, which most intellectuals had long since abandoned. In a land like China, where the literati were regarded as the natural rulers of men, this disaffection of the intellectuals was a telling sign of Kuomintang failure.

Resentment of Censorship and Cultural Control by the Kuomintang

June 2, 1943
Archives copy: 893.00/15038

I find, after my return from the United States, bitter and outspoken resentment by Chinese intellectuals of present censorship and cultural control by the Generalissimo personally and by the Kuomintang. This can best be exemplified by stories and instances gleaned from conversations with many Chinese friends.

After the Chinese motion picture based on Vespa's "Se-

cret Agent of Japan"* had been completed, it was shown to
the Generalissimo. Sections of the picture showing Manchurian guerrillas were ordered by him to be cut out because they
were not Kuomintang guerrillas. Other sections of the picture
were retaken to show pictures of the Generalissimo and Sun
Yat-sen hanging on office walls. This was done in the offices
of the Chinese American Institute of Cultural Relations. . . .

A recent very popular play by a highly respected playwright was banned in the midst of a successful run. The plot
concerned a base hospital in which honest and idealistic doc-
tors and nurses ousted a corrupt and inefficient administrative
staff and took over the running of the hospital. The play had
no particular political significance, but the Generalissimo said
that it was critical of Chinese officials. . . .

Newspapermen generally are bitter over the prohibition
against publishing news of many aspects of China's affairs.
This, they agree, is the cause of the unhealthy concentration
on foreign affairs, in both news and editorial comment. Among
taboo subjects are: internal politics, critical discussion of the
government's price-control measures, discussion of famine-
relief inadequacies, mention of agrarian unrest now prevalent
in many provinces, any phase of the Communist question,
charges of corruption and inefficiency, reprinting of foreign
comment on China when critical. After the *Ta Kung Pao* was
suspended for its article on the Honan famine, even it has tried
to avoid trouble. . . .

Chinese engineers and college professors with whom I
traveled last summer were frank in their hatred of Ch'en Li-fu
and the Ministry of Education. Practically all had scornful remarks regarding political intrigue in their institutions. Several
times I heard "new C-C stories" told with great relish and
amusement. These generally concerned the failure of the Ministry to put one of its men in a desired position. . . .

The scornful reaction of the intellectuals to the Generalissimo's book *China's Destiny* has already been described in a
report on that book. Several of my friends boast of having
not read it. Another remarked that it was "about what one
would expect of a man who had had only a second-rate education in Japan and then had been a stock broker in Shanghai."

---

* A sensationalist exposé by a former Italian agent for the Japanese.

The new Minister of Propaganda, Chang Tao-fan, commands no respect and is spoken of as a feudalist, meaning one who culturally looks back to China's classical age.

The reaction of intellectuals who have been required to attend the Central Training Camp, a political training course, is embarrassment and obvious dislike. One man, an engineer trained in the United States, remarked after "graduation" that the course was "hard on the muscles but easy on the brain." He and a group who had also finished the course ridiculed the extreme military discipline, the childish way in which they (all mature men of considerable rank and responsibility) are treated, the reading aloud of names for such offenses as not making beds in just the required manner, the elementary digesting of lectures into simple slogans that had to be learned by repetition. A Western-trained man laughed as he recalled a lecture in which the trainees had been adjured not to use foreignisms in speech, such as the very common "Mr." and "Miss."

There is an increasing tendency to refer to the Generalissimo as "Mr. Chiang" rather than the usually customary title of "Chairman. . . ."

There is bitter and cynical feeling against the efforts of Ch'en Li-fu, Chang Tao-fan and others, such as H. H. Kung, to turn the country back toward Confucianism. Since they consider Confucianism to have been the stultifying force that prevented progress in China, they regard these efforts as an indication of the fundamental reactionarism of the Kuomintang. They dislike the present tendency to quote from the writing of Confucian scholars of the late Manchu dynasty, such as Tseng Kuo-fan and Chang Chih-tung—with his doctrine that Chinese learning is the substance, Western learning is for practical use. The Chinese literary and intellectual renaissance, it is commonly said, is dead.

Early in 1944 Service had a pair of interviews with one of the most famous critics of the Kuomintang and its anti-Communist policies: Madame Sun Yat-sen, now a (largely honorary) Vice Chairman of the People's Republic of China. "She was extremely popular. She became almost a tourist attraction. A lot of important visitors to Chungking, generals and so on, used to try to pay a call on her, if they were able to get an introduction." On the other hand, she was not able to exert much influence on Chinese politics: "She did not go out much in Chungking. People were able to go in and see her, but they had to be willing to be in the doghouse. She was regarded as being outside the pale." Below are extracts from Service's memos on the two conversations.

Conversation with Madame Sun Yat-sen

February 14, 1944
Archives copy: 893.00/15282

I called on Madame Sun by appointment on the afternoon of February 10th. She was more outspoken and apparently nearer to being bitter than on any of the previous four or five times that I had met her. . . .

She has recently been invited by "several organizations" to visit the United States. (She did not name these but I was given the impression that they were relief bodies, particularly those supporting her work in China, such as the American counterpart of the China Defense League.) She had planned to accept this invitation and hoped to leave early in March. She has, however, been bluntly told that she will not be permitted to go abroad.

She believes the reason for this refusal is the violent reaction of her family and high Kuomintang officials to the publication in *Reynold's Weekly,* a British Labor magazine, of a report that she had sent a message to bodies in the United States, describing the blockade against the Communists and calling for its removal so that medicines and other supplies could reach the Communists and so that all Chinese could be given an equal chance to fight Japan. Following the receipt in Chungking of copies of the article, she was separately visited by Wu Teh-chen, Ho Ying-ch'in and Chang Chih-chung.*

---

* These men were, respectively, Secretary-General of the Kuomintang, Minister of War, and Director of the Political Affairs Department of the Military Affairs Commission.

Their line, which she characterized as childish lecturing, was to upbraid her for "spreading baseless rumors," "appealing to foreigners," "washing China's dirty linen in the foreign press," and so on. She admitted that she had written concerning the blockade to American friends and supporters, but pointed out that everyone has always known that these are her views and that her organization, the China Defense League, is primarily interested in getting relief to the Communist-controlled areas. She mentioned that her family was "very annoyed. . . ."

Madame Sun's relations with her own family and the leaders of the Kuomintang can be considered a gauge of the trend of relations between the Kuomintang and the liberal groups. I could not help getting the impression that Madame Sun's position is now a strained and difficult one and that she is more than ever a prisoner. She implied this in a rather defiant remark when discussing the displeasure over her efforts to have the anti-Communist blockade lifted: "All they can do is to keep me from traveling."

Discussion with Madame Sun

March 5, 1944
Archives copy: 893.00/15320

The following are notes of a conversation with Madame Sun Yat-sen on the afternoon of March 4, 1944.

When I arrived to meet my appointment, the Minister of Propaganda was calling on her. He left immediately. She laughed at my apologies, saying that it had been a trying talk and had lasted far too long. The Minister had called with a Chinese translation of the article in *Time* for February 14 containing quotations from a message sent by her to the United States. The Minister's line was that she was spreading abroad untruths and wild rumors about a Chinese domestic problem. . . . [The message quoted in *Time* was the same as that reported by *Reynold's Weekly* and mentioned in the despatch above.]

The Minister had also called to try to persuade her to

accept a compromise on a radio address which she had agreed to give on Sun Yat-sen's birthday. The invitation to give this address had come from Pearl Buck and other influential persons in America. It was to be a part of an anniversary program in the United States. After she had accepted, she was asked to submit her proposed text for approval. She did this and it was heavily censored (she blamed the Minister of Propaganda). She thereupon refused to give the address. Her remark to me was that she was willing to change an offensive word here and there but that she absolutely would not compromise on principles. After her original acceptance it would be difficult for the propaganda authorities to explain her failure to give the address. The Minister had had no success in his mission and she was not sorry for him. (Madame Sun emphasized that this matter was to be treated as confidential.) . . .

Mention of the recent rumor that T. V. Soong had been arrested brought a laugh and the remark that it would be a good thing if he were arrested and tried, because this might clear the atmosphere. Replying to a suggestion of at least the need of accusation of a crime before one can be tried, she said that almost anything can be called a crime if necessary. The manner in which she made the remark gave the definite impression that the Generalissimo had made some specific charges against T.V. She went on to say that it might be rather nice if she and T.V. could be interned together.

This thought that she might be interned was apparently on her mind because she mentioned it again at a later point in the conversation. Dr. Kung, she said, was much worried about her. He had said: "What if they intern you if you keep on talking?" She had replied that she would welcome it.

Tai Li was mentioned twice. Early in the conversation she asked (quite irrelevantly to the subject just discussed) whether I had heard that Tai was very unhappy. As I was ignorant, she explained that he was having a lot of trouble because he had lost so much revenue by having tax and smuggling control taken away from him.

Later she remarked that the brother of a woman who acts as her secretary was in a concentration camp in Kiangsi. (The man's name is Liao [Ch'eng-chih]. He is a son of Liao Chung-kai, one of the original Kuomintang leaders. The case is well known because of the family's prominence.) She went on to say that Tai is now using some of the Chungking dugouts for prisons and that this had been made known by the following incident. A prisoner in one of these dugout dungeons had succeeded in having smuggled out a note to a lawyer friend who is influential. The lawyer had gone to Tai Li, who denied that such a prison existed. The lawyer, however, pressed the matter and insisted on visiting the site. Tai then claimed ignorance, blaming subordinates. . . .

Discussing Yü Yu-jen (president of the Control Yuan) going to Chengtu, she said that he had tried to resign for the past two years. She added that liberals such as Yü and Feng Yü-hsiang are unhappy but can do nothing. In reply to a suggestion that perhaps Pai Ch'ung-hsi might be included in this group, she denied with rather surprising vigor that he was a real liberal. She did not elucidate. . . .

One Chinese official who made no secret of his dissatisfaction with Chiang Kai-shek's regime was Sun Fo, president of the Legislative Yuan and son of Sun Yat-sen. Beginning in 1944, Sun Fo began a conscious policy of visible criticism of the regime in an apparent attempt to establish himself as a liberal alternative to Chiang.

"Sun Fo was not a terribly heavyweight guy. Just what he thought he was going to achieve is difficult to say. But he tried to make himself the spokesman of the left, the radicals, the liberals. Whether this was because he saw Russia coming up and realized that China was going to have to do business with her, or just what it was is not clear. Sun had a reputation of being a liberal, but he was also something of a bellwether. His views, therefore, were important."

In February 1945, Sun Fo had an interview with Captain Paul Linebarger, a former professor, then in G-2 (Intelligence), who had excellent contacts with the Kuomintang due to his father's service as an adviser to Sun Yat-sen. Sun Fo's views on how the impasse in Kuomintang-Communist relations should be broken coincided rather closely with those of Service, who filed this brief memo on Linebarger's conversation.

Views of Dr. Sun Fo

February 17, 1945
Amerasia Papers, p. 1347

On September 8, 1944, Dr. Sun Fo, President of the Legislative Yuan, was interviewed by Captain Linebarger. Several points from Captain Linebarger's report of Dr. Sun's remarks are interesting in view of the new breakdown of Kuomintang-Communist negotiations.

"The Generalissimo counts on getting American help and on being able to maintain his position without reference to the Chinese people. Therefore the responsibility rests ultimately on the Americans in that the United States is the only factor which has power to change the situation.

"Dr. Sun thought that if the Generalissimo were *told,* not asked, about American aid to the Communists and guerrillas, this would do more than anything else to make the Generalissimo come to terms with them. . . . Otherwise the Generalissimo would continue to hold out for terms which, though legally correct, would mean abandonment of all Northern and Eastern China to the puppets and Japanese. To my interpolation that this might be what some leaders wanted—namely puppet supremacy so that a quick postwar amalgamation with the Wang regime could be effected—Dr. Sun made no comment but smiled ruefully."

One military man with a flamboyant past but little remaining power was Feng Yü-hsiang, the "Christian General" who was said to have baptized his troops with a fire hose during his heyday in the 1920s. Feng was a terribly attractive, earthy sort of fellow who was very much on the outside of the Chungking leadership. His membership of the Military Affairs Commission was politically meaningless. In mid-1944 he asked Service and Paul Linebarger to come visit him, in an obvious attempt to attract the attention of Stilwell's headquarters. Stilwell and Chiang Kai-shek were then locked in what was to be their final battle, and Feng was anxious to express his support for Stilwell's position as he understood it.

Interview with Marshal Feng Yü-hsiang—
Necessity of Improvement of Condition
and Leadership of the Chinese Army

June 6, 1944
Personal copy

Lieutenant Linebarger and I received invitations late last evening, through Marshal Feng Yü-hsiang's secretary, to have breakfast with the Marshal this morning.

Marshal Feng, as you know, considers himself a friend of America and a sort of advocate of the people of China. It was his secretary, sent I am sure by the Marshal, who gave us the first information concerning incidents arising from delays in paying for land for airfield construction at Chengtu (see my memorandum of February 11, 1944*). I was sure therefore that he had some motive in extending this breakfast invitation.

The motive, it developed, was to say that China would be unable to fight unless something was done to improve the condition and leadership of the Chinese army, that this concerned the cause of the United Nations, and that it could not be brought about unless American influence was exerted on the Generalissimo.

The Marshal led up to this very gradually. He explained his work of promoting the movement for voluntary contributions to the government. The people, he said, are patriotic. The trouble has been that they have not been taken into the confidence of the government; they have been given orders, but the need of their participation and contributions has not been explained to them in personal terms. When their individual interest is explained to them in a democratic way they are eager to help, either with money or by volunteer service—as the success of his movement has amply demonstrated.

He then went on to discuss American criticism of China. He said that *all* of this criticism was correct, that all of it was

* Service's February 11 memo has not been printed here. But see his February 26 memo on the same subject, pp. 26–32.

good, and that it was welcomed and appreciated by all but a very few of the Chinese people.

From this he developed the theme of the friendship between China and the United States, especially now that we are fighting together as allies and our interests are so closely linked that the victory or defeat of one is the victory or defeat of the other. America, he said, is not fighting in China for her own interests alone but for those of China; Pearl Harbor would not have happened if America had not refused to sacrifice the interests of China and give up her determination to help China.

This relationship between the two countries has become so close that America, as a friend and an ally in a common cause, has a legitimate and vital interest in China's affairs, particularly in China's ability to continue fighting.

But the condition of China's army has become such that it cannot fight effectively unless a drastic change is brought about.

The fault lies primarily with the present leadership of the army. In the past the great majority of the commanders were men who had risen from the ranks. They knew their men and their junior officers. Being themselves men of the people, they could command their soldiers' respect and allegiance. This is no longer true. The new generation of officers and commanders do not come from the ranks of the common soldiers of the people. After graduation from military academy, they seek staff or bureaucratic jobs. Then after a short period and by means of personal or political influence they get appointments to the Staff College (*lu chün ta hsueh*). From that they become in a short time field commanders. But they know nothing of fighting, have no interest in fighting, and cannot lead their troops effectively because they have no contact or sympathy with the men under them.

From this rotten system come the evils of graft and corruption all through the higher ranks, of leading a soft life while their men starve to death, of engaging in trade, of the callousness toward human life that can result in the present terrible conditions of conscription and the treatment of new recruits. He mentioned as a typical instance a story of 2,000 recruits sent from Szechwan to Hunan. To take charge of the movement a force of 1,000 escort, officers, grooms, etc., were required. But of the 2,000, 500 deserted, 500 died on the road, 500 arrived sick, and only 500 useful men were delivered. And by the time the escort had arrived back in Szechwan, it had lost one fourth of its strength.

These officers do not know how to lead; they may have book learning but they are *"wai hang"* (outside the profession). As long as they run the army, the lives of recruits will continue to be squandered, the men will continue to starve and desert, the soldiers will continue to hate their officers and to be without knowledge of what they are fighting for. For armies such as these, guns will not be of any use.

China has some good officers and commanders. They have fought bravely and well. But instead of being rewarded and advanced, they are held back and passed over by younger men who have influence and are graduates of the new system. Some of these men are Li Tsung-jen, Feng Chih-an, Liu Ju-min (he mentioned another, whose name has escaped me). These men have fought consistently in the front lines. They are good leaders but they do not get recognition. The records of men like T'ang En-po who are the products of the new system, never started at the bottom and so lack the contact with the men, speak for themselves.

The only man who can bring about this needed change to give the Chinese army real leadership is the Generalissimo. But he doesn't know the true condition and no Chinese can tell him. The only outside influence that can and has a right to exert pressure on him is the United States. He hopes therefore that General Stilwell and the Ambassador as the representatives of the United States will make frank and strong efforts to "change the heart of the Generalissimo." This "changing of the Generalissimo" is the only hope for China and for the effective participation of China in our joint cause.

He gave no hint, directly or inferentially, of what should be done if the "heart of the Generalissimo" could not be changed. There was certainly no implication that the Marshal was tired of the leadership of the Generalissimo. It was the men around the Generalissimo whom he attacked. Significantly, there was no reference to the impending visit of Vice President Wallace or to the present state of affairs in the Kuomintang-Communist impasse.

The Marshal made this exposition in the most earnest and serious manner. He said that while these were his convictions, which he would stand by, he would prefer that they not be given publicity. He asked specifically that you* and Stilwell and the Ambassador be informed, and categorically approved the circulation of his views within the official channels of the United States government. In an evident endeavor to be wholly correct, he gave one of his cards to Lieutenant Linebarger to be transmitted to you, and another to me to be transmitted to the Ambassador. (Lieutenant Linebarger has read this report and his concurrence in it stands in lieu of a separate report.)

Comment:

Feng is known to be a bitter critic of Ho Ying-ch'in. While he was careful not to mention any name critically except that of T'ang En-po, the logic of his argument is that it is an attack on Ho and the men whom Ho has pushed ahead, mostly graduates of the *lu chün ta hsueh*—which is a Ho pet.

Not all of the criticism of the Chungking leadership was simply verbal. Late in 1943 a group of young generals began plotting for some sort of action to bring about a change in the political situation. The details of the plot remain obscure to this day. It appears that a kidnapping of the Generalissimo, after the model of the Sian mutiny, was contemplated. Service wrote several reports on the plot, one of which is printed here.

Young Generals Group

February 10, 1944
Personal copy

The following reports are submitted in continuation of previous memoranda regarding the formation and exposure of

---

* Apparently Brigadier General Thomas Hearn, Stilwell's Chief of Staff.

a group within the Chinese army which had the intention of bringing pressure on the Generalissimo to make certain important Government changes.

Guenther Stein (*Manchester Guardian* and *Christian Science Monitor*), in an interview with General Feng Yü-hsiang about ten days ago, inquired whether the current story of an officers group was true. The General asked: "What is your version?" Stein then recounted a rather extreme story of the affair (which he says he had heard from several reliable Chinese contacts) mentioning, for instance: the intention to kidnap Chiang in Kunming, the demands that Ho Ying-ch'in, H. H. Kung and the Ch'en brothers be removed, and the subsequent arrest and execution of sixteen generals. General Feng's only comment was: "Your report is substantially correct."

Today I mentioned the affair to Madame Sun Yat-sen, asking her opinion of the effort of certain (Kuomintang) quarters to cast the blame for it on the Communists. She said that she knew that such a group had existed, that it had caused a great deal of concern in the "highest places" (apparently a reference to her brother-in-law, the Generalissimo), that there had been "a lot" of arrests, that they were not yet satisfied that they had completely uncovered its ramifications because it was widespread and included a considerable section of the army, and that it actually involved a threatened coup d'état. The attempt to blame the Communists, she said, was absurd because the plot was thoroughly "Fascist" in spirit and objective. She added that if the Kuomintang believed its own story that Communist intrigue could have such influence in the army, it would not now be willing to negotiate with the Communists.

White (Luce Publications) has the following explanation of the affair which he says comes from a "high and reliable Whampoa (military) source." "General Ho Ying-ch'in has been trying to institute a General Staff system, modeled after the German, throughout the Chinese army. Under this system, representatives of the General Staff (under Ho Ying-ch'in) would be in a position to more or less dictate to field commanders to whom they were attached, even though the field commanders might be senior in rank. To carry this out, Ho has been using the graduates of the Staff College (*lu chün ta* *hsueh*), which is under Ho's domination. Attempts to set up the system have created friction in the army especially under commanders, such as Ch'en Ch'eng, who are unfriendly to Ho. The staff officers, finding themselves unable to accomplish very much (and possibly with what they might have considered tacit approval of Ho), decided to take matters into their own hands. The present conspiracy was started by sixteen members of the 9th class of the Staff College, all of whom have been arrested." This story agrees in some particulars with other reports. It also explains some seeming inconsistencies: that General Chang Chih-chung (see my memorandum of February 3*) does not name Ho Ying-ch'in as one of the targets; and that General Ch'en Ch'eng is reported by some sources to have been responsible for exposing the plot. However, the report of motivation hardly seems satisfactory and the Whampoa source is probably not unprejudiced.

These reports bring the number of important non-Communist sources from which this story has come to more than ten. It is understandable that the Chinese, for "face" reasons, may refuse to admit *officially* the existence of such dissension within the army. It is significant, however, that not a single source which I have approached has been without knowledge of it.

* Not printed.

FOREIGN AFFAIRS: SINO-SOVIET RELATIONS

As World War II entered its final phase, it was clear to all that Allied victory was inevitable and that the critical postwar problems in the international arena would involve relations among the Allies. In Asia, this meant that China, the United States and Russia would have to learn to live with one another. Clearly, Sino-Soviet relations would be critically important.

Kuomintang policies toward the Soviet Union had already gone through several flip-flops, each closely linked to KMT policies toward the Chinese Communists. From 1923 to 1927 the KMT and the Soviets were intimately allied as Stalin supplied arms and advisers to the Kuomintang armies, enabling them to accomplish the unification of China after years of rampant warlordism. Following Chiang's anti-Communist coup of April 1927, the Soviet advisers were expelled, and Kuomintang policy was guided by its leader's virulent anti-Communism. This continued until Chiang's kidnapping at Sian in 1936 opened the doors to a new period of United Front. In August 1937, after the Marco Polo Bridge incident sparked full-scale war between China and Japan, a Sino-Soviet nonaggression pact was signed. This was followed by financial agreements which would give China $250 million in loans, and military agreements under which some two hundred Soviet "volunteers" flew combat missions against the Japanese and five hundred Soviet advisers worked with the Chinese army. During the early years of China's resistance to Japan, while the United States was still selling scrap metal which fed the Japanese war machine, Russia was clearly the best ally China had.

By 1941, all this had changed. The New Fourth Army incident marked the breakdown of the United Front between the Kuomintang and the Chinese Communists. Relations with the Russians turned equally sour, and the advisers and "volunteers" were withdrawn to prepare for the anticipated attack by Germany. Once

Pearl Harbor brought the United States into the war, Chungking felt no further need for Russian friendship or support.

One critical place where the issue between Chungking and Moscow came to be joined was Sinkiang, the sparsely populated Central Asian province of mountains and desert with its extensive and ill-defined borders with the Soviet Union and Outer Mongolia. Since 1933, Sinkiang had been dominated by the warlord Sheng Shih-ts'ai, who cooperated closely with the Soviet Union. Despite the severity of some of Sheng's police measures, the province had prospered from trade agreements with Russia and Russian assistance in the exploitation of the oil fields at Tushihshan. Sheng himself had benefited from extensive Soviet military assistance. Most important for the predominantly non-Chinese and often anti-Chinese population of the province, Sinkiang was spared the rule of the Kuomintang. Then, in 1942, with Russia occupied on its western front and the United States promising to become the dominant power in the Pacific, Sheng switched sides and moved to ally himself with Chungking. Soon hundreds of Kuomintang officials were moving into his capital of Urumchi (Tihua), bringing with them new tax burdens, inflation and a drying up of the trade with Russia. Reaction from the non-Chinese populace was not long in coming, and soon a local uprising by Kazaks on the Mongolian border developed into a full-fledged crisis in which allegedly Russian (but possibly Mongolian) planes bombed Chinese forces in a disputed area of the Sinkiang-Mongolian border. When the Chungking Government tried to get the U.S. Army involved by sending observers to survey the bombing damage, Service was asked to prepare a study of the problem. This report, the most extensive of a number of memoranda he wrote on the Sinkiang incident, indicates Service's very real fears that Chiang was following a fatally antagonistic policy toward Russia. His advice that the United States not get involved in this conflict was one of the few suggestions of his that Washington had the wisdom to accept.

Situation in Sinkiang

April 7, 1944
Archives copy: 761.93/1771

It is obvious that the Chinese, though greatly concerned over the bombing incident and the situation in Sinkiang, are still confused and undecided as to the policy which they should adopt.

An official of the International Publicity Board in a private talk with a well-known foreign correspondent on the evening of April 5 admitted the general veracity of the Tass story* and other reports tending to show Chinese provocation. He made the definite statement that Chinese troops had actually crossed the border into Outer Mongolia. He explained these actions on the basis of Chinese conviction that relations between Russia and Great Britain and the United States were strained and that it was to China's interest to promote this tension. He pointed out that Chinese authorities in Sinkiang had kept the British and American authorities there fully informed of their version of the matter and that efforts had been made to interest the British and American governments. Finally, the Chinese had prepared a lengthy statement and were about to release it in Chungking when the strong and obviously official Tass report appeared and got in the "first word."

*　　　*　　　*

This explanation of the whole affair as a Chinese effort to complicate relations among the United Nations, even though coming from what must be considered a good Chinese source, can hardly be accepted as sufficient. Chinese motives may actually be several:

1. The Central Government wishes to establish its undisputed control over the whole of Sinkiang.

* When the incident began in March, the Chinese immediately charged Russia with aggression. The Soviet Union broke its silence on April 3 with a major Tass article charging Chinese incursions into Mongolian territory and vowing to honor its mutual-assistance pact with Outer Mongolia to combat Chinese aggression.

This recovery of Sinkiang is an important part of Chinese irredentism, which from a slightly different viewpoint amounts to feudalistic imperialism. The Kuomintang regards its successful completion as a race against time—the day when Russia has recovered sufficiently from her crisis in the West to seek again to draw Sinkiang into her sphere of influence.

The establishment of this control involves:

(a) Establishing direct administrative control over the whole of the province. Important in this connection is the area, apparently north of the main watershed of the Altai Mountains in the northern tip of Sinkiang, which is claimed by both Sinkiang and Outer Mongolia. . . .

(b) Breaking up stubborn and largely independent racial minorities such as the Kazaks. One of the main centers of the Kazak population is this disputed Altai region, where they have lived in the past with little governmental control.

(c) Overcoming continuing local opposition to Central Government control. The majority of the population of Sinkiang is non-Chinese, and Chinese control there has always been unstable. It is reported that the people are not taking enthusiastically to the present Chinese attempt to reassert this control. There are stories, for instance, that there have been disturbances in which some of the recent Chinese settlers, transported to Sinkiang by the Central Government, have been killed. Contributing causes to such trouble, it may be assumed, are the limited amount of irrigable land in Sinkiang and the historic tendency of the agricultural Chinese to encroach upon and destroy the grass lands upon which the livelihood of the nomadic population depends. . . .

2. The Chinese may wish to feel out Russian policy. This is important from a number of aspects:

(a) In regard to Outer Mongolia. The Kuomintang considers Outer Mongolia to be definitely a part of China, and it is determined, as a part of its announced mission to restore China's freedom and territorial integrity, to bring about its eventual return to Chinese control. . . .

[Service then examines the legal, historical and moral basis for the Chinese claims to Outer Mongolia. He concludes with this assessment of the Mongols' views on the subject.]

. . . It would not be surprising, therefore, to find that the Mongols, as the Tibetans and probably the non-Chinese population of Sinkiang, hate and fear the Chinese and are determined to maintain their independence.

(b) In regard to the Chinese Communist problem. The Kuomintang believes that the Chinese Communists have been in the past, and may be again in the future, supported by the Soviets. They may consider that the firmness of Russian policy in Outer Mongolia can be taken as an indication of Russian interest and aims with respect to the Communists.

(c) In regard to Russian plans in Sinkiang, in Manchuria, in China as a whole, and for eventual participation in the Far Eastern war. It may be argued, for instance, that if Russia intends to take a benevolent part in the war, if she does not intend to seek her own selfish interests, and if she wants to have as her neighbor a strong, independent and friendly China (under the Kuomintang), then she will support China's territorial integrity and not dispute Chinese claims to actual—rather than theoretical—sovereignty over such areas as Outer Mongolia.

3. Present Chinese leadership may wish to stimulate anti-Russian feeling, both in China and abroad.

The Kuomintang Government, and many other Chinese, fear Russia and regard her as a greater enemy—certainly potentially—than Japan. With their traditional, and apparently unshakable, habit of playing off one party against another, these elements dislike evidences of closer British-Soviet-American understanding, and welcome signs of differences and disunity. They count for support on the anti-Communist sentiments of the controlling British conservatives and a large part of the American people. . . .

4. The Government seeks an opportunity to rally Chinese nationalism and to provide a diversion of attention from failings in other directions.

This follows naturally from the third point mentioned above. If things are not going well at home (which is very definitely the case in China at present), there can be nothing better than finding a foreign scapegoat toward which to divert attention. The Government has sought to give a boost to national morale by making much of the recovery of Sinkiang and the plans for the development of the whole Northwest; now it can claim that this is threatened by Russia. If the Chinese Communists and Japan can be brought into the picture, so much the better. Worthy of note in this connection is the apparently sudden emergence of rumors of a Soviet–Japanese–Chinese Communist understanding, of arrangements between the Communists and the Japanese for a Communist corridor to Outer Mongolia, of fighting between the Communist and Central Government forces in north Honan, and of shipments of Soviet arms to the Communists by air. These stories come from many sources, including the highest officials. But there is as yet no evidence of their having any basis in fact. . . .

This explanation of the Sinkiang situation as having direct Central Government motivation may be considered too dogmatic. But it is hardly probable that Sheng Shih-ts'ai, weakened by the withdrawal of his former mainstay—Russian military forces and aviation—and certainly preoccupied with the maintenance of his position in the face of growing Central Government control, would independently, or even willingly, seek trouble for himself by campaigning against the redoubtable Kazaks and attempting to establish his frontier in areas known to be disputed with Outer Mongolia. As mentioned in my memorandum of March 22nd, some well-informed Chinese believe that Sheng was under direct orders from the Generalissimo to create a military base in this area, strategic for possible future pressure on Outer Mongolia. The fact cannot be denied that China, in the face of internal troubles and a stagnant war effort, is showing an amazing concentration on peripheral problems—Tibet, Northwest development, the status of North Burma, and even the borders of Indochina and Thailand. Also it cannot be denied that China's relations with Russia have steadily deteriorated to a point of tension: there was bickering and bad feeling over the withdrawal of Russian interest from Sinkiang; the movement of Russian planes and trucks in China has been practically stopped; Russian military advisers are no longer welcomed or consulted; trade and barter are at a near standstill, and Russia claims that the Chinese have not lived up to their promises; attempted transport arrangements have so far been a failure; Chinese feeling against Russia has become more outspoken; and, as mentioned before, the Chinese lost no time in trying to exploit the anti-Russian angles of the present incident.

Crediting the Chinese with at least a lack of concern over complicating their own and their allies' relations with Russia may also be objected to on the ground that China is anxious to have Russia enter the war against Japan. I do not believe that such is actually the case. General Chinese public opinion may desire to have Russia enter the war at an early date in the hope that this will ensure the speedy defeat of Japan. But the Kuomintang's leaders, I suggest, give only lip service to this idea. On the contrary, if they are as calculating as we must assume they are, they will very much prefer to have Japan defeated by the United States, which they hope will continue to be friendly to the Kuomintang and opposed to the spread of Communist influence in China. By the same reasoning, the Kuomintang dreads the active participation by Russia in the defeat of Japan because this will give Russia an undeniable voice in Far Eastern affairs and will greatly increase her prestige and the influence of Communism with the people of China. We can expect, therefore, that as American strength in the Pacific increases and our war against Japan progresses favorably—as it is doing at present—the Chinese Government will become more and more anti-Russian.

These may have been the Chinese motives in Sinkiang. What has been the Chinese success?

*   *   *

The pretext has been provided for sending large Central Government military forces into Sinkiang. These may, by force, overcome any unorganized local resistance and break up minority groups such as the Kazaks inside of Sinkiang. They should also ensure—perhaps after a period of maneuver and face saving—the eventual removal of Sheng Shih-ts'ai and his replacement by a nominee of the Central Government.* They probably will not, however, be able to establish the disputed boundary claimed by China, because the Outer Mongols, even without direct Soviet participation, appear to have an efficient and well-equipped military force. There is also the danger that Central Government military control may prove a boomerang by provoking rebellion in Sinkiang, either spontaneously from the resentment of the largely Mohammedan population, or

---

* Service was predictably prescient in this forecast: in August 1944, Sheng was transferred to a meaningless post in Chungking's Ministry of Forestry and Agriculture.

through Russian connivance and support of such leaders as the mysterious General Ma Chung-ying—reportedly "kept" by the Russians for the past ten years for just such a possible eventuality.* Chinese concern is shown by the numerous rumors of Ma's appearance and by the anxiety to get the Chinese Forty-second Army—one of General Hu Tsung-nan's best units —to Sinkiang as rapidly as possible. All trucks in Kansu are reported to have been commandeered for this purpose.

Russian policy, at least in regard to Outer Mongolia, appears to have been clearly tested. It is obvious that the Russians intend to stand by Outer Mongolia and to keep the country free—in other words, an autonomous republic under Soviet influence.

This stand which the Russians have been maneuvered into taking may convince some sections of Chinese and foreign opinion that Russia has sinister designs in China and the rest of East Asia. But if the Chinese expected active British and American support, they have so far been disappointed. The foreign press seems to have given the matter little notice. The United States has shown little desire to complicate its relations with an important ally over what appears to be a border incident, possibly arising from Chinese provocation. And we have declined the bait of modified involvement by sending representatives to investigate, under Chinese auspices. . . .

The occurrence of this incident, and the likelihood of its repetition in other forms if the Chinese leaders continue in their present course, raises the important question of the attitude which the United States should adopt toward Sino-Soviet differences. In a broader sense this question involves our overall relations with both Russia and the present Chinese Government.

We must be concerned with Russian plans and policies in Asia because they are bound to affect our own plans in the same area. But our relations with Russia in Asia are at present only a subordinate part of our political and military relations

---

* Again, Service was quite correct. A full-scale rebellion broke out in November 1944 and was stopped short of capturing Urumchi only when the Soviet Consul offered to mediate. The KMT was never to regain control of the area lost to the rebels. Ma Chung-ying, however, seems not to have been centrally involved.

with Russia in Europe in the overall United Nations war effort and postwar settlement. We should make every effort to learn what the Russian aims in Asia are. A good way of gaining material relevant to this will be a careful firsthand study of the strength, attitudes and popular support of the Chinese Communists. But in determining our policy toward Russia in Asia we should avoid being swayed by China. The initiative must be kept firmly in our hands. To do otherwise will be to let the tail wag the dog.

As for the present Chinese Government, it must be acknowledged that we are faced with a regrettable failure of statesmanship. Chiang's persisting in an active anti-Soviet policy, at a time when his policies (or lack of them) are accelerating economic collapse and increasing internal dissension, can only be characterized as reckless adventurism. The cynical desire to destroy unity among the United Nations is serious. But it would also appear that Chiang unwittingly may be contributing to Russian dominance in Eastern Asia by internal and external policies which, if pursued in their present form, will render China too weak to serve as a possible counterweight to Russia. By so doing, Chiang may be digging his own grave; not only North China and Manchuria, but also national groups such as Korea and Formosa may be driven into the arms of the Soviets.

Neither now, nor in the immediately foreseeable future, does the United States want to find itself in direct opposition to Russia in Asia; nor does it want to see Russia have undisputed dominance over a part or all of China.

The best way to cause both of these possibilities to become realities is to give, in either fact or appearance, support to the present reactionary government of China beyond carefully regulated and controlled aid directed solely toward the military prosecution of the war against Japan. To give diplomatic or other support beyond this limit will encourage the Kuomintang in its present suicidal anti-Russian policy. It will convince the Chinese Communists—who probably hold the key to control, not only of North China, but of Inner Mongolia and Manchuria as well—that we are on the other side and that their only hope for survival lies with Russia. Finally, Russia will be led to believe (if she does not already) that American aims run counter to hers, and that she must therefore protect herself by any means available: in other words, the extension of her direct power or influence.

It is important, therefore, that the United States have the following aims in its dealings with China:

1. Avoid becoming involved in any way in Sino-Soviet relations; avoid all appearance of unqualified diplomatic support to China, especially vis-à-vis Russia; and limit American aid to China to direct prosecution of the war against Japan.

This may involve soft-pedaling of grandiose promises of postwar aid and economic rehabilitation—unless they are predicated on satisfactory reforms within China.

2. Show a sympathetic interest in the Communists and liberal groups in China. Try to fit the Communists into the war against Japan.

In so doing, we may promote Chinese unity and galvanize the lagging Chinese war effort. The liberals, generally speaking, already consider that their hope lies in America. The Communists, from what little we know of them, also are friendly toward America, believe that democracy must be the next step in China, and take the view that economic collaboration with the United States is the only hope for speedy postwar rehabilitation and development. It is vital that we do not lose this good will and influence.

3. Use our tremendous and as yet unexploited influence with the Kuomintang to promote internal Chinese unity on the only possible and lasting foundation of progressive reform.

There is no reason for us to fear using our influence. The Kuomintang knows that it is dependent on us; it cannot turn toward a Japan approaching annihilation; it is inconceivable that it will turn toward communistic Russia; and Great Britain is not in a position to be of help. American interest in the Chinese Communists will be a potent force in persuading Kuomintang China to set its house in order.

The Communists would undoubtedly play an important

part in a genuinely unified China—one not unified by the Kuomintang's present policy in practice of military force and threat. But it is most probable that such a democratic and unified China would naturally gravitate toward the United States and that the United States, by virtue of a sympathy, position and economic resources, would enjoy a greater influence in China than any other foreign power.

THE CRISIS OF 1944

In 1944, Chiang Kai-shek's China seemed to be literally crumbling. There was famine and unrest in the countryside, with growing resentment of high taxes, brutal conscription policies and inflation. Critics were everywhere: journalists, intellectuals, members of other minor parties, and even some officials and military officers. Early in the year there was the Young Generals plot. Then there was a growing chorus of criticism in the American press. Soon the Sinkiang incident brought Sino-Soviet relations to a crisis. And Sino-American relations were none too friendly as Chiang Kai-shek balked at Stilwell's every attempt to get China to commit the forces promised at Cairo for the retaking of Burma and the opening of the Burma Road. But it was the spectacularly successful Japanese offensive of 1944 which made the most shattering impact. By the end of the year, China had lost all of its East China airfields, and the Japanese had completed their link-up by rail all the way from North China through Hankow and on down to Canton.

The impression of many that the China front was stable and largely inactive from 1939 to 1944 was not really accurate. A brief report by Service in February 1944 gives a good indication of the extent of Kuomintang slippage. Even before the 1944 offensive, the Kuomintang had slowly but surely been losing ground to both the Japanese and the Communists (though when it lost to the Communists, the KMT preferred to regard it as having been lost to the Japanese).

Gradual Growth of Japanese Occupied Area in China; Refusal of Central Government to Admit Existence of Free Chinese Guerrilla Governments in Certain Areas

February 11, 1944
Archives copy: 740.0011 QW/3760

1. At a recent press conference of the Chinese Government spokesmen, Guenther Stein (*Manchester Guardian* and *Christian Science Monitor*) asked for and received a summary report of the extent of Japanese occupation of the war-area provinces. He desired this information to supplement similar data which he had received from the same official Chinese sources for the years 1939 to 1942. All of these reports, tabulated and covering the period January 1939 to October 1943, are summarized on the attached sheet.

2. These figures show a slow but steady decrease in the number of free *hsien* and a corresponding increase in the number of *hsien* predominantly or completely under Japanese control. Inasmuch as the beginning of the period, January 1939, is after the fall of Canton and Hankow and the completion of the Japanese penetration into China, this slow growth of the Japanese-occupied area apparently indicates a gradual expansion and consolidation of Japanese occupation. Japanese expansion between January 1942 and October 1943 may be largely pushing forward of occupied zones in south Chekiang and south Anhwei. However, Communists and other travelers from North China admit that the Japanese have also been making slow progress there by their tactics of blockade and the pushing forward of lines of blockhouses around the guerrilla bases.

3. It is interesting to note that the Government spokesman omits Hopei (where Communist-led guerrillas are active) from his statistics. This is apparently in conformity with the Government's propaganda line that the Communists are insignificant and are not fighting the Japanese. In reply to a question regarding the omission of Hopei, the spokesman specifically said that Hopei is *entirely under Japanese occupation,* the same as Manchuria, and is therefore not a war zone.

4. Actually much of Hopei is under Chinese control, though of Communist rather than Central Government inspiration. For instance, a British refugee from Peiping recently arrived in Chungking after spending over a year and a half in a well-organized governmental area in the western part of the province. Domei has recently reported several minor campaigns against the Communists in south, east and west Hopei.

5. This willingness of the Central Government to give up some of its best publicity material—the permanent Communist guerrilla area through which [the British missionary-educator] Mr. [William] Band escaped extends to within thirty miles of Peiping—is an indication of the bitterness now existing between the two factions.

ADMINISTRATIVE CONDITIONS IN THE *Hsien*
OF TWELVE WAR ZONE PROVINCES

	Total number of hsien	Free hsien (A)	Partly occupied hsien (B)	Predominantly occupied hsien (C)	(D)	Entirely occupied hsien (E)
Jan. 1939	924	622	41	223	17	21
Jan. 1940	924	499	41	334	34	16
Jan. 1941	924	473	31	327	30	63
Jan. 1942	924	459	33	324	49	59
Oct. 1943	924	422	36	351	45	70

The provinces are: Kiangsu, Chekiang, Anhwei, Kiangsi, Hupeh, Hunan, Shantung, Shansi, Honan, Fukien, Kwangtung, Suiyuan. "Hopei & Chahar excluded for unusual conditions."

(A) Totally free from enemy occupation.
(B) Magistrate still holding office in his *hsien*.
(C) Magistrate still exerts some control from office in another place than the original *hsien* town.
(D) Magistrate removed his office to neighboring *hsien* but still wields some influence in his original *hsien*.
(E) Magistrate lost all influence over *hsien*.

In April 1944 Japan began its final offensive in China, code-named ICHIGO. It first swept through famine-ravaged Honan to close the gap in the Peking–Hankow railroad. In about one month, the thirty-four Chinese divisions in the province were utterly routed and the Japanese rested in Hankow, poised to push on toward the South. Then, in late May, the Japanese resumed their attack, which would ultimately capture the length of the Canton–Hankow railway and the South China airfields at Hengyang, Kweilin and Liuchow. General Stilwell had long warned that if Chennault's Fourteenth Air Force ever became effective enough to really hurt the Japanese, Japan would simply move to capture the airfields. He was, of course, right; and Chennault's claim that his planes would protect their own bases was nonsense. But Chiang Kai-shek preferred to rely on Chennault's promises and American air power rather than the reform of the Chinese army, which Stilwell was urging. In the following despatch, Service describes the extent of the disaster which Chiang had brought upon himself.

Though the ultimate economic effects of the Japanese offensive may not have been as severe as Service predicted, he was reflecting the estimates of several competent economists and also the general mood in Chungking, which was strictly "gloom and doom, dark and foreboding." For a while there was genuine fear that Japan's armies might turn west and take Chungking itself. Even Chennault's own propagandists, in their effort to get more Hump tonnage "were painting the situation in the most catastrophic terms. His aide, Joseph Alsop, made frequent trips up to Chungking, and no one was more gloomy and pessimistic than Joe Alsop —'The end has come!'—in his usual apocalyptic sort of way."

Economic and Political Effects of Japanese Success in a Major Drive in Southeast China

June 2, 1944
Amerasia Papers, pp. 554–56

The Chinese Government spokesman at the press conference on May 31 issued a statement that the present Japanese drive in Hunan was the beginning of an attempt to seize the whole of the Canton–Hankow railway. This campaign had been nervously predicted for some time. With its actual commencement, the prevalent Chinese mood has become one of great alarm. Some Chinese even go so far as to doubt whether the Chungking Government will be able to survive the effects of Japanese success in "cutting the country in two." All agree that the effects will be most serious.

Whether or not it is accepted that the Japanese actually do intend to take and hold the Canton–Hankow rail line, it now seems obvious that the Japanese are undertaking a major campaign of more than usual "training maneuver" proportions. We may assume that their objectives are the capture of the Canton-Hankow line as far south as Hengyang, the dispersal of the Chinese armies on both sides of that line and the destruction of American air bases in that area. It seems likely that these objectives can be attained. It therefore becomes pertinent to consider their economic and political effects on China.

ECONOMIC

1. *The rich rice-producing areas of Hunan and Kiangsi will be lost.* The effects will be great whether this loss is permanent or only temporary. The four great granaries of Free China have been Szechwan, the Honan plain, and the Hunan and Kiangsi lake plains. Honan has already been lost. Hunan has helped to support the troops around Ichang and a part of the population in the Kwangsi-Kwangtung area. Kiangsi has helped supply the Chinese forces in East China.

2. *Trade will be disrupted.* This will involve not only goods imported from the Hunan-Kiangsi area (cotton, tea, ramie, porcelain) but also a very important trade from the occupied areas. This prospect has had an immediate effect on the market in Chungking. Goods show a tendency to be withdrawn from the market for hoarding, and prices are going up.

3. *There will be a large influx of refugees* from the fighting zones into the constantly more restricted area of Free China.

4. *Similarly, the forcing westward of the Chinese armies will mean additional forces dependent on a smaller and poorer area.* This will result in greater burdens of taxation and conscription on the farmers of the remaining Free China.

5. *Chinese currency* in the areas occupied by the Japanese will become useless and *will move westward into Free China,* adding to the currency already in circulation there.

6. *All of these factors will work to accelerate inflation and increase economic difficulties in Free China.*

POLITICAL

1. *There will be a lowering of morale* caused by these further defeats, the obvious ineffectiveness of the Chinese army and the increased feeling of blockade and helplessness.

2. *The Central Government will be weakened* by the loss of two of its important base areas. The possession of these has hitherto enabled it to maintain forces which can be utilized, if only by the threat of their existence, to keep the provincial groups under control.

3. *The local interests,* as a result of this weakening of the Central Government, *will increase in relative power* and independence. The Yunnan, Szechwan, Kwangsi and possibly other interests will be better able to capitalize on the greater dependence on them of the Central Government.

4. *General unrest will be stimulated* by the overall weakening and discrediting of the Government and by its greater inability to cope with the heightened economic crisis. This factor, linked to the growing independence of the provincial interests, will probably cause increased opposition by such groups as the landlords and local gentry to efforts to extend or even maintain Central Government control in the field of taxation and local government. The jump in inflation will hit the official and intellectual classes. Government efficiency will suffer, and political criticism and opposition to the Kuomintang Government can be expected to increase.

5. *Agrarian unrest will be greatly increased* by the necessity of increased taxation and requisitioning of food to support larger armies in the smaller area remaining under the control of the Central Government. This may be crucial in relatively poor agricultural areas such as Yunnan, Kweichow and Kwangsi. Even in Szechwan, the last really rich area left to the Government, the farmers have apparently at times and in some localities been near the verge of violent resistance to heavy taxation. A second major factor which will bring about unrest will be probable greater demands for conscripts to rebuild the shattered armies. Szechwan will now be the last great

reservoir of manpower. And conscription, like taxation, has already been the cause of incipient revolt.

CONCLUSIONS

The effects of a major Japanese victory in Southeast China must of course be added to those of the Japanese drive into Honan (see memorandum of May 12)* and will in one sense be cumulative. Thus the effect of the loss of the rich agricultural base of Honan is heightened by the loss of Hunan and Kiangsi.

Taken together, the adverse effects of these Japanese victories are so numerous and potentially so important that the question becomes legitimate: Will the Chinese Government collapse?

My own view is that although disintegration, chiefly from internal economic causes, will be greatly hastened, the Central Government, even though reduced to Kweichow, Yunnan, Szechwan, Shensi and Kansu, will still, for at least a considerable time, be able to maintain itself. But this government will be weakened by violent inflation, by the necessity of temporizing with local interests, and by the continual threat of agrarian revolt. Its weakness seems likely to grow and its collapse, even though it will not come soon, may become only a matter of time.

It goes without saying that the usefulness and potentiality of such a government as an effective military ally will be very small.

* Not printed.

POLICY RECOMMENDATIONS

In March 1944 Roosevelt decided to send his Vice President, Henry Wallace, on an official visit to China. The Chungking Embassy was informed in May that the visit was planned for late June. General Stilwell was then in Burma and not likely to return to meet with Wallace. On the chance, however, that Wallace might ask the Army Headquarters to brief him, Service began to draw up a briefing paper. After several drafts and suggestions from colleagues in Chungking, his memorandum grew to rather substantial proportions. It stood, however, as a summary of all the reports from Chungking and the field which he had written in the previous three years, plus his own suggestions for American policy.

The report never served its intended purpose. Though it was given to Wallace upon his arrival, the Vice President's busy schedule gave him no chance to discuss it—if indeed he ever read it. It was, however, forwarded to Washington through the usual State Department channels. In Washington, Service's memo arrived just as the crisis leading to Stilwell's removal was coming to a head. His analysis seemed particularly relevant and the report got wide distribution: it was reproduced by the O.W.I. and the O.S.S. and circulated through their bureaucracies, as well as through Army, Navy and State. Though few of his recommendations were accepted, the State Department commended Service for his "timely and able analysis and his constructive suggestions."

The Situation in China and Suggestions
Regarding American Policy

June 20, 1944
Service, pp. 200–15

I. THE SITUATION IN CHINA IS RAPIDLY BECOMING CRITICAL.

A. The Japanese strategy in China, which has been as much political as military, has so far been eminently successful.
Japan has had the choice of two alternatives:

1) It could beat China to its knees. But this would have required large military operations and a large and continuing army of occupation. And there was the danger that it might have driven the Kuomintang to carry out a real mobilization of the people, thus making possible effective resistance and perhaps rendering the Japanese task as long and costly as it has been in North China.

2) Or Japan could maintain just enough pressure on China to cause slow strangulation. Based on the astute use of puppets, the understanding of the continuing struggle for power within China (including the Kuomintang-Communist conflict), and the knowledge that Chiang expects to have the war won for him outside of China by his allies, this policy had the advantage that as long as the Kuomintang leaders saw a chance for survival they would not take the steps necessary to energize an effective war. It would thus remove any active or immediate threat to Japan's flank, and permit the accomplishment of these aims at a relatively small cost.

Japan chose the second alternative, accepting the gamble that the Kuomintang would behave exactly as it has. Like many other Japanese gambles, it has so far proved to have been nicely calculated. China *is* dying a lingering death by slow strangulation. China *does not* now constitute any threat to Japan. And China *cannot,* if the present situation continues, successfully resist a determined Japanese drive to seize our offensive bases in East China.

B. The position of the Kuomintang and the Generalissimo is weaker than it has been for the past ten years.
China faces economic collapse. This is causing disinte-

gration of the army and the government's administrative apparatus. It is one of the chief causes of growing political unrest. The Generalissimo is losing the support of a China which, by unity in the face of violent aggression, found a new and unexpected strength during the first two years of the war with Japan. Internal weaknesses are become accentuated and there is taking place a reversal of the process of unification.

1) Morale is low and discouragement widespread. There is a general feeling of hopelessness.

2) The authority of the Central Government is weakening in the areas away from the larger cities. Government mandates and measures of control cannot be enforced and remain ineffective. It is becoming difficult for the Government to collect enough food for its huge army and bureaucracy.

3) The governmental and military structure is being permeated and demoralized from top to bottom by corruption, unprecedented in scale and openness.

4) The intellectual and salaried classes, who have suffered the most heavily from inflation, are in danger of liquidation. The academic groups suffer not only the attrition and demoralization of economic stress; the weight of years of political control and repression is robbing them of the intellectual vigor and leadership they once had.

5) Peasant resentment of the abuses of conscription, tax collection and other arbitrary impositions has been widespread and is growing. The danger is ever-increasing that past sporadic outbreaks of banditry and agrarian unrest may increase in scale and find political motivation.

6) The provincial groups are making common cause with one another and with other dissident groups, and are actively consolidating their positions. Their continuing strength in the face of the growing weakness of the Central Government is forcing new measures of political appeasement in their favor.

7) Unrest within the Kuomintang armies is increasing, as shown in one important instance by the "Young Generals conspiracy" late in 1943. On a higher plane, the war-zone commanders are building up their own spheres of influence and are thus creating a "new warlordism."

8) The break between the Kuomintang and the Communists not only shows no signs of being closed, but grows more critical with the passage of time; the inevitability of civil war is now generally accepted.

9) The Kuomintang is losing the respect and support of the people by its selfish policies and its refusal to heed progressive criticism. It seems unable to revivify itself with fresh blood, and its unchanging leadership shows a growing ossification and loss of a sense of reality. To combat the dissensions and cliquism within the Party, which grow more rather than less acute, the leadership is turning toward the reactionary and unpopular Ch'en brothers clique.

10) The Generalissimo shows a similar loss of realistic flexibility and a hardening of narrowly conservative views. His growing megalomania and his unfortunate attempts to be "sage" as well as leader—shown, for instance, by *China's Destiny* and his book on economics—have forfeited the respect of many intellectuals, who enjoy in China a position of unique influence. Criticism of his dictatorship is becoming more outspoken.

These symptoms of deterioration and internal stress have been increased by the defeat in Honan and will be further accelerated if, as seems likely, the Japanese succeed in partially or wholly depriving the Central Government of East China south of the Yangtze.

In the face of the grave crisis with which it is confronted, the Kuomintang is ceasing to be the unifying and progressive force in Chinese society, the role in which it made its greatest contribution to modern China.

C. The Kuomintang is not only proving itself incapable of averting a debacle by its own initiative; on the contrary, its policies are precipitating the crisis.

Some war-weariness in China must be expected. But the policies of the Kuomintang under the impact of hyper-inflation and in the presence of obvious signs of internal and external weakness must be described as bankrupt. . . .

1. *On the internal political front the desire of the Kuomintang leaders to perpetuate their own power overrides all other considerations: the result is the enthronement of reaction.*

The Kuomintang continues to ignore the great political drive within the country for democratic reform. The writings of the Generalissimo and the Party press show that they have no real understanding of that term. . . .

On the contrary, the trend is still in the other direction.

Through such means as compulsory political training for government posts, emphasis on the political nature of the army, thought control and increasing identification of the Party and Government, the Kuomintang intensifies its drive for *"Ein Volk, Ein Reich, Ein Führer"*—even though such a policy in China is inevitably doomed to failure.

The Kuomintang shows no intention of relaxing the authoritarian controls on which its present power depends. Far from discarding or reducing the paraphernalia of a police state —the multiple and omnipresent secret-police organizations, the gendarmerie, and so forth—it continues to strengthen them as its last resort for internal security. (For the re-enforcement of the most important of these German-inspired and Gestapo-like organizations we must, unfortunately, bear some responsibility.)

Obsessed by the growing and potential threat of the Communists, who it fears may attract the popular support its own nature makes impossible, the Kuomintang, despite the pretext —to meet foreign and Chinese criticism—of conducting negotiations with the Communists, continues to adhere to policies and plans which can only result in civil war. In so doing it shows itself blind to the facts: that its internal political and military situation is so weak that success without outside assistance is most problematic; that such a civil war would hasten the process of disintegration and the spread of chaos; that it would prevent the prosecution of any effective war against Japan; and that the only parties to benefit would be Japan immediately and Russia eventually. Preparations for this civil war include an alliance with the present Chinese puppets which augurs ill for future unity and democracy in China.

2. *On the economic front the Kuomintang is unwilling to take any effective steps to check inflation which would injure the landlord-capitalist class.*

It is directly responsible for the increase of official corruption, which is one of the main obstacles to any rational attempt to ameliorate the financial situation. It does nothing to stop large-scale profiteering, hoarding and speculation—all of which are carried on by people either powerful in the Party or with intimate political connections. . . .

It refuses to attack the fundamental economic problems

of China such as the growing concentration of land holdings, extortionate rents and ruinous interest rates, and the impact of inflation.

3. *On the external front the Kuomintang is showing itself inept and selfishly short-sighted by progressive estrangement of its allies.*

By persistence in tactics of bargaining, bluff and blackmail—most inappropriate to its circumstances—and its continuing failure to deal openly and frankly and to extend wholehearted cooperation—which its own interests demand—the Kuomintang is alienating China's most important ally, the United States. It has already alienated its other major potential ally, Soviet Russia, toward which its attitude is as irrational and short-sighted as it is toward the Communists. The latest example of this is the irresponsible circulation of the report that Soviet Russia and Japan have signed a secret military agreement permitting Japanese troop withdrawals from Manchuria.

It is allowing this situation to develop at a time when its survival is dependent as never before upon foreign support. But the Kuomintang is endangering not only itself by its rash foreign policy: there are indications that it is anxious to create friction between the United States and Great Britain and Russia. When speedy victory—and any victory at all—demands maximizing of agreements and the minimizing of frictions, such maneuvers amount to sabotage of the war effort of the United Nations.

4. *On the military front the Kuomintang appears to have decided to let America win the war and to have withdrawn for all practical purposes from active participation.*

Its most important present contribution is to allow us—at our own and fantastic cost—to build and use air bases in China. . . .

It fails to make effective use of American equipment given to it as it also failed with earlier Russian supplies. Equipment brought into China has often not been transported to the fighting fronts. In other cases it has been known to have been hoarded or diverted to nonmilitary purposes. . . .

It has allowed military cooperation to be tied up with irrelevant financial demands which can only be described as a form of blackmail. . . .

It remains uncooperative and at times obstructive in American efforts to collect vital intelligence regarding the enemy in China. This attitude is exemplified by the disappointing fruits of promised cooperation by Chinese espionage organizations (toward which we have expended great effort and large sums); by the continued obstruction, in the face of agreement, to visits by American observers to the actual fighting fronts; and by the steadfast refusal to permit any contact with the Communist areas. . . .

In its own war effort a pernicious and corrupt conscription system works to ensure the selection and retention of the unfit—since the ablest and strongest can either evade conscription, buy their way out or desert. It starves and maltreats most of its troops to the degree that their military effectiveness is greatly impaired and military service is regarded in the minds of the people as a sentence of death. At the same time it refuses to follow the suggestion that the army should be reduced to the size that could be adequately fed, medically cared for, trained and armed. It bases this refusal on mercenary political considerations—the concentration on the continuing struggle for power in China, and the ultimate measurement of power in terms of armies.

For the same reason it refuses to mobilize its soldiers and people for the only kind of war which China is in a position to wage effectively—a people's guerrilla war. Perhaps our entry into the war has simplified the problems of the Kuomintang. As afraid of the forces within the country—its own people—as it is of the Japanese, it now seeks to avoid conflict with the Japanese in order to concentrate on the perpetuation of its own power.

The condition to which it has permitted its armies to deteriorate is shown most recently by the defeat in Honan, which is due not only to lack of heavy armament but also to poor morale and miserable condition of the soldiers, absence of support by the people—who have been consistently mistreated—lack of leadership, and prevalent corruption among the officers through such practices as trade with the occupied areas.

If we accept the obvious indications that the present Kuomintang leadership does not want to fight the Japanese any more than it can help, we must go further and recognize that it may even seek to prevent China from becoming the battleground for large-scale campaigns against the Japanese land forces. This helps to explain the Kuomintang's continued dealings with the Japanese and puppets. Thus the Kuomintang may hope to avert determined Japanese attack, maintain its own position and power, save the East China homes of practically all of its officials, and preserve its old economic-industrial base in the coastal cities.

If this analysis is valid, it reveals on the part of the Kuomintang leadership—which means the Generalissimo—a cynical disregard of the added cost of the inevitable prolongation of the war in American lives and resources.

D. These apparently suicidal policies of the Kuomintang have their roots in the composition and nature of the Party.

In view of the above it becomes pertinent to ask *why* the Kuomintang has lost its power of leadership; *why* it neither wishes actively to wage war against Japan itself nor to cooperate wholeheartedly with the American Army in China; and *why* it has ceased to be capable of unifying the country.

The answer to all these questions is to be found in the present composition and nature of the Party. Politically, a classical and definitive American description becomes ever more true: the Kuomintang is a congerie of conservative political cliques interested primarily in the preservation of their own power against all outsiders and in jockeying for position among themselves. Economically, the Kuomintang rests on the narrow base of the rural gentry-landlords, the militarists, the higher ranks of the government bureaucracy, and merchant-bankers having intimate connections with the government bureaucrats. This base has actually contracted during the war. The Kuomintang no longer commands, as it once did, the unequivocal support of China's industrialists, who as a group have been much weakened economically, and hence politically, by the Japanese seizure of the coastal cities.

The relation of this description of the Kuomintang to the questions propounded above is clear.

The Kuomintang has lost its leadership because it has lost touch with and is no longer representative of a nation which, through the practical experience of the war, is becoming both more politically conscious and more aware of the Party's selfish shortcomings.

It cannot fight an effective war because this is impossible without greater reliance upon and support by the people. There must be a release of the national energy such as occurred during the early period of the war. Under present conditions, this can be brought about only by reform of the Party and greater political democracy. What form this democracy takes is not as important as the genuine adoption of a democratic philosophy and attitude; the threat of foreign invasion is no longer enough to stimulate the Chinese people and only real reform can now regain their enthusiasm. But the growth of democracy, though basic to China's continuing war effort, would, to the mind of the Kuomintang's present leaders, imperil the foundations of the Party's power because it would mean that the conservative cliques would have to give up their closely guarded monopoly. Rather than do this, they prefer to see the war remain in its present state of passive inertia. They are thus sacrificing China's national interests to their own selfish ends. . . .

The Kuomintang cannot unify the country because it derives its support from the economically most conservative groups, who wish the retention of China's economically and socially backward agrarian society. These groups are incapable of bringing about China's industrialization, although they pay this objective elaborate lip service. They are also committed to the maintenance of an order which by its very nature fosters particularism and resists modern centralization. . . .

E. The present policies of the Kuomintang seem certain of failure: if that failure results in a collapse of China it will have consequences disastrous both to our immediate military plans and our long-term interests in the Far East.

. . . The present policies of the Kuomintang seem certain to fail because they run counter to strong forces within the country and are forcing China into ruin. Since these policies are not favorable to us, nor of assistance in the prosecution of an effective war by China, their failure would not of itself be disastrous to American interests. For many reasons mentioned above we might welcome the fall of the Kuomintang if it could immediately be followed by a progressive government able to unify the country and help us fight Japan.

But the danger is that the present drifting and deterioration under the Kuomintang may end in a collapse. The result would be the creation in China of a vacuum. This would eliminate any possibility in the near future of utilizing China's potential military strength. Because the Japanese and their puppets might be able to occupy this vacuum—at much less cost than by a major military campaign—it might also become impossible for us to exploit China's flank position and to continue operating from Chinese bases. The war would thus be prolonged and made more difficult.

Such a collapse would also initiate a period of internal chaos in China which would defer the emergence of a strong and stable government—an indispensable pre-condition for stability and order in the Far East.

China, which might be a minor asset to us now, would become a major liability.

F. There are, however, active and constructive forces in China opposed to the present trends of the Kuomintang leadership which, if given a chance, might avert the threatened collapse.

These groups, all increasingly dissatisfied with the Government and the Party responsible for it, include:

the patriotic younger army officers

the small merchants

large sections of the lower ranks of the Government bureaucracy

most of the foreign-returned students

the intelligentsia, including professors, students and the professional classes

the liberal elements of the Kuomintang, who make up a sizable minority under the leadership of such men as Sun Fo

the minor parties and groups, some of which, like the National Salvationists, enjoy great prestige

the Chinese Communist Party, and

the inarticulate but increasingly restless rural population.

The collective numbers and influence of these groups could be tremendous. A Kuomintang official recently admitted that resentment against the present Kuomintang Government is so widespread that if there were free, universal elections, 80 percent of the votes might be cast against it. But most of these groups are nebulous and unorganized, feeling—like the farmers —perhaps only a blind dislike of conditions as they are. They represent different classes and varying political beliefs—where they have any at all. They are tending, however, to draw together in the consciousness of their common interest in the change of the *status quo*. This awakening and fusion is, of course, opposed by the Kuomintang with every means at its disposal.

The danger, as conditions grow worse, is that some of these groups may act independently and blindly. The effect may be to make confusion worse. Such might be the case in a military *putsch*—a possibility that cannot be disregarded. The result might be something analogous to the Sian incident of 1936. But the greater delicacy and precariousness of the present situation would lend itself more easily to exploitation by the most reactionary elements of the Kuomintang, the Japanese or the puppets. Another possibility is the outbreak, on a much larger scale than heretofore, of unorganized and disruptive farmers' revolts. A disturbing phenomenon is the apparent attempt now being made by some of the minority parties to effect a marriage of convenience with the provincial warlords, among the most reactionary and unscrupulous figures in Chinese politics and hardly crusaders for a new democracy.

The hopeful sign is that all these groups are agreed that the basic problem in China today is political reform toward democracy. This point requires emphasis. It is only through political reform that the restoration of the will to fight, the unification of the country, the elimination of provincial warlordism, the solution of the Communist problem, the institution of economic policies which can avoid collapse, and the emergence of a government actually supported by the people can be achieved. *Democratic reform is the crux of all important Chinese problems, military, economic and political.*

It is clear beyond doubt that China's hope for internal peace and effective unity—certainly in the immediate future (which for the sake of the war must be our prior consideration) and probably in the long-term as well—lies neither with the present Kuomintang nor with the Communists, but in a democratic combination of the liberal elements within the country, including those within the Kuomintang, and the probably large section of the Communists who would be willing, by their own statements and past actions, to collaborate in the resurrection of a united front. . . .

II. IN THE LIGHT OF THIS DEVELOPING CRISIS, WHAT SHOULD BE THE AMERICAN ATTITUDE TOWARD CHINA?

It is impossible to predict exactly how far the present disintegration in China can continue without spectacular change in the internal situation and drastic effect on the war against Japan. But we must face the question whether we can afford passively to stand by and allow the process to continue to an almost certainly disastrous collapse, or whether we wish to do what we legitimately and practically can to arrest it. We need to formulate a realistic policy toward China.

A. The Kuomintang and Chiang are acutely conscious of their dependence on us and will be forced to appeal for our support.

We must realize that when the process of disintegration gets out of hand it will be to us that the Kuomintang will turn for financial, political and military salvation. The awareness of this dependence is the obvious and correct explanation of the Kuomintang's hypersensitivity to American opinion and criticism. The Kuomintang—and particularly the Generalissimo—know that we are the only disinterested, yet powerful ally to whom China can turn.

The appeal will be made to us on many grounds besides the obvious, well-worn, but still effective one of pure sentiment. They have said in the past and will say in the future that they could long ago have made peace with Japan—on what are falsely stated would have been favorable terms. They have claimed and will claim again that their resistance and refusal to compromise with Japan saved Russia, Great Britain and ourselves—ignoring the truth that our own refusal to compromise with Japan to China's disadvantage brought on Pearl Harbor and our involvement before we were ready. They have complained that they have received less support in the form of materials than any other major ally—forgetting that they have done less fighting, have not used the materials given, and would not have had the ability to use what they asked for.

Finally, they have tried and will continue to try to lay the blame on us for their difficulties—distorting the effect of American Army expenditures in China and ignoring the fact that these expenditures are only a minor factor in the whole sorry picture of the mismanagement of the Chinese economy.

But however far-fetched these appeals, our flat refusal of them might have several embarrassing effects:

1) We would probably see China enter a period of internal chaos. Our war effort in this theater would be disrupted, instability in the Far East prolonged, and possible Russian intervention attracted.

2) We would be blamed by large sections of both Chinese and American public opinion for "abandoning" China after having been at least partly responsible for its collapse. (In a measure we would have brought such blame upon ourselves because we have tended to allow ourselves to become identified not merely with China but also with the Kuomintang and its policies. Henceforth it may be the better part of valor to avoid too close identification with the Kuomintang.)

3) By an apparent abandonment of China in its hour of need, we would lose international prestige, especially in the Far East.

On the other hand, if we come to the rescue of the Kuomintang on its own terms, we would be buttressing—but only temporarily—a decadent regime which by its existing composition and program is incapable of solving China's problems. Both China and we ourselves would be gaining only a brief respite from the ultimate day of reckoning.

It is clear, therefore, that it is to our advantage to avoid a situation arising in which we would be presented with a Hobson's choice between two such unpalatable alternatives.

B. The Kuomintang's dependence can give us great influence.

Circumstances are rapidly developing so that the Generalissimo will have to ask for the continuance and increase of our support. Weak as he is, he is in no position—and the weaker he becomes, the less he will be able—to turn down or render nugatory any coordinated and positive policy we may adopt toward China. The cards are all in our favor. Our influence, intelligently used, can be tremendous.

C. There are three general alternatives open to us:

1) We may give up China as hopeless and wash our hands of it altogether.
2) We may continue to give support to the Generalissimo, when and as he asks for it.
3) We may formulate a coordinated and positive policy toward China and take the necessary steps for its implementation.

D. Our choice between these alternatives must be determined by our objectives in China.

The United States, *if* it so desired and *if* it had a coherent policy, could play an important and perhaps decisive role in:

1) Stimulating China to an active part in the war in the Far East, thus hastening the defeat of Japan.
2) Staving off economic collapse in China and bringing about basic political and economic reforms, thus enabling China to carry on the war and enhancing the chances of its orderly postwar recovery.
3) Enabling China to emerge from the war as a major and stabilizing factor in postwar East Asia.
4) Winning a permanent and valuable ally in a progressive, independent and democratic China.

E. We should adopt the third alternative—a coordinated and positive policy. This is clear from an examination of the background of the present situation in China and the proper objectives of our policy there.

The first alternative must be rejected on immediate military grounds—but also for obvious long-range considerations. It would deprive us of valuable air bases and a position on Japan's flank. Its adoption would prolong the war. We cannot afford to wash our hands of China.

The results of the second alternative—which, insofar as we have a China policy, has been the one we have been and are pursuing—speak for themselves. The substantial financial assistance we have given China has been frittered away with negligible if any effect in slowing inflation and retarding economic collapse. The military help we have given has certainly not been used to increase China's war effort against Japan. Our political support has been used for the Kuomintang's own selfish purposes and to bolster its shortsighted and ruinous policies.

The third, therefore, is the only real alternative left to us.

Granted the rejection of the first alternative, there is no longer a question of helping and advising China. China itself must request this help and advice. The only question is whether we give this help within a framework which makes sense, or whether we continue to give it in our present disjointed and absent-minded manner. In the past it has sometimes seemed that our right hand did not know what the left was doing. To continue without a coherent and coordinated policy will be dissipating our effort without either China or ourselves deriving any appreciable benefit. It can only continue to create new problems, in addition to those already troubling us, without any compensating advantages beyond those of indolent short-term expediency. But most important is the possibility that this haphazard giving, this serving of short-term expediency, may not be enough to save the situation; even with it, China may continue toward collapse.

F. This positive policy should be political.

The problem confronting us is whether we are to continue as in the past to ignore political considerations of direct military significance, or whether we are to take a leaf out of the Japanese book and invoke even stronger existing political forces in China to achieve our military and long-term political objectives.

We must seek to contribute toward the reversal of the present movement toward collapse and to the rousing of China from its military inactivity. This can be brought about only by an accelerated movement toward democratic political reform within China. Our part must be that of a catalytic agent in this process of China's democratization. It can be carried out by the careful exertion of our influence, which has so far not been consciously and systematically used.

This democratic reform does not necessarily mean the overthrow of the Generalissimo or the Kuomintang. On the contrary—if they have the vision to see it—their position will be improved and the stability of the Central Government increased. The democratic forces already existing in China will be strengthened, the reactionary authoritarian trends in the Kuomintang will be modified, and a multiparty United Front government will probably emerge. It is almost certain that the Generalissimo and the Kuomintang would continue to play a dominant part in such a government.

It goes without saying that this democratization of China must be brought about by, and depend on, forces within the country. It cannot be enforced by us—or by any foreign nation. For us to dictate "democracy" would not only be paradoxical, it would also open us to the charge, which the Japanese and reactionary elements would exploit, of being "imperialistic." Our task therefore is to find means of exerting our political influence in indirect and sometimes unassuming ways and of showing to the Kuomintang and the people of China our benevolent and serious interest in democracy.

The popular desire for democracy in China is already strong. We can be sure that as our attitude becomes clear, and as our desire that China itself should be the prime mover in bringing about reform becomes apparent, steady progress will be made. . . .

III. THE IMPLEMENTATION OF THIS POLITICAL POLICY, THOUGH DIFFICULT IN SOME RESPECTS, IS PRACTICAL AND CAN BE CARRIED OUT BY MANY MEANS.

A. Diplomatic finesse will be required in the execution of this policy in such a way as not to offend the strong current of genuine nationalism (as distinguished from the chauvinism of the Kuomintang) which characterizes almost all sections of the Chinese people. . . .

B. There must be effective coordination of the policies and actions of all American government agencies concerned in these dealings with China.

The present lack of effective cooperation between the various government agencies—State, War and some of the newer autonomous organizations—detracts from the efficient functioning of each, and weakens American influence when it is most needed.

It must be recognized—and it will be even more the case under the policy proposed—that *all our dealings with, and all our activities in, China have political implication.* Coordination is absolutely essential for the achievement of unity of policy and synchronization of action. Its attainment will require intelligent and forceful direction both in Washington and in Chungking.

The logical person to coordinate activities in Chungking is

obviously, because of the broad issues involved, the Ambassador. Similarly the corresponding person in Washington might be the chief of the China Section of the State Department, who would watch the whole field for the President or a responsible Cabinet member. Positive action, of course, would depend on constant and close consultation, both in Washington and in the field, between the representatives of the State, War, Navy and Treasury departments and the other agencies operating in China.

C. Since all measures open to us should not be applied simultaneously, there should be careful selection and timing.

Some measures will be simple and immediately useful. Others should be deferred until primary steps have been taken. Still others will be more forceful or direct, and their use will depend on the Kuomintang's recalcitrance to change its ways. We must avoid overplaying or underplaying our hand.

D. Specific measures which might be adopted in the carrying out of this positive policy include the following:

1. *Negative:*
a) Stop our present "mollycoddling" of China:
   by restricting lend-lease
   cutting down training of Chinese military cadets
   discontinuing training of the Chinese army
   taking a firmer stand in the financial negotiations, or
   stopping the shipment of gold

Any or all of these restrictive measures can be reversed as the Generalissimo and the Kuomintang become more cooperative in carrying on military operations, using equipment and training supplies, being reasonable on financial questions, or allowing us freedom in such military requirements as establishing contact with the Communist areas.

b) Stop building up the Generalissimo's and the Kuomintang's prestige internationally and in the United States. Such "face" serves only to bolster the regime internally and to harden it in its present policies. Our inclusion of China as one of the "Big Four" served a useful purpose in the early stage of the war and as a counter to Japanese racial propaganda but has now lost its justification. . . .

Abandonment of glib generalities for hard-headed realism

in our attitude toward China will be quickly understood—without the resentment that would probably be felt against the British. We can make it clear that praise will be given when praise is due.

c) Stop making unconditional and grandiose promises of help along such lines as UNRRA, postwar economic aid and political support. We can make it clear without having to be very explicit that we stand ready to help China when China shows itself deserving. . . .

d) Discontinue our present active collaboration with Chinese secret-police organizations, which support the forces of reaction and stand for the opposite of our American democratic aims and ideals. This collaboration, which results in the effective strengthening of a Gestapo-like organization, is becoming increasingly known in China. It confuses and disillusions Chinese liberals, who look to us as their hope, and it weakens our position with the Kuomintang leaders in pressuring for democratic reform.

2. *Positive:*

a) High government officials in conversations with Chinese leaders in Washington and in China can make known our interest in democracy and unity in China and our dissatisfaction with present Kuomintang military, financial, and other policies.

b) We should take up the repeated—but usually insincere—requests of the Kuomintang for advice. . . .

c) We should seek to extend our influence on Chinese opinion by every practical means available.

The Office of War Information should go beyond its present function of reporting American war news to pointing up the values of democracy as a permanent political system and as an aid in the waging of war against totalitarianism. We should attempt to increase the dissemination in China, by radio or other direct means, of constructive American criticism. . . .

A second line is the active expansion of our cultural relations program. . . .

Other, more indirect lines, are the expansion of our American Foreign Service representation in China to new localities (since each office is in some measure a center of American influence and contact with Chinese liberals and returned students from the United States); and the careful indoctrination of the American Army personnel in China to create, by example and their attitude toward Chinese, favorable impressions of America and the things that America stands for. Where contact between American and Chinese military personnel has been close, as in Burma, the result has apparently been a democratizing influence.

d) We should assist the education of public opinion in the United States toward a realistic but constructively sympathetic attitude toward China. The most obvious means would be making background information available, in an unofficial way, to responsible political commentators, writers and research workers. . . .

e) We should maintain friendly relations with the liberal elements in the Kuomintang, the minor parties and the Communists. This can—and should for its maximum effect—be done in an open, aboveboard manner. The recognition which it implies will be quickly understood by the Chinese.

Further steps in this direction could be publicity to liberals, such as distinguished intellectuals. When possible they may be included in consideration for special honors or awards, given recognition by being asked to participate in international commissions or other bodies, and invited to travel or lecture in the United States. A very effective action of this type would be an invitation to Madame Sun Yat-sen from the White House.

We should select men of known liberal views to represent us in O.W.I., cultural relations, and other lines of work in China.

f) We should continue to show an interest in the Chinese Communists. This includes contact with the Communist representatives in Chungking, publicity on the blockade and the situation between the two parties, and continued pressure for the dispatch of observers to North China. At the same time we should stress the importance of North China militarily—for intelligence regarding Japanese battle order, Japanese air strength, weather reporting, bombing data and damage assessment, and air-crew evasion and rescue work. We should consider the eventual advance of active operations against the Japanese to North China, and the question of assistance to or cooperation with Communist and guerrilla forces. If our reasonable requests based on urgent military grounds do not receive a favorable response, we should send our military observers anyway.

g) We should consider the training and equipment of provincial or other armies in China in cases where we can be satisfied that they will fight the Japanese.

h) We should continue to press—and if necessary insist—on getting American observers to the actual fighting fronts. We should urge, and when possible assist, the improvement of the condition of the Chinese soldier, especially his treatment, clothing, feeding, and medical care.

i) We should publicize statements by responsible government officials indicating our interest in Chinese unity and our attitude toward such questions as the use of American Lend-Lease supplies by the Kuomintang in a civil war. It is interesting, for instance, that Under Secretary Welles' letter to Browder regarding American interest in Chinese unity was considered so important by the Kuomintang that publication in China was prohibited.*

This program is, of course, far from complete. Other measures will occur to the policy agency and will suggest themselves as the situation in China develops.

E. Most of these measures can be applied progressively.

This is true, for instance, of the various negative actions suggested, and of the conversations, statements, and other lines of endeavor to influence public opinion in China. A planned activity of encouragement and attention to liberals, minor-party leaders and the Communists can advance naturally from stage to stage.

F. The program suggested contains little that is not already being done in an uncoordinated and only partially effective manner.

What is needed chiefly is an integration, systematic motiva-

---

* On October 12, 1942, Sumner Welles gave a memorandum on U.S. China policy to Earl Browder, General Secretary of the Communist Party of the United States, who had accused the State Department of encouraging the Kuomintang in its anti-Communist policies. The memorandum, which was made public by Browder, is printed in *Foreign Relations, 1942,* pp. 248–49.

tion, and planned expansion of activities in which we are already, perhaps in some cases unconsciously, engaged. We *do,* for instance, try to maintain contact with liberal groups; we *have* expressed the desire to send observers to the Communist area; we *have* a weak cultural relations program; and the O.W.I. *has* made some attempts to propagandize American democratic ideals.

G. The program constitutes only very modified and indirect intervention in Chinese affairs.

It must be admitted that some of the measures proposed would involve taking more than normal interest in the affairs of another sovereign nation. But they do not go so far as to infringe on Chinese sovereignty. If we choose to make Lend-Lease conditional on a better war effort by China, it is also China's freedom to refuse to accept it on those conditions. We do not go nearly as far as imperialistic countries have often done in the past. We obviously do not, for instance, suggest active assistance or subsidizing of rival parties to the Kuomintang—as the Russians did in the case of the Communists.

Furthermore, the Chinese Government would find it difficult to object. The Chinese have abused their freedom to propagandize in the United States by the statements and writings of such men as Lin Yu-tang. They have also, and through Lin Yu-tang, who carries an official passport as a representative of the Chinese Government, engaged in "cultural relations" work. They have freely criticized American policies and American leaders. And they have attempted to dabble in American politics —through Madame Chiang, Luce, Willkie and Republican congressmen. They have had, and will continue to have, freedom to try to influence public opinion in the United States in the same way that we will try to do it in China.

THE STILWELL CRISIS AND
THE "NEED FOR REALISM"

By the fall of 1944, Sino-American relations had reached a critical juncture with a dispute over the person and the role of General Joseph Stilwell. Although President Roosevelt had been the strongest advocate of Chiang Kai-shek's inclusion in the Allied "Big Four," and had been responsible for the considerable "face" given to the Generalissimo at the Cairo Conference of November 1943, Chiang's vacillations at Cairo and his exorbitant demands for loans, aircraft and increased tonnage over the Hump in the months following Cairo had significantly cooled the President's feelings for the Generalissimo. On April 3, with Chiang refusing to commit his American-trained and -armed YOKE forces to the battle on the Salween front in Burma, Roosevelt bluntly informed him that

> A shell of a division opposes you on the Salween. Your advance in the west cannot help but succeed. To take advantage of just such an opportunity, we have, during the past year, been equipping and training your YOKE Forces. If they are not to be used in the common cause, our most strenuous and extensive efforts to fly in equipment and furnish instructional personnel have not been justified.*

Two weeks later, after a direct threat to cut off Lend-Lease supplies, the Chinese finally committed their forces to Burma. But by midsummer, with the Chinese army crumbling under the Japanese offensive in Central China, Roosevelt was ready to suggest the most drastic of remedies. In a July 6 message to Chiang, FDR wrote:

> The extremely serious situation which results from Japanese advances in Central China, which threaten not only your

---

* Charles F. Romanus and Riley Sunderland, *Stilwell's Command Problems* (Washington: Department of the Army, Historical Division, 1958), p. 310.

Government but all that the U.S. Army has been building up in China, leads me to the conclusion that drastic measures must be taken immediately if the situation is to be saved. The critical situation which now exists, in my opinion calls for the delegation to one individual of the power to coordinate all the Allied military resources in China, including the Communist forces.*

The President continued that despite Chiang's known feelings for Stilwell, "I know of no other man who has the ability, the force, and the determination to offset the disaster which now threatens China and our over-all plans for the conquest of Japan."

The issue was now joined, but Chiang temporized and persuaded Roosevelt to send a personal representative, Major General Patrick J. Hurley, to arrange the details of Stilwell's new command. By the time Hurley reached China, Service was already in Yenan. He had, however, been the interpreter when Roosevelt's July 6 message was personally delivered to the Generalissimo. He knew, therefore, that there was a major dispute between the United States and China over the issue of Stilwell's powers and responsibilities. What he did not know was that Hurley was slowly switching to Chiang's side in the dispute, and the issue was becoming not Stilwell's powers but whether Stilwell was to remain in China at all. Service did not learn this until October 9, when Hurley's aide, Colonel E. J. McNally, an old friend of Service's when they were both studying Chinese in Peking, arrived on a junket to Yenan—the Communist capital having become an unusually popular sightseeing attraction. Service and Colonel David Barrett, commander of the U.S. Military Observer Section (the Dixie Mission) in Yenan, cornered McNally to get filled in on events in Chungking. "He said the issue was not command, but the issue was whether Stilwell would stay at all. The Generalissimo had dug in his heels and demanded his recall. Well, hell, Dave and I were pretty excited about this: it seemed the height of folly, perhaps partly because we hadn't been kept fully informed. But for the issue to become not command but the life or death of Stilwell himself. . . . he was going to have his head cut off. So I went and sat down and in my agitated state, fulminated! You might say that the effect of McNally's bombshell was all the greater because we were so completely in ignorance."

* *Ibid.*, p. 383.

The report which Service wrote is one of his strongest pleas for a new U.S. policy toward the Kuomintang. Friends who later read it in Washington were shocked and even a little apprehensive: "More people said to me: 'Jesus, Service! I read that thing of yours, and I certainly agree with you, but it is going to get you in a lot of trouble.'" Their fears were not unfounded. In November 1945, when Hurley dramatically resigned the ambassadorship to China to which he had been appointed a year earlier, he cited this report in particular as evidence of a plot by "the professional Foreign Service men" who wished "not to uphold but to cause the collapse of the Government of the Republic of China."* This charge would later be picked up by Congressman Walter Judd and others and formed a foundation for McCarthy's accusations in the early fifties.

The report was a memorandum addressed to General Stilwell personally. Service was acting here in his capacity as political adviser to Stilwell, and was urging a strong negotiating stance toward Chiang. In discussing the possible collapse of the Kuomintang Government, he was certainly not *advocating* it, he was not even *predicting* it; he was simply arguing that we should not weaken our negotiating stance out of fear of a Kuomintang collapse. Secondly, what Service was suggesting was not necessarily anything very radical or new. American "realism" in its dealings with Chiang had been increasing all year. Stilwell held views quite similar to those of Service. The President himself, when he conferred privately with Stilwell at Cairo, had asked: "How long do you think Chiang can last?" And when Stilwell indicated doubt as to the Generalissimo's ability to withstand a sustained Japanese offensive, FDR replied: "Well then, we should look for some other man or group of men to carry on."†

Finally, and most important, Service's confidence that the collapse of the Kuomintang Government, even if it occurred, would not mean the collapse of China's resistance was founded on his long experience in the provinces and in the field in China. He realized that even if the Chungking Government collapsed, provincial and local governments and armies would continue. China had not been effectively unified since the end of the Em-

* *Tydings*, p. 1984.
† Barbara W. Tuchman, *Stilwell and the American Experience in China* (New York: Macmillan, 1971), p. 410.

pire in 1911. It was not effectively unified in 1944, even with full U.S. support for the Generalissimo at the top. To some degree, the existence of the Chungking Government even hindered the war effort, as when Chiang blocked the sending of supplies to a provincial commander like Hsueh Yueh, who was putting up a dogged resistance to the Japanese offensive in Hunan. It was, then, precisely Service's intimate knowledge of and experience with the workings of the Chinese political system which allowed him to make these recommendations. But he was not to be heard. Hurley, who had been in China for barely a month and had no understanding of China whatsoever, was to have the ruling voice. Before Stilwell even received Service's memo, he was recalled and on his way back to the States.

The Need for Greater Realism in Our Relations with Chiang Kai-shek

To: General Stilwell, Commanding General, USAF-CBI

October 10, 1944
Amerasia Papers, pp. 1014–17

1. You have allowed me, as a political officer attached to your staff, to express myself freely in the past regarding the situation in China as I have seen it. Although in Yenan I am only a distant observer of recent developments in Chungking and Washington, I trust that you will permit the continued frankness which I have assumed in the attached memorandum regarding the stronger policy which I think it is now time for us to adopt toward Chiang Kai-shek and the Central Government.

2. It is obvious, of course, that you cannot act independently along the lines suggested. The situation in China and the measures necessary to meet it have both military importance and far-reaching political significance; the two aspects cannot be separated. Because of this interrelation, and because of the high level on which action in China must be taken, there must be agreement and mutual support between our political and military branches. But this will be ineffective without clear decision and forceful implementation by the President.

3. It is requested that copies of this report be transmitted, as usual, to the American Ambassador at Chungking and Headquarters, USAF-CBI, for the information of Mr. Davies.*

MEMORANDUM

Our dealings with Chiang Kai-shek apparently continue on the basis of the unrealistic assumption that he is China and that he is necessary to our cause. It is time, for the sake of the war and also for our future interests in China, that we take a more realistic line.

The Kuomintang Government is in crisis. Recent defeats have exposed its military ineffectiveness and will hasten the approaching economic disaster. Passive inability to meet these crises in a constructive way, stubborn unwillingness to submerge selfish power-seeking in democratic unity, and the statements of Chiang himself to the People's Political Council and on October 10, are sufficient evidence of the bankruptcy of Kuomintang leadership.

With the glaring exposure of the Kuomintang's failure, dissatisfaction within China is growing rapidly. The prestige of the Party was never lower, and Chiang is losing the respect he once enjoyed as a leader.

In the present circumstances, the Kuomintang is dependent on American support for survival. *But we are in no way dependent on the Kuomintang.*

We do not need it for military reasons. It has lost the Southern airbases and cannot hold any section of the seacoast. Without drastic reforms—which must have a political base—its armies cannot fight the Japanese effectively no matter how many arms we give them. But it will not permit those reforms because its war against Japan is secondary to its desire to maintain its own undemocratic power.

---

* Service sent most of his reports from Yenan with this distribution: The first copy would go either to Stilwell or G-2 in Chungking; the second to the Ambassador; and the third to John P. Davies, the senior of the Foreign Service officers attached to the headquarters of the U.S. Army Forces, China-Burma-India Theater, and usually stationed in Delhi. In the despatches below, Service's note on distribution has been deleted.

On the other hand, neither the Kuomintang nor any other Chinese regime, because of the sentiment of the people, can refuse American forces the use of Chinese territory against the Japanese. And the Kuomintang's attitude prevents the utilization of other forces, such as the Communist or provincial troops, who should be more useful than the Kuomintang's demoralized armies.

We need not fear Kuomintang surrender or opposition. The Party and Chiang will stick to us because our victory is certain and is their only hope for continued power.

But our support of the Kuomintang will not stop its normally traitorous relations with the enemy and will only encourage it to continue sowing the seeds of future civil war by plotting with the present puppets for eventual consolidation of the occupied territories against the Communist-led forces of popular resistance.

We need not fear the collapse of the Kuomintang Government. All the other groups in China want to defend themselves and fight Japan. Any new government under any other than the present reactionary control will be more cooperative and better able to mobilize the country.

Actually, by continued and exclusive support of the Kuomintang, we tend to prevent the reforms and democratic reorganization of the Government which are essential for the revitalization of China's war effort. Encouraged by our support, the Kuomintang will continue in its present course, progressively losing the confidence of the people and becoming more and more impotent. Ignored by us, and excluded from the Government and joint prosecution of the war, the Communists and other groups will be forced to guard their own interests by more direct opposition.

We need not support the Kuomintang for international political reasons. The day when it was expedient to inflate Chiang's status to one of the "Big Four" is past, because with the obvious certainty of defeat, Japan's Pan-Asia propaganda loses its effectiveness. We cannot hope that China under the present Kuomintang can be an effective balance to Soviet Russia, Japan, or the British Empire in the Far East.

On the contrary, artificial inflation of Chiang's status only adds to his unreasonableness. The example of a democratic, nonimperialistic China will be much better counterpropaganda in Asia than the present regime, which, even in books like *China's Destiny,* hypnotizes itself with ideas of consolidating minority nations (such as Tibet and Mongolia), recovering "lost territories" (such as the "Southern Peninsula"), and protecting the "rights" and at the same time national ties of its numerous emigrants (to such areas as Thailand, Malaya and the East Indies). Finally, the perpetuation in power of the present Kuomintang can only mean a weak and disunited China—a sure cause of international involvements in the Far East. The key to stability must be a strong, unified China. This can be accomplished only on a democratic foundation.

We need not support Chiang in the belief that he represents pro-American or democratic groups. All the people and all other political groups of importance in China are friendly to the United States and look to it for the salvation of the country, now and after the war.

In fact, Chiang has lost the confidence and respect of most of the American-educated, democratically minded liberals and intellectuals. The Ch'en brothers, military and secret-police cliques which control the Party and are Chiang's main supports are the most chauvinist elements in the country. The present Party ideology, as shown in Chiang's own books *China's Destiny* and *Chinese Economic Theory,* is fundamentally antiforeign and antidemocratic, both politically and economically.

Finally, we need feel no ties of gratitude to Chiang. The men he has kept around him have proved selfish and corrupt, incapable and obstructive. Chiang's own dealings with us have been an opportunist combination of extravagant demands and unfilled promises, wheedling and bargaining, bluff and blackmail. Chiang did not resist Japan until forced by his own people. He has sought to have us save him—so that he can continue his conquest of his own country. In the process, he has "worked" us for all we were worth.

We seem to forget that Chiang is an Oriental; that his background and vision are limited; that his position is built on skill as an extremely adroit political manipulator and a stubborn, shrewd bargainer; that he mistakes kindness and flattery for weakness; and that he listens to his own instrument of force rather than reason.

Our policy toward China should be guided by two facts. First, *we cannot hope to deal successfully with Chiang without being hard-boiled.* Second, *we cannot hope to solve China's problems* (which are now our problems) *without consideration of the opposition forces*—Communist, provincial and liberal.

The parallel with Yugoslavia has been drawn before but is becoming more and more apt. It is as impractical to seek Chinese unity, the use of the Communist forces, and the mobilization of the population in the rapidly growing occupied areas by discussion in Chungking with the Kuomintang alone as it was to seek the solution of these problems through Mikhailovitch and King Peter's government in London, ignoring Tito.

We should not be swayed by pleas of the danger of China's collapse. This is an old trick of Chiang's. There may be a collapse of the Kuomintang Government, but it will not be the collapse of China's resistance. There may be a period of some confusion, but the eventual gains of the Kuomintang's collapse will more than make up for this. The crisis itself makes reform more urgent—and at the same time increases the weight of our influence. *The crisis is the time to push—not to relax.*

We should not let Chiang divert us from the important questions by wasting time in futile discussions as to who is to be American commander. This is an obvious subterfuge.

There is only one man qualified by experience for the job. And the fact is that *no one who knows anything about China and is concerned over American rather than Chiang's interests will satisfy Chiang.*

We should end the hollow pretense that China is unified and that we can talk only to Chiang. This puts the trump card in Chiang's hands.

Public announcement that the President's representative had made a visit to the Communist capital at Yenan would have a significance that no Chinese would miss—least of all the Generalissimo. The effect would be great even if it were only a demonstration with no real consultation. But it should be more than a mere demonstration: we must, for instance, plan on eventual use of the Communist armies and this cannot be purely on Kuomintang terms.

Finally, if these steps do not succeed, we should stop veiling our negotiations with China in complete secrecy. This shields Chiang and is the voluntary abandonment of our strongest weapon.

Chinese public opinion would swing violently against Chiang if he were shown obstructive and noncooperative with the United States. We should not be misled by the relatively very few Kuomintang die-hards: they are not the people. The Kuomintang Government could not withstand public belief that the United States was considering the withdrawal of military support or recognition of the Kuomintang as the leader of Chinese resistance.

More than ever, we hold all the aces in Chiang's poker game. It is time we started playing them.

PART II

The Communist Areas

The old order changeth, yielding place to new.

—Tennyson,
Morte d'Arthur

From the time of his assignment to the Chungking Embassy in 1941, Service made a clear and conscious decision to concentrate on the Chinese Communists and the Kuomintang's relations with them. "It was a simply careerist decision. To be noticed and advanced in the Foreign Service, one had to write notable reports. That meant finding an area of special competence and concentrating on it. Not being an economist capable of specializing in that area, and being quite sick of the pro-KMT propaganda put forth by many, I decided that the key internal political problem which I could handle adequately and well was the CCP and its relations with the KMT."

Between 1937 and 1939, there had been frequent foreign visitors traveling to the Communist areas, and Chou En-lai and other Communist leaders spent much of their time in the United Front capital of Hankow. After the fall of Hankow, and especially after the New Fourth Army incident of January 1941, the KMT blockade had cut off most sources of direct information on the Communist-controlled Border Region and guerrilla base areas. Still, Service did his best to keep informed on the CCP by talking to refugees from the coast who had traveled through their areas, by questioning missionaries in the Northwest on the edge of the Border Region, by reading the heavily censored but often informative Communist newspaper in Chungking, by picking up such rumors and word of mouth as circulated among intellectual and journalistic circles in Chungking, and by talking to members of the Communist office in Chungking. In this way, Service became quite cognizant of the growing strength of the Communists, and also of the likelihood of renewed civil war as soon as the war with Japan was ended. But he was also aware of the critical need for firsthand information of the Communist areas.

When Service returned to Washington for consultations in January 1943, he was the first Foreign Service officer to return from Chungking since Pearl Harbor. He found the State Department completely out of touch: "There was Spanish moss hanging from the chandeliers." His recent extensive trip to the Northwest and Honan had convinced him that the Department's rosy view of the Kuomintang was completely unfounded. Thus he wrote the following memorandum, which the reigning patriarch of the Department's Far Eastern Division, Stanley K. Hornbeck, sent back with such marginal comments as "Preposterous," "Ridiculous" and "Scandalous."

Kuomintang-Communist Situation

January 23, 1944
Foreign Relations, 1943, pp. 193–99

An outstanding impression gained during the past eighteen months spent in Chungking and in travel through Southwest and Northwest China is that the most careful study should be given to the internal political situation in China, particularly the growing rift between the Kuomintang and the Communists.

The "United Front" is now definitely a thing of the past and it is impossible to find any optimism regarding the possibility of its resurrection as long as present tendencies continue and the present leadership of the Kuomintang, both civil and military, remains in power. Far from improving, the situation is deteriorating. In Kuomintang-controlled China, the countering of Communism is a growing preoccupation of propaganda, of both military and civilian political indoctrination, and of secret-police and gendarmerie activity. There is not only a rigorous suppression of anything coming under the ever widening definition of "Communism" but there appears to be a movement away from even the outward forms of democracy in government. It is now no longer wondered whether civil war can be avoided, but rather whether it can be delayed at least until after a victory over Japan.

The dangers and implications of this disunity are obvious and far-reaching. Militarily, the present situation is a great hindrance to any effective war effort by China. Its deterioration into civil war would be disastrous. The situation therefore has direct relationship to our own efforts to defeat Japan. At the present time a large and comparatively well trained and equipped portion of the Kuomintang army is diverted from active combat against the Japanese to blockade the Communists. In the north (Kansu and Shensi) the lines are well established by multiple lines of blockhouses, and these large forces remain in a condition of armed readiness. Further south (Hupeh, Anhwei, north Kiangsu) the lines are less clearly demarcated and sporadic hostilities, which have gone on for over two years and in which the Kuomintang forces appear to take the initiative, continue.

On the other side, the Communist army is starved of all supplies and forced in turn to immobilize most of its strength to guard against what it considers the Kuomintang threat. It was admitted by both parties that there was extreme tension in Kuomintang-Communist relations in the spring of 1942. The Communists believe that it was only the Japanese invasion of Yunnan that saved them from attack at that time. The Communists and their friends claim, furthermore, that the Kuomintang is devoting its energies to the strengthening of its control over those parts of China accessible to it rather than to fighting Japan. This strengthening of the position of the Kuomintang will of course assist it in re-establishing its control over areas which will then be opened to it. A logical part of such a policy would be the taking over, as soon as an opportunity is found, of the Communist base area in Kansu-Shensi. Success in this move would weaken the Communists and make easier the eventual recapture by the Kuomintang of the Communist guerrilla zones. To support this thesis the Communist point to the campaign in the more extreme Kuomintang publications for the immediate abolition of the "Border Area." Another factor sometimes suggested as tending to provoke an early Kuomintang attack on the Communists is the desirability, from the Kuomintang point of view, of disposing of them before China finds itself an active ally of Russia against Japan.

The possible positive military value of the Communist army to our war effort should not be ignored. These forces control the territory through which access may be had to Inner Mongolia, Manchuria and Japanese North China bases. The strategic importance of their position would be enhanced by the entry of Russia into the war against Japan. This importance is largely potential, but fairly recent reports of continued bitter fighting in Shansi indicate that the Communists are still enough of a force to provoke periodic Japanese "mopping up" campaigns. Reflection of this is found in the intensive Japanese anti-Communist propaganda campaign in North China in the summer of 1941, although the fact must not be overlooked that Japanese propaganda has emphasized the anti-Communist angle to appeal to whatever "collaborationist" elements there may be in occupied China and to the more conservative sections of the Kuomintang. This activity in Shansi and the difficulties of the Japanese there contrast with the inactivity on most of the other Kuomintang-Japanese fronts.

Aside from the immediate war aspects, the political implications of this situation are also serious. Assuming that open hostilities are for the time being averted, the eventual defeat and withdrawal of the Japanese will leave the Kuomintang still confronted with the Communists solidly entrenched in most of North China (east Kansu, north Shensi, Shansi, south Chahar, Hopei, Shantung, north Kiangsu and north Anhwei). In addition the Communists will be in position to move into the vacuum created by the Japanese withdrawal from Suiyuan, Jehol and Manchuria, in all of which areas there is already some Communist activity. In the rest of China they will have the sympathy of elements among the liberals, intellectuals and students. These elements are of uncertain size but of considerable influence in China; and the Kuomintang's fear of their power, and the power of whatever underground organization the Communists have succeeded in maintaining in the Kuomintang area, is indicated by the size and activity of its various secret-police organs.

But possibly the greatest potential strength of the Communists, and one reason why military action against them will not be entirely effective at the present time, is their control of the rural areas of North China in the rear of the Japanese. Here the Kuomintang cannot reach them and the Communists have apparently been able to carry out some degree of popular mobilization. I am in possession of a secret Kuomintang publication describing the "Communist Control of Hopei." It discusses measures of combating the Communists (by such means, for instance, as the blockade now being enforced) and concludes that if the Communists fail to "cooperate" (i.e., submit to complete Kuomintang domination) they must be "exterminated." I hope to make a translation of this pamphlet, which would appear to have significance as an official Kuomintang indication of the policy it will pursue in these areas. It seems reasonable to question, as some thoughtful Chinese do, whether the people of these guerrilla zones, after several years of political education and what must be assumed to be at least partial "Sovietization," will accept peacefully the imposition of Kuomintang control activated by such a spirit and implemented by military force and the political repression, and secret-police and gendarmerie power, which are already important adjuncts of Party control and which are being steadily strengthened and expanded.

Non-Communist Chinese of my acquaintance (as, for instance, the nephew of the well-known late editor of the *Ta Kung Pao*) consider the likelihood of civil war the greatest problem facing China. They point out that the Communists are far stronger now than they were when they stood off Kuomintang armies for ten years in Central China and that they will be much stronger yet if it proves that they have succeeded in winning the support of the population in the guerrilla zone. They point to numerous recent instances of successful Communist infiltration into and indoctrination of opposing Chinese armies (such as those of Yen Hsi-shan) and wonder whether this will not cause a prolongation of the struggle and perhaps make a victory for the Kuomintang, or for either side, impossible. There is undoubtedly a strong revulsion in the mind of the average, non-Party Chinese to the idea of renewed civil war, and the Kuomintang may indeed have difficulty with the loyalty and effectiveness of its conscript troops.

Belief in the certainty of eventual civil war leads these same Chinese to question whether the United States has given sufficient realistic consideration to the future in China of democracy. The question is raised whether it is to China's advantage, or to America's own interests, for the United States to give the Kuomintang Government large quantities of military supplies which, judging from past experience, are not likely to be used effectively against Japan but will be available for civil war to enforce "unity" in the country by military force. These Chinese also speculate on the position of American troops which may be in China (in support of the Kuomintang army) if there should be civil war; and wonder what will be the attitude of Russia, especially if it has become by that time a partner in the victory over Japan.

But ignoring these problematical implications, there can be no denial that civil war in China, or even the continuation after the defeat of Japan of the present deadlock, will greatly impede the return of peaceful conditions. This blocking of the orderly large-scale rehabilitation of China will in itself seriously and adversely affect American interests. Even if a conflict is averted, the continuance or, as is probable in such an event, the worsening of the already serious economic strains within the country may result in economic collapse. If there is civil war, the likelihood of such an economic collapse is of course greater.

There is also the possibility that economic difficulties may make the war-weary, overconscripted and overtaxed farmers fertile ground for Communist propaganda and thus bring about a revolution going beyond the moderate democracy which the Chinese Communists now claim to be seeking. Such a Communist government would probably not be democratic in the American sense. And it is probable, even if the United States did not incur the enmity of the Communists for alleged material or diplomatic support of the Kuomintang, that this Communist government would be more inclined toward friendship and cooperation with Russia than with Great Britain and America.

For these reasons it would therefore appear to be in the interest of the United States to make efforts to prevent a deterioration of the internal political situation in China and, if possible, to bring about an improvement.

The Communists themselves (Chou En-lai and Lin Piao in a conversation with John Carter Vincent and the undersigned about November 20, 1942) consider that foreign influence (obviously American) with the Kuomintang is the only force that may be able to improve the situation. They admit the difficulty of successful foreign suggestions regarding China's internal affairs, no matter how tactfully made. But they believe that the reflection of a better-informed foreign opinion, official and public, would have some effect on the more far-sighted elements of leadership in the Kuomintang, such as the Generalissimo.

The Communists suggest several approaches to the problem. One would be the emphasizing in our dealings with the Chinese Government, and in our propaganda to China, of the political nature of the world conflict; democracy against Fascism. This would include constant reiteration of the American hope of seeing the development of genuine democracy in China. It should imply to the Kuomintang our knowledge of and concern over the situation in China.

Another suggestion is some sort of recognition of the Chinese Communist army as a participant in the war against fascism. The United States might intervene to the end that the Kuomintang blockade be discontinued and support be given by the Central Government to the Eighteenth Group Army. The Communists hope this might include a specification that the Communist armies recieve a proportionate share of American supplies sent to China.

Another way of making our interest in the situation known to the Kuomintang would be to send American representatives to visit the Communist area. I have not heard this proposed by the Communists themselves. But there is no doubt that they would welcome such action.

This visit would have the great additional advantage of providing us with comprehensive and reliable information regarding the Communist side of the situation. For instance, we might be able to have better answers to some of the following pertinent questions: How faithfully have the Communists carried out their United Front promises? What is the form of their local government? How "Communistic" is it? Does it show any democratic character or possibilities? Has it won any support of the people? How does it compare with conditions of government in Kuomintang China? How does the Communist treatment of the people in such matters as taxation, grain requisition, military service and forced labor compare with that in the Kuomintang territory? What is the military and economic strength of the Communists and what is their probable value to the Allied cause? How have they dealt with problems such as inflation, price control, development of economic resources for carrying on the war, and trading with the enemy? Have the people in the guerrilla area been mobilized and aroused to the degree necessary to support real guerrilla warfare?

Without such knowledge, it is difficult to appraise conflicting reports and reach a considered judgment. Due to the Kuomintang blockade, information regarding conditions in the Communist area is at present not available. Such information as we do have is several years out of date, and has limitations as to scope and probable reliability. Carlson* was primarily a military man and had a limited knowledge of the Chinese language. Most of the journalists who have been able to visit the Communist area appear to have a bias favorable to the Communists. They also suffered from language limitations and were unable to remain in the area for an extended period.

I suggest that the American representatives best suited to visit the Communist area are Foreign Service officers of the China language service. One or two men might be sent. They should combine moderately long-term residence at Yenan or its vicinity with fairly extensive travel in the guerrilla area. It is important that they not be required to base a report on a brief visit during which they would be under the influence of official guides, but that they should have a sufficient time to become familiar with conditions and make personal day-to-day observations.

There is mail and telegraphic communication between Yenan and Chungking, and similar communication between various parts of the Communist area. The officers would therefore not be out of touch with the Embassy and could, if it is thought desirable, make periodic reports.

* Major Evans Carlson, United States Marine Corps, formerly in China.

LIFE IN THE BORDER REGION

It would be eighteen months before Service's notion of sending Foreign Service officers to Yenan would bear fruit, but he and John P. Davies in particular continued to press the idea. After they were attached to Stilwell's headquarters, they gained allies in the U.S. Armed Forces who were anxious to make use of the Communists' extensive network of guerrilla bases behind the Japanese lines for military intelligence against Japan, and for the rescue of American airmen downed behind the lines. In addition, Stilwell and some of his staff—increasingly frustrated in their efforts to collaborate effectively with the KMT armies—were anxious to explore the possibility of coordinating American and Chinese Communist military efforts. In order to do so, they needed firsthand assessments of the Communists' military capabilities. The Chungking Government persistently turned down these requests for access to the Communist regions until the spring of 1944, when it allowed a group of Chinese and foreign journalists to visit Yenan, apparently on the assumption that the press would find life in the Border Region as bitter as the Kuomintang's own propaganda insisted it was. Once the Generalissimo had acceded to the press's request to visit Yenan, it was difficult for him to deny the same access to the U.S. military. Vice-President Henry Wallace's visit to China in June 1944 provided an opportunity to present the American case for a mission to Yenan directly to the Generalissimo. Though Chiang at first tried to evade the issue, Wallace persisted in his efforts to gain approval for the mission. Finally, on the Vice-President's last day in Chungking, the Generalissimo agreed to the dispatch of a U.S. Army Observer Section to Yenan. Since its destination was the "rebel" area of China, it soon acquired the code name "Dixie Mission."

On July 22, 1944, Service flew into Yenan with the first section of the Dixie Mission. He found himself in a new China. The humid heat and fog of Chungking gave way to the dry loess country and bright blue skies of Yenan. Even more impressive than the change in physical setting (which he had seen before in trips to the Northwest) was the change in mood and human atmosphere. The gloom of Chungking, reeling under the Japanese offensive, was in total contrast to the cheerfulness, the confidence and energy so evident in Yenan. Furthermore, for the first time in his long experience in China, Service was part of a foreign group working, living, eating and relaxing together with Chinese with a real sense of cooperation. Relations between the Americans and the Chinese Communists were close and congenial—in total contrast to the situation in Chungking, where officials tended to keep foreigners at a comfortable distance, to deal with them only in very formal settings, and to regard them with a certain amount of suspicion. Service described this change in atmosphere, this new China, in his first despatch from Yenan.

First Informal Impressions of the North Shensi Communist Base

No. 1: July 28, 1944
Foreign Relations, 1944, pp. 517–20.

Although I have been in Yenan only six days, it seems advisable, in view of the availability of mail facilities and their future uncertainty, to try to record a few general first impressions of the Communist Border Region.

In spite of the shortness of the time we have been here, I have had opportunities to meet and talk to a number of Chinese friends, to meet three foreigners who have been resident in the Communist area for some time, and to meet most of the important Communist leaders. In addition I have had the chance to draw on the experience, impressions and notebooks of several foreign correspondents who have spent more than six weeks in Yenan, during which time they have been given every sort of facility to interview personages and collect information.

My own experience is that one enters an area like this, concerning which one has heard so many entirely good but secondhand reports, with a conscious determination not to be swept off one's feet. The feeling is that things cannot possibly be as good as they have been pictured, and that there must be a "catch" somewhere.

It is interesting, therefore, that my own first impressions—and those of the rest of our Observer Group—have been extremely favorable. The same is true of the foreign correspondents, at least two of whom (Votaw and Forman)* could not, by any stretch of the term, have been called "pro-Communist" before their arrival. The spell of the Chinese Communists still seems to work.

All of our party have had the same feeling—that we have come into a different country and are meeting a different people. There is undeniably a change in the spirit and atmosphere. As one officer, born and brought up in China, put it: "I find myself continually trying to find out just how Chinese these people are."

This difference in atmosphere is evident in many ways.

There is an absence of show and formality, both in speech and action. Relations of the officials and people toward us, and of the Chinese among themselves, are open, direct and friendly. Mao Tse-tung and other leaders are universally spoken of with respect (amounting in the case of Mao to a sort of veneration), but these men are approachable and subservience toward them is completely lacking. They mingle freely in groups.

Bodyguards, gendarmes and the claptrap of Chungking officialdom are also completely lacking. To the casual eye there are no police in Yenan. And very few soldiers are seen.

There are also no beggars, nor signs of desperate poverty.

Clothing and living are very simple. Almost everyone except the peasants wears the same plain Chungshan-type uniform of native cotton cloth. We have seen no signs of ostentation in dress, living or entertaining.

Women not only wear practically the same clothes (trousers, sandals or cloth shoes, and often a Russian-type smock), they act and are treated as friendly equals. Their openness and

---

*Maurice Votaw was an American employee in the Chungking Government's Ministry of Information, in Yenan as a correspondent for the Baltimore *Sun*. Harrison Forman was a photographer and reporter for the London *Times* and *Reader's Digest,* who later published a book on his trip to Yenan: *Report from Red China* (New York: Henry Holt and Company, 1945).

complete lack of self-consciousness is at first almost discon-
certing. This does not mean familiarity: the spooning couples
seen in parks or quiet streets in Chungking would seem as out
of place as long gowns, high heels or lipstick.

There are a great number of younger people, both men
and women. This is natural with the universities and various
Party training schools. But there is generally an air of maturity
and seriousness about these students. They have little time, one
learns, for loitering and they have most of them earned their
higher training by hard work, generally for the Party. Those
who are here are here because they want to be, and they expect
work and a very simple life.

These students from all over China, many from the forward bases in the guerrilla zones, and the fact that one meets
Government and military officials from all over North China,
gives the feeling that this is a sort of nerve center of important
happenings. Students continually talk of going back to the villages or the front to carry on their work.

Morale is very high. The war seems close and real. There
is no defeatism, but rather confidence. There is no war-weariness.

One gets a feeling that everyone has a job. The program to
make every person a producer has a real meaning. Those who
do not grow crops work at something like spinning. Each
morning we see our coed neighbors at the university at their
spinning wheels outside their caves.

At the same time there is time for a great deal of talk and
discussion. There are continual meetings.

This leisure is notable in the case of the Party leaders. One
learns that they stay completely out of the government and hold
no routine tasks of this time-consuming character.

People do not talk of going "back to Shanghai" as soon
as the war is over. People have made themselves at home here.

Toward the rest of China, the attitude is one of interest in
conditions there but a sort of detached sympathy because they
know that conditions there are so much worse than here.

There is everywhere an emphasis on democracy and intimate relations with the common people. This is shown in their
cultural work, which is taken very seriously. Drama and music
have taken over the native folk forms of the country people of

this area. Social dancing includes dancing of the local folk dance.

People are serious and tend to have a sense of a mission. But recreation is encouraged. One form of this, just mentioned, is social dancing. At the dinner given for us after our arrival, all the most important leaders joined in the dancing in the most natural and democratic manner.

There is a surprising political consciousness. No matter who one questions—barber or farmer or room attendant—he can give a good description of the Communist program for carrying on the war. We notice that most of the coolies waiting on us read the newspaper.

There is no tension in the local situation—no guards when one enters the city, no garrisoned blockhouses on the hills (as were so apparent in Lanchow in 1943). One hears nothing of banditry or disturbances in the country.

We saw a group of men marching down the road with no armed escort in sight. We were told they were new recruits.

There is no criticism of Party leaders and no political talk.

At the same time there is no feeling of restraint or suppression. Foreigners notice this particularly after they have traveled in Kuomintang North China. We are not burdened with people trying to question us under the guise of making friends. Our interpreters are available when we want them. No one bothers to lock his room. We walk freely where we wish. The correspondents have had no censorship.

The leaders make excellent personal impressions. The military men look and act like capable military men. Mao has more warmth and magnetism than would be expected from the generally poor pictures of him.

The general feeling is of calm self-confidence—self-respect. General Yeh* laughed about the weapons of the Communist armies. "But," he said, "I won't apologize. It was all we had, and we fought with them." Things happen pretty well in a businesslike way.

To the skeptical, the general atmosphere in Yenan can be compared to that of a rather small, sectarian college—or a

* Yeh Chien-ying, chief of staff of the Communists' Eighth Route Army.

religious summer conference. There is a bit of the smugness, self-righteousness and conscious fellowship.

I had a little bit of this feeling during the first few days. Later I found myself agreeing with one of the correspondents, a man who has been long in China, when he said: "We have come to the mountains of north Shensi, to find the most modern place in China."

I think now that further study and observation will confirm that what is seen at Yenan is a well-integrated movement, with a political and economic program, which it is successfully carrying out under competent leaders.

And that while the Kuomintang has lost its early revolutionary character and with that loss disintegrated, the Communist Party, because of the struggle it has had to continue, has kept its revolutionary character, but has grown to a healthy and moderate maturity.

One cannot help coming to feel that this movement is strong and successful, and that it has such drive behind it and has tied itself so closely to the people that it will not easily be killed.

Kuomintang propaganda always placed great emphasis on the alleged poverty of the Communist Border Region, and the KMT attempted with its economic blockade to ensure that its assessment would remain accurate. Since northern Shensi was known to be an unusually poor area of China, and since the blockade meant that the area would be deprived of such usual critical imports as cotton, Service went to the Border Region expecting to find a reasonably desperate economic situation. Remarkably, this proved not to be the case. Not only had the blockade failed to cripple the Communists, but Mao Tse-tung and others seemed almost grateful that the blockade had sparked a production drive which made the Border Region virtually self-sufficient. The Border Region government provided Service with convincing statistics, and foreigners like Michael Lindsay, a British professor from Yenching University, and George Hatem, an American doctor, both of whom had lived in the Communist areas for several years, were able to attest to the dramatic improvement in conditions during their stay in Yenan. From such sources, Service compiled the following report.

Brief Notes on the Economic Situation
in the North Shensi Communist Base

No. 6: August 3, 1944
Amerasia Papers, pp. 729–33

Improvement in Economic Conditions

The all-important fact relative to the economic situation in the Shensi-Kansu-Ninghsia Border Region is its improvement during the past two years.

This fact is everywhere apparent in this area. It is supported by statistics which I have as yet obtained in only very fragmentary form but will submit as soon as possible. It is shown in the improvement in the rations of the army, in the better feeding and clothing of the government and party personnel; and in the almost complete disappearance of cases of malnutrition from the local hospitals—whereas three years ago such cases were numerous.

This improvement in the economic situation has had a great effect on the morale and general stability of this important Communist base. For instance, the physical condition of the Communist army three years ago, according to foreign observers resident in these areas, was very poor; it is now extremely good.

Similar improvement of economic conditions, but probably to a lesser extent, is also reported from other Communist base areas in the guerrilla zones behind the Japanese lines. The general effect therefore has been an increase in the actual and potential effectiveness of the Communists, either to take part in the war against Japan or to resist Kuomintang pressure.

Factors in Improvement

This sweeping improvement has been helped by nature: the crops for the past two years have been good. Indications for the present year are excellent—"nine-tenths" by Chinese calculation, which is well above normal.

The most important factor, however, has been an extremely energetic and widespread campaign on the part of the local government (at the instigation and under the leadership of the Communist Party) to develop agricultural and industrial production.

Effect of Kuomintang Blockade

These measures were, in a sense, forced by the Central Government blockade which permitted the passage of luxuries but rigidly refused importation to all commodities which the Communists lacked and urgently needed. This included commodities formerly not produced in the Border Region such as cotton, paper, rice, sugar and matches.

This blockade had its most serious effects in 1940 and 1941. Surrounded and isolated in an extremely poor, undeveloped area, the Communists found themselves at that time in a precarious condition. It became a question of developing production to a point of reasonable self-sufficiency, or eventually facing the need of capitulation. Some Communists now say that the blockade has contributed to their eventual strengthening by forcing them to heroic measures which otherwise would never have been taken.

The Production Campaign

The production campaign was therefore made an important part of government activity—in point of effort expended, probably the most important. All the Communist talents for propaganda were mobilized and the resourcefulness of their leaders, who had had to meet a somewhat similar but less serious situation in the days of the civil war in Kiangsi, devised new expedients. In the concentration on this goal of increased production and in some of the promotional media utilized, the atmosphere here reminds one of what one read of Russia under the Five-Year Plans.

Favorable Circumstances for the Production Campaign

Certain natural conditions in this area were favorable to the successful carrying out of the campaign. Depopulation as a result of the devastations of Mohammedan uprisings of the last century and famines in the 1920s left a large amount of idle, tillable land. The population of the whole Border Region is only 1,500,000. The loess soil is fertile and can easily be put into cultivation. It was found that cotton and rice, though not formerly produced here to any appreciable extent, could be grown in favored localities.

The population itself was good material for such a campaign. This part of Shensi underwent a land revolution in

1934 when a Soviet form of government was set up. The people took over their land and most of the landlords left. The people therefore have a tradition of independence and initiation, and since they till their own land, have a greater incentive in increasing production. Finally, there was a large proportion of army and party personnel who were available to be thrown into the campaign.

Measures for Increasing Production
The first and most important step was to remedy the manpower shortage by making every person a producer. Theoretically, and in most cases actually, this meant every man and every woman. Tremendous propaganda and education pressure was applied. Mass meetings, lectures, plays, slogans and every other conceivable medium was used. Special pressure was used against the remnants of the local "loafer" class. When social censure proved insufficient, more direct means were applied. The slacker was forced to wear a placard, and so on.

Every government and party organization was set the goal of becoming self-supporting in food and production of cloth. This was applied even to schools and the universities. Fortunately, plenty of land was available. Those who were able to, cultivated the fields. The girls and women learned to spin and weave. Every functionary and student works at least two hours daily.

The troops garrisoning the Border Region were settled on new land, which they put into cultivation.

[Service lists here a series of specific programs to promote spinning, improve agriculture and animal husbandry, establish "Labor Heroes," encourage immigration, and so forth.]

Special emphasis was put on development of cooperative societies of all types, but especially productive. Societies organized under the Chinese Industrial Cooperatives increased in three years from less than 30 to 343. Other cooperative societies have increased the total in this small area to over 800. In some societies, about 340,000 people are in some way concerned. The government has provided the capital for most of this development on a lavish scale, often without exacting interest.

Promotion of labor cooperatives (or labor exchange

groups) has greatly increased agricultural production. Based on an old but discarded system, these groups have become popular among the peasants. A group of men band together to till the soil of each in turn. By joint activity they do this more efficiently and quickly than by individual labor. The time they save is then used for joint activity in opening new land, the products of which are shared in common.

Effectiveness of Campaign
[Service notes improved living standards and an improvement in the dietary staple from millet to wheat.]

Cotton was formerly not produced. Last year the Border Region produced and made into cloth half of its requirements. This year it expects to produce two thirds. The lack of cotton cloth was the greatest single problem in the Border Region.

The army has become practically self-supporting. At least one brigade (one fifth of the forces in the region) is actually presenting a surplus to the government this year: thus its production exceeds its own needs.

According to government reports, 70 percent of its income is now derived from the production of the army and government organizations. This is presumably calculated by assigning a book value to this production and crediting the government accordingly.

Taxes in kind have been reduced by about 12 percent and are considerably lower than in the rest of China.

After considerable research, matches, soap and other articles of daily use are now being produced entirely from local materials. On the whole these are of extremely satisfactory quality.

An important success has been the discovery that paper can be manufactured from a local grass which had no other use. Paper is therefore no longer a problem. . . .

Inflation . . . is not an important factor in the lives of practically all of the population. The salaried classes of government and party students and functionaries are partially self-supporting and have all their necessities provided.

In all superficial aspects, business is booming. The markets are busy. And there is a great deal of construction work going on.

Shortcomings of the Production Campaign

It must not be assumed that the production campaign has been 100 percent successful or that there do not still remain unsolved difficulties.

The tremendous expansion of production was financed largely by the government, and the resultant heavy increase in note circulation added to inflation. As noted above, this tendency now seems to have been arrested and the Border Region [currency] is showing definite signs of appreciating in terms of national currency.

A serious problem is the lack of qualified technical personnel. . . .

Another problem is the continuing and probably insoluble problem of the shortage of many types of equipment needed for industrial development. . . .

It is admitted that the sometimes overzealous enthusiasm, and high-pressure promotion put into the production campaign, coupled with lack of experience, were responsible for some confusion and some poor quality production. For instance, in the early stages individuals often volunteered to produce impossibly high quotas of yarn. The resulting product was too poor to be of any use. These problems are being ironed out with the gaining of experience.

Conclusion

Despite these minor failings, the basic fact remains that the production campaign has been generally, and even spectacularly, successful, and that as a result the economic situation in the Border Region is healthy and improving.

The contrast between these conditions, and the energetically implemented policies which have brought them about, and the conditions and policies obtaining in Kuomintang China is too obvious to need comment.

To a field reporter who had known the prevalence of rural banditry in many parts of Kuomintang China, the clear absence of it in the Communist areas was a phenomenon worthy of analysis. The absence of banditry seemed to confirm the Communist claims of popular support based on social and economic reforms.

Service's report on the subject is printed here with the omission of the details of CCP reforms described in other despatches.

The Communist Success in Eliminating Banditry: Supporting Evidence of Communist Claims of Democratic and Economic Reforms

No. 37: October 2, 1944
Amerasia Papers, pp. 963–67

1. There is attached a memorandum regarding the apparent Communist success in handling the banditry problem in the areas under their control.

2. The memorandum may be summarized as follows:

Summary. All reports indicate an absence of banditry in the Communist-controlled areas. This is a marked contrast to the conditions under the Kuomintang. The Communists credit their solution of this age-old Chinese problem to improvement of the economic condition of the peasants, democratic reforms which have eliminated the feudalistic base for much of the banditry, and mobilization of the entire population into mass organizations for the support of the war. The fact of the absence of banditry seems to be concrete evidence of the truth of these claims. *End of Summary.*

MEMORANDUM

1. All reports of present conditions in the Communist-controlled areas agree in making no mention of banditry. This is true whether the reports come from Communist sources or from foreigners who have passed through those areas. . . .

A recent traveler has been Lieutenant J. Baglio, USAAF, who was rescued by guerrillas after his plane was shot down near Taiyuan and then spent three months with the Eighth Route Army in traveling from central Shansi to Fouping, Hopei, and then to Yenan. Lieutenant Baglio was surprised by a question about bandits and said that he had heard no mention whatever of any.

2. This absence of banditry is of immediate and great

interest to observers of conditions in China during the past several decades and at present in the rest of the country. During the disturbed conditions prevailing since the 1911 Revolution, banditry has been sporadic in almost every section of the country. Some of the areas which the Communists now control, including north Shensi, have been particularly notorious in this respect. . . .

It is also noteworthy because of the contrast of the apparent increase of banditry in most of the areas under Kuomintang control, even far behind the fighting lines. I have found banditry an active concern of travelers in all of the provinces in which I have traveled by road during the past three years: Szechwan, Shensi, Kansu, Kweichow, Yunnan and Kwangsi. . . .

3. This absence of banditry in Communist areas also seems significant because of the reasons usually given for its prevalence in Kuomintang territory: opposition to harsh military conscription; impoverishment by heavy taxation and grain collections; the presence of large numbers of deserting and half-starved soldiers; discriminatory treatment of aboriginal or minority groups (such as the Miao tribes in Kweichow or the Mohammedans in Kansu); and popular resentment of oppressive and corrupt government.

4. Finally, the apparent success in dealing with the problem seems significant because the Kuomintang method of attempting to eliminate banditry by military suppression seems to have had no basic and permanent success.

5. After my interest had been aroused in this problem, I discussed it at length with a number of Communist leaders from the various anti-Japanese bases. These include: General Ch'en Yi, acting commander of the New Fourth Army; General Nieh Jung-chen, commander of the Shansi-Hopei-Chahar Military District; and Dr. Yang Hsiu-feng, chairman of the Shansi-Hopei-Shantung-Honan Border Region Government. Their descriptions of the handling of the banditry problem in their respective areas are strikingly similar. The following is a general summary which is applicable to all the areas.

6. Most of the areas which have come under Communist control during the war were, at the time of occupation, in a chaotic and unsettled condition with banditry rife. . . .

7. Communist measures to cope with this situation fall

into four general categories: economic improvement, mass organization of the people, democracy, and finally, direct action. The elimination of banditry, while an important immediate problem, was not, however, the main or direct reason for these measures. The measures were taken to win the support of the people and to assist in the prosecution of the war. The disappearance of banditry was a natural but subsidiary result. . . .

8. Immediately after gaining control of an area, the Communists start to improve the economic condition of the peasants. First is the reduction of farm rents and interest. . . .

9. Another important process is mass mobilization through intensive and continued propaganda indoctrination. This is put on the basis of organization to resist the enemy and support the war. Banditry obviously becomes an unpatriotic and traitorous activity. Everybody becomes a member of one or more mass organizations: People's Self-Defense Corps, Farmers National Salvation Associations, People's Militia, Youth Vanguards, and so forth. . . .

An important result of this work is the elimination of the old "*min tuan*"* and its replacement by the new "People's Militia," which is a genuine self-protective organization of the people created on a volunteer basis. The *min tuan,* on the other hand, were usually recruited by the wealthy landlords from the loafer and secret-society groups for their own protection. These village toughs were actually the professional bandits. Their tactics combined extortion from those who bought immunity and robbery of those who lived at some distance or would not pay protection money. . . . Under the Communist system, the maintenance of these semi-police, semi-bandit, extortion-squeezing *min tuan* by the landlords becomes unnecessary and impossible.

10. The third process is democratization. The people elect their own local governments. They thus have a greater interest in their protection, and through their own forces, greater ability to enforce it. Since the government is native, it is much better able to keep in touch with the population and to identify and deal with unruly elements. The same fact eliminates corruption and oppressive or discriminatory government. . . .

---

* The traditional, gentry-controlled local militia.

11. Finally, with the creation of a stable democratic government there is strong direct action against any disturbers of the peace who remain. . . . The loafer elements are induced by every sort of pressure, first social and then legal, to engage in active production. The army and the People's Militia are mobilized and used relentlessly, if necessary, against any remaining bandits who refuse to cooperate in the new order of things or who try to enter the area from the outside. These outside groups are classified as "enemy" or "puppet" forces. An important part of this suppression work is the careful protection of people who give information. An interesting sidelight is the treatment of captured bandits. They are given public trial before a village mass meeting and subjected to great social pressure to confess their sins and promise to reform. If they do so, they are given only nominal punishment. Only if they have proved incorrigible are they executed.

12. Lieutenant Baglio, who was a completely fresh and uninformed observer, was asked what he thought were the reasons for the absence of banditry which he reported. His answer, after some thought, was that he "did not see how there could be banditry when everybody supported the army and was busy fighting." This is an interesting reflection of what seemed to a man previously unacquainted with China to be the actual conditions. But it does not go deep enough to explain these conditions of popular support and participation in the war which have, it might almost be said—incidentally, removed banditry.

I suggest that the only satisfactory explanation is the Communist one, and that we can accept the absence of banditry as good evidence of Communist claims of economic and political reforms toward democracy. If the Communists have done nothing more than show an effective way to deal with the scourge of banditry, they have done a great service to the common people of China.

THE CHINESE COMMUNIST LEADERSHIP

One way in which Yenan clearly differed from Chungking was the openness and accessibility of the leaders. "Chungking was a city with all the trappings of a shaggy bureaucracy—moth-eaten and run-down—but still insisting on all its prerogatives. As in Washington, you could tell a man's rank by whether he had a water carafe on his desk, a rug on the floor or a name on the door. The KMT was very insistent on the prerogatives of rank and prestige, and if you were the Second Secretary of the Embassy you could talk to a division chief in the American Bureau of the Foreign Ministry, but you did not talk to the Minister." Yenan was a totally different sort of place. Mao, or Chou En-lai or Chu Teh would often casually drop in on the Americans and chat for hours. Nor was the contact merely social: "If you wanted something done, and you went to the Chief of Staff and he approved, then it would be done, and done quickly. You can't imagine Ho Ying-ch'in functioning the way Yeh Chien-ying did. The comparison is laughable. Ho Ying-ch'in: a beautifully made uniform, tailored, pressed, spotless, starchy. A priggish little man. Pompous. Yeh Chien-ying: simple, baggy clothes, very direct, very open. It is the same openness and directness which you see going back to China now."

General Impression of the Chinese Communist Leaders

No. 21: September 4, 1944
Amerasia Papers, pp. 832–36

A general impression of the leaders of the Chinese Communist Party, as a group, may be of some interest because of

Mao Tse-tung. Presented to John S. Service by Mao on March 15, 1945. Mao's inscription and autograph are on reverse.

謝偉思先生惠存

毛澤東

一九〇五年

三月五日

Chou En-lai. Autographed and presented to John S. Service on April 1, 1945 (as Service was leaving Yenan).

Left to right: *Chou En-lai, Chu Teh, John Service, Mao Tse-tung, Yeh Chien-ying in Yenan, September 1944.*

Since everyone in Yenan was mustered to enlarge and improve the airstrip (in order to better serve the U.S. Army DC-3 that linked the Observer Section with the outside world), the personnel of the Observer Section also volunteered one day's work. Service in central foreground.

A gathering of "fellow provincials," all born in the western Chinese province of Szechwan. Left to right: Yang Shang-k'un, General Ch'en Yi, Captain Whittlesey, General Chu Teh, John Service, Wu Yü-chang and General Nieh Jung-chen.

An "arrival picture" at the Yenan airstrip in late 1944. Left to right, foreground: *General Chu Teh (John Service in background), Colonel D. D. Barrett, Chairman Mao Tse-tung.*

General Lin Piao giving a talk in the summer of 1944 to personnel of the Dixie Mission in Yenan on Communist military organization and operations. Seated figure at Lin's right is Huang Hua (now China's Permanent Representative to the United Nations). Service is at Lin Piao's left. On Huang's right, by the door, is Barrett; next to him is R. P. Ludden.

Discussion just after the Dixie Mission arrived in Yenan. Left to right: *Service, Champion, Barrett, Huang Hua, Chou En-lai, unknown. Churchill on the wall.*

the growing importance of the party they represent, and the certainty that the United States must take it into account in its future dealings with the China situation. Reference is made in this connection to my report No. 20, September 3, 1944, on the subject: "The Need of an American Policy toward the Problems Created by the Rise of the Chinese Communist Party."*

Such a group character study should be based on long acquaintance and careful study. This I cannot claim, having been in Yenan only six weeks.

However, I have had unusual opportunities during that short time to meet and talk to the unprecedentedly large number of the important Communist leaders who are now assembled in Yenan for conferences. A partial list of these leaders, some of whom have not been able to meet in one place for more than ten years, is included in my report No. 15 of August 27, 1944.†

Biographical and individual "Who's Who" data on these and other Communist leaders is being assembled and will be forwarded at a later date. I merely attempt here a general description of the first impressions given by the Communist leaders *as a group*. This is perhaps easier to do with the leaders of the Communists than with the leaders of most other political parties—certainly than of the Kuomintang. There is among them a certain lack of striking individuality, and they seem to show a number of common characteristics. It should be understood, of course, that the picture drawn does not pretend to fit every case.

A general knowledge of the history of the Chinese Communist Party is important to a study of its leaders. The Party's twenty-three years of almost continuous struggle and war have not only affected the attitudes and character of its leaders, they have also helped to determine the type of men who could survive and rise to leadership. It is difficult to understand these men without this background.

A first impression is that of *youth*. Almost all are in the middle forties; a few in the upper thirties. They were college

* See pp. 318–21.
† See pp. 293–94.

students or young military cadets in the early 1920s, a period of great political ferment in both China and Europe.

With this youth there is *physical vigor*. As a group, they are active and fit; none seem soft, flabby or indolent. The half-starved, anemic Chinese intellectual is missing; so is the overfed official and bureaucrat. These men have never had a chance to lead an easy life. They worked in the "underground," or lived through the civil war and the "Long March." All have fought—in the most strenuous kind of warfare, guerrilla operations—and a surprising number carry wounds.

This vitality is not only physical, it is also *intellectual*. The proportion of men with an academic background is very large. Many became Communists while doing postgraduate study in Europe. They arrived at their views logically, they have been schooled in years of debate and discussion, and they have spent their lives in convincing others of the rightness of their unpopular cause. Communism, especially in China, it seems to me, is chiefly an intellectual cause. And in its development in China it has passed through many stages without being completely dominated by a single man or dogma—like Sun Yat-sen and his San Min Chu I.

The knowledge, interests and experience of these men are *well-rounded*. Politics, economics, education, propaganda and culture are to them inseparable parts of a single whole. To these they have been forced to add military science in order to survive. There is among them no one who is merely a military man or an expert in one field such as economics. Every Communist is required to have military training. Many high commanders commenced as political commissars, and vice versa. Most of them have faced successfully the problems of organizing independent and self-sufficient governments under the most difficult and chaotic conditions.

All are men of unmistakably *strong conviction*. The weaker ones have long ago left them. Those remaining are sure that they are fighting for something worthwhile: their *sincerity, loyalty* and *determination* are patent.

This strong conviction seems to give them an *assurance*, a certain *pride* and a strong *self-confidence*. They are not troubled with doubts about themselves or their general policies. They neither apologize for the past, nor obsequiously seek your favor in the present. They are cordial and friendly—but not demonstratively anxious to make a good impression. They seem to know that they have been through hard times and accomplished creditable things, and they are confident—in a quiet but definite way—that they are now on the winning tide.

Related to all these characteristics is what, for lack of a better word, can be described as *toughness*. One realizes that they have *patience* (they have had a long, hard schooling in that); that they will compromise, if it is decided to be for the best long-term interest of the Party; that they will fight when the need arises; and that they can be hard and ruthless if that becomes necessary. One feels that fear or personal interest do not enter into consideration. Their *personal courage* cannot be questioned.

A rather unexpected, and yet strong impression that grows with acquaintance is their *realism* and *practicality*. Far behind are the days when they may have engaged in heated youthful debates on alien and impractical theories. The pure visionaries have left their ranks or been submerged; those who stayed had to be doers. Firmly and universally held is the belief that the test of everything is whether it works—in China. It is difficult to get them to engage in what they regard as "useless" discussions of pure theory. The reaction is: "We cross our bridges when we come to them."

A part of this realism is constant self-examination and *self-criticism*. This is not of the general objectives and policies, but of the specific measures and policies being carried out to advance toward those goals—of the reasons why they failed in the past or are not working out as intended now. This critical examination is of policies, not of personalities. It is carried on by very *free discussion* by all the higher cadres of the Party. But there is also a willingness to accept suggestions from outside the Party—several of the present basic policies have, in fact, such an origin.

This consideration of policies is based on an *objective* and *scientific* attitude. Most of these leaders have a foundation of Western social science. Their outlook impresses one as *modern*. Their understanding of economics, for instance, is very similar to ours. There is no mysticism in their make-up, no vague mouthings of the beauties of ancient Chinese culture,

and no rigid adherence to a hardened dogma. In fact, one hears very little about the San Min Chu I—or any other Chu I.*
As for the ideas that China is "different," that the fundamental economic laws do not apply here, or that "foreigners cannot understand China"—they laugh at them.

Once a specific measure or policy has been found unsuccessful or unsuited to conditions, and after discussion has produced what seems to be a better substitute, there is no hesitation in admitting failure by making a change. This *adaptability* and *willingness to change* has been apparent in every field —military strategy, taxation, land policy, education, mass organization, the promotion of the modern drama and dance, the attempt to romanize the Chinese written language. When it was found that the measures being taken were not suitable to the actual conditions in China, and hence not successful, they were dropped or changed.

Another important characteristic is a *systematic orderliness*. This is both mental and physical. Thinking is *logical*. There is a strong sense of *organization*. Speeches are direct and easy to follow. It is taken for granted that you take notes during an important conversation. People you call on like to know beforehand what you want to discuss so that they can be prepared. Decisions reached are put into writing and confirmed so that there can be no misunderstanding. There is a general businesslike atmosphere and apparent *efficiency*. For every task some particular person is made responsible. Things seem to get done with less fuss and talk than one is accustomed to in China.

In meeting and dealing with these men, one is struck by their being *straightforward* and *frank*. There is no "beating about the bush." If they do not know something, they say so. If they promise something, you feel sure that it can and will be done.

Among these men there seems to be a strong *group feeling* and firm *unity*. They have had to stick together. Evidences of personal criticism, jealous rivalries or cliquism are totally lacking. Personal ambition, if present, is subdued. None gives the impression of being a "politician." They have reached the top

---

* "Chu I" by itself might be translated as "principle" or "-ism."

in a struggle where success depended not on the creation of a political machine, scheming maneuvers or the cultivation of advantageous personal relationships, but on practical achievements.

In their relations with each other and with outsiders their attitude is *democratic*. Rank is of no importance: the Party relationship of comrade seems to be genuine. Toward the higher leaders, there seems to be respect and admiration but no subservience. Living, dress and actions are simple; there is *no pretentiousness*.

One does not think to question the *integrity* and *honesty* of these men; their *incorruptibility* is obvious. Riches could be of no use to them—and could not be concealed in these surroundings. If they had been interested in such things, they would have turned in other directions long ago.

These might all be called positive characteristics. There are also a number of what might be termed negative traits.

One gets a feeling of voluntary *effacement of individuality*. Most refuse to talk about themselves and it is rare to hear a man refer to his own experiences. There is no boastfulness. Most of them are quiet and tend to be reserved. This is to be expected—their lives have been devoted not to the satisfaction of personal ambition, but to the progress of an impersonal cause.

In their thinking and expressions, there is a noticeable *uniformity*. This may be a result of training in Communist thought and of Party discipline. But it must also, partly at least, be due to the fact that the Communist Party has not had to be a catch-all like the Kuomintang. Those who dissented have been free to leave them. In some cases they have been expelled. Those who are left do seem to really think alike.

It may also be noted that there seems to be a *lack of humor*—and what humor there is tends to be grim.* The pre-

---

* To those familiar with stories of Mao's or Chu Teh's earthy sense of humor, this observation might seem a bit strange. What Service meant is that while the Communists might tell amusing stories about old times ("They found it very funny to talk about the old days when they had a price on their heads, or when they were chasing and kidnapping missionaries") they did not talk lightly about important political problems ("You could not kid them about their relations with the Russians").

vailing mood is sober and serious. Again, this is something to be expected. Their whole working life has been a struggle; it is not surprising that they do not find it easy to relax. It is obvious that the Communists themselves seem to recognize this; social amusements such as bridge and dancing are now encouraged.

A surprising absence of what might have been expected in the light of their history is an apparent *lack of vengefulness.* It is true that they are deeply cynical regarding the Kuomintang. But this is apparently not put on a personal plane. Their private and personal grievances are rarely mentioned. It is a common experience, for instance, to ask a man about his family and have him reply in a quiet and matter-of-fact way that he has been unable to hear from them for fifteen years, or that his wife, children, parents and brothers were killed by the Kuomintang. This suppression of personal feelings may be partly because of Party policy, which now calls for cooperation with the Kuomintang and a United Front. It is also partly due to disgust and weariness with the long years of bitter civil war: vengefulness has given way to a deep-seated desire for peace and a chance to work out their program (one gets the strong impression that these men will not *start* a civil war). Finally, it is a reflection of that toughness of character mentioned above: personal interests are to be submerged—"what is past, is past."

Conclusion

The general impression one gets of the Chinese Communist leaders is that they are a unified group of vigorous, mature and practical men, unselfishly devoted to high principles, and having great ability and strong qualities of leadership. This impression—and, I suggest, their record—places them above any other contemporary group in China. It is not surprising that they have favorably impressed most or all of the Americans who have met them during the last seven years: their manners, habits of thought, and direct handling of problems seem more American than Oriental.

THE STRENGTH OF THE CCP

Of all the matters in Yenan which Service observed and reported on, probably the most important was the strength of the Chinese Communist Party and its armies. In 1944 the war with Japan was clearly drawing to a close, and civil war between the KMT and the CCP seemed just over the horizon. If American policy toward China was to be realistic, nothing was more important than an accurate judgment of the likely outcome of such a civil war. Such a judgment, in turn, depended on an accurate assessment of the political and military strength of the Communist forces. Everyone knew that in armament and material, the KMT was superior. But was that superiority enough to outweigh its other obvious weaknesses?

In assessing Communist strength, Service began by attending a series of briefings which had been set up for the Dixie Mission as a whole. "They gave us a blue-ribbon seminar. We had Chu Teh, Yeh Chien-ying, Lin Piao, P'eng Teh-huai, and so on. They harangued us for a day or two days each. It was a remarkable opportunity. Of course it was rather one-sided, but it gave us some things to check against." Service's most extensive reports were on the briefings by Yeh Chien-ying, the Chief of Staff, and P'eng Teh-huai, vice commander of the Eighth Route Army. Service's report on P'eng Teh-huai's three-day briefing, a detailed political-military history of the Eighth Route Army, is too long and repetitious to reprint here. (The report is printed in *Amerasia Papers*, pp. 807–16.) However, the following excerpts from Yeh Chien-ying's two briefings give a fair summary of the size, type, functions and arms of the Communist forces.

Summary of the Situation in North China

No. 10: August 15, 1944
Amerasia Papers, pp. 750–56

1. Enclosed are notes of a talk given by General Yeh Chien-ying, Chief of Staff of the Eighteenth Group (generally known as the Eighth Route) Army, to officers of the U.S. Army Observer Section on August 3, 1944, on the subject: "A Summary of the Situation behind the Enemy Lines in North China."

2. General Yeh's talk was intended as an introduction to a series of following talks by various Communist leaders regarding various regions and different phases of Communist military operations. The talk was informal and rambling, and I have made some reorganization of the material in the interest of logical sequence and the avoidance of repetition.

3. It is understood that the full texts of this and the following talks will be furnished us by the Communist authorities, and that Colonel Barrett or other officers of the section will render detailed reports, particularly on military matters touched upon in them. I will therefore give emphasis to nonmilitary aspects, such as political and economic, and will merely summarize the military side sufficiently to give an understanding of the whole situation.

4. It must continually be borne in mind, however, in this and the following talks, whether dealing with military or other subjects, that in the minds of the Communist leaders, there is no definite distinction between military and nonmilitary spheres. Their military policies and operations cannot be separated from the background in which they have had to work. To create the conditions which can win popular support and thus make possible their continued and successful operations, *the Communists have had to be a political army.* Their whole program of political indoctrination and organization of the people, and of institution of economic policies to unite all classes and yet improve the condition of the poorer groups, is essential to support their warfare. Each part—political, economic and military—is therefore dependent on the other, and of almost equal

importance. None of them can be carried out independently. And in practice all three are carried out by the same men— the Communist army. Understanding of this interrelation of military, political and economic phases of Communist policies is of the utmost importance in any study of the present situation of the Chinese Communists because it is the key to their success. . . .

A SUMMARY OF THE SITUATION BEHIND THE ENEMY LINES IN NORTH CHINA
(General Yeh Chien-ying to U.S. Army Observer Section, August 3, 1944)

Division of control of the enemy rear

We . . . have, practically speaking, the following three important divisions of the Japanese rear: (1) anti-J bases; (2) guerrilla areas; and (3) enemy areas.

In the anti-J bases there is one army (the Communist), one government (the democratically elected government of the people of the area), and the people pay taxes to only one agency (their own government). In the guerrilla areas there are often two armies, two governments, and the people may have two taxes to pay. (Where we know that the people are forced to pay to the Japanese, we do not *require* them to pay to our government. But they often *wish* to do so because they are supporters and participants in our government.) In the enemy areas there is only one government; but even there our army and political workers continue their work underground.

In the division of this territory in the enemy rear, the guerrilla areas are the largest. The enemy areas and our stable anti-J bases are both smaller. Many of the CA* bases cover large unbroken areas—as much as 200 by 100 miles where no Japanese will be found. The Japanese, on the other hand, control few large or broad areas. Their occupation is for the purpose of holding important cities, main communication lines, and to separate or partition our areas. The result is thus long narrow zones of occupation.

The general picture of the division of territory between our fixed bases, guerrilla territory and areas of enemy occupa-

* Communist army.

tion is to a certain degree fluid. During a major Japanese drive a part of a stable base may become guerrilla territory. But as the result of seven years of warfare the situation has become *relatively stable*. The changes that continually occur as the Japanese carry out mopping-up campaigns, or as we counter these drives and recover territory, are comparatively minor.

The recent tendency has been for our areas to grow. . . .

Summary History of War in North China

The history of the war in North China may be briefly summarized as follows:

1. The Japanese drove from North down into Central China in 1937. We came into the theater of operations from the side (the west), drove across the line of J advance, and extended our operations to the Shantung coast and into Kiangsu. We had only one enemy to fight (the Japanese) and had spectacular successes and a very rapid growth.

2. After the fall of Wuhan (October 1938) the enemy had to counter these successes by turning back to strengthen his rear. Japanese attacks on the KMT therefore stopped. The Japanese developed their anti-Communist tactics. At the same time the KMT, jealous and nervous over our successes in North China, sought to recover its lost territory there which it had earlier abandoned. We therefore faced two enemies—the Japanese *and* the Kuomintang. This was our most difficult period. From 1939 to 1942 our bases were reduced.

3. After 1942 there was a change. The KMT troops could not maintain themselves in North China because they lacked popular support and could not adjust themselves to the difficult conditions of active guerrilla warfare. They therefore either withdrew southward or became puppets. Our own military tactics and our political and economic programs were improved through experience. The Japanese were forced to consider other matters than merely the consolidation and defeat of China. Our bases again grew—this time more slowly than in the first stage. . . .

Communist strength

The Communist program for building up and maintaining its bases is very simple. In essence it is the creation of popular support.

Politically—to mobilize the masses and win the support of all classes through democratic methods.

Economically—

      to lighten the people's burden of taxation

      to increase production

      to prevent Japanese exploitation of resources

Militarily—to advance when the enemy advances. (This is the common explanation of CA tactics. It means to not await encirclement and annihilation but to move forward as the enemy attacks, infiltrate and get into his rear to harass his communications and rear.   js)

Our best propaganda agent and helper is the enemy himself.

The strength we have to offer the counteroffensive is not small:

Population in areas under our control and paying taxes
   to our govts 86,000,000
Regular troops on full-time military status 475,000
People's militia, armed, partially trained but still participating in production 2,000,000
Area (est.) in square miles 330,000
Harbors in our present areas 17
Airfields formerly developed or potential 18

Under our *political control* there are:

22 Administrative Area Governments (*hsing-cheng ch'ü*)

85 Supervisory Districts (*chuan-yuan kung-shu*)

585 District (*hsien*) Governments—22 of which are still in the original *hsien* cities

Development and Character of Communist Military Forces

Our military forces are of the following five categories:

     1. Regulars (*cheng-kuei chün*)

     2. Guerrillas (*yu-chi tui*)

     3. People's Militia (*min ping*)

     4. People's Self-Defense Corps (*jen-min tzu-wei tui*)

     5. Armed Working Detachments (*wu kung tui*)

Their differentiation and evolution is as follows:

All able-bodied persons, male and female, generally between the ages of eighteen and forty-five, belong to the People's Self-Defense Corps. This force is not armed and has no military training. It is mobilized when needed for road watching, sentry duty, intelligence, message carrying, rescue and care of wounded, destruction of blockade line and enemy communications, et cetera.

From this Self-Defense Corps, the more able-bodied, brave young men are *voluntarily* recruited into the People's Militia. They are as well armed as circumstances permit—usually not as well as the regulars. Often they have only local muskets, grenades and mines. They receive spare-time training and are organized militarily. They continue in their regular occupation except during times of actual fighting, and do not leave their native localities, even during J occupation. For this reason their membership is secret (as far as people outside the village are concerned) and they wear no uniform.

A stage above the militia are the guerrillas. These are mainly volunteers from the militia, who acquire experience and show combat qualities, and tend to advance toward a regular military status. They are seeded with cadres from the regular army to give them further training and strengthening. Organization is still irregular and detachments vary greatly in size. They operate over a wider area than the militia (who are tied to their own immediate neighborhoods), but they generally do not leave their home region. Generally they are mobilized on a full-time military basis and they are therefore not counted as producers. They are most numerous on the borders of the bases or in actual guerrilla territory.

Armed Working Detachments are a special form developed to cope with conditions on the plains of North China after the Japanese had driven the regulars to the mountains in their great mopping-ups of 1939–1942. They are small, extremely mobile units—often less than twenty men—who work if necessary under cover. They carry arms, but important duties are political work and organization. Because of the difficulty of this type of warfare, only the most highly experienced and dependable fighters and cadres go into these units. They are not uniformed, carry only simple arms, and find concealment by complete merging with the people. Their function is to keep alive resistance in the areas which the Japanese have taken from us, and to prepare the way for the return of our regular forces. Since their organization in 1942 they have been the chief forces responsible for the steady recovery of these plains areas.

The regular forces have grown by volunteer recruitment from the lower categories, such as the militia and guerrillas. They are organized in the normal military manner, are generally uniformed (except sometimes in guerrilla areas) and are in all senses "regular troops." However, they make a practice, when stationed in any spot long enough, to assist in supporting themselves. And they receive no pay.

In operations, the regulars provide the striking force. They are assisted by the guerrillas. The militia and Self-Defense Corps cooperate, especially by harassing activities in the enemy's rear.

There is a good deal of flexibility between these various categories. Regulars may act as or become guerrillas if need arises. Guerrillas sometimes revert to being militia or return home in quiet times or during harvest. There is a steady movement both up and down the scale.

During our twenty years' development we have gone through several phases of military development. At first we were purely guerrillas. As we were surrounded in Kiangsi and the scale of KMT attacks grew, we tended to fight as regulars. During the present war, we have again had to become primarily guerrillas. This was relatively easy because of the extensive guerrilla experience and training of our leaders and cadres. But in the counteroffensive against the Japanese, we must again develop toward regular warfare. This new evolution may present some problems in training, especially in the use of modern weapons and tactics.

The second briefing, also by Yeh Chien-ying, presented a table giving the numbers and arms of Communist forces in various regions, and discussed quite frankly the Communists' weakness in matériel. Unlike the Kuomintang generals, Yeh carefully avoided pleading for American arms to remedy this deficiency.

	Field Forces	L(... Fo...
Shen-Kan-Ning	50,000	
Shansi-Suiyuan	26,000	
Shansi-Chahar-Hopei	35,000	2...
Shantung	42,000	28...
Shansi-Hopei-Honan	50,000	2...
Hopei-Shantung-Honan	17,000	1...
TOTAL: Eighth Route Army	220,000	10(...
Central Kiangsu	19,000	
South Huai	24,000	
North Kiangsu	23,000	
North Huai	18,000	
Hupeh-Honan-Anhwei	22,000	31...
South Kiangsu	6,000	
Central Anhwei	5,000	
East Chekiang	4,000	
TOTAL: New Fourth Army	121,000	31...
East River	3,000	-
Hainan Island	5,000	-
GRAND TOTAL	349,000	131...

1 & al es	Rifles: Field Forces	Rifles: Local Forces	Rifles: Field & Local Forces	Militia
00	30,000	—	30,000	—
00	15,000	} 50,000	} 154,000	} 1,580,000
00	24,000			
00	25,000			
00	29,000			
00	11,000			
00	134,000	50,000	184,000	1,580,000
	11,000			
	15,000			
	14,000			
	11,000			
	14,000	} 16,000		} 550,000
	3,000			
	3,000			
	2,000			
00	77,000	16,000	93,000	550,000
00	2,000	—	2,000	—
00	3,000	—	3,000	—
00	216,000	66,000	282,000	2,130,000

Some of the totals on this table do not equal the sum of
ns. Nonetheless, the original figures have been main-

Strength and Distribution of Communist Forces

No. 17: August 30, 1944
Amerasia Papers, pp. 800–6

1. There are attached notes of a portion of a talk on the growth and organization of the Chinese Communists forces given to officers of the Observer Section by General Yeh Chien-ying, Chief of Staff of the Eighteenth Group Army, on August 4, 1944. The first part of these is a table showing the distribution of the Communist forces. The second part is General Yeh's summary of the deficiencies and strong points of the equipment and organization of the Communist armies. . . .

DEFICIENCIES AND STRONG POINTS OF THE COMMUNIST FORCES
(General Yeh Chien-ying to U.S. Army Observer Section,
August 4, 1944)

1. Comparison of our Eighth Route Army "A Class Regiment," our best-equipped, with the regiments of the Japanese and Kuomintang armies shows the following:

	Japanese	Kuomintang	Eighth Route
Men	3,329	2,447	1,763
Rifles	1,327	810	817
Light Machine Guns	72	81	27–55
Heavy Machine Guns	27	18	6
Grenade Throwers	72	81	15–27
Mortars or Inf. Cannon	10	6	4

2. The Eighth Route Army's *organizational deficiencies* may be summarized as follows:

a. We have practically no special troops such as artillery, engineers or transport units.

b. We are very weak in communications, both in equipment and technical personnel. Our radio net extends down only to the regiments; below that we have to depend on messengers.

This is a serious impediment to the dispersed type of operations that we generally are forced to conduct.

c. There is great diversity in the organization of our units and great variation in strength. Many of the units are of an irregular nature. This makes for difficulty in keeping accurate statistics of strength and in planning and carrying out military operations.

d. Casualties in operations are very high. We are able to save relatively few of our wounded because of the guerrilla nature of our operations and the lack of an adequate medical service. Thus there is a large turnover and constant change of personnel.

e. Casualties among our junior officers are especially high. This is due to our emphasis on active leadership. But it makes it difficult to keep up the quality of training and experience of the officers of these ranks. This is especially true of company and platoon commanders.

f. We completely lack training and experience in the use of new weapons and mechanized equipment. In some engagements, such a Pinghsingkuan, we have had to destroy captured trucks, which could have been useful to us, because of the lack of any men who even knew how to drive them.

We do, however, have certain *organizational advantages:*

a. Our small units with the lightest possible equipment have high mobility and are well adapted to guerrilla warfare.

b. Our units are equipped and trained to operate independently. They exist off the country, and supply is not a problem. This facilitates quick dispersal and mobility.

c. At the same time we are able to coordinate the operations of these individual units through a centralized command which takes in all forces in the area, regular, guerrillas, local detachments, People's Militia, and even the whole population enlisted in the People's Self-Defense Corps.

d. The political work throughout the army guarantees high morale and the absolute carrying out of orders. It gives us also the wholehearted support and cooperation of the people wherever we go.

e. Our army is entirely made up of volunteers.

f. Most of our higher cadres have had long experience—

seventeen years of continuous fighting through the civil and anti-Japanese war. Also, because our expansion has been arbitrarily held down—we still have only the three divisions we started the war with—many of these commanders, of regiments and above, have been in the same grade for many years and know their duties well.

3. *In discussing equipment, there are only deficiencies:*

a. The most immediate and pressing problem is lack of ammunition. The average per rifle is now about 30 rounds. In this connection our standard tables, which allow each man 50 rounds, are of little meaning.

b. We seriously lack automatic weapons which could increase our fire power.

c. We have only a few light mortars and cannon, but no real artillery. Much of the little we have is unusable for lack of ammunition. We need weapons which can attack Japanese blockhouses or fortified positions.

d. Most of our weapons are very old and should be considered obsolescent. This is true of all types.

e. There is no standardization in our weapons. They are of all sizes, types and calibers. This is because we have had to take our weapons where we could find them.

f. The bayonets which we manufacture have to be of soft steel and their quality is poor. This is a serious handicap because our shortage of ammunition forces us to rely heavily on bayonet charges and close-quarters fighting.

g. We have no anti-gas equipment and the enemy has taken advantage of this to inflict over 14,000 casualties, including a number of brigade and division commanders. . . .

5. *Comment*

It is my impression that General Yeh in his discussion of the organizational deficiencies and strong points of the Communist forces is frank and fair, and that his summary of the equipment deficiencies—and inferentially, needs—is, if anything, understatement. General Yeh and the other Communist military leaders have consistently taken the line: "We are not ashamed of what we have done with what we have had. But we know that we could do a great deal more if we had more."

There has been no request for equipment and nothing suggestive of "begging."

The Communists' Eighth Route Army in North China was their largest and most famous fighting force. It was not, however, their only regular army. In 1944 the New Fourth Army operating in Central China was regaining much of the strength it had lost after the New Fourth Army incident and the Kuomintang's capture of its commander, Yeh T'ing, in 1941. As it happened, Service was in an extraordinary position to learn a great deal about the New Fourth Army. Its acting commander, Ch'en Yi (later Foreign Minister of the People's Republic) was a "fellow provincial" of Service; both were born in Szechwan. Furthermore, Ch'en had once been a student at the Chengtu Y.M.C.A., of which Service's father had been the head. Thus Ch'en greeted Service with mock humility as "the son of my teacher." Here was the basis for a firm friendship, and soon Ch'en Yi was speaking quite openly and freely about the past history of the New Fourth Army and some of his hopes for its future expansion. As he spoke it became clear that the Japanese offensive of 1944 would mean not only setbacks for the Kuomintang, but also opportunities for the Communists to expand. Such a development would be of considerable importance to the United States, for at this time most American military planners were anticipating an American landing on the China coast as part of the final campaign to defeat Japan. If the Communists expanded into the Southeast, they, and not the KMT, would be the forces which the United States would meet on the beaches.

Possible Usefulness in Present War
of Old Communist Bases in Southeast China

No. 19: August 31, 1944
Foreign Relations, 1944, pp. 527–32

1. The fact is probably not generally recognized that the present New Fourth Army, the second main military organiza-

tion of the Chinese Communists and numbering some 150,000 regular troops,* was created out of remnants of the old Communist forces left behind in Southeast China when the Communists started their "Long March" in 1934, and that their old bases there are still potential centers of guerrilla resistance.

2. These "rear guards" of the main Communist forces withdrew into a number of mountainous regions especially suited to guerrilla warfare, usually along provincial boundaries, where in operations on a limited scale they were successful in resisting Kuomintang attempts at extermination which continued up to 1937. At the beginning of the Sino-Japanese war, with the creation of the Kuomintang-Communist United Front, a general amnesty was issued by the Central Government to these forces and they were amalgamated into a new special unit, the New Fourth Army, for guerrilla operations against the Japanese in the lower Yangtze Valley. . . .

3. A number of Communist leaders have made passing reference to the possible potential usefulness of these old bases in Southeast China from which the New Fourth Army was organized. . . .

4. With these statements in mind, I took the occasion of a private conversation with General Ch'en Yi, on August 25, to draw him out on the history of these old guerrilla bases.

General Ch'en talked most interestingly and at great length. He himself spent the period 1934–1937 in the areas on the Kwangtung-Hunan and Kwangtung-Kiangsi borders, mostly in the vicinity of Nanhsiung (Namyung), with a high Kuomintang price for his head, usually only a small band of guerrillas with him, moving continually through the hills and villages to elude and harass the surrounding Government forces, and often having hairbreadth escapes from capture or death. His personal experiences, many of which I have heard only from others, would make a most thrilling book.

The chief interest of General Ch'en's story, however, is that it shows that it was the support of the local people that made possible this continued resistance against seemingly overwhelming Government forces. The Communist Party was able

* See my report No. 17, August 30, 1944. [Footnote in original. See pp. 208–11.]

to maintain its underground organization in the villages. In some small remote districts it actually kept its own governments. The villages cooperated actively with the guerrillas by warning them of the movements of the Government troops, by sheltering them when possible, and by smuggling food and supplies to them when they were forced to take to the hills. The Government was finally forced to adopt the measure (later used by the Japanese in Manchuria and more recently in parts of North China) of forcing the peasants to live only in stockaded and guarded villages. . . .

5. These old remnant bases of the Communist forces are shown, in blue, on the attached map. . . .*

6. The details of present conditions in most of these areas are not now known to the Communists. Since the "New Fourth Army Incident" of January 1941, the members of the New Fourth Army have been regarded by the Central Government as rebels and have been unable to return to or have direct contact with these old base areas in which most of their homes are located.

By the Kuomintang agreement under which the New Fourth Army was organized, these home bases were not to be interfered with. The existing local governments were not to be disturbed. Landholdings were not to be forcibly changed. The families of the men who left the bases to form the New Fourth Army were not to be molested.

The Communists claim that this agreement was violated even before the "Incident." The governments (which had been only on the village or possibly in a few cases *hsien* level) were reorganized by the Kuomintang; the land was given back to the landlords (as it had been earlier in the rest of the former Communist areas); and in many cases the families of known members of the New Fourth Army were arrested and subjected to violence.

Resistance broke out in all or most of the areas. In some the Kuomintang was successful in crushing it by military force. But in other areas, the Communists are sure, sporadic resistance against the Central Government still continues. It is

* This map was not attached to the file copy of this document. See, however, the map in this book.

undoubtedly on a small scale and Communists claim to find confirmation in occasional newspaper reports of banditry and Government bandit suppression in these old base areas.

7. After this history of these old bases, I made the comment that if the expected Japanese attempt to open the Canton–Hankow railway is successful, these areas (ignoring the two which are north of Hankow) would perhaps be freer of strong Kuomintang control. General Ch'en gave me a sharp and seemingly surprised look and said with some excitement: "That is just what we are considering."

The general then went on about as follows:

After the New Fourth Incident and the definite break with the Kuomintang, and especially after they learned that the Kuomintang was trying to liquidate these old bases, many of the old cadres and officers of the New Fourth Army demanded that they be allowed to return and carry on the old fight for their homes. The Communist authorities did not permit this, but instead continued their movement north of the Yangtze River, where they have remained except for the small force that moved into East Chekiang after the Japanese occupation in 1942.

Now, however, the Communists are considering this question. If the Japanese close the Canton–Hankow line, the Kuomintang forces east of the railway will be weakened and cut off from supplies. Since they have proved in North China their inability to live and fight under guerrilla conditions, they may lose most of the territory to the Japanese (if the Japanese want to take it) without much of a fight. This seems all the more likely because of the indications —in the Honan and Hunan fighting—that the fighting ability of the Kuomintang forces has sunk to a new low. It will also be likely because the Kuomintang forces will have not the support of the people in these areas, but more likely their active resistance.

But this section of Southwest China may be of great importance to the war against Japan because it must be the site of American landings. If the Kuomintang cannot hold it, the Communists can. They could easily send officers and old cadres into the old bases from their present operating areas in the Yangtze Valley. Organization and training would be incomparably easier than it was in North China. The organizers would be natives of the areas who know it well from the long years of civil war and subsequent guerrilla fighting. The people would be already indoctrinated and eager to mobilize under a democratic regime. The arms would be plentiful from the Kuomintang forces who have been defeated and scattered all through the area by the Japanese. In six months the Communists could be sure of at least 100,000 well organized and effective guerrilla fighters.

So far the Communists have not decided to do this because they want to avoid more trouble with the Kuomintang, which would consider such expansion an aggressive act by the Communists and resist it violently. The Communists are not afraid of this competition with the Kuomintang, but it would be a stage closer to civil war, and it would interfere with fighting the Japanese.

Now, however, the situation may be changing. The possible near collapse of the Kuomintang in these areas, and the importance of the areas to the United Nations war effort must be considered.

8. It would be a mistake to assume that the Communist consideration of the problem is all on the high-minded and unselfish plane that is indicated here. I have suggested, in paragraph 9 of my report No. 15, August 27, 1944,* that this particular question is a part of the general problems which the Communists are now studying. If the Kuomintang is going to continue the trend it now shows—determination on elimination of the Communists—then the Communists, in order to prepare to defend themselves, may take the initiative by actively trying to extend their influence. If the Kuomintang is going to collapse as a force able to actively resist Japan, the Communists may take the leadership by trying to organize these regions for guerrilla warfare in conjunction with American landing forces.

9. This second possibility is of possible direct military importance to American forces that may have to operate in Southeast China. If the Kuomintang is going to prove a hopelessly "broken reed" as far as holding this section of China is concerned, we may be able to find an effective ally in the Communists.

The Communists would not need much in the way of supplies. They will have the support of the local people because they will *be* the local people. They already have a small existing nucleus in the East River area. There is another at present in east Chekiang. But the expansion here contemplated would go far beyond those areas and fairly well cover the southeastern provinces. There are at least two areas where these old

* See pp. 294–95.

bases lie on the coast where contact might be made and supplies landed.

10. But if these forces are to be organized and ready in time to be of any use, there must be a quick decision and speedy action on our part.

Several days after his first report on the growth of the New Fourth Army, Service sat down to analyze the reasons for its success. In doing so, he stressed in particular its "popular democratic appeal." This reference to democracy left Service open to any number of subsequent attacks. The most voluminous and complete work on Sino-American relations in this period accuses Service of a "misunderstanding of democracy," which according to the author necessarily implies "more than one center of power competing for the consent and support of the governed through constitutional process."* As Service put it: "The bright Ph.D.s have pointed out that I obviously didn't understand American political terms. But these were not political-science tracts or theses. I and the other Foreign Service officers were writing hurriedly and not for publication or a general readership. We were using shorthand terms—terms that were familiar or in current use. In the back of our minds (and the minds of those who were reading these reports in Chungking and Washington) was a comparison to conditions in the KMT areas. We were not talking about textbook democracy, but about democracy in the Chinese context. Democracy meant more than popular support. It meant more than simply serving the interest of the people. It meant also giving the people a share in the government so that they felt that they were a part of it."

Ultimately, what Service meant by "democratic" is best clarified by the way he described the Communist policies in his report.

* Tang Tsou, *America's Failure in China, 1941–1950* (Chicago: University of Chicago Press, 1963), pp. 204–5.

The Growth of the New Fourth Army:
An Example of the Popular Democratic Appeal
of the Chinese Communists

No. 22: September 4, 1944
Amerasia Papers, pp. 836–42

1. The growth of the Chinese Communist armies during the present war has proved them to be an extremely powerful political instrument because this spectacular development would not have been possible without the support of the people of the areas in which they have operated. This widespread popular support must, under the circumstances in which it has occurred, be considered *a practical indication that the policies and method of the Chinese Communists have a democratic character.*

2. This may seem to be jumping to an *ipso facto* conclusion.

(a) It might be assumed, for instance, that a patriotic desire to fight the foreign invader was responsible for this popular support. This is partially true.

But to the Chinese peasant (who is the only important class involved, both because of his overwhelming numerical superiority in China and because the Communists have had to operate entirely away from the cities) the idea of active *personal* resistance was entirely new. In the past the peasant had regarded all governments merely as something to be endured; there was little, as far as he was concerned, to choose from between them; and even if one was slightly better or worse than another, it was no concern of his and there was nothing he could do about it.

So the peasant needed a great deal of education and indoctrination—and some tangible evidence that it would benefit his own interests—before he was willing to take up arms. The fact that the Communists were able to accomplish this— while the Kuomintang was not—indicates a closeness to and an ability to appeal to the common people in terms which they understand. This is something akin, at least, to democracy.

(b) Furthermore, the people, if they were willing to fight,

almost always—certainly in the early years of the war—had two choices: they could fight with either the Kuomintang *or* the Communists. It would have been more natural for them to have turned to the Kuomintang because it was *the* government. Instead they turned to the Communists, who have come more and more to be regarded and treated by the Government as rebels. It would seem therefore that the peasants received better understanding and treatment from the Communists. This, again, is a *prima facie* indication of democracy. At least it can be said, on this basis, that the people must regard the Communists as more democratic than the Kuomintang.

(c) It might be argued that the Communists have the advantage of a "cause," that they use such direct appeals as distributing the land of the landlords to the peasants, that they spread a rabble-rousing Communism, or that they have found an equivalent of the fervor which gave such impetus to the Taipings or the Boxers. But, in fact, this argument is never heard. Even the Kuomintang does not bother to advance it. If they did, it would be refuted by the evidence of every foreign observer who has traveled through the Communist guerrilla areas. The Communists are not even actively preaching *Communism*—though it cannot be denied that they are, sometimes by not too subtle means, trying to create support for the Communist *Party*.

(d) It can also be claimed this popular support is chiefly due to the Communist skill in propaganda. The Communists *are* masters of this art, and it does have a part—but only a relatively small one. The war has lasted more than seven years —longer than mere propaganda without positive results could hope to hold the stolid and practical Chinese peasant. Furthermore, the guerrilla warfare into which the Communists have drawn their supporters is the type which is hardest of all military forms on the peasant because the whole area is continually a battleground.

(e) Another argument, little heard because it is so obviously untenable, is that the Communists have *forced* the people to support them and to join their armies. But the Communist armies were small when the war began; they did not have the military power necessary to have forced the people. Their armies, relatively speaking, are still small. They are, for instance, much smaller than the Kuomintang uses to *garrison* areas of equivalent size far in the rear and away from any enemy. It is obvious therefore that the Communist army does not need large forces to maintain its own rear—as it would if it carried out Kuomintang policies of conscription and taxation and was plagued by the same resultant problems of banditry and internal unrest. It is also true that these relatively small regular forces could not successfully fight off the Japanese and hold these areas unless they had the active assistance and participation of the people in large irregular auxiliary forces, which can only, by their nature, be voluntary. The Communists claim over 2 million local volunteers, the People's Militia, who are an active force in resisting and harassing the enemy. This figure may be exaggerated—though the evidence we have so far been able to gather indicates that Communist statistics of this nature are not inflated. But an organization of this type cannot be created and made effective by the threat of military force. And the Kuomintang does not even claim to have such an organization.

3. The conclusion therefore seems justified that the peasants support, join and fight with the Communist armies because they have been convinced that the Communists are fighting for their interests, and because the Communists have created this conviction by producing some tangible benefits for the peasants.

These benefits must be improvement of the social, political or economic condition of the peasants. Whatever the exact nature of this improvement, it must be—in the broader sense of the term as the serving of the interests of the majority of the people—toward democracy.

I believe that this success of the Communist forces in winning the support of the people is particularly well shown in the history of the New Fourth Army (hereafter referred to as N4A). This force has not received the publicity given to the development of the Eighth Route Army, which was visited by a number of foreign journalists and other observers early in the war. In many ways, however, its growth has been even more remarkable.

4. The N4A was not organized until 1938. It was formed out of remnants of the old Red Army who had been scattered among numerous isolated areas in South and Central China since the withdrawal of the main Communist forces from

Kiangsi at the end of 1934 (see my report No. 19, August 31, 1944, paragraph 2*). This was therefore an entirely new force with no background of unified organization; it could hardly compare with the Eighth Route Army, which at the outbreak of the war was already a well-organized army in being.

When organized, the N4A had a strength of only 12,000 officers and men; this is small compared with the 80,000 of the Eighth Route Army in 1937. Weapons and equipment were insufficient and mostly old: many of them were dug up from the ground where they had remained buried during the years of Kuomintang suppression. The new arms promised them by the Central Government were never forthcoming; all they ever received was a small amount of ammunition. Likewise the recruits that had been promised by the Central Government to fill their ranks were never turned over to them.

This new army was immediately thrown into action and was assigned the lower Yangtze Valley, where it was to attack already important and heavily garrisoned Japanese areas. In these areas, or close to them, there were also Kuomintang troops. The N4A Army thus had much less favorable opportunities for expansion than the Eighth Route Army, which had first occupied large, almost empty areas behind the Japanese lines, from which the Central Government forces had withdrawn and which the Japanese had left very lightly guarded as they moved south.

Having this greater freedom, the Eighth Route Army was able, as early as 1938, to establish stable bases to support its operations. When the Kuomintang, in the years 1939–1942, made an attempt to recover this territory, the physical difficulties of distance and interposing Japanese lines made it impossible for the Kuomintang to bring great strength against them. But the N4A, operating partly in Kuomintang territory much more easily accessible to the Central Government, was subjected to much stronger Kuomintang pressure and was forced to change its bases of operations several times. The result has been that most of the present N4A bases date from only 1940 or 1941. This is a serious handicap to the Communist method of growth by the mobilization of local support through a comprehensive political and economic program.

* See p. 212.

The N4A not only had to move, it also suffered heavy losses in conflicts with the Central Government troops. There have been sporadic small engagements and several of considerable size. In the largest of these, the "Incident" of January 1941, the N4A suffered about 7,000 casualties. Furthermore, since that time the N4A has been "illegal" by official mandate of the Central Government. Recruits joining it therefore know that they will be regarded by the Kuomintang as rebels and that this official vengeance will extend to their families. The Eighth Route Army has also suffered under this opprobrium, but to a much lesser extent.

What was the actual development of the N4A under these apparently unfavorable conditions?

At the end of its first year (spring 1939) the original strength of 12,000 had grown to 35,000. Operations extended from Shanghai to Hangchow, from Nanking to Hsuchow, and from Hsuchow west along the Lunghai railway to the vicinity of Kaifeng. Equipment had been brought in by recruits and captured from the Japanese.

By the spring of 1942, strength had risen to 100,000 regulars. Operations in the area between the Yangtze and the Lunghai railway had been extended to the Kiangsu coast; it had also moved forces into the Japanese-occupied areas around Hankow.

By the spring of 1944 the regular strength of the N4A had increased to 152,000 men, armed with 93,000 rifles, and supported by an organized People's Militia of 550,000. Operations had been extended into east Chekiang and into south and west Hupeh. Stable base areas had been created with a total population, paying taxes only to Communist-controlled governments, of about 30,000,000. All of these bases had withstood large-scale Japanese attacks, and some areas had not been penetrated by the Japanese for over two years.

In this development the N4A has increased its size by more than twelve times. In a slightly longer period the Eighth Route Army has increased sixfold.

5. These results have been achieved by a force which started from almost nothing. It has grown as it went along, out of the people. It has been an orphan, without any powerful, well-established government with large resources behind it. It has had to supply itself entirely.

During much of its history it has shared areas with or been in close proximity to Kuomintang troops. Despite the advantages of supply, re-enforcements and Government support, those Kuomintang forces did not have any such increase. To the contrary, they grew steadily weaker and most of them have by now disintegrated, turned puppet or withdrawn. They have never carried out an offensive against the Japanese, and they have shown repeatedly that they cannot successfully withstand Japanese attack.

6. General Ch'en Yi, acting commander of the N4A (General Yeh T'ing is still regarded as commander, although he has been a prisoner of the Kuomintang since 1941), insists that the success and growth of the N4A is wholly due to its policy toward the people. The most important of these were the following:

(a) First it was necessary to win the people's confidence, in a military sense. Fortunately the original cadres were old and experienced guerrilla fighters. In their first engagements, the Japanese were not used to their tactics and were unprepared and overconfident because of their easy defeats of other Chinese troops. During the first year they [N4A] had uniform success; after that they had newly trained and capable forces. The Communists always follow the policy of using their best troops in important engagements, holding their newer troops as reserve or to throw in after the enemy is retreating, to give them experience.

(b) The first step after coming into an area is intensive propaganda to explain the war and secure popular support.

(c) This is followed by the creation of mass organizations of the people. These include farmers, youth, women, militia, and so on. All of these are for the purpose of carrying out some function in resisting the enemy. But they are also encouraged to interest themselves in their own problems. For instance, the farmers are told that in the well-established guerrilla bases, rents and interest have been reduced.

(d) Through and from these mass organizations, democratically elected governments are set up. At first these are on the village level. As the area becomes stabilized the system is extended until the *hsien* governments, and finally the base governments, are elected by the people. Nominations and elections are carried out in general village meetings.

(e) As soon as some sort of government control is established, rents and interest are reduced. This is done moderately. The minimum standard is 37½ percent for rent. But in the first stage, rents are not usually reduced by more than one quarter. This is to avoid driving the landlords away and into the Japanese camp. In many areas into which the N4A has gone, the power of the landlords has been very great and they have been able to hang on to their control and even in some areas to dominate the local governments. In such areas the Communists move slowly by strengthening the organization of the people until they gain control by democratic methods.

(f) Taxes are reduced because of the moderate requirements of the N4A and the elimination of corruption through popular election of officials.

(g) Taxation is made moderately progressive. At present the poorest approximately 20 percent of the farmers pay no tax. The highest rate on the rich landlords usually does not exceed 35 percent.

(h) Banditry is vigorously attacked and the welfare of the people is improved by the maintenance of peace and order. In addition to direct attack, the other policies of the Communists are effective in removing this old burden of banditry.

(i) As important as any of these is the practical demonstration of the unity of the army and the people. The army takes as one of its major tasks the protection of the people (to the degree that this often determines its military operations). It takes positive measures to prevent enemy interference with the sowing and harvest. It actually assists, when possible, in farm work. When and where able, its troops produce a part of their own needs. It avoids any sort of arbitrary demands on the people, pays for what it takes, and replaces breakage or damage. It helps the people cope with disasters such as breaks in dikes. In times of poor crops it reduces its own rations to the level of subsistence of the people. It continually harps on the idea that the army and people are "one family."

(j) There is never any forced conscription. Except for the encouragement of the formation, on a volunteer basis, of such organizations as the militia, it avoids, in the early stages of its control of an area, any attempt at recruiting.

(k) Within the army it takes special measures to care for families of soldiers; emphasis is given to care of wounded;

such practices as beating of soldiers are prohibited; and there is a democratic relationship—outside of purely military matters —between officers and men.

(1) Various other phases of the program include women's rights, intensive advancement of popular education, promotion of all types of cooperative societies, and so on.

7. General Ch'en, with whom I have had several long talks on these general subjects, can be excused if he paints an exaggeratedly pretty picture.

The fact remains that the Communists have been successful in winning the support of the people in the areas in which they operate, while the Kuomintang has not. General Ch'en laughingly says that the Communists should thank the Kuomintang for coming into the same areas, because they have provided the people with a basis for comparison.

We cannot yet say with certainty that the Communist claims of democratic policies are true. But that they are at least partially true is the only reasonable explanation of the popular appeal which the Communist armies have shown.

Several days after his report on the appeal of the New Fourth Army, Service wrote a similar report analyzing data on Communist control in all of the guerrilla base areas. It was another attempt to assess the appeal of the CCP, here noting in particular the Party's ability to attract students and liberal intellectuals who fled the Japanese occupation and joined the guerrilla-area governments established by the Communists. There was no question, in Service's mind, that the CCP was the "undisputably dominant political factor," and that the army was an arm of the Party, but he was impressed by their moderate policies and their strict adherence to the United Front.

The Development of Communist Political Control in the Guerrilla Bases

No. 26: September 10, 1944
Amerasia Papers, pp. 867–75

Summary: Communist influence predominates in the guerrilla bases because the Communists took the lead in establishing the governments, because there has been no important organized political opposition within the areas, and because the Communists have been supported by the peasants and liberals. The Communists have used their influence in a democratic way and to further democratic ends.   *End of Summary.*

1. The Chinese Communist Party has overwhelming political influence in the various guerrilla bases. In effect, this influence amounts to control. Although the governments of these bases are nominally independent of each other, their form of organization, and their policies and administrative programs, are all similar. Furthermore, these policies are identical with those of the Communist Party.

It is sometimes suggested that this fact of Communist control is a refutation of Communist claims of democracy. Considering the history, political development and present situation of these bases, I do not believe that this criticism is valid.

2. The political history of the guerrilla bases has been discussed at length with a number of Communist leaders. These include:

> Liu Shao-ch'i: Member of the Political Bureau, Communist Party
>
> Lin Pai-ch'ü: Chairman of the Shen-Kan-Ning Border Region Government
>
> Nieh Jung-chen: Commander of the Shansi-Hopei-Chahar Military Region   (General Nieh played a leading part in the establishment of the government of the Shansi-Hopei-Chahar Border Region, which is identical in extent with the Military District.)
>
> Ch'en Yi: Acting Commander of the New Fourth Army

> Chu Jui: Political Commissar of the Shantung Military District
>
> Yang Hsiu-feng: Chairman of the Government of the Shansi-Hopei-Honan-Shantung Border Region (At the outbreak of the war Dr. Yang was a professor in the National Normal University at Peiping and a member of the National Salvationist Group. He was a leader of the first popular resistance in central Hopei. He joined the Communist Party in 1939.)

3. From these talks it appears that the political development in the different bases has followed a generally similar pattern. I have therefore attempted to give a generalized account of this development which will fit all of the bases. . . .

4. The political development of the Communist bases has been, in general, along the following lines.

There had never, even before the war, been much political progress in the area which has come under the influence of the Communist Party. All of it is rural. Much of it is mountainous, isolated and backward in every respect. Shansi, Shantung and several other sections were "warlord satrapies" where the Kuomintang had never been able to develop a widespread and effective organization. What formal Kuomintang organization did exist in all these Northern provinces was expelled by Japanese pressure in 1935 (by one clause of the Ho-Umetsu Agreement*). In none of them had the Kuomintang, which was (a) chiefly Southern and Central Chinese and (b) tied to the large cities, established itself on a broad base among the rural population. And in none of these provinces had there been permitted the development of any other political party. Political control had always been from above, by small groups: there was no political foundation for democracy.

As the Japanese army advanced through North China at

---

* On June 10, 1935, the Nationalist Chinese Minister of War Ho Ying-ch'in signed a secret agreement with General Umetsu Yoshijiro, the commander of the Japanese North China garrison, under which the Chinese were to withdraw most of their troops from Hopeh and abolish KMT and patriotic anti-Japanese organizations in the area. When news of this KMT appeasement policy leaked out, Ho became a principal target of patriotic student protests.

227 The Communist Areas

the beginning of the war, most of the provincial and local governments collapsed. The officials and leading Kuomintang members—usually the same men—fled south with the Central Government troops. Many of the wealthy landlords also fled south, or took refuge in the large cities where there were foreign Concessions or which, even under Japanese occupation, were relatively quiet. North China, outside of the large Japanese-occupied cities, became a political void.

The Communist armies rapidly overran these areas in their westward advance during late 1937 and 1938 which extended from Shensi to the sea. They came in *behind* the Japanese into this political vacuum. Some areas they had to fight for; but many fell into their hands because the Japanese had ignored them or had passed on in their swift southern advance which they hoped would defeat the Central Government and bring an early end to the war.

After occupation, it was necessary that organized governments be set up to administer these areas and to enable them to serve as supporting bases for the Communist armies. The Political Department of the Eighth Route Army (in other words, the Communist Party) set about this task as rapidly as possible. Intensive propaganda and indoctrination of the peasants could create support for the army's government. But it could not immediately produce leaders. . . .

The *only* important, politically conscious and experienced group that the Communists found in the areas and willing to join them, were large numbers of liberals and intellectuals. Most of these were university professors and students from the great educational center of Peiping. Since the student demonstrations there in December 1935, they had been demanding resistance against Japan. In the first great tide of war enthusiasm they had left Peiping and other cities ahead of the Japanese occupation and gone into the countryside to organize popular resistance. Most of these groups had stayed behind after the Government and its defeated armies fled south. But they were not organized, and were operating individually or in small groups with whatever followings their eloquence could attract.

A few of these people were Communists. A larger number were nominally Kuomintang members. Many belonged to no party. But the great majority of them were strongly liberal and in favor of the Communist plan of people's guerrilla warfare based on democracy. This was, in fact, what they were already actively trying to start. The need of coordination and the organization of governments which could serve as bases was obvious. Most of these groups therefore willingly—by inclination, and by the logic of circumstances—accepted Communist leadership and joined with them on a United Front basis. . . .

The "democratic" nature of these first governments was "confirmed" by the followings of the Communist armies and these liberal groups, and by numerous mass meetings organized by them—which often went through the gesture of voting (by acclamation) for the government which had been set up.

The liberals were very useful in this early stage for providing the bulk of the immediately needed administrative officials and *hsien* magistrates. As democratic machinery was not yet set up, they were appointed to these posts by the government, or in very newly occupied areas by the political officers of the army (who, among many other duties, fulfill the function of our Army's civil government officers).

Most of the partisan bands which had gathered around the liberals were absorbed into the Communist army; this was one important source of their rapid growth in this early stage of the war.

The Communists were not only the leaders in setting up these governments, they were also the only group ready with a complete and well-thought-out program. They were preparing for a long war and had determined that they would fight behind the enemy lines with guerrilla tactics. . . .

In brief, the Communist plan was the following. The apathetic peasant had to be aroused by convincing him that he had something immediate and concrete to fight for. It was also necessary to create a well-rounded, productive, self-sufficient base that could survive being cut off from the cities. This demanded the support of *all* classes, and the return and cooperation of the landlords, local capitalists, handicraft entrepreneurs and merchants. These conditions dictated moderate policies. Even if there had not been the United Front pledges to the Central Government, extreme policies would frighten away what little local capital existed and leave the base economically disorganized and unable to support the army. Politically it was also desirable to bring all classes into unified resistance and to prevent the possibility of division by the Japanese. The most effective measure as far as the farmer was concerned was the reduction of rents and interest. But this reduction was to be moderate and *limited,* and the government would protect the interests of the landlord by guaranteeing the payment of these reduced rates. Private enterprise was guaranteed noninterference and was offered assistance to increase production. Thus the fears of the landlord-merchant group would be calmed. Finally, democracy would be instituted. This would interest all groups in joining the government, through the democratic process, in order to protect or advance their own interests in such matters as rent-and-interest reduction and taxation.

The Communist leaders stress the importance and precedence of these measures: *first and basic,* limited rent-interest reduction to win the active support of the peasants, who are the bulk of the population; *second,* democratic self-government to bring all classes, particularly the landlord-merchants, into active participation and hence support of the government. This conception of the importance of democracy as a means of obtaining the participation and support of the capitalist groups is interesting and significant in the study of present and probable future Communist policies. They have no illusions that China can hope to build a proletarian state in anything like the near future. . . .

The program worked out as intended. As the governments became well established and showed ability to withstand Japanese attack, and as the peasants through education (by the Communists) in their new democratic powers began to exhibit interest in more drastic rent-interest reduction and progressive taxation, the landlord-capitalist group was driven to active participation to preserve its own interests.

Within one year most villages were under elected governments. By 1939–1940 the democratic election of *hsien* governments was general. And by 1942 most of the bases were governed by popularly elected People's Political Councils.

In all of these grades of government there is substantial, though not large, representation of both the landlord-capitalist and peasant-laborer groups. This landlord-capitalist participation has been rewarded (by means of Communist support) with some reduction of the early high tax rates on large incomes, and more extensive government assistance to private productive enterprise.

This institution of political democracy has not, however, been accompanied by political development along definite Party forms.

The landlord-capitalist element has formed pressure groups, without unified Party organization or leadership. Their main object has been merely the preservation of their own interests.

The Kuomintang has not established itself in an organized manner because (1) it had no strong original foundation in the regions, and (2) the central Kuomintang authorities (Chungking) have generally taken the attitude that these are "traitor areas" and "illegal" governments. When the Kuomintang *has* tried to come back into some of these areas, it has done so with the backing of military force and Government mandates abolishing the governments already set up and functioning. . . .

The increasingly politically conscious peasants have tended to gravitate toward the Communist Party. This can be regarded as natural. In the first place they regard the Communists as responsible for setting up the bases and for the practical improvement in their social-political-economic condition. In the second place, there is no other party with anything to offer the peasants or actively seeking their support. Even if the Kuomintang were active in these areas, it could give little practical attraction to the peasant.

It must, of course, be recognized that the Communists have controlled all political indoctrination and propaganda and have not discouraged this tendency of the peasants to regard them as their benefactors. Furthermore, the Communist Party has actively expanded its Party organization in its newly won areas and has established branches down to the villages. Of the approximately one million present members of the Party, it is claimed that more than one-half are peasants. It is reasonable to assume that most of these are in North China.

The only other important group, the liberal-intellectuals, has also failed to set up a separate Party organization. They have remained in close support and cooperation with the Communists. Some have actually joined the Communist Party. But it seems that this tendency is not at present encouraged—since the overwhelming domination of the Communist Party is something that the Communists, for political reasons described be-low, wish to avoid—and that many of those outside the Com-munist Party might as well, as far as thinking goes, be con-sidered in it.

Even without Party organization or their own following, this liberal-intellectual group has remained politically important as holders of elective offices. Reasons for this can be assumed to be: (1) the shortage of men in the areas with their qualifications of education and experience; and (2) during their first, ap-pointed terms they generally made a good impression on the people by their patriotic enthusiasm, democratic leanings and honesty. Thus many of them have continued to hold posts as magistrates and high administrative officials.

The actual situation, therefore, is that no strong opposition has developed to the Communists and they have remained the undisputably dominant political factor.

This dominance tended to become so pronounced that in 1940 the Communist Party decided, as a purely Party measure, to restrict itself to one-third of the membership of any elective government body, and to advocate that the other two-thirds be divided between Kuomintang and non-Party members. The one-third limitation on the Communists was a maximum, not a minimum limit. It was hoped that this would improve the all-round representative character of the governments, thus helping to keep the support of the numerically small landlord-merchant groups and countering Kuomintang charges of monopoly and violation of the United Front.

This self-restriction of the Communist Party has not had much effect on its leading role. It generally elects its solid one-third (in a few areas it actually continues to hold slightly over this ratio in the People's Political Councils). The Kuomintang representation is made up of *individuals* who were former of-ficials or Kuomintang members but now have no Party machine back of them and are usually of liberal tendencies. It is usually difficult to find enough of these persons, with suitable quali-fications, who are willing to join the government: with the present situation between the two parties, a "regular" Kuomin-tang member knows that he jeopardizes his Party standing and will be accused by Chungking of being a "Communist" if he participates in an "illegal" "Communist" government. As a result the Kuomintang (it would be more correct to say "nominal Kuomintang") representation in most governments is below the sought-for one-third. The remainder of the government is then made up of a few representatives of the landlord-merchant groups (who may also find some representation through the Kuomintang members) and a larger number of the liberal-intellectuals.

The typical composition, then, is one-third Communists, plus a few liberal Kuomintang (or ex-Kuomintang) members, plus a large number of liberal-intellectuals, and finally a relatively small group of the landlord-merchant group.

With this strong representation and a predominantly liberal and sympathetic majority, it is not surprising that the Communists have been the chief initiators of the policies followed by the base governments. Furthermore, since the Communist Party holds the same dominant position in each government, and since it is the one connecting link between these separate governments, it has secured the adoption by all of them of its program.

5. Related to this development of predominant Communist influence in the guerrilla bases are a number of other factors which should be mentioned, even though detailed study of some will be left for following reports. . . .

The Communists have accepted and incorporated into their own program some proposals put forth by other groups. An example was the policy to "refine the army and reduce the government" (generally translated as "rationalization"), which was originally introduced into the Shen-Kan-Ning People's Political Council by a landlord representative.

[Here Service discusses policies covered in the preceding despatch.]

Finally, the army is the army of the Communists. This is important because the political effect of the Eighth Route and New 4th armies is tremendous. This effectiveness comes in several ways. The Political Department, which is used in indoctrination of the people, especially of newly occupied areas, is highly organized and experienced, and under wholly Communist leadership (contrary to the rest of the army). But even greater than this direct effect is the example of the behavior and attitude of the army toward the people, its volunteer character, its completely different attitude of unity with the people, its high morale, and the fact that it fights.

6. I have attempted to show that the political control of the Communist Party in the guerrilla bases has developed from its leadership in establishing and holding these bases, the absence of strong opposition, the adoption of moderate, democratic policies which have benefited the great majority of the population, and political astuteness combined with control of propaganda and the influence of the army. The *policies* of the Communist Party have been democratic, and there is little which under the circumstances can be called undemocratic in its *methods*.

The question may be asked whether the Communists would have been so democratic in method if they had been faced with stronger opposition. The question is hard to answer because there has never been a strong opposition willing to cooperate on a democratic basis. In the one area where the Kuomintang has an organization, it has been allowed its own newspaper and other democratic freedoms. But this opposition was weak. In areas where the Kuomintang came in with military force to oust the Communists, the Communists won out because they had the democratic support of the people. The Kuomintang did not have this support and was unable to obtain it. This fact, together with difficulties connected with the war, forced the Kuomintang to withdraw.

The next question is logically the future. I believe that the Communist influence with the people in the guerrilla bases is now so great, and rests on such a strong democratic basis, that the Communists will be willing to contest their political control there with any other party *on a democratic basis;* and that they will accordingly content themselves with democratic methods— including freedom of propaganda—provided that the other party or parties do the same.

Service had been briefed by the Communist leaders on the extent, nature, tactics and history of their armies; he had talked extensively to Ch'en Yi and others about the political program of the Communists in their guerrilla areas; but he did not yet have clear independent verification of the popularity or political strength of the CCP in the base areas. The first reliable independent information was to come from an American Army doctor, Major M. A. Casberg, who in seven weeks had trekked a thousand miles through the guerrilla areas, and from three American correspondents who had visited a base area in northwest Shansi. All had observed the Eighth Route Army in combat and were able to witness at first hand the degree of popular support for the Communist armies. This is Service's report on their findings.

American Officer and Foreign Correspondents Report Active Popular Support of the Eighth Route Army at Front

No. 38: October 9, 1944
Amerasia Papers, pp. 1004–11

1. The return of Major M. A. Casberg and three foreign correspondents from an extended trip to Northwest Shansi gives us additional reports based on direct observation of conditions in the Communist areas behind the Japanese lines to add to those of Lieutenant Baglio and other foreign travelers.

2. Major Casberg's full report (Medical Organization and Equipment of the Chinese Communist Forces behind the Japanese Blockade Line, dated October 15, 1944)* is of the greatest interest not only because of his findings regarding the medical work of the Communist army, but also because of necessary incidental description of conditions he found in the fighting zone. I hope that his report can be made available to the State Department and other interested agencies. Major Casberg was actually with the Communist forces during several important engagements and assisted in the care of Chinese (and

---

* There is no explanation for Casberg's postdating of his report, but this is indeed the date on the original report, and Service's No. 38 is also clearly of October 9.

captured Japanese) wounded. I attach a few excerpts of his report which are illustrative of general conditions.

3. There is also attached a summary of conversations with the three foreign correspondents (Harrison Forman—London *Times* and *Reader's Digest,* Maurice Votaw—Baltimore *Sun,* and I. Epstein—*New York Times* and *Time-Life*) reporting their general impressions. The correspondents and Major Casberg covered the same general territory but did not travel together until the last part of their trip.

4. The important gist of the impressions of both Major Casberg and the correspondents is that there is active, aggressive resistance of the Japanese, and that this is based on complete unity and solidarity of the people and the Eighth Route Army.

5. It may be possible to criticize the reports of these observers on the ground that they are not military men. Major Casberg, however, is an extremely careful, sober observer who has spent most of his life in the Orient. The three correspondents have all been many years in China, and Epstein speaks excellent Northern Chinese. Discussion of military qualifications is, however, beside the point. The chief significance of their reports is the political fact that the Communists have the complete support of the local population. This political fact is the basis for military strength.

(Excerpts)*

MEDICAL ORGANIZATION AND EQUIPMENT OF THE CHINESE COMMUNIST FORCES BEHIND THE JAPANESE BLOCKADE LINE

by M. A. Casberg, Maj., M.C.—October 15, 1944

2. RELATIONSHIP OF THE EIGHTH ROUTE ARMY AND THE LOCAL POPULACE

One of the most impressive facts gleaned from this trip was the complete solidarity of the soldiers and the civilians. This solidarity increases as one approaches the front. On every occasion that I witnessed contacts between soldiers and peasants,

* All deletions (indicated by asterisks) were done by Service in his original despatch.

whether individually or in larger groups, there was evidenced a genuine friendship.

* * * The villagers are very generous in supplying the needs of the soldiers, all food being paid for in full. In the morning before leaving the village the soldiers sweep up all rubbish, replace furniture such as doors used for beds and leave things in good order.

b. On numerous occasions I witnessed peasants from surrounding villages bring in gifts to the soldiers. These gifts were frequently quite substantial consisting of sheep, goats, chickens, eggs, baskets of grain, fruit, shoes (handmade by the peasant women) and various other items. * * * On returning to the village where we were camped I again saw these same peasants. They had brought gifts for the Eighth Route Army soldiers, coming out practically from under the shadow of the Japanese blockhouse.

c. When marching through villages it was quite a common sight to see the schoolchildren gather along the streets and sing for the passing soldiers. I have seen villagers walk up to the soldiers passing through and give them gifts of food such as ears of corn, fruit and bread.

3. THE PEOPLE'S MILITIA

* * * My discussions will be limited to observations of this organization as it functions at the front. In brief, this unit is an organization of peasants banded together and cooperating with the Eighth Route Army to fight the Japanese. In some ways it resembles the Minutemen of our Revolutionary War days, for they are really civilians, receiving no pay and wearing no uniforms. Their support comes from their farms. Each member has a rifle (some of which are of very ancient vintage), and three or four hand grenades. It is not an uncommon sight to pass a field and see a stack of guns and grenades in one corner while the farmers are working nearby.

a. One cannot travel very far near the front without meeting the People's Militia, for at intervals averaging two to three miles are guards who are members of this organization and who check the passes of all travelers. * * * This is a great aid to the army, for it prevents the passage of unauthorized personnel such as spies.

b. Villages near the front are organized by the People's Militia for rapid evacuation. These minutemen keep constant watch over Japanese strongpoints and spread the alarm the moment the enemy starts on the march. * * * I have observed the complete evacuation of Kuantou, the headquarters of the Eighth subdistrict, accomplished in two hours. The cattle were driven into the hills, valuables hidden, and women and children safely evacuated. Members of the People's Militia mined all the approaches while others took up vantage points along the tops of the surrounding hills to snipe at the enemy. Because of inferiority in numbers and equipment the peasant cannot meet the Japanese in open combat but must wage guerrilla warfare, thus harassing the enemy and giving the villagers time to escape to safety.

Many of the villages in this area have elaborate caves which extend a distance of two to four miles underground, built as a means of escape from the raiding parties of the enemy. The soft loess soil of this region makes such construction possible. I examined one of these hideaways which had been used on several occasions by the village and was shown where two Japanese soldiers had been killed as they attempted to gain entrance. The numerous narrow twists and turns, both in the vertical and horizontal planes, made it very easy to defend. There were several secret entrances and exits quite a distance from the village, and numerous air vents leading out through the hill above kept the air pure. In the depths of the tunnel were many side caves with sufficient room to house the entire village of around two hundred people. In the event of the approach of the enemy, the women, children and valuables are quickly stored in the cave and only two or three men armed with rifles and hand grenades remain with them to take care of the defense. The rest of the able-bodied men hide up in the hills and snipe at the enemy. These caves are also used to hide the harvested crops from the Japanese. Wounded soldiers have often found refuge in such caves.

c. Mine warfare has been converted into an effective weapon by the People's Militia, so much so that in many areas the Japanese are afraid to venture far from their blockhouses, or if they do so, are forced to follow stream beds and keep away from paths. * * * I have passed through villages near Japanese strongpoints where mines were buried every night. The People's Militia collect scrap metal (such items as old temple bells) and present this to the ordnance factories for which in return they receive mine casings. These they fill with homemade black powder and attach homemade detonators. * * *

d. The Eighth Route Army depends to a great extent on the People's Militia for intelligence. While I was behind the Japanese lines in the Eighth subdistrict the military men in our party could give me daily information of the exact movements of the enemy around us. This was obtained from this organization of "minutemen" who sent runners every few hours from points where enemy intelligence could be gained. When we attacked a blockhouse we knew not only the exact number and size of the firearms, the exact number of the soldiers both Japanese and puppet, but also in many cases even the names of the soldiers. Besides gaining military intelligence, the members of the People's Militia also act as guides for the soldiers of the Eighth Route Army. Much of the fighting is done at night and the terrain is rough, so it is a great advantage for the soldiers to have as guides men who have been born and raised in the vicinity and know every inch of the ground.

4. EIGHTH ROUTE ARMY COMBAT

[This final extract from Major Casberg's report covers a few combat operations which he observed. The opening lines indicate his general impression: "There have been numerous accusations by the Kuomintang that the Eighth Route Army is not fighting the Japanese. From my observations I am convinced that nothing could be farther from the truth."]

MEMORANDUM: SUMMARY OF TALKS WITH HARRISON FORMAN, M. VOTAW, AND I. EPSTEIN, CONCERNING IMPRESSIONS GAINED ON TRIP TO GUERRILLA BASE BEHIND ENEMY LINES IN NORTHWEST SHANSI.

(Note: This is a summary of rough notes made during three lengthy conversations lasting for several hours. Every point made by the correspondents was illustrated by numerous anecdotes and observed incidents. Space prevents the quotation of these.)

The fighting we observed was in the Eighth subdistrict of the Shansi-Suiyuan Military Base of the Eighth Route Army. It is an area about 75 miles in diameter, just to the west of Taiyuan, with a population of 400,000, including two *hsien* cities of 20–30,000 each. The whole area is under effective Eighth Route Army control but is completely surrounded by a ring of over 100 Japanese blockhouse strongpoints—108 at the start of the recent campaign.

The enemy forces were 5,800 Japanese and 3,000 puppet troops distributed among these strongpoints. Reserves for the Japanese forces can normally be drawn from the Taiyuan garrison.

Chinese forces in the area are: 1 Brigade (4–5,000 men) of the regular forces of the Eighth Route Army; 3,000 local guerrillas (irregular forces on full-time military status operating under the Eighth Route Army); 12,000 People's Militia (farmers who work on their farms when not carrying out military duties). This official figure for the People's Militia is probably an understatement. At one time we saw 600 men mobilized from only four *hsiang* (a *hsiang* is a small subdivision of a *hsien*).

The truth is that practically the whole able-bodied population is combatant, or available for cooperative work such as transportation of wounded and collection of intelligence.

During the six weeks' campaign, of which we saw only a small part, twenty-eight of these surrounding blockhouse strongpoints were taken and destroyed. Eight of these were taken during the two weeks we were in the area. We were present or close to the taking of four.

After our observation of several important engagements, especially the raid on Fenyang, we find on our return that the newspaper reports err on the side of understatement. Thus, for instance, the number of rifles—by our own observation—captured at Fenyang was seventy instead of the reported thirty. Claims of casualties and Jap prisoners were correct. Our whole trip proved that reports given us in Yenan before our trip about conditions were correct.

The campaign had several motives: to protect the harvest and stave off the expected Japanese foraging by taking the initiative and tying the Japanese to their blockhouses; to eliminate a number of blockhouses which menaced certain districts, obtruded into the base area or interfered with free movement of the people and military forces; to extend the base area. Advantage was taken of the fact that the Japanese had committed forces in a mopping-up campaign in southeast Shansi and hence did not have readily available reserves to put into this area.

The whole campaign was planned and directed from one headquarters, extended over the whole subdistrict, and showed excellent coordination and coperation of all the forces involved.

Generally the People's Militia carried out preliminary work by blockade or reduction of outlying defenses. The regulars provided a mobile striking force which was not brought onto the scene until the final assault. The regulars were continually on the move.

The People's Militia participated in actual fighting, in evacuation of wounded and in transportation—besides doing guard and intelligence work. Some blockhouses were actually taken by the militia without the aid of the regulars.

There was never any question of lack of cooperation between militia and regulars. Militia seemed to take the whole thing as a great sport. Militia keep what equipment they capture, and receive a share of that taken in joint operations. They receive basic training from the regulars and are given recognition (such as the gift of a rifle) for specially meritorious or brave service.

Peasant ingenuity and initiative in the use of the wooden cannon, land-mines, booby traps, caves and tunnels, etc., is amazing.

All the regulars we saw had Japanese arms. A very large number of the People's Militia also have rifles. We were surprised by this.

There is no question of the desire of these people to fight. Every village has been invaded by the Japanese; most are in complete ruin.

Morale, of both army and people, could not possibly be higher. The enthusiasm and spirit of the people has to be seen to be believed. There was constant fraternization between the soldiers and the people in the most spontaneous and friendly manner.

Intelligence cover is absolute. We were at all times within

ten or fifteen miles of Japanese strongpoints. We at times slept within one mile of Japanese blockhouses. The officers at all times had complete knowledge of the whereabouts and exact strength of Japanese forces in the area.

Mutual confidence between the people and army regarding security is absolute. Every indication pointed to that fact that the population is so united that there are no spies or subversive groups in the villages. When townspeople came out from Japanese-occupied Fenyang to bring gifts to the troops, a public meeting was held at which we were introduced to the crowd. The people were merely told not to mention our presence after they returned. All this time 300 Japanese were within five miles of us.

There was no banditry and no mention of deserters. We talked to many soldiers privately: all said that they had volunteered, liked the army, and gave very good reasons for their fighting. The idea that they are the army of the people is firmly imbedded. Most of the soldiers are local boys.

We saw many troops engaging in production work—yarn making, field work, etc.

We saw eight Japanese prisoners taken. Several were wounded and were given treatment ahead of the Chinese wounded.

During our stay 150 puppet troops were taken prisoner. Their arms are taken away but they are allowed to return if they wish. One group desired to stay but said that their families in Fenyang would suffer; the Communists sent into the town and brought the families out. Forty puppets deserted and came over to the Communist, bringing their guns: they were allowed to keep these and when Forman took their pictures he found these puppets' guns still loaded. They could have captured the headquarters.

Nobody showed any hesitation in talking freely. They had sensible opinions and seemed well informed on the war in general. Every subheadquarters puts out a news bulletin which is spread in many ways.

The people spoke of Yen Hsi-shan's troops as bandits and robbers. They also compared their present condition favorably with their former condition under Kuomintang troops. The Kuomintang generally is anathema. Everybody, even in private, did not vary from the story that things were good now and terrible under the old Government.

Practical democracy is obvious on every hand, in relations of army to the people, in the local governments, in the people's concern over their own affairs. We saw many of these elected officials of the villages and mass organizations who were obviously ordinary farmers. There is great pride in their independence and ability to run their own affairs.

We were surprised by the large number of young people of college or middle school student class who were actively working with the army or in local governments. These are chiefly in political and organizing work.

These men and the Party workers are in the closest possible touch and sympathy with the common people. There is no barrier of class or education between them. They lead the same life and engage in productive work with their hands.

We also encountered a large number of former officers and soldiers in the Kuomintang armies now members of the Eighth Route Army. Some of them were the most enthusiastic "converts" we met. The brigade commander of this subdistrict, for instance, was a former Kuomintang battalion commander.

There is no question of the unity of the population. Some people bringing voluntary presents to the troops were well dressed and apparently the local well-to-do. We saw instances where local gentry were elected officials.

We saw no slogans mentioning Communism, and heard no mention of it as a political doctrine. There is, however, good feeling toward the Communist Party. People everywhere spoke of the Eighth Route Army as "our army." Propaganda is specific and related to current problems, such as the production campaign.

Political indoctrination of the troops is obviously extremely effective but, again, not Communistic in content. Political leaders are of very high caliber and play an important part, not only in indoctrination and morale building but also in actual leadership. There is complete and detailed explanation by the political director of each engagement before it takes place, describing its significance and relation to the whole situation. After the engagement there is another meeting of the political director with the men, analyzing the engagement and giving criticism or praise. The officers and political director obviously know each man intimately, as an individual. After a private soldier was killed in one engagement we saw a brief and simple but very moving memorial service by his unit. His commander and political officer made short speeches of appreciation, mentioned things that he had done, and put over the idea that his memory was an inspiration to his comrades. You could not help but feel that this poor boy—a farmer's son—was important.

There is great emphasis everywhere on education, both of the troops and people. We saw primary schools close to the enemy, ready for evacuation as a body at moment's notice under the leadership of the armed teacher.

The physical condition of the troops is superb. They are "rugged." At one time we marched rapidly for nine hours in rain and on a slippery road without a single halt. No one out of our company of 130 men dropped out. Earlier reports of the mobility of the Communist forces are not exaggerated. No officer below regimental commander rides a horse.

Discipline is excellent but not forced. We saw no punishment. Relations between officers and men are democratic and friendly. Both eat and dress alike and take the same hardships. They obviously know and trust each other.

The men are adequately and neatly clothed, though shoes and clothes are often patched. Their care of their weapons was "loving."

A chance to fight is welcomed. There is no hanging back. Our orderly who accompanied us from Shensi begged to be allowed to stay behind because he had been in the army several years without a chance to fight. His request was granted, to his great delight.

Chinese casualties, by our own observation, are much lighter than those of the enemy because the initiative is in the hands of the Chinese. Most of their operations are at night and depend on surprise. They attack only when conditions are all in their favor. When the Japanese send out parties, they withdraw and resort to harassing, sniping and use of landmines and booby traps.

Economic conditions are not what could be described as "good" because the country was poor to start with and has all been subject to the depredations of the Japanese. But they are at least not worse off than they were before the Japanese came, and much better than under Japanese occupation. The people everywhere speak of the advantages of the reduction of rent and interest, progressive tax, participation of the army in production to lighten the burden on the people, etc. The average rate of taxation is much lower than before the war.

There has been a tremendous development of cooperative labor. This is within the village, between soldiers and the people, and even between villages. For instance, if one village's crops are ready to harvest before those of the surrounding villages, the men from those other villages will help in getting the work done expeditiously. Later, when their crops are ready, this service will be reciprocated. This greater speed due to organization is important in frustrating Japanese foraging raids. Harvesting time has been reduced greatly. There has been created a strong cooperative group spirit.

We could not find any criticism or opposition to the present order. This is obviously a people's movement. It is clearly gaining strength and solidarity.

When Service returned to Yenan in 1945, he had enough data from non-Communist sources, especially downed American airmen, to summarize the extent of Communist influence in the Japanese-occupied areas of China. The picture was quite conclusive and he expressed it succinctly: the Communists controlled virtually all of the countryside of occupied China.

Verification of Communist Territorial Claims by Direct American Observation

No. 17: March 17, 1945
Foreign Relations, 1945, pp. 287–89

Summary: Almost all of the important Communist-held areas in North and Central China have now been visited by American Army observers or rescued American air crews. All evidence verifies Communist claims of controlling substantially all of the countryside of "occupied" China. *End of Summary.*

Ever since the arrival of the U.S. Army Observer Section in Yenan and the establishment of direct contact with the head-quarters of the Communist armies, there has been some hesi-tancy to accept the Communist claims to have effective control of the countryside of those parts of North and Central China which are under nominal Japanese occupation. Until we had seen for ourselves, such hesitancy was justified; the extent of Communist claims surprised even those who had made efforts to collect all previously available information on their activities.

Due to lack of personnel, absence of facilities such as air assistance, and the slowness of overland travel by foot, the Ob-server Section has made relatively slow progress in inspecting the various Communist bases behind the Japanese lines. Officers of the Section have, however, covered northwest and northeast Shansi, southeast Shansi and west Hopei (including visits to the Peiping and Paoting areas).

Officers of other organizations have visited the Hankow area and north Chekiang.

But by far the greatest aid to our verification of the extent of the Communist areas has been the large number of American airmen (now some seventy) who have dropped to safety in those areas.

The attached map* shows the approximate routes traveled by American observers on assigned missions and by these rescued airmen. (Although a number of flyers have been rescued in the East River Communist area near Canton, their routes are not shown because the area is relatively small and well known.)

It will be noted that routes traveled include all of the major Communist bases except the Shantung Peninsula (which ap-parently has not been the scene of air activity). From their points of rescue some of the air crews have traveled as far as 1,000 miles through Communist-held territory.

Crews have traveled under Communist protection from the seacoast near Shanhaikuan (just south of the border of Man-churia) around Peiping to Yenan. Others have landed on the coast of north Kiangsu and traversed that province and Anhwei. Another party dropped just across the river from Nanking and was brought to Shansi.

* Not found in Department files.

The Communists have rescued men near Shanghai, Hankow, Canton, Nanking and Taiyuan—all important Japanese-held bases in China. Flyers have dropped safely within a mile of Japanese airfields or blockhouses.

Over a hundred American crossings of Japanese-held railways have been made safely.

It is axiomatic that it is difficult to hide an Anglo-Saxon traveling through China. But except when crossing railways or in areas very close to the Japanese, practically all travel was done by day without any attempt at concealment. In fact, public celebrations, mass meetings and speeches along the way were customary. Newspapers published in the base areas noted the passage of American visitors. Some of the parties did not even take the bother of exchanging their American Army uniforms for Chinese clothing.

Passage across solidly held areas of Chinese control, in which there were no Japanese forces, sometimes took a week or more of steady travel.

The rescued aviators I have had a chance to talk to have agreed with the officers of the Observer Section in their favorable impression of the Communist forces with which they had contact. The so far unequaled opportunities for extensive observation enjoyed by these men makes the collection and compilation of their reports a most important source of information concerning the Chinese Communists.

The following conclusions are now justified:

(1) We must accept as substantially correct the Communist claims to control the countryside of North and Central China behind the line of Japanese penetration.

(2) Our past consideration of this territory as "Japanese-occupied" should be revised. The Japanese hold only a thin skeleton; the rest of the area is controlled by forces on our side.

By early October 1944, after some eleven weeks in Yenan, Service was convinced of the strength and vitality of the Communist movement. By then, the initial briefings by the various military leaders had been checked and verified in any number of interviews and conversations with new-found friends like Ch'en Yi, political leaders from the guerrilla areas, downed airmen, foreign refugees from the coast, Major Casberg and the American correspondents. The conclusion of all was unanimous: here was a revolutionary movement with a political strength that would not be vanquished. On this, Service was unequivocal: in the event of a civil war, "a Communist victory will be inevitable." That was a fact which any realistic American policy toward China would have to come to terms with. Service wrote this report in his best succinct style in hopes that it might reach the eyes of the men making policy in Washington. If it ever reached them, it was ignored.

The Present Strength and Future Importance of the Chinese Communists

No. 39: October 9, 1944
Amerasia Papers, pp. 1011–13

1. There is attached a memorandum regarding the present strength and future importance of the Chinese Communists.

Summary: The Japanese are being actively and successfully opposed in Communist-controlled areas. This opposition is possible and successful because of total mobilization and unity of army and people. This in turn is possible because of a peaceful revolution under Communist leadership which has improved the political, economic and social status of the peasant. He will fight in future, if necessary, to keep these things he is fighting for now. As the Japanese cannot defeat these forces of the people, neither can the Kuomintang. Force will throw the people into the arms of the Communists; democracy will leave the Communists with a great base for political influence. The Communists are certain to play a large, if not dominant, part in China's future.   *End of Summary.*

2. At present this Communist strength, based on popular support, provides a military power for which means should be found to permit its coordination with our war against Japan.

3. But even more important is the consideration that this popular support gives the Communists political power which will make them a continuing and potent force in China. This is a fact which American policy must take into account.

THE PRESENT AND FUTURE STRENGTH
OF THE CHINESE COMMUNISTS

Reports of two American officers, several correspondents and twenty-odd foreign travelers regarding conditions in the areas of North China under Communist control are in striking agreement. This unanimity, based on actual observation, is significant. It forces us to accept certain facts, and to draw from those facts an important conclusion.

The Japanese are being actively opposed—in spite of the constant warfare and cruel retaliation this imposes on the population. This opposition is gaining in strength. The Japanese can temporarily crush it in a limited area by the concentration of overwhelming force. But it is impossible for them to do this simultaneously over the huge territory the Communists now influence.

This opposition is possible and successful because it is total guerrilla warfare aggressively waged by a totally mobilized population. In this total mobilization the regular forces of the Communists, though leaders and organizers, have become subordinate to the vastly more numerous forces of the people themselves. They exist because the people permit, support and wholeheartedly fight with them. There is complete solidarity of army and people.

This total mobilization is based upon and has been made possible by what amounts to an economic, political and social revolution. This revolution has been moderate and democratic. It has improved the economic condition of the peasants by rent-and-interest reduction, tax reform and good government. It has given them democratic self-government, political consciousness and a sense of their rights. It has freed them from feudalistic bonds and given them self-respect, self-reliance and a strong feeling of cooperative group interest. *The common people, for the first time, have been given something to fight for.*

The Japanese are being fought now not merely because

they are foreign invaders but because they deny this revolution. *The people will continue to fight any government which limits or deprives them of these newly won gains.*

Just as the Japanese army cannot crush these militant people now, so also will Kuomintang force fail in the future. With their new arms and organization, knowledge of their own strength, and determination to keep what they have been fighting for, these people—now some 90 million and certain to be many more before the Kuomintang can reach them—will resist oppression. They are not Communists. They do not want separation or independence. But at present they regard the Kuomintang—from their own experience—as oppressors, and the Communists as their leaders and benefactors.

With this great popular base, the Communists likewise cannot be eliminated. Kuomintang attempts to do so by force must mean a complete denial of democracy. This will strengthen the ties of the Communists with the people: a Communist victory will be inevitable. If, as the Communists hope, the Kuomintang turns to democracy, this established popular support will ensure influential Communist participation in national affairs. If the Kuomintang continues its present policy of quarantine without itself instituting thoroughgoing democracy, the better condition of the common people in the Communist areas will be an example constantly working in Communist favor.

From the basic fact that the Communists have built up popular support of a magnitude and depth which makes their elimination impossible, *we must draw the conclusion that the Communists will have a certain and important share in China's future.*

I suggest the further conclusion that unless the Kuomintang goes as far as the Communists in political and economic reform, and otherwise proves itself able to contest this leadership of the people (none of which it yet shows signs of being willing or able to do), the Communists will be the dominant force in China within a comparatively few years.

CHINESE COMMUNIST POLICY
TOWARD THE KUOMINTANG

In the 1940s, China was not to see a single year of peace. Throughout the long and devastating war against Japan, China lived with the specter of civil war lurking on the horizon, waiting only for the international struggle to end so that the internal battle could begin. Service's concern over this disastrous prospect was evident as early as January 23, 1943, in his memorandum on the "Kuomintang-Communist Situation," and it continued to be visible in many of his despatches from Yenan.

Civil war between the KMT and the CCP was clearly not in the best interests of the United States. If it broke out before the end of the war against Japan, it would destroy all possibility of effective resistance to Japan on the mainland. Even if postponed until the end of the war, a civil war which both sides regarded as either inevitable or desirable meant that both would save their strength for the coming showdown rather than use it against Japan. Already there was incontrovertible evidence that the KMT held back large quantities of U.S. arms instead of committing them against the Japanese during the 1944 offensive in Central China. There were also clear humanitarian reasons which made the United States—and especially a man like Service, who had spent so much of his life in China—anxious to spare that country from the ravages of another bloody war. Finally, Service was convinced that in a civil war the Communists would be the certain victors. Given the long exclusive American support of the Kuomintang, there was no reason to believe that a victorious CCP would have friendly feelings toward the United States.

If civil war was to be avoided, the only alternative path was negotiations. The KMT and the CCP had been involved in sporadic negotiations since the initiation of the United Front in 1937. After the New Fourth Army incident, efforts to bring the two sides together temporarily collapsed. Armed conflict between the two sides increased. In October 1942, Lin Piao joined the CCP's permanent representative in Chungking, Chou En-lai, in an attempt to work out a *modus vivendi* with the KMT. No progress was made, and with tensions between the two parties increasing notably in 1943, Lin and Chou both returned to Yenan in June. For a while it seemed that the KMT, at least, was bent on immediate conflict, but a September speech by Chiang Kai-shek, in which he told the KMT Central Executive Committee that "the Communist problem is purely a political problem and should be solved by political means," helped significantly to cool things down.

In May 1944, Lin Pai-ch'ü (also known as Lin Tsu-han), the Chairman of the Border Region government, flew to Sian and then Chungking to resume negotiations with the KMT. The selection of Lin rather than the higher-ranking Chou En-lai indicated the CCP's doubts of the KMT's willingness to reach a genuine settlement. Equally significant was the fact that the Communists' proposals were now notably stronger than before. Whereas in 1942–1943 Lin Piao had asked KMT authorization of only twelve divisions in four armies, in 1944 Lin Pai-ch'ü wanted eighteen divisions in six armies. As Communist strength continued to increase rapidly in 1944, the Communists' negotiating posture grew correspondingly tough. Service's despatches from Yenan reflect that progressive hardening of CCP policy. While he initially wrote of the CCP's "policy of self-limitation," a month later he would speak of the Communists' "refusal of reconciliation" with the KMT.

Some of the first real indicators of CCP policy toward the KMT were the interviews that Mao and the other Communist leaders had granted to foreign correspondents then in Yenan. Many of these reporters were close friends of Service's, and they allowed him to copy their notes of the interviews. Several feared that stories filed from Chungking would be blocked by the KMT censors, and they were anxious that news of these interviews get out. Service's despatch, transmitting their interviews and two interviews of his own, is the longest he sent from Yenan (28 pages in printed form). Since much of the material is repeated in talks Service himself later had with Mao and others, the correspondents' interviews and Service's interview with Chou En-lai have been severely edited here. Still, these interviews include important statements on CCP-KMT relations, and sections are reproduced. Service's interview with Lin Piao is printed in its entirety.

Views of Communist Political and Military Leaders

No. 3: July 30, 1944
Amerasia Papers, pp. 690–717

1. There are transmitted memoranda of the following interviews and conversations with prominent Communist political and military leaders:

    a. Mao Tse-tung, July 14, Interview with Guenther Stein.

    b. Mao Tse-tung, July 18, Interview with Maurice Votaw.

    c. Chou En-lai, July 28, Conversation with the undersigned.

    d. Gen. Chu Teh, June 25, Interview with Guenther Stein.*

    e. Gen. Chu Teh, July 8, Interview with Guenther Stein.

    f. Gen. Chu Teh, July 15, Interview with Maurice Votaw.*

    g. Gen. Chu Teh, July 21, Interview with I. Epstein.

    h. Gen. Lin Piao, July 27, Conversation with the undersigned.

2. It is believed that these interviews, most of which were given privately and off-the-record to the foreign correspondents now at Yenan, provide an authoritative and up-to-date summarization of the views of the Communist leaders in regard to relations between the Kuomintang and the Communist Party, the conduct of the war against Japan, and most of the political and economic problems confronting China. . . .

[a.]
EXCERPTS FROM GUENTHER STEIN'S NOTES OF INTERVIEW
WITH MAO TSE-TUNG, JULY 14, 1944

During its twenty-three years of history the Chinese Communist Party has not changed its fundamental or basic policy.

---

* Not printed.

There have been superficial changes on account of the coming together or falling apart of classes or political groups within the country.

This basic policy is New Democracy—carrying out the revolution of national independence, democracy and people's livelihood, by the masses of the Chinese people and on the basis of private property.

The Kuomintang carried out its "purge" of 1927 because the Communist Party was resolutely carrying out this program of New Democracy as embodied in Sun Yat-sen's Manifesto of the First Kuomintang Congress. The Kuomintang was afraid.

We were forced to go into the hills. Our guerrilla warfare grew from small to large scale. During this period we practiced the Soviet system, but on a democratic—not the socialist Soviet—basis. We did not confiscate all capitalistic private property; on the contrary, we protected it. We only confiscated land of feudal landlords to distribute to peasants, who then held it as their own. We did not organize collective farms because that would have been impossible in China. The slogan that tillers should own their own land was Sun Yat-sen's. Wallace on his recent trip has said the same thing. . . .

In the past seven years we have followed the Gmo's* division of tasks: the KMT to take care of the regular fronts; we to take care of the rear. In fact, there are two battlefields in China: front and rear. We have persuaded the peasants not to confiscate land, and the landlords to accept reduction in rents in order to win over the landlords to our fight against Japan. The one-to-three system† is also to unite the landlords and capitalists against Japan. . . .

Our old program of land confiscation—modified inasmuch as the landlord got a share—was not bad at the time. The basic demand of the masses was concentrated on their desire for land. Sun Yat-sen advocated it. But it is not suitable to wartime because the landlords wish to be anti-Japanese, but a policy of confiscation may drive them into the other camp. The peasants see the simple truth that rent reduction makes it pos-

---

* Generalissimo Chiang Kai-shek.

† Also known as the "three-thirds system," whereby local government councils were to be 1/3 Communist, 1/3 Kuomintang and 1/3 non-Party members.

sible for the landlords to remain, and helps to isolate the Japanese. After a few experiences of land confiscation in some areas early in the war, the peasants saw that this policy ultimately harmed them. A policy of rent concessions by the landlord and guarantee of payment of rent by the tenant results in successful and genuine cooperation. This policy is not merely opportunistic; it is the only possible one.

This policy was first suggested by comrades in lower Party organizations. It was adopted as a Party policy. If China is democratized and there is a parliament, it might be made law all over the country. If this rent reduction is carried out all over the country, it will of course be a great advance. But it will still be a step behind ownership by the tillers. However, under a democratic system there will be means to consider peaceful and gradual transfer of ownership. For example landlords may be able to transfer investments into industrial development. The important thing is that we can devise methods beneficial to both sides.

The possibility of confiscation cannot be ruled out, because it depends on internal peace. Civil war will probably be followed by outright confiscation—by the masses themselves.

Of course there were brutalities during the civil war. We had many different kinds of people. But we learned the value of magnanimity, and which policies were correct and which incorrect. "Man's experience is practical dialectics." Actually the principle of private ownership was well protected in the villages in the Soviet period. Only a few childish comrades tried to establish collective farms. But these cases were rectified because the peasants were against it. The policy of free trade was practiced in the cities. Goods were taxed only once. There was a progressive tax according to profits. In many cases no taxes were collected in order to help trade to develop. A few overzealous comrades in isolated areas overtaxed trade and ultimately suffered loss by it, because we needed trade. Not only confiscation of merchants' goods but also of profits is suicidal.

It is a matter of mutual benefit to adopt proper treatment of capital after the war. This applies not only to Chinese capital but also to foreign capital. Private capital must have opportunity for broad, liberal development. We need industrial development. We want to substitute the principle of free trade between nations for the Jap principle of colonization of China. We should substitute the policy of developing modern industries, raising the productive power of the peasants and increasing purchasing power for the policy of curbing development of industry and worsening the living conditions of the peasants to the point of causing them to lose interest in developing production: of industrial progress instead of industrial backwardness. (This is a reference to the working of present KMT economic policies.) It is our hope that the peasants, after procuring land, will have more interest in increasing productivity. . . .

We have three irrevocable demands: fight against Japan, democracy, national unity.

The North China masses do not want the reduction in our armies that the KMT now insists upon. There is no one to hold our positions if our armies are to be reduced.

After the war there should be proportional demobilization on a ratio of six KMT men to one Communist soldier.

The people of China's 19,000 villages should elect 19,000 village governments. Then the governments above will be elected either by direct suffrage or by representatives of the people, according to Sun Yat-sen. Election and service should be regardless of Party membership. The Manifesto of the First Kuomintang Congress means democracy, that the government belongs to the people and cannot be monopolized by the few. These problems are simple if we follow Sun Yat-sen. . . .

There is no likelihood of a complete breakdown of the National Government before the end of the war.

If the Kuomintang attacks us, we will retreat a little. If they continue to attack us, we will fight. We will have to defend ourselves. We will never fire the first shot. We must do everything to prevent incidents. The Chinese people, the majority of the Kuomintang, and the Allied powers should try to prevent them. CKS would not welcome allied mediation.

It is still early to discuss an Allied Supreme Commander. CKS probably would not agree to Allied command and would want only foreign advisers. We would be willing but the Allies would first have to have the approval of CKS. . . .

. . . We accept critically the long tradition of China—inheriting that which is good and rejecting that which is bad. We do the same with things coming from abroad. We have accepted such things as Darwinism; the democracy exemplified by Washington and Lincoln; the eighteenth-century philosophy of France; the materialism of Feuerbach; Marxism from Germany; and Leninism from Russia. We accept anything from abroad that can be good for and useful to China. We reject bad things, such as Fascism. Such things as the type of Communism practiced in Russia are not to be adopted in China, for the conditions in China are not ripe. Conditions are not present for the introduction of Communism. But if there is something good, we do not refuse to accept it for fear of criticism. Science knows no boundaries. . . .

In political science we have learned democracy from abroad. But Chinese history, too, has its democratic tradition. The term Republican was originated in the Chou Dynasty 3,000 years ago. Mencius said: First the people, then the State, then the Emperor. The Chinese peasant has a rich democratic tradition. The hundreds of large and small peasant wars have been rich in democratic meaning. An example from history is described in the famous novel *Shui Hu Chuan*. The question of adopting proper forms in accepting and evaluating Chinese history and foreign conditions is very important. There must not be blind following. The one-to-three system of government representation suits present and actual conditions in China. . . .

Since July 1943, when conditions around the Border Area became tense, there have been no large-scale attacks by Kuomintang troops. But there have been continuous acts of disruption and disturbances on the part of the blockading troops. From January 1944 to April 1944 there were seventy-three such cases. This is an average of two every three days.

The Communist Party has no intention whatsoever of overthrowing the rule of the Kuomintang. I have explained to the Chinese correspondents that we sincerely wish that the Kuomintang would make progress. Progress by the Kuomintang would be beneficial to the people and the nation, and also the Communist Party. . . .

We have criticized the National army and conditions in Kuomintang China. But we believe in criticism and constantly and seriously criticize ourselves. Our only limitation is that the criticism must have a valid cause. Before July 1943 we withheld our criticism of the Kuomintang for a long time, because we hoped that relations between the two parties would be improved. Then there was the July incident (of the Kuomintang military threat) and we therefore had quite extensive criticism during July, August and September. In September 1943 the 11th Plenary Session of the Kuomintang advocated that differences with the Communist Party should be settled by political means. From then until May of this year we refrained from criticism. Recent criticism is for the following reasons: first, that our army did not fight well and resist the enemy offensive; second, criticisms from Washington and London were much sharper than our own and pointed out the danger of China stopping her resistance. They spoke of the danger of collapse, and the fact that the loss of Hengyang will result in prolongation of the war and the sacrifice of more American lives. We have not yet said these things in our articles. Also the newspapers in the Great Rear [KMT areas] were strong in their criticisms. We criticize because of the seriousness of the situation for the nation. But the Kuomintang press continues to put out slanders and calumnies against us, that we are murderers and arsonists, that we have made a secret agreement with the Japanese. By comparison with what has been said against us, I would say that we have been very polite. . . .

In 1927 the Kuomintang carried out a "purge," driving the Communists from the army, party and government. On April 12, 1927, the dissolution of the trade unions began. After the purge the civil war began. The great majority of the National army was sent on military expeditions against the Communists. The system of political work in the Kuomintang armies was abolished; with it came a lowering of morale.

In 1937 came the restoration of Communist-Kuomintang cooperation. Its practical effectiveness was seen in the early stage of the war of resistance. Political work in the army was restored. No Communist work was permitted in the Kuomintang armies but it was carried on there by a great number of youths. The patriotic work of the people and popular movements, though under restrictions, were allowed to develop.

Therefore during these two years the morale of the Kuomintang was comparatively good. After the fall of Wuhan the Japanese changed their policy. Their main attack was shifted to the Communist forces. Toward the Kuomintang their policy was enticement. The Kuomintang alleged that the Communists intended to make peace with Japan. But the Japanese, knowing the impossibility of this, never said anything of the kind. Instead they openly declared that the Communists were their main enemy. Then the 5th Plenary Session of the Kuomintang in 1939 passed a resolution to curb the Communist Party. Since then an anti-Communist atmosphere has undone the coordination of 1937–1938. Not only the Communist Party but the people also have had to face oppression and suppression. In the army, political education for nationalism was greatly cut down; education for democracy was reduced to nought. Not only this: there has been a great deal of anti-Communist education in the army. As a result conditions have worsened: relations between the officers and the men, and between the army and the people, have deteriorated.

In order to change the situation we must go to the root of the trouble. It is necessary for the Kuomintang to revise its fundamental policy. It must adopt a policy of unity with the people in the fields of politics and economics. Only then can the military situation change. I sincerely hope you and all other friends desirous of helping the Chinese people will help the Kuomintang to realize the new situation. Our hopes are for unity and democracy.

Naturally the Generalissimo is recognized as the President of China. We have and will continue to stick to our promises. First, not to overthrow the Kuomintang. Second, not to confiscate land. Third, our democratically elected governments to be local governments under the National Government. Fourth, our troops to be part of the National army under the National Military Council.

[c.]

REPORT BY JOHN S. SERVICE OF CONVERSATION WITH
CHOU EN-LAI, JULY 28, 1944

I called by invitation on General Chou En-lai on the morning of July 27 and spent about three hours in private conversation with him. General Chou, who was for several years the Communist representative in Chungking, is usually referred to in Yenan as "Vice Chairman." Apparently, however, his only official or Party post is that of member of the Politbureau, or Standing Committee, of the Central Executive Committee of the Chinese Communist Party. His influence in the political councils of the Party is reputedly second only to Mao Tse-tung, and if the Communists had a foreign minister he would be the most likely candidate. Having known him for some time in Chungking, our conversation was from the start on a very frank and cordial basis. Too long to report in detail, I mention only the gist of details of possible interest.

I mentioned that the morning's Chungking broadcast had carried a statement by the Government spokesman (given at the press conference of July 26) that considerable progress had been made in the Kuomintang-Communist negotiations. Chou appeared amused. He pointed out that the Kuomintang terms of June 5, which had been presented in answer to the Communist proposals of May 22 (presented by Lin [Pai-ch'ü] in Chungking on that date, refused by the Kuomintang delegates, then later forwarded by letter from Lin) left little ground for agreement. The Communists find particularly unacceptable the Kuomintang's refusal of any political commitments (except the vague promise of "after the war"); the demand that the Communist armies be limited to ten divisions (100,000 men) and the remainder (370,000) be *disbanded* (even though they are holding territory against the enemy); and that all territory now held by the Communists in excess of that authorized (presumably all territory south of the old course of the Yellow River) be turned over to the Central Government (even though its inability to hold them has been proved in the past and it now is unable to get forces into them).

When it became obvious after the Kuomintang submitted its terms that a great deal of negotiation would be necessary, the Communists asked the Kuomintang to send suitably authorized representatives to Yenan to talk with the top Communists. The Kuomintang refused. The Communists then suggested that Lin Tsu-han return to Yenan for consultation. The Kuomintang then used every sort of pressure to prevent Lin from leaving Chungking.

It is apparent that the Kuomintang will not make reasonable concessions, that a compromise is impossible, and that the

Kuomintang has entered into the talks primarily for their propaganda value and to make an impression on foreign opinion, especially American. Here and several times later he referred to the Kuomintang as completely unrealistic. . . .

In 1944 the Kuomintang's two alternatives are to seek compromise on its own terms or to continue to delay. Even though there was little hope of the first being successful, nothing would be lost and there would be gains from the propaganda standpoint.

Delay, in the mind of the Kuomintang, means an eventual conflict. The Kuomintang hopes that it will be in a position at the end of the war, with newly reorganized, trained and equipped armies, to liquidate the Communists in a summary fashion.

The Communists do not welcome this delay in settling their difficulties with the Kuomintang because their only objective is the speedy defeat of Japan. To accomplish this there must be democratization and mobilization of the country. They will not, therefore, agree to giving up what they have accomplished toward these ends. And if the Kuomintang prefers delay to present settlement, the Communists do not fear it because they know that they are getting stronger as the Kuomintang gets weaker and because the Kuomintang, if it continues its present course, cannot mobilize the popular support which it will need. . . .

We turned to discussion of conditions in Kuomintang China, and after Chou described the tendency there in gloomy (but not particularly new) terms, I asked his opinion regarding the likelihood of a collapse. In reply he suggested that Kuomintang China was more like a tuberculosis patient than a man suffering from a disease such as cholera; that there would continue to be a steady decline; but that there probably would be no sudden break or collapse. (He liked this tuberculosis analogy and used it again later.)

[Chou's estimate of Japanese aims in their current offensive follows here.]

As gloomy as the situation admittedly is, Chou thought that it would get worse and that the Generalissimo would wait until then before taking any drastic action. He emphasized that the Generalissimo did not face problems until forced to (as at Sian in 1936), that he was an opportunistic drifter, that he was surrounded by unbelievably stupid, second-rate men (as one of many examples he pointed to the selection of "empty-headed" Shang Chen as military representative in Washington), and that there were obvious shortcomings in his education and understanding of such things as democracy and economics. Nonetheless, he insisted, the hope is still present, although small, that the Generalissimo will "see the light" and make an about-face. But if the Generalissimo does not do this before next year, it will be "too late."

[Chou then discussed reforms which he felt the KMT should carry out.]

I asked his ideas on what the United States could do to help China. He believed that press comment and criticism, even though not liked by the people in power, were still influential. An even better means, however, of making our influence felt might be through personal contacts at very high levels. Wallace's visit had been very useful; we should use the opportunity to work hard on H. H. Kung while he is in the United States. We would find Kung a much more useful person in this respect than T. V. Soong.

Having in mind Chu Teh's suggestion to Stein of an Allied Supreme Commander in China, I asked whether this would be advisable or practical. He replied with a strong affirmative but qualified it by saying that the time for the suggestion had not yet come; we should wait until American supplies and men are coming into China in significant magnitude and the counteroffensive is actually in sight. The Commander should be American and would be welcomed by the Communists, if agreed to by the Central Government.

Regarding the possible enlargement of the scope of activities of the present Observer Section, Chou said that such expansion toward active collaboration would of course be welcomed by the Communists but would, unless there was a radical change, be opposed by the Central Government. However, the door was now opened a crack and it might be possible, by following a slow and careful course, to move toward modified collaboration. For this reason the granting of permission for the Observer Group was a milestone. (I was interested that here, as well as in other parts of the conversation, Chou was careful to recognize the authority of the Central Government and the at least potential leadership of the Generalissimo. He obviously had no expectation that we were going to immediately start on a program of direct support of the Communist forces.)

Chou was interested in a number of subjects: Wallace's views; American-Soviet relations; reports of efforts to improve Sino-Soviet relations; American progress in the Pacific; and American views in regard to the future strategy of the war against Japan. He refused to accept my suggestion that internal deterioration in China and our rapidly growing naval strength would reduce the importance of the China theater of land warfare. His opinion was that the Japanese army in China and Manchuria would still have to be defeated. He seemed to think that Russia would eventually enter the Far Eastern war but avoided committing himself. . . .

[e.]

EXCERPTS FROM INTERVIEW OF GENERAL CHU TEH WITH GUENTHER STEIN, JULY 8, 1944

(Interview given for publication, but permission to release later canceled by General Chu.)

"The China theater must be brought under one Allied Supreme Commander for the sake of the counteroffensive against Japan. . . . I don't hesitate to say that in the interest of the fullest unification of our armies under Generalissimo Chiang Kai-shek, an impartial inter-Allied command is absolute necessity both for China and for the Allies, both for victory and postwar peace.

"The Chinese people would welcome an inter-Allied high command and cooperate wholeheartedly with it as we would ourselves. In fact, this is what they hope for, because their two only objectives in the war are the same as those of the Allies —that is: the quickest possible common victory and democracy. No, they will not consider anything like 'loss of face' as being involved, just as the British people do not mind American high command. They see the necessity for inter-Allied direction of the war against Japan and realize that the Chinese high command is unqualified to command modern allied forces.

"Thorough reorganization of the Central Government's armies by Generalissimo Chiang Kai-shek on basis of genuine democratic reform of Government's policies, with adoption of fair measures for equal treatment of all armies of China in connection with full understanding between Chungking and Yenan, would of course help very much indeed. But unfortunately this is still no more than a hope as yet. Even when and if this hope comes true, the urgent necessity for Allied supreme command still remains. It should in fact be Allied command of all operations against Japan. . . ."

[g.]
EXCERPTS FROM CHU TEH INTERVIEW BY I. EPSTEIN, JULY 21, 1944

Epstein opens with an introductory description of the Communist army and the country in which it operates. He goes on to a description of Chu Teh which I find rather good in catching the unassuming, simple and homely character of the man.

"Chu Teh himself is a stocky, shambling, kindly man of fifty-eight with a head of thick black hair and large tranquil eyes setting off a broad face whose understanding simplicity has almost invariably reminded observers of the main characteristics of Abraham Lincoln. Nothing in his appearance suggests the intrepid field leader and strategist of some of the world's boldest and bitterest military campaigns. Rather, he looks like everybody's father come home after a long hard satisfying day's work, leaning back in unbuttoned relaxation and talking with a quiet smile and ripe homespun wisdom of things he knows so well from experience so long and intimate that they have become part of him. . . ."

[In answer to Epstein's question on the present military situation in China, and possibilities of its improvement, Chu Teh said:]

The improvement of China's situation can come only through change of political, economic, military policies, including . . . establishment of a democratic political structure based on the United Front. Militarily, stop should be put to present civil war indoctrination so that all troops have only one aim—to defeat the enemy—and the spy system in the army should be abolished. Under these conditions and with Allied help in equipment to both fronts ("regular" and behind the lines) we can achieve consolidation and simultaneous counterattack in front and rear of enemy. . . .

Our guerrillas with supplies could—if supplied properly—damage many more of these than an equal weight of bombs. The tactical employment of aircraft in coordination with ground troops should play a subordinate role until the ground troops are sufficiently improved to cooperate with the air force and render such cooperation fruitful. . . .

[h.]
REPORT BY JOHN S. SERVICE OF CONVERSATION WITH LIN PIAO, JULY 27, 1944

At the dinner last evening I met General Lin Piao, commander of the 115th Division of the Eighteenth Group Army. He remembered our meetings in Chungking in November 1942 and May 1943 while he was there in a vain attempt to settle points of friction between the Central Government and the Communist armies.

General Lin spoke with some heat of those wasted months and dryly remarked that Lin Tsu-han was now having the same experience. He described the Kuomintang as without any sincere intention of coming to an agreement and bitterly referred to the Kuomintang demand that the Communist armies be drastically reduced as the equivalent of helping the Japanese by turning over to them the guerrilla zones of North and Central China.

General Lin, who was the commander of the Communist forces in the 1937 victory of Pinghsingkuan, went on to say that reports from the front indicated that fighting quality of the Japanese troops in North China had deteriorated considerably in the past two or three years; that Communist operations this year had been very successful; and that a great deal more could have been accomplished if the Communists had had more and better arms.

I was called away to meet someone else and our conversation did not last more than ten minutes.

The conversation seems worth reporting for two reasons:

1. The Communist military leaders whom we have met so far have been very circumspect in avoiding direct pleas for arms and equipment. They seem conscientiously to avoid giving any impression of "begging." The familiar refrain of "tanks, planes and heavy artillery" is noticeable by its absence. General Lin's remarks are as close as I have heard to a definite statement of the desire to receive arms.

2. It is my impression—confirmed by the experience of the newspaper correspondents who have been in Yenan for six weeks and who have interviewed most of the leading Communist figures—that the military leaders are far more outspoken in their bitterness and criticism of the Central Government than are the civilian leaders such as Mao Tse-tung and Chou En-lai. The "Party line" at present seems to avoid direct criticism of the Generalissimo and the Kuomintang. There are reports that there are occasional difficulties in keeping the military men in line with this policy and that several "reprimands" have had to be given. This divergency between the civilian and the military attitude was apparent when Lin Piao was in Chungking in 1942, just as it is apparent now.

———————

Service's first analytical despatch on CCP-KMT relations was a very preliminary attempt to interpret the Communists' United Front tactic. It was based in large measure on conversations he had had with Michael Lindsay and Guenther Stein, both of whom had been in the Border Region far longer than he. While it is perhaps the most speculative and least persuasive piece of analysis Service did on the CCP, it does reflect the fact that the Communists' preferred path to power was unquestionably through intermediate stages, such as coalition government with an ability to control their own areas. Of all the Communist leaders, Mao Tse-tung was the man who throughout his career had been most inclined toward the tactic of the United Front, and in 1944 he seemed anxious to continue the tactic. Service here asks the question: Why?

The Communist Policy toward the Kuomintang

No. 5: August 3, 1944
Foreign Relations, 1944, pp. 562–67

While there are a large number of political subjects of great importance to be observed in the Communist areas (such as the form of their governments, their political program, and their political indoctrination of the people), the problem of greatest immediate urgency, and the only one which I have had as yet even a slight opportunity of studying, is the attitude of the Communist Party toward its differences with the Kuomintang.

In comment on a conversation with General Lin Piao, a memorandum of which was attached to my report No. 3 of July 30, I noted the outspoken and apparently irreconcilable bitterness of the Communist military leaders toward the Generalissimo and the Kuomintang as contrasting with the more moderate and reserved attitude of the civilian political leaders.

The policy of these political leaders, who appear to have unquestioned control over the military leaders in policy matters, continues to be: adherence to the United Front; full mobilization to fight Japan; abandonment of any purely Communist program; and recognition of the Central Government and the leadership of the Generalissimo. This attitude has been clearly expressed by Mao Tse-tung in recent interviews and by Chou En-lai in his talk with me on July 27, memoranda of which were also transmitted with my report No. 3.

This professed policy of the Communist Party presents a number of anomalies. It is generally assumed, for instance, that the driving power of any political party is the struggle for political power. This should be even more true of a Communist party which, theoretically at least, is revolutionary in nature. Why, then, at a time when it is apparently growing in strength, and in the face of the obvious and serious deterioration in China and the growingly questionable capacity for leadership of the Kuomintang and the Generalissimo, should the Communist Party insist on a policy of self-limitation? Certainly the Kuomintang has given ample provocation for it to give up its adherence to the United Front. And it would seem that conditions in Kuomintang China had reached such a stage that further effective resistance against Japan is doubtful under its leadership and the Party might reasonably be justified in playing its own hand. Instead of holding mass meetings and offering to send troops to defend Sian (as was done during the critical period in the middle of June), would it not be more logical for the Communists to hope for, or even work for, the defeat and collapse of the Kuomintang?

The question therefore presents itself: Are the Communists sincere in this policy?

The indications are that they are sincere. Except for the months from July to September 1943, when they seriously thought they were in danger of attack by the Kuomintang, they have not talked of violent opposition to the Kuomintang. Impartial observers have never been convinced of Communist attacks on Government forces. But there have been instances of Kuomintang attacks. And the Kuomintang's record of its relations with the puppets and even the Japanese in those guerrilla areas does not bear close examination. The Communists steadfastly stick to the line that civil war would be a tragedy which must be avoided at any cost—although some observers believe that it would be difficult if not impossible for the Kuomintang to defeat them. They will not permit any suggestion that China should be divided or that they should hold one section of it, such as North China, more or less independently. Propaganda wall slogans in Yenan (long antedating our arrival) call for both parties to unite to resist Japan. There are reports that military leaders too outspoken in their criticism of the Central Government have been required to temper their statements—similarly some Party members have been disciplined for becoming "left deviationists" by going beyond the Party line in advocating such reforms as collective farms. Finally and very significantly, even the Kuomintang has not made more than weak and unconvincing efforts to claim that the Communists have attempted to foment or capitalize on the agrarian unrest in Kuomintang China, or that there is any large-scale Communist activity outside of the areas of their military operations in North and East China.

What, then, is the explanation of this Communist policy? And what is their expectation of their place in China during the fairly near future—say the next few decades?

I suggest that there may be two explanations of Communist policy. The first, based on theoretical grounds, is the one given by the Party leaders (though never, as far as I know, completely to any one foreign observer). The second, arising out of practical political considerations, may be too cynical and would certainly be rejected by those leaders. Both, I think, make some sense. And both would seem to show that the Party is under far-sighted, careful leadership and strong discipline.

Theoretical Explanation of Communist Policy

The Chinese Communist Party claims that it is Marxist. By this the Communists mean that their ideology, their philosophical approach and their dialectical method are based on Marxist materialism. Marxism thus becomes to them chiefly an attitude and approach to problems. It is a long-term view of political and economic development to which all short-term considerations of temporary advantage or premature power are ruthlessly subordinated.

This interpretation of Marxist materialism means to them a certain logical development of economic society. It also means that this natural sequence cannot be short-circuited. To try to do so would be disastrous and a violation of their basic principles of strategy.

Thus socialism, in their view, cannot be evolved at one jump from the present primitive agrarian society of China. It can come only after considerable development of the Chinese economy and after it has passed through a stage of at least modified capitalism.

Their Communism, therefore, does not mean the immediate overthrow of private capital—because there is still almost no capitalism in China. It does not mean the dictatorship of the proletariat—because there is as yet no proletariat. It does not mean the collectivization of farms—because the political education of the peasants has not yet overcome their primitive individualistic desire to till their own land.

Furthermore, the Communists see the existence of their politically advanced party in an economically backward country as a unique opportunity to so lead and direct economic development that the abuses of capitalism which lead to violent revolution can be avoided. The problem is to have the economic revolution catch up to and keep pace with the more rapid political revolution. By democracy, they hope to prevent the exploitation of the working and peasant classes and the need for class revolution. By orderly and progressive solution of China's basic land question, they seek to remove the possibility of a land revolution. By the encouragement of such institutions as cooperatives, they can assist productive development in a way suitable to a country lacking in capital, modern industry and communications, and at the same time educate the people toward socialism. By encouragement of private capital, they can increase national wealth and raise the standard of living, but at the same time, by democratic controls, avoid the abuses of powerful private monopolies that have created problems in purely capitalistic states.

All facets of present Communist policies seem to fit into this framework. For instance: the substitution of rent reduction for the former policy of confiscation not only helps to keep the support of the landlord interests and to unify all groups in support of the war, it also serves to make industrial investment more attractive to the landlord-capitalist class by restricting their profits from land investment. The policy is already having this effect in the North Shensi Border Region.

So although the Chinese Communist Party aims at eventual socialism, it hopes to arrive at this not through a violent revolution, but through a long and orderly process of democracy and controlled economic development. This democracy will be of a progressive—or what would generally be called radical—type. The economic development will be partly socialistic, partly private. The first is essential to the second: the desired economic development can come about only under democracy.

This long-term approach therefore determines for the Communists their present policy toward the Kuomintang. Since they believe in democracy, they advocate multiparty participation in politics. They accordingly seek compromise with the Kuomintang and hope that the progressive elements within the Kuomintang will rise to the occasion to make such a compromise possible. To this end, they refuse to exploit what seems to be a present opportunity to seek the overthrow of the Kuomintang. And for this reason they seek to avoid civil war; even if they win after a long struggle, the country's development will be set back by loss of time and destruction of resources.

At the same time, the Communists take the view that this

desirable compromise with the Kuomintang will be wasted if they are forced to give up the progress that they have already made toward these democratic goals. Therefore, while they accept provocation and abuse, they will make no concessions of principle, because to make such concessions would be a violation of their long-term policy and a turning back in the pursuit of their ultimate objectives.

By this view the Communist Party becomes a party seeking orderly democratic growth toward socialism—as it is being attained, for instance, in a country like England—rather than a party fomenting an immediate and violent revolution. It becomes a party which is not seeking an early monopoly of political power but pursuing what it considers the long-term interests of China. It bases this seemingly "idealistic" policy on a rigid interpretation of materialism, which holds it to be a violation of those materialistic principles to attempt to force the country into socialism before the natural development of the country's economy makes socialism possible.

Practical Explanation of Communist Policy

Almost everything that the Communist Party is doing and advocating can also be explained from a practical point of view. This starts from the assumption that the Party is actually seeking power and that this aim provides the motivation for its policies. In very brief and exaggerated form this interpretation might be as follows.

The Communists actively support the war because this gives them an opportunity to mobilize, organize and indoctrinate the people, and to create and train an efficient army.

They operate by preference in the areas behind the Japanese lines because there they are relatively free from Kuomintang interference.

Such policies as the abandonment of land confiscation are useful temporary expedients to help them carry on the war and to win unified popular support in the areas of their operations. It also has strong propaganda appeal in other areas.

Their espousal of democracy appeals to the great majority of the people of China and is a good club for beating the Kuomintang. They realize that popular support must be their principal weapon against the superior arms of the Kuomintang in any contest of strength.

271   The Communist Areas

Their democratic claims, their engagement in guerrilla warfare behind the enemy lines, and their proclamation of liberal economic policies based on private property are also useful in appealing to foreign sympathy and in winning the foreign support which they realize will be necessary, at least for a time, in the economic rehabilitation and development of China following the war.

At present, time is working in favor of the Communists. As conditions in the rest of China worsen and the Kuomintang becomes weaker, the Communists, both relatively and absolutely, are growing stronger. It is unnecessary, therefore, for them to take active steps to capitalize on this situation in Kuomintang China. They can afford to sit back and wait. If things continue as they are now going, time will bring the collapse of the Kuomintang, leaving the Communists the strongest force in China. They will then be free, immediately or gradually as circumstances seem to dictate, to revert to their program of Communism.

Comment

It is difficult to make a clear-cut choice between these two explanations of Communist policy. It is probable that something of both enter into the actual formulation of Communist strategy. The bellicoseness of the Communist generals inclines one toward acceptance of the second explanation. Even the almost over-adroitness of the Communists in the field of public relations and propaganda inclines one at times to be suspicious of them.

But on the other hand, the apparently genuine attempts of the Communists to avoid any civil war now or after the present war are hard to fit into the second explanation. And the impressive personal qualities of the Communist leaders, their seeming sincerity, and the coherence and logical nature of their program lead me, at least, toward general acceptance of the first explanation—that the Communists base their policy toward the Kuomintang on a real desire for democracy in China under which there can be orderly economic growth through a stage of private enterprise to eventual socialism without the need of violent social upheaval and revolution.

If this view is correct, it follows that the policies of the Chinese Communist Party will not run counter to the interests of the United States in China in the foreseeable future, and that the Party merits, so far as possible, a sympathetic and friendly attitude on our part.

Service's next despatch on Communist-Kuomintang relations, less than two weeks after his analysis of the CCP policy of "self-limitation," dealt specifically with the negotiating terms of the two parties. The Communist terms had been spelled out in a statement by Chou En-lai, printed in the Communist Party organ, *Chieh-fang jih-pao* (*Liberation Daily*). We have printed here only portions of Service's brief covering despatch to the translation of Chou's statement. The despatch is particularly interesting not only for its stress on the "tough and hard-boiled" Communist stance but also for what it reveals about the remarkable informality and frankness with which the Communist leaders soon came to treat Service: he was present while Mao and Chou discussed the content of the proposed statement and the manner of its release.

Statement by Chou En-lai on Kuomintang-Communist Negotiations

No. 9: August 14, 1944
Amerasia Papers, pp. 739–46

1. Attached is a translation* of a statement by General Chou En-lai regarding the present state of the current Kuomintang-Communist negotiations. This statement was published in the *Chieh-fang jih-pao,* the official organ of the Chinese Communist Party at Yenan, on August 13, 1944. It is a complete history, from the Communist point of view, of the negotiations, and a clear summarization of the main points of difference between the two parties. . . .

Chou En-lai's authorship, and the publication of the statement—in the most prominent position—in the *Chieh-fang jih-pao,* are sufficient indication of its importance. Moreover,

* Not printed.

I happened to be present on August 11 when General Chou and Chairman Mao Tse-tung together decided to issue the statement and agreed on its general outline. It is interesting that they discarded the suggestion that it be issued through an interview with the foreign correspondents now in Yenan. . . .

5. The strong tone of General Chou's statement, as well as other recent publicity, such as charges that General Yen Hsi-shan is having dealings with the Japanese (being reported on separately) and the August 12 editorial in the *Chieh-fang jih-pao* on the fall of Hengyang (reported in my No. 8 of August 13*), would seem—superficially at least—to be indications that the Communist Party has either abandoned hope of, or is no longer interested in, the success of its negotiations with the Kuomintang. But Communist leaders themselves deny this. They admit that chances look slim but insist that they still desire a settlement. The Kuomintang, however, understands only one thing—force. Therefore, after having tried to be reasonable, the time has now come to be tough and hard-boiled. This tactic has a better chance of success with the Kuomintang leaders than continued argument and discussion. (This is the gist of views expressed by several Communists, including General Ch'en Yi, acting commander of the New Fourth Army, with whom I had a private conversation this afternoon.)

My own opinion is as follows. The Communists would be glad to have a reconciliation with the Kuomintang—but only on the basis of something very closely approaching their own terms. They have decided that the Kuomintang is not going to make any substantial concessions or try to meet those terms. They are therefore now chiefly concerned with trying to "get the jump" on the Kuomintang in preventing the Kuomintang from trying to create the impression that the Communists are responsible for failure to come to an agreement.

In September, the Communists publicly revealed, first in a speech by Lin Pai-ch'ü (Lin Tsu-han) to the People's Political Council in Chungking, then in a *Liberation Daily* article, the critical issue on

* Not printed.

which negotiations were stalled. That issue was the reorganization of the Chungking Government into a genuine coalition government (significantly, the same issue which stalled for so long the negotiations in Vietnam). The Kuomintang wished the Communists to place their armies under the command of Chungking. The Communists refused to do this until they had a genuine and effective voice in the Chungking Government, and a guarantee of democratically elected local governments—which they knew would give them power in the Border Region and the guerrilla areas. With negotiations stalled on that point, the Communists decided to release their terms to the public and lash out at the Kuomintang in the process.

Communist Comment on Kuomintang-Communist Negotiations and Need for Reorganization of the Central Government

No. 30: September 21, 1944
Amerasia Papers, pp. 882–83

1. There are attached translations of two news items* which occupied the most prominent positions on the front page of the *Chieh-fang jih-pao,* the Communist Party newspaper published at Yenan, on September 20, 1944. These stories were both included in the English news broadcast from Yenan on the same date.

2. The first item charges the Kuomintang with suppressing the news of the proposal made by the Communist representative in the People's Political Council for the reorganization of the Central Government. At the date of writing, the full text of Mr. Lin Tsu-han's statement to the People's Political Council has not been received in Yenan. It is assumed, however, that it has been made available to the Embassy.

3. The second article repeats at some length the Communist arguments that the Kuomintang has no sincere intention of reaching a reasonable settlement with the Communists

* Only the first, very brief item is printed here.

in the interest of the war against Japan. It accuses the Kuomintang of trickery and evasion, and of being willing to weaken the forces of the country even though this may aid the enemy. It then goes on to present the view that the military and administrative unity which the Kuomintang claims is its sole aim is utterly impossible without complete reorganization of the Government and the high command to ensure that that unity is used to further the good of the country and to aid the prosecution of the war.

4. The whole article is strongly phrased. Its meaning is to make superfluous further discussions on the plane, which the Kuomintang seems to have tried to maintain, of settling *limited* outstanding problems, such as the giving of supplies to a certain number of Communist troops. The Communist statement, taken at its face, is tantamount to a refusal of reconciliation and military cooperation with the present Kuomintang Government.

5. It need not be assumed that the Communists will necessarily adhere to this uncompromising stand. They believe, however, that internal pressure for reform and the present unsatisfactory situation of the Kuomintang make this a favorable time to push this proposal into the open. It is the first time that the reorganization of the Government and the high command have been discussed in the Communist press in definite terms. If domestic dissatisfaction continues and foreign reaction is not unfavorable, it can be expected that this Communist pressure will be continued and intensified.

6. It has been obvious that the Kuomintang-Communist negotiations on the lines proposed by the Kuomintang had no chance of success and that the Communists never expected (or intended) them to be successful. The effect in Yenan of this proposal for government reorganization has been to take attention away from the negotiations and to push them into the background. They are now generally regarded as of no practical importance.

7. The general attitude of leaders in Yenan toward the coming of the five-man commission of the People's Political Council seems to be one of satisfaction without any elation or high hopes. They point out that whether or not the commission can accomplish anything on its return to Chungking de-

pends entirely on the attitude of the Generalissimo, which has not yet shown any satisfactory signs of a change. In other words, it is not lack of knowledge which is responsible for the Kuomintang's attitude toward the Communists.

Enclosure:

NEW CHINA NEWS AGENCY (YENAN)
ENGLISH NEWS BROADCAST, SEPTEMBER 20

(Translation from *Chieh-fang jih-pao,* Yenan, September 20)

Yenan, September 19.—The Kuomintang propaganda organizations have issued a grossly mutilated and distorted version of the report given by Comrade Lin Tsu-han to the People's Political Council on September 15 concerning Kuomintang-Kungchantang* relations. For example, the original speech contained the demand for the reorganization of the existing autocratic government of the Kuomintang into a coalition government of all parties and groups in China for the benefit of unity and the war effort, but this passage was completely deleted by *Central News*. The full text of Comrade Lin's speech will be published as soon as it is received.

One interesting indication of the popular attitude toward the Kuomintang in the Border Region was the celebration of Chinese National Day on October 10. Service had managed to make himself somewhat of an expert on staged demonstrations in his years in China. He had been in Sian in the fall of 1942 when Wendell Willkie visited that city, and had gone out early in the morning to listen to the people complaining about the *pao-chia* officials forcing them to attend the demonstrations. He had watched as the local gendarmerie coached them on how to cheer the visiting American. They apparently did their job well, for Willkie left much impressed by the "spontaneous demonstration" of Chinese affection.

* For a brief period in 1944, partly in response to repeated foreign suggestions that they abandon the provocative label "Communist," the CCP in its English broadcasts used its romanized Chinese name: *Kungchantang.*

Service had, then, considerable grounds for comparison when, in a deleted summary of his despatch, he called the Yenan celebration the "best organized and all-inclusive . . . celebration of a National Anniversary which I have seen in China." From a political standpoint, the considerable public ridicule of the Kuomintang was clearly significant. But his report was also an interesting account of a holiday in Yenan.

Celebration of October 10 in Yenan

No. 42: October 11, 1944
Amerasia Papers, pp. 1021–24

Commencing on the 8th, the customary Chinese type of temporary *ornamental arches* were erected on the streets by various public organizations and government bureaus. There were perhaps twenty of these, enough to make quite a showing on Yenan's three streets. Gates to main government offices were similarly decorated.

Flags were of course flown by shops and government offices. (Yenan is a much beflagged town. It is the custom to hang out the flags every Sunday. The flag is of course the Chinese national—"white sun, blue sky, red earth"—flag. The Kuomintang Party flag has not been seen. And the Communist Red flag is not used.)

During the night of October 9 and on the morning of the 10th, the town was literally covered with *slogan posters*. All were handwritten and most on colored paper—generally pink or green. Several features of these posters are characteristic and hence worthy of being mentioned:

1. Subjects are current and specific. They refer definitely to the present situation, generally to the immediate war situation, the Kuomintang-Communist negotiations, or the proposal for reorganization of the Government.

2. While showing obvious inspiration or guidance in the general similarity of line, there is great variety in actual form and phraseology. Few slogans are identical.

3. Furthermore, there is great diversity of source. Numerous organizations join in the campaign, each government or

Party office covers its immediate neighborhood, and every shop puts up one or two posters—"signing" its own name. Many shops put out lanterns with slogans written on them. But the fact that not all did this would seem to indicate lack of compulsion.

4. While relating directly to the current situation, the general tone was not inflammatory against the Kuomintang. Nothing approached "Down with the Kuomintang Government." Perhaps the closest was "Stop False Democracy: Carry Out True Democracy." Of course the very large number calling for freedom of the press, of speech, of person, et cetera, are implied criticism of the Kuomintang. Other slogans called for recognition of the Communist governments and military forces (without, however, referring to them as Communist). And a number referred to the broader aspects of the war by asking for better cooperation with the United States, Soviet Russia and Great Britain (always mentioned in that order—a probable indication of official orders). There were no slogans mentioning Communism, but some demanding "true" carrying out of the San Min Chu I.

There was a general *holiday*. The weather was fine and the town had a really festive appearance. The streets were filled with people among whom the presence of a large number of peasants was noteworthy (in most parts of China it is doubtful whether the farmers even know there is a celebration). Women and children were dressed in their "feast clothes" and indeed that was the general atmosphere. There was apparently no effort by the police, as I have observed in some Chinese cities, to force shops to observe the holiday. Many were closed—with slogans pasted over their fronts—but others were open and did a good business with the holiday crowds.

Periodically through the day there were small *parades* through the streets by propaganda corps from various organizations, each led by a small native band and followed by a crowd.

One of these carried large maps showing the situation of the war in the Pacific and in China—emphasizing the Kuomintang losses of territory and the recent growth of the guerrilla bases.

Two other groups contained native folk play (*yang ko*) troupes who gave these popular singing-dancing performances (with modern propaganda stories) at points of public congregation.

Another parade included three actors representing Dr. H. H. Kung, Ho Ying-ch'in and the Kuomintang's C-C politicians. There was great laughter as these figures appeared and seemingly no lack of comprehension on the part of the crowd. "Kung" was a fat man, made fatter by a pillow at the right place, wearing a long Chinese silk gown and round black cap (the trademark of a merchant), with National currency $100 bills pinned on his stomach. "Ho Ying-ch'in" was dressed to look like a Japanese military dandy. The C-C was represented by a Kuomintang petty officer, wearing the usual Kuomintang Party uniform, including the old felt hat, and made up to look like a gangster.

With some of these parading troupes there were distributed mimeographed handbills. These were eagerly sought after, and the person handing them out, generally a girl, was surrounded by people. One which I received may be translated as follows:

"The Eighth Route Army, New Fourth Army and South China Guerrilla Detachment are maintaining the three fronts of North, Central and South China. They have set up fifteen anti-Japanese Democratic Bases and freed 90,000,000 people.

"Of the 1,300,000 Japanese and puppet (traitor) troops in China we are resisting 1,100,000 (five sixths); the Kuomintang troops are resisting 200,000 (one sixth). But they are being defeated every day."

WHO SHOULD BE ABOLISHED?

WHO IS RESISTING SUCCESSFULLY?

WANGCHIAP'ING PROPAGANDA CORPS OCTOBER 10

The day was filled with *meetings*—although plans for a really large outdoor mass meeting was abandoned because recent rains had delayed the completion of the harvest.

In the morning there was an official reception at the Shensi-Kansu-Ninghsia Border Region government headquarters, at which all important government, military and Party officials were present, and to which the Observer Section, foreign correspondents and other foreigners in Yenan were invited.

Among other guests were two elderly Mongols, said to be from the Ordos region.

In the afternoon there was a large meeting in the auditorium of the Border Government, seating over a thousand. We were not officially invited to this but I was told that I would be welcome to attend if interested. I did so and found a seat among the crowd in the rear of the hall. The audience was apparently made up of government and Party workers, and representatives of local governments and mass organizations. The latter two categories, common people elected to their posts, seemed to make up perhaps 40 percent of the total. Many of them were typical shopkeepers or old farmers. There seemed to be no particular seating arrangement, all groups being mixed. It was interesting to note that young men near me, apparently Party workers, took pains (in a very friendly way) to make sure that some of these old farmers knew who the speakers were and what in general was going on.

Above the speakers were the usual pictures of Churchill, Stalin, Sun Yat-sen, Roosevelt and Chiang. (The exact order may not be correct. But Sun Yat-sen, as always, was in the center.) Behind the speakers were large crossed Chinese flags.

There was very little ceremony at the opening of the meeting. The presiding officer, the commissioner of Civil Affairs of the Border Government, briefly explained the significance of the day and called on General Chu Teh, commander of the Eighth Route Army, to make a few remarks.

General Chu's talk was a remarkable performance. He is a large, unpretentious, shambling man with a broad, pleasant but strong, peasant face. He spoke entirely extemporaneously, without any excitement or oratorical effects, almost in a conversational manner, in simple, direct earthy language of the people, full of homely simile and common sayings. Talking of things the people knew, the history of the past thirty-odd years, he dealt little with theory and -*isms* but instead of what the people themselves had experienced during this time. Attention was profound and it was obvious that he held his audience completely. With quiet humor, sly rather than bitter, he managed to demolish the Kuomintang by ridicule which kept the audience breaking out into spontaneous laughter. After talking about Yuan Shih-k'ai's unsuccessful efforts to make himself Emperor, and the attempts of Ts'ao K'un, Tuan Chi-jui, Wu P'ei-fu* and others to do the same in fact if not in name, he ended up on the line: "And if Chiang Kai-shek doesn't look out, he is going to find himself among them." The audience "ate it up."

The next speaker was General Chou En-lai. He read a prepared speech which was obviously intended to be an important statement of Communist Party policy toward the Kuomintang and present internal problems of China. This was in clear, direct language (though not the talk of the people which Chu had used), but the delivery, while avoiding dramatics, was slightly formal and strained and did not get the enthusiastic response which General Chu had seemingly so effortlessly received. Attention was good and applause frequent. But it seemed to be more of organized applause, started and led by the uniformed (political worker) section of the audience. The content of General Chou's speech is discussed in my report No. 44 of October 14.†

The final speaker was Li Ting-ming, vice chairman of the Border Government and acting head in the absence of Lin Pai-ch'ü in Chungking. His background as wealthy landlord (which he still is), former minor government official under the Kuomintang, and organizer of local *min tuan* forces which fought the Communists in the civil war is interesting. I did not stay to hear all of his talk, which because of his age and weak voice could hardly be heard from where I sat, but he started on the theme, referring to the Kuomintang, that "You can't go on fooling the people."

---

* Yuan Shih-k'ai was the first President of the Republic of China 1912–1916), who died after the failure of an attempt to make himself Emperor. Ts'ao, Tuan and Wu were all warlords who after Yuan's death each made a brief and futile attempt to establish his supremacy in the Peking Government.

† Not printed. In his summary of Chou's speech, Service gave this statement of the Communists' new tough policy toward the KMT: "There must be an end of the Kuomintang's one-party despotism and personal dictatorship. There must be created a truly national government of all parties and groups. This should be done through an emergency national conference. Without full power to reorganize and control the military high command, this coalition government will be useless. There can be no disbanding of active anti-Japanese forces and governments. We have the right to demand that these forces receive a share of foreign aid proportionate to the enemy forces they oppose." (See *Amerasia Papers*, p. 1069).

A dinner in the evening given by the Border Government for the Observer Section and other foreigners, like the dance at headquarters the evening previously, can hardly be classed as part of the general program.

But during the evening there were numerous other meetings and *dramatic performances*. In the large open-air theater of the Merchants Association, where folk plays were to be given, the populace (carrying their own stools and often blankets) had started congregating three hours before the performance was to commence. American newsreels were shown to a large audience at the Eighth Route Army headquarters auditorium. Regular plays were given in at least three other places.

The play which Colonel Barrett and I attended, along with General Chu Teh, was an adaption into opera form of a modern play by the well-known playwright Kuo Mo-jo which, though historical, had obvious relation to the situation in China. The villain was a king who refused to use his large army to attack the enemy, keeping it inactive. The hero was a Minister, beloved of the people's, truly patriotic, and concerned over the danger to the country, who by a ruse ousted the field commander, took over the army, and defeated the enemy (thus saving the country), only to return to death at the hands of the tyrant.

The Party *newspaper,* the *Chieh-fang jih-pao,* of course devoted a good deal of space to the day. The editorial and several special articles, one by the Kuomintang elder, Hsu Fan-t'ing, accused the Kuomintang of forgetting the ideals for which Sun Yat-sen had overthrown the Manchus. The editorial, I suggest, would be worth translation by the Embassy as an effective piece of Communist propaganda.

At the same time that Chou En-lai was publicly enunciating the CCP's negotiating stance in his October 10 speech, both Chou and Mao had private conversations with Service which underscored their belief that there was no hope of an early agreement with the Kuomintang. Quite clearly, both men felt that time was on their side and that by waiting patiently their position could only become stronger.

Comments of Chairman Mao Tse-tung and General Chou En-lai on the Internal Situation in China

No. 43: October 12, 1944
Foreign Relations, 1944, pp. 636–40

1. There are enclosed memoranda of informal conversations with Chairman Mao Tse-tung and General Chou En-lai on October 9 and 12, 1944.

2. *Summary:* Both men reflect confidence and willingness to wait for what they regard as the inevitable turn of events in favor of the Communists. They believe that any decisive American pressure to clear the situation in China must await the results of the Presidential election. At present the Generalissimo has hardened his attitude and there is no immediate hope for reconciliation or for the creation of a national government. The Communists will continue to follow behind the Japanese advance into new territories and have already moved into east Honan Mao and Chou seemed to disagree on whether the Communists would accept limited participation in a Kuomintang Government not based on complete reform.   *End of Summary.*

MEMORANDUM OF CONVERSATION WITH CHAIRMAN MAO TSE-TUNG

October 10, 1944

Mao Tse-tung and his wife were at the small impromptu dance at headquarters last evening. Both were in fine humor, dancing repeatedly with each other and with most of the others present in a manner which, remembering Mao's normally quiet and reserved bearing, can only be called gay.

Early in the evening, Mao came over and sat beside me during a lull between dances and started a conversation which lasted for perhaps twenty minutes.

He commenced by jokingly congratulating me on the American reply to Chinese criticism of the small quantity of American aid. As I was at a loss, he explained the article in the evening paper quoting a "release of the State Department" (see my report No. 41 of October 10*). I insisted that there must have been some mistake, that the State Department could not possibly have issued the supposed statement, and that there were no other indications that we were taking such a strong line with the Kuomintang.

He switched to the subject of Kuomintang-Communist relations and admitted that the Kuomintang was not yet ready to compromise and there was hence no immediate hope for the proposed Emergency National Congress and the reorganization of the Government.

To my query regarding what the Communists would do, he replied: "We will wait. We have a long training in patience." He then suggested that if there was going to be any direct American pressure on the Kuomintang it would be delayed until after the President's re-election, since inasmuch as the President had built Chiang up, he would do nothing to discredit him—thus perhaps stirring up the "friends of China" and making China policy a political football—until after the election was safely over. Laughingly, he asked about the President's chances.

Turning serious, he repeated what he had said before— that the Communists would risk no friction with the United States and would therefore "keep in step" with American policy. Laughing again, he asked what American policy was toward the Kuomintang and Communists.

I suggested that it was really the Japanese who determined the Communist policy and future, that the more territory the Japanese occupied and the harder they pushed the Kuomintang, the stronger the Communists became. He admitted the partial truth of this, saying that the Communists would "recover any territory lost by the Kuomintang," and that their forces had already moved into east Honan from both north and south. He intimated that the Communists would also go into Southeast China if Kuomintang control there disintegrated. But, he insisted, the Communists will not compete with the Kuomintang

* Not printed. In his report, Service explains that the Communists' shortwave receivers had picked up a radio bulletin of the State Department Foreign Service, and had mistaken the bulletin's summary of domestic newspaper editorial comment for an official statement of the State Department. After Service's intervention, the *Liberation Daily* printed a correction and apology. (See *Amerasia Papers*, pp. 1017–20.)

for territory which it still holds, and while they recognize that Japanese crushing of the Kuomintang may mean eventual advantage, the Communists realize that this will be outweighed by immediate disadvantages to the Allied war against Japan. The Communists therefore seek cooperation on the basis of democratic unity, believing that this is the key to successful prosecution of the war and the resolution of China's internal political problems.

Mao then asked about Major Casberg's impressions gained on his recent trip. I mentioned that he had noted friendly relations and practical cooperation between the army and peasant population. His reply was: "Of course. We wouldn't be here, or alive today, if we didn't have the support of the common people (*lao pai hsing*)." From this he went on to develop the theme of the importance to the Allied victory in France of the support—for intelligence, scouting and even in sabotage and military operations—of the population, that this would be lacking in a landing or operations by American forces in Kuomintang territory, but that it could be provided by the mobilized population of the Communist areas.

I turned back to the subject of Kuomintang-Communist relations and suggested the hypothetical possibility that the Kuomintang might eventually be willing to invite several of the Communist leaders to accept posts in the Kuomintang Government, perhaps as cabinet ministers. Without hesitation, he said that this would be useless, that the C-C and other conservative Kuomintang cliques would still have full control of the lower government structure, and the Communist participation on this basis would only help the Kuomintang to deceive the Chinese people and foreign opinion. Communist participation would have to be conditioned on thoroughgoing reform and governmental reorganization.

He returned to the idea that the Communists would wait for a period. He then mentioned Yugoslavia, saying that time had eventually proved the falseness of Mikhailovitch's claims to be fighting only the Germans, that Tito had had to assist general knowledge of Mikhailovitch's motives and actions, that the Communists also had a great number of absolute proofs of Kuomintang complicity with the Japanese and puppets, that they had so far withheld publication in the hopes of the Kuomintang being willing to compromise and cooperate, but that if it finally became certain that the Kuomintang had no such intention, the material would be published. To my queries as to how the Communists would know when there was no longer hope for Kuomintang compromise, he would make no comment except: "The time has not yet come; there is still a little hope."

CONVERSATION WITH GENERAL CHOU EN-LAI

October 12, 1944

General Chou dropped in informally, stayed to lunch, and talked for some time afterward. Most of the conversation was on general subjects. But the following points may be of interest.

He analyzed the Generalissimo's October 10 speech as the most reactionary and uncompromising that Chiang has made for a long time. The first point—"China cannot be judged by normal standards because she is a revolutionary country"—is aimed primarily at domestic critics. The second and third—"the war cannot be won without China," and "we still have ample strength of our own"—are directed at foreign critics. The fourth point—"talk of disunity and civil war is the attempt of the enemy and traitors to prevent our victory"—is flung at the Communists. He pointed out that there was no recognition of foreign aid, no reference to internal political problems (except the obvious inclusion of the Communists among the traitors), and no mention of democracy or government reform.

He thought that the speech marked a new recent hardening of the Generalissimo's attitude. He based this on four supporting indications: (1) Recent reports that a plenary session of the Kuomintang's Central Executive Committee would be called in the near future—presumably to discuss reconciliation with the Communists and governmental reorganization—have now died down. (2) The Generalissimo is reported to have made an attempt—through Wu Teh-chen—to muzzle Sun Fo. (3) Although it was announced on October 2 that the PPC* Investigatory Commission would come to Yenan within a week, no definite date has yet been set for their departure from Chungking. (4) There have been several recent instances of severe internal censorship.

* People's Political Council.

He believed there is no immediate hope for results in the Kuomintang-Communist negotiations, or for any promising reorganization of the government.

He said that the Communists would "wait a month or two" before deciding their next move. By that time the Presidential election may have permitted a more definite American policy, and the Japanese drive toward Kweilin and Liuchow will have either succeeded or failed. If those cities are lost and the Japanese continue their advance, country-wide pressure on the Kuomintang for reform will be greatly increased.

He suggested that the Generalissimo's policy, being continually on a short-term basis, now depends on the hope that Germany will be defeated within a month or two, that by that time the United States will be attacking the Philippines, and that the Japanese drive—and the critical attention of the Chinese people—will be diverted to the impending events on the China coast. He thinks that the *Ta Kung Pao* editorial about the opening of the "Second Front" (the landing on the coast) is obviously officially inspired.

To a hypothetical question regarding possible Communist participation on a very limited basis in the present government, he reiterated the points in his October 10 speech that governmental reorganization had to be complete, and that the new government would have to have the authority to reorganize and control the high military command. He then recalled the experiences of himself and other opposition figures in accepting posts under the Kuomintang Government which meant no authority but rather a muzzle. He went on, however, to say that the Communists would consider any proposal carefully and might not necessarily refuse it, even though the participation offered was small. He drew the parallel of the People's Political Council. The Communists knew that the Council was intended to be a sham and had no authority, and the seats offered them were not proportionate to their relative strength. But they accepted them because it gave them a chance to make their views known and was a small opening wedge (they hoped) toward cooperative participation in national affairs. (General Chou's attitude was quite different from Mao Tse-tung's rather snap statement that the Communists would not participate unless there was a thorough reorganization.)

COMMUNIST POLICY TOWARD
THE UNITED STATES

The Communists were clearly, in 1944, a rapidly expanding political and military force, confident of their own future and not inclined to make unnecessary compromises with a moribund Kuomintang. As Service's friend and colleague John Paton Davies was to put it, "The Communists are in China to stay. And China's destiny is not Chiang's but theirs."* This being the case, it was essential to discover precisely what their attitude toward the United States was and would be.

Indications of CCP policy in this regard came mainly from conversations and interviews with the Communist leadership, several of which have been printed in the preceding section. Fortunately Service, from his concentration on Communist affairs during his days in Chungking, was not unknown to the Communist leaders. Service had often talked with Chou En-lai in Chungking, and Chou's secretary, Ch'en Chia-k'ang, was something of a personal friend. "I liked Chinese, generally speaking. I liked these people, and apparently some of them liked me. Of course, they recognized me as an official of the American government, but they sensed that I was genuinely interested and to some extent sympathetic to their point of view. I never made any attempt to talk as if I were a Communist or give them any idea that I was a Communist. There was never any suggestion of my being a comrade. But they apparently concluded that I was a reasonably fair political reporter. On the other hand, I wasn't simply a newspaper reporter, who just sat and wrote down everything that was said. When we had talks, there was give-and-take. I expressed views and disagreements and criticisms, so they were not simply using me as a recording device to pass their views on. They also had a chance to know my views. And my views

* John Davies memorandum, "Will the Communists Take Over China?" *Foreign Relations of the United States, 1944: China*, p. 671.

were in line with most liberal American opinion. The CCP program —their United Front policies and coalition government—were things that a lot of Americans, and certainly myself, felt were the best policy. These liberal sympathies, of course, were one of the things which ultimately trapped us in the 1950s."

In any case, Service was clearly identified by the Communists as the leading civil official in the Dixie Mission and the man with whom political and diplomatic affairs should be discussed. At formal dinners, Service would usually sit on one side of Mao Tse-tung, with Dave Barrett on the other, next to Chu Teh, commander of the Eighth Route Army. It was on such an occasion, at the dinner welcoming the Dixie Mission to Yenan, that Service had his first talk with Mao Tse-tung.

Desire of Chairman of Communist Central Committee for Continued American Representation of Diplomatic Character at Yenan

No. 2: July 28, 1944
Foreign Relations, 1944, pp. 522–23

1. There is enclosed a memorandum of a conversation with Mao Tse-tung, Chairman of the Central Committee of the Chinese Communist Party, on the evening of July 26, 1944.

2. Chairman Mao expressed the hope that a representative of the State Department might be regularly stationed at Yenan, even after the possible withdrawal of American military observers. He stated that the reason for this hope is that the time of greatest danger of a Kuomintang attack on the Communists will be soon after the cessation of hostilities against Japan.

3. In expressing this hope, Chairman Mao inferentially agrees with the statements of Communist representatives in Chungking that they believe that American observers in the Communist areas will prove an important factor in preventing an open conflict between the Kuomintang and Communist parties.

MEMORANDUM OF CONVERSATION
WITH CHAIRMAN MAO TSE-TUNG

July 27, 1944

During the welcome dinner given last evening to our Observer Group I was seated beside Chairman Mao Tse-tung. Neither before nor after dinner was there opportunity for private conversation, but during the meal the Chairman made a number of personal remarks to me.

He repeated earlier general remarks of pleasure at our arrival. Very kindly he added an indication of pleasure at my inclusion in the Observer Section, saying that he had heard of my interest in Chinese politics from General Chou En-lai and Mr. Tung Pi-wu and knew that I had been a friend of the Communist Delegation in Chungking.

He said that he understood that I was an adviser on the staff of General Stilwell but that I still retained some connection with the Embassy. I confirmed this and added that for reasons which he could understand I was here nominally in my military capacity only, although any reports I might write on political subjects would be seen by the Ambassador.

He asked whether I would remain here permanently. I replied that being attached to a group which was here primarily for study and investigation, I could make no definite reply as to the length of my stay but that it was our hope that it would be found worthwhile for representatives of our headquarters to be stationed in Yenan and that such representatives would probably include civilian advisers.

He asked whether there was a possibility of the State Department setting up a consulate at Yenan. I suggested that there were a number of practical difficulties—the first being the small number of Americans in the area. He agreed but said that he had raised the question because an American military group would withdraw from Yenan immediately after the cessation of hostilities against Japan, which was just the time of greatest danger of a Kuomintang attack and civil war.

He said that he understood that Vice President Wallace had secured the Generalissimo's approval for the despatch of our group and asked whether there had been other previous attempts to get such permission. I suggested that there were a number of topics which I would like to discuss with him at his leisure, though none of them would be called official business. He gave a good-natured laugh and said that after I had gotten settled down, we would have a good chance to "exchange ideas."

I then asked about the progress of the Kuomintang-Communist talks in Chungking. He said that there was no progress and that the Kuomintang now would not let Lin Tsu-han return.

———

Service's first talk with Mao had been brief, and for good reason. Despite the overture to establish a U.S. consulate in Yenan, Mao was apparently not quite ready to commit himself to a major rapprochement with the United States. The United States was, after all, one of the "imperialist powers," and the Chinese Communist Party had risen to prominence on a policy of anti-imperialism. It was essential, therefore, for Mao to have the entire Party firmly behind him as he attempted to establish friendly relations with the country which he knew would be the dominant power in the postwar Pacific. Thus Mao put off any early meeting with Service and invited him to "get acquainted first."

While Service was getting acquainted, and after each side had looked the other over to some extent, there was—unbeknownst to Service or anyone else in the Dixie Mission—a meeting of the CCP leadership which produced, on August 18, a Central Committee directive entitled "On Diplomatic Work."* As an internal Party document intended for the use and information of local cadres who might come in contact with members of the Dixie Mission, it is a significant indication of the seriousness and sincerity of the CCP overtures to the United States.

The directive viewed the arrival of the Dixie Mission as signaling "the beginning of our participation in the unified international anti-Fascist front [and] the start of our diplomatic work." It noted that the motives for the dispatch of the U.S. Army mission were primarily military: for intelligence and rescue of air crews, but "On the basis of military collaboration it will later be possible to establish cultural and then political collaboration." The directive then goes on to describe the types of collaboration which would be welcomed: military ("military personnel and armed forces of the

* This secret directive was published by the Russians in *Problemy Dal'nego Vostoka*, No. 1 (March 1972), pp. 184–87.

Allied powers may enter the territory of our regions"), political ("we welcome the dispatch of diplomatic missions to our Border Region"), cultural ("we welcome the establishment of branches of their information and government press agencies in Yenan"), religious ("we permit foreign priests' entry into the Border Region"), and economic ("under conditions of observance of the principle of mutual advantage, we welcome international capital investments and technical cooperation"). It concludes with certain guidelines to be observed in contacts with the Americans. The CCP was to maintain the initiative, while "refraining from making requests" for arms and ammunition. Cadres were to "observe caution and manifest directness." Finally, "The Allies should be received warmly and modestly. It is necessary to refrain from excessive luxury while avoiding indifference."

Once Mao had the Party committed to his policy of rapprochement with the United States, he was ready to talk with Service. Mao sent word on August 22 and the interview took place the next day. From Service's report, there is no question that this was indeed a major *démarche* by the Chinese Communist Party attempting to establish friendly relations with the United States both during the war and in the postwar period. Mao's suggestion that Service fly immediately to Chungking to present his report to the Ambassador is an indication of the importance he saw in this interview. Unfortunately, Service's conviction that the substance and significance of Mao's overture would be quickly appreciated in Chungking and Washington was not completely warranted. This despatch was not forwarded from Chungking until September 28 and not received in Washington until October 24.

Interview with Mao Tse-tung

No. 15: August 27, 1944
Foreign Relations, 1944, pp. 602–14

1. There is attached a memorandum of a conversation on August 23, 1944, with Mao Tse-tung, Chairman of the Central Committee of the Chinese Communist Party. This memorandum is necessarily a summarization, inasmuch as the conversation lasted for six hours, but it has been prepared from notes made during the interview.

2. Chairman Mao believes that the influence of the United States in China can be decisive if applied now and that American policy is accordingly a vital concern to the Chinese people. He therefore wants to know what that policy is, or is likely to be. He raises the questions of American policy toward the problem of China's democracy, toward the Communist Party, and toward the civil war that he considers inevitable if democracy is not achieved during the present war.

3. Specifically, Chairman Mao seeks American support of a proposal that a new national government be set up by the calling of a conference of all leading political groups in China.

4. The meeting was on the initiative of Chairman Mao and he directed the conversation. His attitude was friendly and informal, and I believe that he spoke with frankness. Certainly his statements were direct and revealing. I consider them the clearest indication we have yet received of Communist thinking and planning in regard to the part they hope to have in China's national affairs in the near future.

5. There are a number of indications that the Communists believe that in the near future they will be faced with the making of important decisions in regard to their future line of action. Now assembled in Yenan are most of the important leaders, not only of the central Party and army organizations, but also of the bases and armies in the field. These include:

P'eng Teh-huai: Vice Commander of the Eighth Route Army in command of the Field Headquarters, Southeast Shansi

Nieh Jung-chen: Commander in Chief of the Shansi–Hopei–Chahar Military District

Ch'en Yi: Acting Commander in Chief of the New Fourth Army

Lin Piao: Commander of the 115th Division, Eighth Route Army

Yang Hsiu-feng: Chairman of the Shansi–Hopei–Shantung–Honan Border Region Government

Lo Jui-ch'ing: Chief of the Political Department of the Field Headquarters, Eighth Route Army

Chu Jui: Communist Party Secretary for Shantung

This list is incomplete and includes only better-known names. It does not, of course, include the majority of the top Communist leaders, such as Mao Tse-tung, Chou En-lai, Po Ku, Wang Ming, Liu Shao-ch'i, Chu Teh and Yeh Chien-ying, who are now, as normally, in Yenan.

6. These men obviously did not come here in connection with the Observer Section—some have been on their way since March 1944, when it could not be known that we might be coming to Yenan. When questioned about this unprecedented concentration of influential leaders, the Communists merely say that they are here for conferences to prepare for the counter-offensive.

7. Despite this disinclination to go into detail regarding the character of these conferences, it is obvious that the Communists are considering the problems connected with:

(*a*) the weakening of the Kuomintang and the deterioration of conditions in Kuomintang China;
(*b*) the probable development of the closing stages of the war in China;
(*c*) the probable strategy of the Kuomintang toward the Communists in these last stages and immediately afterward.

8. Related to these problems is the present attempt to negotiate a compromise with the Kuomintang. The Communists have now practically given up hope (if they ever had any) that these will be successful without strong outside pressure on the Kuomintang. Japanese military pressure, it seems, will not be enough to overcome the Kuomintang's anti-Communism.

9. Also related, if the Kuomintang is going to collapse or if it is going to be in a position to be aggressively anti-Communist at the end of the war, is the problem of preparation by improving the Communist position. This may have an effect on Communist participation in the war. They are not going to stop fighting. But they may be more interested in directly extending their control, and less willing to sacrifice their strength and advantages to overall United Nations strategy. It may, for instance, decide whether the Communists extend their operations into the area east of the Pinghan railway, which has now been cut off from direct Kuomintang control (see paragraph 1 of my report No. 7, August 4, 1944*) or whether they attempt to take

* Not printed.

advantage of the Japanese campaign along the Canton–Hankow line to re-establish their old bases in Southeast China (this will be discussed in greater detail in my despatch No. 19 of August 31*). Both of these expansions can be justified as definite aids to the war against Japan. But in present circumstances they will mean more friction with the Kuomintang and moving closer to a condition of actual civil war. The question must therefore be considered whether this is desirable, and whether the United States desires and will support such vigorous Communist activity.

10. Basic to all these problems, the Communists believe, are the policies and actions of the United States. We have the ability to bolster the Kuomintang and keep it in power; we will determine the development of the war in the China theater; we can, if we wish, prevent civil war and force the Kuomintang toward democracy. These American policies will decide whether the Communists must play a lone hand and look out for themselves, or whether they can be assured of survival and participation in a democratic China, and so cooperate wholeheartedly in the war. The Communists want our understanding and support: they are anxious to do nothing to alienate us or compromise that support.

11. The most important question—and at present the greatest unknown—to the Communists, therefore, is American policy. This orientation toward the United States is clear. The Communists do not, for very practical reasons, expect that Soviet Russia will be able to play a large part in China. And they believe, for the sake of China's unity on a democratic basis, that this Russian participation should be secondary to that of the United States.

INTERVIEW WITH MAO TSE-TUNG, AUGUST 23, 1944

(After a short general conversation Mao said that he would like to talk about Kuomintang–Communist relations. The following is the gist of his remarks.)

The relationship between the Kuomintang and the Communist Party is the key to the problem of China. In the first

* See pp. 211–16.

stage, from 1922 to 1927, there was cooperation. This made possible the success of the Northern Expedition and the rise to power of the Kuomintang. But as soon as the Kuomintang got that power it sought to monopolize it; it turned against and tried to exterminate us. The result was the second stage—the ten years of civil war from 1927 to 1937. The third stage, a return to cooperation, was impelled by the imminence of the Japanese invasion. It has continued precariously up to the present.

This cooperation of the third stage was not entered into gladly or willingly by the Kuomintang. Its acceptance by the KMT has never been sincere or wholehearted. It was forced on the KMT by five factors:

1. The Japanese attack
2. The pressure of foreign opinion
3. The enduring strength of the Communists—exploited at Sian
4. The will of the people of China—to resist Japan
5. The internal weakness of the KMT—which made it unable to defeat us.

The end of the war (and even its approaching end) will bring a shift in these forces.

The defeat of Japan will eliminate the most powerful and positive of these factors.

The Communists are stronger than before. In this way it can be said that their influence for unity and against civil war is greater. But as long as the KMT is under its present type of leadership this greater Communist strength makes the KMT more determined on Communist elimination. This can work only up to a certain point: if the Communists are too strong, the KMT will not dare to attack them. But the KMT leaders are so grasping for power that they may take long chances.

The people of China are still inarticulate and politically repressed. They are kept so by the KMT. The liberals, students, intellectuals, publicists, newspaper interests, minor parties, provincial groups and modern industrialists (who have been disillusioned and see no future for themselves in Kuomintang bureaucratic industrialization) are numerous. But they are disorganized, disunited and without power. Over them, Chiang holds the bayonets and the secret police.

The Kuomintang is an amorphous body of no definite character or program. The liberal groups within it have no strong leader, no rallying point, and no aggressive platform. If they did have these, they would have no way, under present circumstances, of reaching the people. The controlling leaders of the Kuomintang, though divided into jealous cliques, are all anti-Communist and antidemocratic. They are united by their selfish determination to perpetuate their own power.

Considering these factors alone, it seems inevitable, if the country drifts along under the present leadership, that there will be Kuomintang-provoked civil war.

We Communists know civil war from bitter experience. We know that it will mean long years of ruin and chaos for China. China's unity, her stabilizing influence in the Far East, and her economic development will all be delayed. Not only the Chinese but also all nations having interests in the Far East will be affected. China will become a major international problem. This vitally concerns the United States.

One thing certain is that we Communists dread civil war. We abhor it. We will not start it. We will do our best to avoid it—even though we know that as things now are (provided that the KMT does not receive foreign help) we would eventually win. But the Communists are of the people. The people's interests are our interests. The people will not submit for long to the despotic Fascism which is now apparent in Chungking and Sian, and which is foreshadowed even more menacingly in books like Chiang's *China's Destiny*. If the people fight, the Communists must fight along with them.

The hope for preventing civil war in China therefore rests to a very great extent—much more than ever before—on the influence of foreign countries. Among these, by far the most important is the United States. Its growing power in China and in the Far East is already so great that it can be decisive. The Kuomintang in its situation today must heed the United States.

American policy in China therefore becomes not merely a matter of concern to Americans alone; it is also a question of the most vital interest to the democratic people of China. The Chinese people, accordingly, are interested in three general questions.

First, is there a chance of an American swing-back toward isolationism and a resultant lack of interest in China? Are Americans to close their eyes to foreign problems and let China "stew in her own juice"? We Communists feel that this problem will not arise if Roosevelt is re-elected.

(This and other questions about the United States were addressed directly to me. I therefore made it clear, in the most explicit terms, that I had no official authority and that my replies were only my purely private and completely unofficial opinions.

(On the above points, I mentioned America's long and special interest in China; the fact that we would have no internal reconstruction problem as a result of war destruction; that on the contrary our greatly expanded economy and our more international outlook would impel us to seek trade and investment beyond our borders; that it was therefore unlikely that we would become isolationist or unconcerned about China; and that I doubted whether administration of the country by either Republicans or Democrats would fundamentally affect our China policy.)

Second, is the American government really interested in democracy—in its world future? Does it, for instance, consider democracy in China—one fourth of the world's population—important? Does it want to have the government of China really representative of the people of China? Is it concerned that the present government of China, which it recognizes, has no legal status by any law and is in no way representative of the people of China? Chiang Kai-shek was elected President by only ninety members of a single political party, the Kuomintang, who themselves cannot validly claim to represent even the limited membership of that party. Even Hitler has a better claim to democratic power. He was selected by the people. And he has a Reichstag. Does the United States realize the obvious fact that the present Kuomintang has lost the confidence and support of the Chinese masses? The important question, however, is not whether the American government realizes this fact, but whether it is willing to try to improve the situation by helping to bring about democracy in China.

(I referred to the numerous official American statements regarding unity in China and our general hope for democratic development in all countries. I mentioned the apparent trend of at least an important part of American opinion as shown in recent critical articles in the American press.)

It is obvious that the Kuomintang must reform itself and reorganize its government. On its present basis it cannot hope to fight an effective war. And even if the war is won for it by the United States, subsequent chaos is certain.

The government must broaden its base to take in all important groups of the people. We do not call for full and immediate representative democracy; it would be impractical. And under Kuomintang sponsorship and control, it would be an empty fraud. But what can and should be done—at once—is to convene a provisional (or transitional) National Congress. To this all groups should be invited to send delegates. These delegates must not be selected and appointed by the Kuomintang, as in the past. They must be genuine representatives—the best qualified leaders. They should include the Communist Party, all minor parties, the intellectual groups, newspaper interests, students, professional groups, central organizations of cooperative societies, labor and other mass organizations.

A workable compromise for the distribution of strength might be that the Kuomintang would have one half of the members, all others together the other half. It would have to be agreed beforehand, for reasons of practical politics, that the Generalissimo would be confirmed as Temporary President.

This Provisional Congress must have full power to reorganize the Government and make new laws—to remain in effect until the passage of the Constitution. The Government should be directly responsible to the Congress. Its functions and powers might be somewhat like those of the British House of Commons.

The Provisional Congress would also have full charge of the preparations for full democracy and constitutionalism. It would supervise the elections and then convene the National Congress. It would then turn over its powers and pass out of existence.

Is the American government willing to use its influence to force the Kuomintang to carry out such a proposal? Is the American government willing to make the proposal and actively support it?

(Chairman Mao made the suggestion that this matter was

of such importance that it would warrant my making a trip to Chungking to present it to the Ambassador. I said that the Ambassador would be fully informed. I also suggested that we had already heard this general proposal from other quarters in Chungking.

(Subsequently, on August 26, I learned in a conversation with Chou En-lai that the Politbureau of the Communist Party was considering the making of this proposal to the Kuomintang. They would base it on the Kuomintang's refusal to discuss the Communist demands for democracy in their present negotiations on the ground that they are "too abstract.")

Third, what is the attitude and policy of the American government toward the Chinese Communist Party? Does it recognize the Communist Party as an active fighting force against Japan? Does it recognize the Communists as an influence for democracy in China? Is there any chance of American support of the Chinese Communist Party? What will be the American attitude—toward the Kuomintang and toward the Communists—if there is a civil war in China? What is being done to ensure that the Kuomintang will not use its new American arms to fight a civil war?

(These questions, especially the points raised in the second and third, formed the framework of our further conversation. I returned to a number of points for further amplification and discussion.

(Regarding the question of "support" of the Communist Party, I pointed out that the question was obscure and, in any case, premature inasmuch as the Communists themselves publicly supported the Central Government and Chiang Kai-shek.)

We Communists accepted KMT terms in 1936–1937 to form the United Front because the foreign menace of Japan threatened the country. We are, first of all, Chinese. The ten years of inconclusive, mutually destructive civil war had to be stopped in order to fight Japan. Even though we had not started the civil war, we took the lead in stopping it. Also, the foreign countries recognized the KMT and Chiang; they did not support us. But the United Front was not all one-sided: The KMT also promised political reforms—which they have not carried out.

Our support of Chiang does not mean support of despotism; we support him to fight Japan.

We could not raise this question of recognition before. In a formal sense it is still premature. We only ask now that American policy try to induce the Kuomintang to reform itself. This would be a first stage. It may be the only one necessary: if it is successful, there will be no threat of civil war.

But suppose that the KMT does not reform. Then there must be a second stage of American policy. Then this question of American policy toward the Communists must be raised. We can risk no conflict with the United States.

We can ignore the question of the supply of American arms now which can be used by the KMT in a future civil war. But must we expect a repetition of past history. In the early days of the Republic, the Powers recognized only Peking —long after it was apparent that the only government that could claim to represent the people of China was that in Canton. Nanking was not recognized until after the success and completion of the Northern Expedition. Now the internal situation in China is changing. The lines are not yet clearly drawn. But a somewhat similar situation may develop. Will the United States continue to give recognition and support to a government that in ineffectiveness and lack of popular support can only be compared to the old Peking Government?

(I suggested the diplomatic impossibility of withdrawing recognition from a government that had not committed a directly unfriendly act, the obvious undesirability of working behind a recognized government to support an opposition party, and finally the delicacy of the whole problem of interference in the domestic affairs of another country.)

America has intervened in every country where her troops and supplies have gone. This intervention may not have been intended, and may not have been direct. But it has been nonetheless real—merely by the presence of that American influence. For America to insist that arms be given to all forces who fight Japan, which will include the Communists, is not interference. For America to give arms only to the Kuomintang will in its effect be interference because it will enable the Kuomintang to continue to oppose the will of the people of China. "Interference" (Mao noted his objection to the term because of its having no meaning in this situation) to further the true interests of the people of China is not interference. It will be welcomed by the great mass of the people of China because they want democracy. Only the Kuomintang is against it.

We do not ask the stopping of all aid to the KMT forces. The effect would not be good on the war. The KMT would collapse and the American landing in China will be more difficult.

(Chou En-lai in a subsequent conversation developed the following themes along related lines: (1) The giving of American arms only to the KMT is sure to mean civil war; (2) We must not ignore the possibility that Japan may try to end the war by a "surrender" to Chiang Kai-shek. This will be a trick on the other Allies and will in effect be a compromise based on Japan's desire to keep a weak Kuomintang rather than a strong, unified and democratic government in China; (3) The only way to be sure of decisively winning the war in China and avoiding civil war is to give arms to both Kuomintang and Communists.)

(I raised the question of how American influence could be exerted effectively, expressing skepticism about "dictation" to Chiang. Mao vigorously rejected my suggestion.)

Chiang is in a position where he must listen to the United States. Look at what happened in Honan, is happening now in Hunan, and shows every sign of happening in Kwangsi! Perhaps it will be Yunnan next. Look at the economic situation! Chiang is in a corner.

Chiang is stubborn. But fundamentally he is a gangster. That fact must be understood in order to deal with him. We have had to learn it by experience. The only way to handle him is to be hard-boiled. You must not give way to his threats and bullying. Do not let him think you are afraid; then he will press his advantage. The United States has handled Chiang very badly. They have let him get away with blackmail—for instance, talk of being unable to keep up resistance, of having to make peace, his tactics in getting the $500-million loan, and now Kung's mission to the United States and the plea for cloth. Cloth! Are we or are we not fighting the Japanese? Is cloth more important than bullets? We had no cotton here in the Border Region and the KMT blockade kept us from getting any from the parts of China that did have it. But we got busy and soon we are going to be self-sufficient. It would be a hundred times easier for the KMT, and if they were a government that had an economic policy, they would have done it themselves.

With Chiang you can be friendly only on your own terms. He must give in to constant, strong and unified pressure. Never relax on your objectives: keep hammering at him.

The position of the United States now is entirely different from what it was just after Pearl Harbor. There is no longer any need or any reason to cultivate, baby or placate Chiang. The United States can tell Chiang what he should do—in the interest of the war. American help to Chiang can be made conditional on his meeting American desires. Another way for American influence to be exerted is for Americans to talk American ideals. Every American official meeting any Chinese official, in China or in the United States, can talk democracy. Visits like Wallace's give good opportunities; there should be more of them. Kung's presence in the United States should not be wasted.

Every American soldier in China should be a walking and talking advertisement for democracy. He ought to talk it to every Chinese he meets. American officers ought to talk it to Chinese officers. After all, we Chinese consider you Americans the ideal of democracy.

(I suggested that the use of our Army as a political propaganda force was alien—and that we had nothing corresponding to the Communist Political Department to indoctrinate the troops and direct such work.)

But even if your American soldiers do not actively propagandize, their mere presence and contact with Chinese has a good effect. We welcome them in China for this reason. The Kuomintang does not. It wants to segregate them and keep them from knowing what conditions really are. How many American observers do you have now in the front lines? We are happy to take your men anywhere. The KMT is worried about the effect of a lot of Americans in China. They fear an American landing only second to their fear of Russian participation.

The presence of Americans is good in another negative way.

If Americans are scattered widely, they will have a restraining effect on the Kuomintang. It will be more difficult for the KMT to start trouble. An example is Kunming. It has become a center of liberal thought and student freedom because the KMT doesn't dare to arrest and throw the students into concentration camps under the eyes of so many Americans. Compare this with Sian, where Americans are very few and the secret police unrestrained.

Criticism of the Kuomintang in American periodicals is good. Its effect may not be immediately apparent. Sometimes it may even seem temporarily to have a bad reaction. But if it is fair (the KMT will know if it is), it causes the KMT to hesitate and think—because they need American support.

Finally, any contact you Americans have with us Communists is good. Of course we are glad to have the Observer Section here because it will help to beat Japan. But there is no use in pretending that—up to now at least—the chief importance of your coming is [not] its political effect on the Kuomintang.

(I noted his emphasis on American landing in China and suggested that the war might be won in other ways and a landing not necessary.)

We think the Americans must land in China. It depends, of course, on Japanese strength and the developments of the war. But the main Japanese strength is in the Yangtze Valley and North China—not to speak of Manchuria.

If the Americans do not land in China, it will be most unfortunate for China. The Kuomintang will continue as the government—without being able to be the government.

If there is a landing, there will have to be American cooperation with both Chinese forces—KMT and Communist. Our forces now surround Hankow, Shanghai, Nanking and other large cities. We are the inner ring; the KMT is further back.

If there is to be this cooperation with both Communist and KMT forces, it is important that we be allowed to work in separate sectors. The KMT is too afraid of us to work with us. Their only concern will be to checkmate us. When we are in separate sectors, the U.S. Army can see the difference: that we have popular support and can fight.

(I questioned whether open civil war was, as he had suggested, inevitable if the KMT was not restrained or induced to reform.)

We can say that civil war is "inevitable but not quite certain." Subjectively, the present KMT leaders are determined on the elimination of the Communists. They are afraid of us just as, and for the same reason as, they are afraid of the people. Objectively, there are factors—the five mentioned at the beginning of the talk—which restrain the KMT. The strongest of these—the Japanese—will be out of the picture. Another—strong because outside and independent of the KMT —is foreign opinion. But it is now unpredictable. The KMT still hopes that foreign influence may be on its side.

The KMT is already busy preparing pretexts for civil war. The more you know of us and conditions in our areas, the less value these pretexts will have.

So the KMT may resort to indirect methods of attack. It will be hard to define or set a line to its aggression.

But if the KMT undoes the progress that has been accomplished in our areas, if they take away the new democratic rights of the people, the people will resist and will demand our help.

Another line of KMT action will be through the puppets. The puppets will turn back to the KMT—claiming to have been "patriotic" all the time. The KMT will then use the puppets to hold the cities and areas from which the Japanese withdraw. They will incite the puppets to attack us and to create friction.

(Chou En-lai carries this line further by suggesting that this may be a part of the possible fraudulent Japanese surrender to Chiang: the Japanese will turn over their arms to the puppets (or the KMT) on the condition that the Communists will be liquidated.

(This may seem at first a little far-fetched. The only possible comment is that the forces involved in this situation are so complicated and their hatreds so intense that almost anything is possible.)

The fact is clear, even to the Kuomintang, that China's political tendency is toward us. We hold to the Manifesto of the First Kuomintang Congress. This is a truly great and democratic document. Sun Yat-sen was no Communist. The Manifesto is still valid. It will not quickly pass out of date. We will hold to it even if the KMT should collapse because its general policies are good and suited to China. Everything we have done, every article of our program, is found in that document.

Of course, we do not pretend that we are perfect. We still face problems of bureaucracy and corruption. But we do face them. And we are beating them. We welcome observation and criticism—by Americans, by the KMT or by anyone else. We are constantly criticizing ourselves and revising our policies toward greater efficiency and effectiveness.

Our experience proves that the Chinese people understand democracy and want it. It does not take long experience or education or "tutelage." The Chinese peasant is not stupid; he is shrewd, and like everyone else, concerned over his rights and interests. You can see the difference in our areas—the people are alive, interested, friendly. They have a human outlet. They are free from deadening repression.

(I queried his emphasis on the importance of the United States and his neglect to consider Russia.)

Soviet participation either in the Far Eastern war or in China's postwar reconstruction depends entirely on the circumstances of the Soviet Union. The Russians have suffered greatly in the war and will have their hands full with their own job of rebuilding. We do not expect Russian help.

Furthermore, the KMT because of its anti-Communist phobia is anti-Russian. Therefore KMT-Soviet cooperation is impossible. And for us to seek it would only make the situation in China worse. China is disunified enough already! In any case Soviet help is not likely even if the KMT wanted it.

But Russia will not oppose American interests in China if they are constructive and democratic. There will be no possible point of conflict. Russia only wants a friendly and democratic China. Cooperation between America and the Chinese Communist Party will be beneficial and satisfactory to all concerned.

(I jokingly remarked that the name "Communist" might not be reassuring to some American businessmen. Mao laughed and said that they had thought of changing their name but that if people knew them they would not be frightened.)

The policies of the Chinese Communist Party are merely liberal. Our rent reduction is from the old 80–70–60 percent

down to the legal (by unenforced Kuomintang law) 37½ percent. Even this we only try to accomplish gradually because
we don't want to drive away the landlords. Our limit on interest is 10 percent a year. This is not extreme—though it is much
lower than it used to be.

Even the most conservative American businessman can
find nothing in our program to take exception to.

China must industrialize. This can be done—in China—
only by free enterprise and with the aid of foreign capital.
Chinese and American interests are correlated and similar.
They fit together, economically and politically. We can and
must work together.

The United States would find us more cooperative than
the Kuomintang. We will not be afraid of democratic American influence—we will welcome it. We have no silly ideas of
taking only Western mechanical techniques. Also we will not
be interested in monopolistic, bureaucratic capitalism that sti-
fles the economic development of the country and only en-
riches the officials. We will be interested in the most rapid
possible development of the country on constructive and productive lines. First will be the raising of the living standard
of the people (see what we have done here with our limited
resources). After that we can come to the "national defense
industry" that Chiang talks of in his *China's Destiny*. We will
be interested in the welfare of the Chinese people.

America does not need to fear that we will not be cooperative. We must cooperate and we must have American help.
This is why it is so important to us Communists to know what
you Americans are thinking and planning. We cannot risk
crossing you—cannot risk any conflict with you.

After more than two months in Yenan and many more interviews with Mao and the other Communist leaders, Service was
ready to sit down and write his own analysis of Communist foreign
policy. The critical question of course was the Chinese Communists'
relations with the United States and the U.S.S.R. Basing his analysis
in large measure on the Rectification (*cheng-feng*) Movement then in
progress in the Communist areas, he argued that the Chinese Communists were moving away from dogmatic Marxism, that they were

stressing their "Chinese" nature, and that they were sincere in their desire for friendly relations with the United States. He warned however, that "This does not preclude their turning back toward Soviet Russia if they are forced to in order to survive [an] American-supported Kuomintang attack." It was a warning which would go tragically unheeded.

The Orientation of the Chinese Communists toward the Soviet Union and the United States

No. 34: September 28, 1944
Amerasia Papers, pp. 939–46

1. There is attached a memorandum on present policies of the Chinese Communists as they affect and are indications of present Chinese Communist orientation toward the Soviet Union and the United States.

2. This memorandum may be summarized as follows:

Summary: Politically, any orientation which the Chinese Communists may once have had toward the Soviet Union seems to be a thing of the past. The Communists have worked to make their thinking and program realistically Chinese, and they are carrying out democratic policies which they expect the United States to approve and sympathetically support.

Economically, the Chinese Communists seek the rapid development and industrialization of China for the primary objective of raising the economic level of the people. They recognize that under present conditions in China, this must be accomplished through capitalism with large-scale foreign assistance. They believe that the United States, rather than the Soviet Union, will be the only country able to give this economic assistance and realize that for reasons of efficiency, as well as to attract American investment, it will be wise to give this American participation great freedom. *End of summary.*

3. The *conclusion,* which is the continual statement of the Communist leaders themselves, is that American friendship and support is more important to China than Russian. The

Communists also believe, of course, in the necessity of close and friendly relations of China with the Soviet Union, but they insist that this should involve no conflict in interests between the United States and the Soviet Union.

4. This apparent strong orientation of the Chinese Communists toward the United States may be somewhat contrary to general expectation—which may be too ready to emphasize the Communist name of the Party. Apart from what may be called the practical considerations that the United States will be the strongest power in the Pacific area, and America the country best able to give economic assistance to China, it is also based on the strong Communist conviction that China cannot remain divided. I believe that the Chinese Communists are at present sincere in seeking Chinese unity on the basis of American support. This does not preclude their turning back toward Soviet Russia if they are forced to in order to survive American-supported Kuomintang attack.

POLICIES OF THE CHINESE COMMUNISTS AFFECTING THEIR
ATTITUDES TOWARD THE SOVIET UNION
AND THE UNITED STATES

A. POLITICAL

1. The attempt to make Chinese Communist thinking more Chinese

There is apparent in the major statements of theory by Communist leaders during the past several years an effort to get away from slavish attempts to apply Russian communism to China. The emphasis is laid on realistic study of China itself.

The strongest intellectual movement within the Communist Party has been against the "three great faults" of subjectivism, sectarianism and pedantic formalism. The most important of these, judging from the attention given to it, is subjectivism, which is interpreted to include the dogmatic application of foreign theories unsuited to existing conditions in China. The attitude set forth as correct is "objectivism"—the application of theory on the basis of exhaustive study of actual facts and true conditions. The general effect of this movement has been to take the communism out of Chinese Communist thinking, at least in regard to the immediate future of China.

Examples of such Communist statements are numerous. Perhaps one of the best is a lecture entitled "How to Change the Way We Study," given by Mao Tse-tung to high Party workers at Yenan in May 1941. This lecture is now included in a volume of selected papers which is required textbook for all Communist Party cadres. The following is a partial quotation:*

"No one has begun in a really serious manner the study of the political, economic, military and cultural history of China during the past century, the period of real significance.*** Many of our comrades regard this ignorance or partial knowledge of our own history, not as a shame, but on the contrary as something to be proud of.*** Since they know nothing about their own country, they turn to foreign lands.*** During recent decades many foreign-returned students have made this mistake. They have merely been phonographs, forgetting that their duty is to make something useful to China out of the imported stuff they have learned. The Communist Party has not escaped this infection.

"We study the teachings of Marx and his followers. But the way that many of us learn those teachings is in direct opposition to their spirit.*** Marx, Engels, Lenin and Stalin teach us to study seriously the existing conditions, starting from the actual objective circumstances, not from our subjective wishes. But many of our comrades are acting directly contrary to this guiding principle.

"*** Many comrades learn the truths of Marx-Leninism merely for the sake of Marx-Leninism.*** Although they can quote at length from Marx, Engels, Lenin and Stalin, yet they cannot apply their learning to the concrete study of Chinese history and the present conditions in China; they cannot analyze and solve problems that arise from the Chinese Revolution.

"These people, who are unscientific in attitude, who only know how to recite dogmas, who have degrees but no real knowledge*** are a practical joke on real Marx-Leninism."

* This translation has been made by Communist sources in Yenan. I have, however, checked it roughly by reading the Chinese original. [Footnote in original.]

2. *The application of Marxism to China*

I attempted in my report No. 5 of August 3, 1944,* to describe the Chinese Communist application of Marxist ideology to China. The gist was that the Chinese Communist Party in its present program has abandoned everything except the doctrine of historical materialism and the belief in the eventual socialistic society.

That exposition was based on very incomplete study and fragmentary statements by various Communist leaders. It was confirmed, however, in a striking way by Po Ku (generally referred to by the Kuomintang by his original name, Ch'in Pang-hsien) in a conversation on September 3, 1944. Po Ku's comments are of interest, not only because of his position as a member of the Political Bureau and former Chairman of the Communist Party's Central Committee, but also because he is a Russian-returned and usually described in Kuomintang "analyses" of the Communists as the leader of a "pro-Russian clique." My notes of Po Ku's remarks are as follows:

"We regard Marxism not as a dogma but as a guide. We accept its historical materialism and its ideological method. It furnishes us with the conclusions and the objectives toward which we strive. This objective is the classless society built on socialism—in other words, the good of the individual and the interests of all the people.

"But to try to transplant to China all of Marx's description of the society in which he found himself (the Industrial Revolution of Europe in the nineteenth century) and the steps (class struggle and violent revolution) which he saw would be necessary for the people to escape from those conditions, would not only be ridiculous, it would also be a violation of our basic principles of realistic objectivism and the avoidance of doctrinaire dogmatism.

"China at present is not even capitalistic. Its economy is still that of semifeudalism. We cannot advance at one jump to socialism. In fact, because we are at least two hundred years behind most of the rest of the world, we probably cannot hope to reach socialism until after most of the rest of the world has reached that state.

* See pp. 266–72.

"First we must rid ourselves of this semifeudalism. Then we must raise our economic level by a long stage of democracy and free enterprise.

"What we Communists hope to do is to keep China moving smoothly and steadily toward this goal. By orderly, gradual and progressive development we will avoid the conditions which forced Marx to draw his conclusions of the necessity (in his society) for class struggle: we will *prevent* the need for a violent revolution by a peaceful planned revolution.

"It is impossible to predict how long this process will take. But we can be sure that it will be more than thirty or forty years, and probably more than a hundred years. . . ."

3. The Communist political program is democracy

Changing from theory to practice, the Communist political program is simple democracy. This is much more American than Russian in form and spirit.

Communists now are prone to deny that they were Communistic even in the early days of their rule in Kiangsi. I am not competent to discuss this. But the fact was that their governments were organized as Soviets during that period.

Starting in August 1935, the Communists reversed their basic policy on the basis of the United Front line. Since that time—for over nine years—they have adopted the San Min Chu I (as set forth by Sun Yat-sen in the Manifesto of the First Kuomintang Congress), have abandoned the Soviet type of government, and have sought cooperation of all groups based on democratic rights of the whole people.

[Service then reviews the moderate United Front policies of the CCP, which have been covered in earlier despatches.]

4. There is little aping of Soviet Russia and little evidence of strong ties to Russia

Not only in theory and policy, also in the atmosphere and daily scene in Yenan there is little direct evidence of Soviet influence. Except in speeches within the Party, there is little reference to Communism or to Marx and the other patriarchs of Communism. In Party institutions there are pictures of Marx and occasionally of Engels and Lenin, but these are rare. Stalin's picture is common but usually placed alongside those of Mao Tse-tung, Chu Teh, Sun Yat-sen, Chiang Kai-shek, Roosevelt and Churchill.

The Communist newspaper gives considerable prominence to Russian war news but not more than it does its news of American victories and much less than it does to the operations of the Communist armies.

Soviet influence is obvious in the organization of the Communist Party, but the same can be said of the Kuomintang. . . .

The Soviet symbols of the hammer and sickle are almost never seen. In fact, the casual observer sees little to remind him of Russia or to make him think that the Chinese Communists are particularly attached to Soviet Russia or, as suggested by the extreme faction of the Kuomintang, in any way a front for the Russian Communists.

It cannot be said, on the other hand, that the Chinese Communists are trying to ape American models (except in the surprising ways of social dancing and a mild interest in bridge and poker). In fact, they are imitating nobody. Their emphasis is on being Chinese. And in this they seek to come down to the level of the common people. There is no hocus-pocus such as the Kuomintang insists on of weekly Sun Yat-sen Memorial Meeting, no formal posting of Sun Yat-sen's (or any one else's) picture to be bowed to before every meeting, no ceremonial of repeating Sun Yat-sen's will, no standing every time someone's name is mentioned. The Russian-inspired romanization of the Chinese language has been dropped. Except for limited audiences of the Party cadres, the Western drama has been abandoned for a popularization and development of the native Northern Chinese folk plays and dances. Music has been made native. In every sphere the Communists have made the most strenuous efforts to go native and to approach the mass of the people in terms that they will understand.

B. ECONOMIC

Following views chiefly Po Ku, supplemented by talks with Mao and Liu Shao-ch'i.

1. The Communists agree that China must industrialize

The Communists are just as convinced as the Kuomintang (and everyone else) that China must industrialize.

Where the Communists differ from the Kuomintang is in their motivation and emphasis. One gains the impression from *China's Destiny* and much of the present thinking in Chungking that the primary objective of China's industrialization is defense—in other words, national power. The Communists place this second. First in their minds (at least in their talk) is welfare. Unless the living standards of the people are raised, there can be no real foundation for either economic or political progress. The first great expansion, the Communists claim, should therefore be in light, consumer industry and communications. More gradually and slowly there can be built up a heavy industry (or as *China's Destiny* calls it, a National Defense) base.

The Communists also place greater emphasis on the idea that China will probably always be predominantly an agricultural country, that China's agricultural resources and problems must therefore not be neglected, that China does not have the material resources to be a first-rank heavy-industry country.

2. China can industrialize at present only on a capitalistic basis

China's basic condition at present is still semifeudalism. To get rid of this is the first important step. From this it is impossible to step at once to socialism because there is neither the political nor economic foundation. The Chinese people are not yet ready for socialism and will not be for a long time to come. To talk of socialism now is impractical. The next stage in China's advance must be capitalism. In this capitalism must be given the freest possible opportunity to develop the country economically. China's weakness now is the underdevelopment of capitalism.

3. Foreign assistance will be necessary to bring about this industrialization

China not only lacks enough native capital to finance large-scale industrialization, it also lacks an adequate industry to serve as a starting point for this industrialization, [and] it lacks experience and technical personnel. The end of the war will see these conditions accentuated. China will be suffering from ruinous inflation, from the disorganization and destruction brought by the war. It is probable that the Japanese will complete the destruction of the rudimentary Chinese industry before they withdraw or are defeated.

These conditions make it impossible for China to follow Russia's example of building herself. Backward as Russia was after the Revolution, she had far more of a modern industrial base than China will have. Low as were the living standards of the Russian people, they were not as low as the irreducible minimum of the great majority of the Chinese people, and it was therefore possible for the Soviets to depress those living standards even further to raise the capital for their industrialization. But even Russia accomplished what she did only with terrific sacrifices. She did not do it on her own resources because she wanted to, but because she had to. China, even if she were able to accomplish such a herculean feat, will be under no such compulsion to do so. The attempt would be foolish.

4. Soviet Russia will be unable to give this needed large-scale economic assistance to China

After the war, Russia will have a great part of her country to rebuild. Her own reconstruction and the continuation of her own internal development which was interrupted by the war will continue for a long time. Published reports indicate that the reopening of the mines in the Donbas Basin may take as long as two or three years of work. The report of Mr. Johnson, the president of the American Chamber of Commerce, of his talks in Moscow indicate that Russia herself will seek large-scale assistance from the United States after the war in imports of materials and machinery. These will have to be financed by loans.

It is therefore obvious that Russia will have neither surplus capital nor technical personnel available to assist us in the industrialization of China.

5. The United States is the only country which will be able to help China

Even if Russia were able (which she will not be) to assist China, the United States will be the logical country to play the greatest share. American resources will be tremendous. They have been geared to huge exports during the war. America will have industrial plants which will not be needed and can be exported whole. She will have capital to invest and the necessary technical personnel. In addition, her sea communications with China are better than those from European Russia. America faces on the Pacific. Siberia is still under development.

American ties with China are strong. America has all of China's good will. For reasons of China's internal unity it will be better for America to play the major role in this economic development.

The other European countries will be engaged in reconstruction of their own countries. They will not have capital to invest. The same will be true to some extent of Great Britain, whose large-scale participation in China will in any case be less welcome than America's.

6. *Great freedom must be given to foreign capital in this economic development of China*

Since our goal is the most rapid possible development of Chinese resources, communications and industry, we must make investment attractive to foreign capital. We cannot reasonably expect China to reap all the profit.

The logic of our moderate treatment of landlords and merchants, and limited reduction of rent and interest in order to obtain the support of these groups in a United Front which can strengthen our bases economically, will hold good. If we carried out drastic reduction of rents, or confiscation of land and restriction of private business, we would cut off our own noses and weaken our bases by driving out these necessary capitalistic groups.

We must therefore give foreign capital very wide freedom of opportunity.

Experience has shown us that government enterprises in our own areas cannot yet be operated efficiently. Our army factories are not as efficient as privately run factories.

We believe that Chungking's efforts to create a bureaucratic industry (for instance, the enterprises of the National Resources Commission and the monopolies of H. H. Kung) are proving the same thing. They may enrich Kung and a few others. But they are rotten with favoritism, graft and inefficiency. They are *not* the best means to bring about this economic development.

POLICY RECOMMENDATIONS

Mao Tse-tung's clear attempt to interest the United States in some alternative to its policy of exclusive support for the Kuomintang, coming as it did on top of the accumulating evidence of growing Communist strength and confidence, helped to spur Service to some explicit policy recommendations. While a junior officer in the Foreign Service would not normally be making policy recommendations of his own, Service, in his anomalous position as political reporter and adviser to Stilwell, had already made one long policy recommendation (in his June 20, 1944, memorandum*), and that had been extraordinarily well received in the Department. Now, with firsthand knowledge of the Chinese Communists and their movement, he was to go a good deal beyond his June 20 recommendations and urge that the United States "take a more or less active part in influencing China's internal affairs."

While in June he had spoken primarily of expanding our cultural relations program, maintaining friendly relations with liberal elements in the Kuomintang, expressing our interest in democracy and continuing "to show an interest in the Chinese Communist," now Service was directly advocating that U.S. military aid go not only to the KMT but also to the Chinese Communists. Furthermore, it is clear from the Yenan reports that Service's concern was not so much with the war against Japan, which by then seemed certain to be won by U.S. island-hopping across the Pacific. Now his concern was the near certainty of civil war in China and the danger that in that civil war exclusive U.S. support for the KMT might commit us to a hopeless cause. Above all, he urged that our relations with the Kuomintang be determined by an intelligent understanding of the effect they would have on future relations with the Chinese Communists.

* See pp. 138–57.

The Need of an American Policy toward the Problems Created by the Rise of the Chinese Communist Party

No. 20: September 3, 1944
Foreign Relations, 1944, pp. 615–18

An important development in China during, and partly as a result of, the war against Japan has been the phenomenal growth and spread of influence of the Chinese Communist Party. It is now in control of most of North and a part of Central China, and is the only active force carrying on the war there against the Japanese. It claims, probably with some foundation, the effective government of 86 million people—about one fifth of the population of China.

This development has come at the same time as an apparent loss of vitality of the Kuomintang, and a deterioration of conditions in the areas under its control. These have had serious effects on the prosecution of the war by the Central Government.

This shift in the balance of Chinese political forces has resulted in internal tension—due primarily to the Kuomintang's fear of losing its monopolistic power—which has brought about a situation practically equivalent to civil war. This has had further depressive effects on the Kuomintang's will and ability to fight Japan, and will be an impediment to the unity, democratic progress and economic rehabilitation of China which the United States (not to speak of the great majority of the Chinese people) hoped for.

Without the intercession of external factors, it now seems inevitable that this tension will result in catastrophic civil war—probably soon after the defeat, chiefly by our efforts, of Japan.

Even though such a civil war would be immensely harmful to our own interests, we must consider that we would be accused —with much justification—of having contributed to it by our present arming of the military forces of the Kuomintang.

These various circumstances may force the United States, despite its natural disinclination, to take a more or less active part in the influencing of China's internal affairs. Our influence in China will never be greater than it is now; and progress of events in this part of the world will not allow delay. The crisis will increase as the defeat of Japan is approached. It may therefore be necessary in the very near future for the United States to decide on a definite policy in regard to the problems created by the rise of the Chinese Communist Party.

The ramifications of these problems do not need emphasis. They are of great and immediate military importance, but they are also highly political in their short and long term effects.

For instance, we may well decide, on the basis of what the Chinese Communist military forces have achieved and their apparent potentialities for contributing to the defeat of Japan, that those military forces deserve our active support—probably in the form of military supplies.

It may not be necessary for us to give this support directly and against the opposition of the Kuomintang. Our diplomatic influence, quietly but firmly exerted, or the growingly obvious deterioration of its own position, may impel the Kuomintang to share its power with a more truly representative national government. This presumably would have to include the Communists. There would then be a new United Front, the present blockade of the Communist areas would be ended, and the Government itself should give the Communist forces, as a part of the national armies, some share of American supplies. Present indications, however, do not encourage hope of such a reversal of attitude by the Kuomintang. It is probable, even if a nominally national government is set up, that the Kuomintang would continue to block any aid to the Communist forces. Should we, under these circumstances, insist on giving this military aid?

The giving of any American military support to the Communists, whether directly or by some indirect means as mentioned above, would be certain to have an important effect on the political situation in China. The Communist army is as much a political as a military force. These dual characteristics cannot be separated. And this political nature cannot be taken away— even by incorporation of the Communist forces into the National army. Our support would be generally interpreted as an indication of American approval. And by improving the military effectiveness of the Communist forces, it would increase their claimable share in winning the war. Both of these factors would raise the prestige of the Communist Party and ultimately its influence in China.

This boosting of the Communists might swing the balance

of political forces in China far enough so that the Kuomintang would be forced to reform its policies and—even more important —the manner of their execution, to change its present reactionary leadership, and thus to move toward the cooperation with the Communists which would lead toward unity, democracy and national strength. These are the effects we would hope to have result.

We could not, however, ignore the possibility that the present Kuomintang leadership—apparently lacking in statesmanship and thoroughly selfish for power—will not, even under these conditions, release its stranglehold on the Party. If the Kuomintang thus refuses to reform itself, it will be courting suicide. It will, indeed, be questionable whether it can in this form survive the crisis of the present war. If it does survive, we can at least be confident that we will have prevented, by our moral and material support of the Communists, the civil war that would otherwise have been certain.

If this possibility of the collapse of the Kuomintang— chiefly through its own intransigeance—is admitted, we must consider what forces would rise to take its place in China. At present it appears certain that the strongest of these would be the Communist Party, and that after a fairly short period it would succeed in unifying the country.

Even if the Communist Party does not have this opportunity to rise to control, we must expect, because of the vitality it is showing and the popular support it has won, that it will be influential in China and an important element in the democratic structure which must, as an alternative, be created.

We can limit ourselves to these two possibilities of (*a*) Communist control of the country, or (*b*) important Communist political participation, because it is now apparent that the present Kuomintang cannot unaidedly exterminate the Communists, and because it can be taken for granted that we will not willingly, or knowingly, give this aid. The Communist Party, therefore, under any circumstances, must be counted a continuing and important influence in China.

Whichever possibility—control or influential participation —is realized, it is obvious that the nature, policies and objectives of the Chinese Communist Party are of vital long-term concern to the United States.

Answers to these questions, and the determination of our

proper policy toward the Chinese Communist Party—whether we use our diplomatic influence in its favor, whether we remain neutral, or whether we ignore the Communist Party and continue our support only of the Kuomintang—should be determined, in part at least, by the study of: (1) the actual accomplishments of the Communist Party; (2) its policies, both present and what they may be expected to be in future; and (3) the quality and capacity of its leadership.

The military accomplishments of the Chinese Communist Party during the present war, and the fact that these depend on a political base of popular support which the Communists have created, are now fairly well known. I have touched on these subjects in my reports nos. 6 (August 3), 10 (August 15), 17 (August 30), 18 (August 31) and 19 (August 31).* Colonel Barrett has also submitted a number of reports on the Communist participation in the war, the development of their main bases, and the quality of their military forces and arms. In addition a series of reports will be submitted on specific phases of Communist accomplishments: the extent of democracy in the areas under their control; their methods for the creation of popular support; their political use of the army; the organization and working of their governments; their educational program; their legal system; the economic developments in their bases, and so on. Because of the importance of the time element, the logical order will in some cases be reversed by submitting generalized reports before the completion of basic specialized studies.

To commence work on the other two proposed points, there are being attempted in following reports: (1) an analysis of present Communist policies and probable extensions into the future; and (2) a general group impression of the personality, character and apparent capability of the leaders of the Communist Party.

––––––––––––

An even more specific policy recommendation by Service was exclusively directed to the question of aid to the Chinese Com-

---

* All save No. 18 (on a briefing by P'eng Teh-huai) are printed above. See pp. 183–87 (No. 6), 200–5 (No. 10), 208–11 (No. 17), and 211–16 (No. 19).

322   *Lost Chance in China*

munist armies. Here once again, though Service included a list of military reasons for such a move, he indicated the primacy of political considerations by listing them first. The key to the policy recommendation was the fact that the KMT was then clearly aiming in the direction of civil war, and the only way to prevent that catastrophe for China and the international relations of the Pacific basin was to make civil war an unattractive alternative for the Kuomintang: ". . . the aid we give the Communists will almost certainly make it impossible for the Kuomintang to start a civil war."

Desirability of American Military Aid to the Chinese Communist Armies

No. 16: August 29, 1944
Foreign Relations, 1944, pp. 618–22

The U.S. Army has made a start in cooperation with the military forces of the Chinese Communists. So far this has been passive on our part—the tapping of Communist intelligence sources and the rescue of American air crews. The obvious success which this halfway cooperation has had should lead logically to the consideration of more active measures.

Such active cooperation would begin with our furnishing basic military supplies now desperately lacked by the Communist forces. It should be supported by training in the effective use of these supplies. It should be planned to lead, as the war in China develops into its late stages, to actual tactical cooperation of Communist with air and other ground forces.

The physical difficulties of supplying the Communist forces admittedly will be great. These difficulties can be overcome. But the decision to start this cooperation will involve questions of both military and political policy. It is sure, to begin with, to meet the strong and obstinate opposition of the Kuomintang. We must decide whether the gains we can reasonably expect from aiding the Communists will justify the overcoming —or disregarding—of this Kuomintang opposition.

The decision, I suggest, depends on the following considerations:

A. Political

We are now enough acquainted with conditions in China, and sufficiently experienced in cooperation with the Kuomintang, to say that the Kuomintang—as it is today—is weak, incompetent and uncooperative.

The chief concern of the politically blind and thoroughly selfish leaders of the Kuomintang is to preserve their tottering power. Lacking popular support and afraid to carry out reforms necessary to gain it, the Kuomintang knows that its miserable and dispirited conscript armies cannot stand combat against the Japanese. But its power depends, in its present narrow view, on the preservation of those armies and the equipment which it hopes we will give them. Lacking any effective economic policies, the Kuomintang is allowing the country to drift rapidly toward an economic collapse. It fears that this process will be accelerated by any large-scale military operations—by itself or by us—in China.

The Kuomintang therefore fears, and seeks to avoid, the further attrition of its resources by large-scale involvement in the war. It wants to have the war won for it—outside of China. It fears, second only to its fear of Russian participation, a large-scale extension of American military operations onto the Chinese mainland.

The situation as far as the Chinese Communists are concerned, is just the opposite. The war has given them the chance to grow and greatly extend their influence. They have acquired real popular support and mobilized an important part of the population of North China by convincing the people that this is their war and that they must take a part in it. The fact that their aggressive participation in the war against the Japanese has given the Communists their chance to come to by far their greatest power is of great importance. The Communists realize that if they play a major part in winning this war they will greatly strengthen not only their domestic but also their international position. For these, if for no other more idealistic and patriotic reasons, the Communists really want to fight.

Against this background, the following conclusions can be drawn:

(a) The limitation of our support and supplies to the Kuomintang will not win us an effective and wholehearted ally.

(*b*) Instead, it will only encourage the Kuomintang in its present undemocratic tendencies. While it may help to prolong the Kuomintang's precarious power, it is doubtful, as long as the Kuomintang refuses to reform, whether it can for long delay the inevitable internal crisis. It may even encourage its Fascist-minded leaders to embark on a civil war which could only be disastrous to China, to postwar peace in this part of the world, and to our peaceful interests here.

(*c*) The impartial support of both Kuomintang and Communists will make effective at least one force, the Communists, which is really interested in fighting.

(*d*) Such impartial support will actually be a constructive influence in China. The Kuomintang will be forced to compete not only for our support but for that of the Chinese people. We may thus help to stimulate the Kuomintang toward reform.

(*e*) Finally, the aid we give the Communists will almost certainly make it impossible for the Kuomintang to start a civil war. At the same time we will not likely be contributing to a Communist-provoked civil war; their policies are against civil war, the weapons they want from us (in contrast to those asked for by the Kuomintang) are light and simple rather than heavy offensive weapons, and, if the progress of the Kuomintang which our policy should promote is realized, civil war will be unnecessary.

Summing up: If the Kuomintang is actually what it claims to be—democratic and sincerely anxious to defeat the Japanese as quickly as possible—it should not oppose our insistence on giving at least proportional aid to the Communists. It is not too much to say that the strength of Kuomintang opposition will be a measure of the desirability of support of the Communists.

B. Military

Although we have not yet completed field observations in the actual fighting zones, enough is now known about the Communists to warrant the drawing of a number of conclusions. These are supported by the results of such cooperation as we have already received from the Communists. But above all else is the incontrovertible fact that the Communists, starting from almost nothing at the beginning of the war, have not only maintained but greatly strengthened themselves in a very large area of North and Central China, where they continue to tie down considerable Japanese forces.

(*a*) The Communist forces hold strategic positions along and in very close proximity to all the Japanese communication lines north of the Yangtze River. The map of their positions speaks for itself. Communist claims are supported by their furnishing of intelligence and by their rescue of American air crews. From these positions they have access to the main cities and can cut the railways. As our control of the China Sea becomes more complete, these communications will become more important. They will, for instance, be vital to the Japanese if we make a landing anywhere in South China —or even if Hankow is attacked.

(*b*) The Communist forces are capable and experienced in mobile and guerrilla warfare and have the morale and determination to carry out such operations.

(*c*) They have the popular support of the people in the areas concerned which is necessary to the conduct of such operations on a wide scale and over a protracted period. This popular support gives them great manpower reserves of a useful, because voluntary and already partially trained, type.

(*d*) Their matériel requirements are simple and moderate. With them, a little will go a long way. They fully realize that they are unable [to use], and the conditions of their terrain and operations prevent them from using, heavy and complicated modern equipment.

(*e*) The furnishing to the Communists of moderate quantities of supplies will not only improve their effectiveness (making it possible, for instance, for them to take isolated blockhouses or to hold a bridge long enough to carry out proper destruction), it will also enable them to add to their supplies, as they have done in the past, by the capture of quantities of Japanese equipment. Their position inside the areas of Japanese occupation and the tactics they employ facilitate this self-supply.

(*f*) The tonnage of supplies given to the Communist forces, even though not large, will be much more effective in disrupting communications, sabotaging industries and supplies, and killing Japanese than the same tonnage put into the supply of the air forces for similar purposes. Air bombing is not only wasteful and often ineffective; it will also require, with the distance of targets in North China from our useful bases, great expenditures of gasoline, maintenance supplies and other equipment. A much better job could be done in destroying and keeping out of use a Japanese railway, for instance, by numerous coordinated guerrilla attacks along an extended stretch of line. Japanese garrisons not only on the railway itself but all through the occupied territory would have to be increased if the Communist forces had sufficient supplies to make them effective. Japanese losses and expenditures in equipment in these operations would be much greater than suffered from isolated bombings.

(g) The use of the Communist forces for this guerrilla warfare and the demolition of communications in the far rear of the Japanese would permit concentration of the air force on other important tasks. For instance, before a coastal landing the Communists over a considerable period could be given sufficient supplies and trained in their use. When the landing is about to be, and after it has been made, the air force can devote itself to direct support because the already equipped and prepared Communist forces will be able to relieve it of the responsibility of attacking and disrupting the communications from Manchuria to the Yangtze.

Conclusion:

Consideration of all these political and military factors, I propose, warrants the extension of American military aid to the Chinese Communist armies.

PART III

The Debate
with Hurley

Take note, take note, O world!
To be direct and honest is not safe.

—Shakespeare,
Othello

After Stilwell's recall to the United States on October 19, 1944, Service was ordered back to Washington to report on his stay in Yenan and to participate in any possible discussions of our policy toward China. When he passed through Chungking, Service met briefly with Ambassador Clarence Gauss. Gauss, discouraged by Chiang Kai-shek's blunt refusal of any compromise with the Communists and distressed by the flamboyant independence of President Roosevelt's personal representative, Pat Hurley, asked Service to inform the State Department of his intention to resign. Thus the two senior American representatives in China were on their way out, the victims of the Generalissimo's intransigence.

Clearly, this was a major watershed in American policy toward China and the Kuomintang. Nobody sensed this more clearly than Service and such colleagues in the Foreign Service as John P. Davies: "After Stilwell's recall, I really felt that we were headed down the wrong track. Both Davies and I felt we were making a serious mistake in tying ourselves to the Kuomintang and giving in to Chiang. So as time went on, I certainly became much more of an advocate of a policy position. After the Stilwell affair, most of us felt that it was worth sticking our necks out."

In sticking their necks out, the executioner whom the young Foreign Service officers would confront was Patrick J. Hurley. During his October 1944 stopover in Chungking, Service had spoken briefly with Hurley and tried unsuccessfully to educate the general about the Chinese Communists. He also knew enough about Hurley's handling of the Stilwell crisis to advise President Roosevelt's confidant, Harry Hopkins, that Hurley's appointment as Ambassador to succeed Gauss would be a "disaster." Unfortunately, this advice was disregarded. On November 17, 1944, Roosevelt appointed Hurley Ambassador to China. Thus when Service returned to China in mid-January 1945, he knew that he would be, in a sense, involved in a debate with Hurley.

We have already seen some of the documents which form part of this "debate." "Chiang Kai-shek," said Hurley, "asserts that he desires to unite the military forces of China . . ."* Hurley believed Chiang, but as Service pointed out in his memo on "Chiang Kai-shek's Treatment of the Kwangsi Clique," the Generalissimo's policy "actually increased disunity." Hurley claimed that "The strength of the armed forces of the Chinese Communists has been exaggerated. The area of territory controlled by the Communists has been exaggerated."† Yet Service's "Verification of Communist Territorial Claims by Direct American Observation" was able to establish that "We must accept as substantially correct the Communist claims to control the countryside of North and Central China behind the line of Japanese penetration." Then there were the critical issues of 1945: the negotiations between the KMT and the CCP, and the very much related problem of Sino-Soviet relations.

* *Foreign Relations, 1944,* p. 699.
† *Foreign Relations, 1945,* pp. 432–33.

THE LIKELIHOOD OF KMT-CCP RECONCILIATION

Service remembers well his first meeting with Hurley on October 23, 1944. Stilwell had just been recalled, and General Hurley, having failed in his mission to bring Stilwell and the Generalissimo together, was now seeking to heal the even greater breach between the KMT and the CCP. At Hurley's request, Service called to brief him on the Communists' new and tougher negotiating terms, on which Service had frequently reported from Yenan. "It was like the famous talk that Hurley had with Mike Mansfield*: fifty-seven minutes Hurley, three minutes Service. He went on saying, 'Don't worry, I'll bring these two sides together. They [the Communists] are going to get American arms. That's what I'm here for. . . . I've had experience with this sort of thing. I know it's going to be tough, but I've done this before.' Hurley never read any of my reports on the CCP's new terms, and while I tried to tell him that the Communists were going to be very tough and hard-boiled and were not going to yield on what they thought were the essentials, I never really got a chance to get through."

Hurley's ignorance and inability to listen to professional advice had tragic consequences. In November he flew to Yenan, agreed to Mao Tse-tung's terms for a coalition government and even strengthened them with a few clauses of his own. Then he returned to Chungking, got talked out of the agreement by Chiang Kai-shek and ended up wholeheartedly supporting Chiang's position in the negotiations. Hurley reported himself "convinced that Chiang Kai-shek personally is anxious for a settlement with the so-called Communists."† His subsequent insistence on exclusive U.S. support

* Reporting on his trip to China in November–December 1944, Congressman Mike Mansfield reported to President Roosevelt that "I saw Major General Pat Hurley and we had a very long talk. He talked for two hours and forty-seven minutes, and I talked for thirteen minutes, which was about right." (See *Foreign Relations, 1945*, p. 8.)

† *Foreign Relations, 1944*, p. 699.

for the KMT meant that Chiang had no incentive to compromise. Consequently, all Hurley's efforts did nothing to heal the breach between the two parties. If anything, they made matters worse.

Throughout the entire period Hurley remained blissfully ignorant of the issues which divided the two parties. To him there were no real differences of principle between the KMT and CCP. With the negotiations thoroughly bogged down in February 1945, he would report that "two fundamental facts are emerging: (1) the Communists are not in fact Communists, they are striving for democratic principles; and (2) the one-party, one-man personal government of the Kuomintang is not in fact Fascist, it is striving for democratic principles."* He saw the Chinese Communists as comparable to Oklahoma Republicans like himself: "outs, who wanted to be the ins and . . . the only difference between Oklahoma Republicans and the Chinese Communists was that the Oklahoma Republicans were not armed."† He seemed totally incapable of comprehending the centrality of the Communists' demand for a coalition government in Chungking if they were to subordinate their military forces to the Central Government. Hurley gave this account of T. V. Soong's reaction to the draft agreement Hurley and Mao had signed in Yenan on November 10, 1944:

> Dr. Soong immediately said, "You have been sold a bill of goods by the Communists. The National Government will never grant what the Communists have requested." He then pointed out all the defects he found in the proposal, only one of which seemed to have any merit and that was that the Communists really meant to say that they desired a coalition administration whereas they had actually asked for a change in the name of the Chinese Government [to Coalition National Government]. This seemed to me to be trivial and could easily be corrected.‡

By mid-February, negotiations had clearly come to an impasse, though Hurley's report to the Department managed to detect signs that were "very encouraging."§ Chou En-lai, sensing quite correctly that Hurley was not accurately reporting matters to Wash-

---

* *Foreign Relations, 1945*, p. 211.
† Senate Committees on Armed Services and Foreign Relations, 82nd Congress, 1st Session, *The Military Situation in the Far East* (Washington: G.P.O., 1951), pp. 2420–21.
‡ *Foreign Relations, 1945*, p. 195.
§ *Ibid.*, p. 229.

ington, sought out Service to relay his concern over the state of the negotiations.

Failure of Kuomintang-Communist Negotiations

February 14, 1945
Amerasia Papers, pp. 1337–38

According to Chou En-lai, the Kuomintang-Communist negotiations have again resulted in an impasse. At a conference on February 13, with Ambassador Hurley, Wang Shih-chieh and Chou En-lai present, the Generalissimo said that he would not agree to anything except a "political consultative committee." This would be composed of members of the various parties but would have no powers or position in the government.

This empty and disappointing proposal is unacceptable to all of the opposition groups. All it permits is further talk, without commitments or limitation of the power of the Kuomintang. It is irreconcilably far from the Communist proposal of an inter-party conference with power to reorganize the Government and prepare for constitutional government. It is even a step backward from the type of inter-Party organ which had been the basis for discussion by the Kuomintang representatives as a ludicrously misnamed "war cabinet."

In view of this debacle, Chou is planning to return to Yenan as soon as possible. He seems to think that the Communists will demonstrate their good intentions by agreeing to participate in this Kuomintang-proposed committee, despite its futility. He would not commit himself regarding plans to proceed with setting up a Federative Council of all the Communist area governments. He gave the impression that the Communists were quite willing to wait for another period.

Before leaving Chungking, Chou will issue a statement setting forth the Communist position. A joint statement by the Communists, League of Democratic Parties and democratic wing of the Kuomintang (headed by Sun Fo) is also under consideration. These three groups have maintained close liaison and unity throughout, although the League and democratic wing were excluded from the actual negotiations.

Chou believes that Chiang does not expect Russian participation in the Far Eastern war (there is also a local rumor
that Soong wants to go to Russia to try to settle outstanding and
potential problems), that Chiang is confident of continued
American support as indicated by the statements and actions of
the Ambassador, that he has been strongly encouraged by the
announcement of the Five-Power Conference in April, and that
he will therefore continue to stall. If Chiang's international position remains strong, the Kuomintang will then, through its Party
Congress in May, proceed to offer "democracy" to the country
on its own terms.

Chou seemed anything but depressed. He believes that the
new breakdown of the negotiations has clarified the main issue,
revealing Chiang's determination to give no concessions which
can limit his power or substantially change the *status quo*. Chou
feels that the onus for the breakdown lies clearly on the Kuomintang, even in the eyes of the Ambassador. And his optimism
reflects the Communist confidence in the future.

Chou refused to sign a joint statement (which he believes
to have been prepared by the Ambassador with revisions by
T. V.) which tried to strike an optimistic note regarding the
negotiations. He said that it was entirely favorable to the Kuomintang and did not present the true facts.

An interesting footnote is that on February 12, Hollington
Tong urged a reliable and very well known American correspondent to include in a despatch the statement that the negotiations were proceeding well and were likely to succeed.

Influential members of the Kuomintang Government generally
did not speak openly of their plans for civil war with the Communists. Some of their American supporters, however, were willing
to speak quite freely about "liquidating the Communists." One of
these was General Chennault's P.R. man, Captain Joseph Alsop,
whose voice regarding U.S. policy in Asia has long been both loud
and regrettably influential.

Views of Captain Alsop

February 28, 1945
Amerasia Papers, pp. 1372–73

Captain Alsop often reflects the sentiments of T. V. Soong and other important Chinese to whom he is very close. The following views expressed by him in a private conversation on February 24, 1945, may therefore be of some interest.

Alsop, who has been very critical in the past of both General Stilwell and Ambassador Gauss, was pleased over recent improvement in American political and military relations with the Central Government. He was sure that the Chinese will cooperate 100 percent "as long as they are treated decently."

I suggested that several phases of the situation—the obvious feeling of strength of the Central Government, countered by aggressive actions of the Communists such as moving into South China—did not augur well for "getting on with the war against Japan."

Alsop vehemently replied that such concentration on the war against Japan in China was "naïve," the issues being much deeper. He explained that Japan will be destroyed by other means; the real problem to be faced by the United States is the rise of Russia and the probable destruction of any balance of power in Asia.

I said that the prosecution of the war against Japan is, however, the chief concern of the American commander in China.

He emphatically refuted this, saying that "Any American commander who put this immediate objective, and his own personal desire to make a name for himself, ahead of fundamental long-range American national interests should be flogged from his post."

He developed his thesis as follows:

We are childish to assume that the Chinese Communists are anything but an appendage of the Soviet Union, that they are really willing to accept any compromise or coalition short of complete control of China, or that they can be swung into cooperation with our interests. Attempts to arrange a reconciliation in China, or to utilize Communist military forces, are therefore dangerous and "idiotic."

Our only correct policy, accordingly, is to support the Central Government, giving it all the aid possible (on a much larger scale than at present), helping it to create a strong army, and then assisting (by our own forces if necessary) in unifying the country, liquidating the Communists, and establishing a strong government.

To back up China, we must adopt a strong policy toward Russia. Russian dependence on our military supplies and their desire for postwar economic assistance enables us to "buy them off." At the same time, our political concessions to Russia in Europe and our acceptance of Russia prohibitions against, for instance, participation in the war in Finland and the Balkans, gives us basis to "tell the Russians that they must stay out of China."

Alsop refused to accept my suggestion that it was unrealistic, in view of his own certainty of Russian designs in Asia and close relationship to the Chinese Communists, to assume that the Russians would accept such a prohibition or "buying off." We Americans, he said, are alone in failing to realize that all relationships between countries are on a basis of power politics and that we must play the game the whole way in the preservation of our own interests.

To my suggestion that the guns of the Central Government might have difficulty in dealing with the mass opposition engendered by several years of Communist control of most of occupied China, he was skeptical. He believed, however, that "really capable American statesmanship," which we have not yet had applied to China, would be able to persuade the Central Government of the advantages of progressive liberalism.

American public reaction to our involvement in civil war in China he thought would not be serious when the American public had the "true picture"—i.e., the danger of Communism and Russian dominance. "Of course," he admitted, "magazines like the *New Republic* will work themselves into a frenzy."

In November and December 1944, soon after his victory over Stilwell, Chiang made a number of important changes in his cabinet. Most notably, Ho Ying-ch'in was removed as Minister of War (but retained as Chief of Staff), and H. H. Kung was replaced as Minister of Finance and acting president of the Executive Yuan. With this, Chiang apparently rid himself of two of the most widely disliked men in the Chungking government. Hurley was much impressed. But Service's more practiced eye looked below the cabinet level to the sorts of appointments which were being made to the local war areas. There he detected an unmistakable pattern of continuing rigid anti-Communism, and clear preparations not for reconciliation with the CCP, but for civil war.

Recent Appointments by the Generalissimo Contradictory to Announced Intentions of Peaceful Settlement of Internal Issues

March 22, 1945
Amerasia Papers, pp. 1439–41

Summary: A number of recent appointments of reactionary military men who have been associated with anti-democratic or secret police groups seem to point to preparations for civil war and thus cast doubt on the Generalissimo's professed democratic and peaceful intentions. *End of Summary.*

It is the continual plea of the Generalissimo and his supporters that he sincerely wishes to do everything possible to bring democratic unity to China and to avoid civil war, and that "his good intentions should be trusted."

In the political field, these intentions are as yet unimplemented. They remain the promises that have been made many times already.

On a more practical level, an indication of the Generalissimo's intentions can be found in the nature of a number of recent appointments. These appointments are too similar in character and too numerous to be accepted as coincidental. Regarded in any light, they are ominous.

*   *   *

Ho Ying-ch'in has been placed in command of the field forces of the Chinese army, the most important parts of which are the Burma and Salween divisions, and the units being trained and equipped with American help in Yunnan. These should constitute the strongest military weapon that Chiang has ever had and are his great hope for the "unification" of China. That Ho, archconservative and bitter enemy of the Communists and liberals of China, should be placed in direct command is a measure of Chiang's trust, and a guarantee that they will resist any liberal groups. Convincing the American public that the removal of Ho from his post as Minister of War was a concession to American and liberal Chinese disapproval was one of the best pieces of propaganda the Chinese have done. Actually, Ho is more important than ever.

Liu Shih has been given command of the 5th War Zone. His reputation as a fighter is low, his personal ineptitude is notorious, and his complaisance in the corruption of subordinates while garrison commander of Chungking is well known. But he is a strong Central Government man, of the Ho Ying-ch'in group, and his politics are completely reactionary. His 5th War Zone is important because of Communist expansion into the newly occupied Japanese areas in Honan and Hupeh.

Hu Tsung-nan has been made acting commander of the newly expanded and very important 1st War Zone. This long-standing foe and perpetual blockader of the Communists has thus been strengthened. He now holds the northern front against the Communists from Kansu to south Hopei.

Li P'in-hsien has been appointed to command the newly activated 10th War Zone. This zone lies to the east of the Peiping–Hankow railway in territory almost completely occupied by the Communist New Fourth Army. Li has already been fighting the Communists for control of this area for the past several years. He can be counted on to continue to do so.

Ku Chu-t'ung has been placed in charge of the Generalissimo's field headquarters in the Southeast to have control of all Central Government forces in that area. He keeps his old position as commander of the 3rd War Zone. Another bitter anti-Communist (he was in command of the forces who attacked the Communists in the notorious New Fourth Army incident of January 1941), he can be expected to do his best to check Communist growth around Shanghai and Nanking and to resist popular uprisings which may put those cities in the hands of the Communists.

T'ang En-po has been given command of the newly organized Kweichow-Kwangsi-Hunan Border Forces. T'ang is regarded as one of the most uncompromising enemies of the Communists. His force is adjacent to the new Japanese occupied areas in Hunan and Kiangsi into which the Communists are now penetrating. The Kuomintang regards this as particularly dangerous because these are old Communist bases. T'ang's policies were indicated by a public statement soon after he assumed his post that all arms in the hands of the people should be collected.

Chan Chak has been appointed mayor of Canton—after it has been liberated. Admiral Chan is an important member of Tai Li's organization and was Tai's representative in Hongkong until its fall. He has not had experience in civic administration and does not appear to have special qualifications for coping with the problems of restoring municipal government and public services, or of handling the inevitably serious matters of relief and rehabilitation. The answer to Chan's appointment is obviously the fact that the Communists have a guerrilla base near Canton, which neither the Central Government nor Japanese have been able to wipe out and from which the Communists expect to gain control of Canton. Chan's announced first task is to organize a guerrilla force as near Canton as possible— ostensibly to cooperate with the American landing. Chan's qualification as mayor of Canton seems to be that he is a Gestapo internal-security man.

A mayor for Swatow is also reported to have been selected but his name is still unknown.

Ho Kuo-kuang is reported to have been appointed chairman of the still future government of Formosa. General Ho is a former commander in chief of the Chinese gendarmerie, an important element of the Kuomintang's police government whose activities are antidemocratic and extralegal. Since the Chinese gendarmerie is a conscious imitation of the notorious Japanese internal-security organization, the people of Formosa are not likely to have the privilege of untrammeled democratic freedom. General Ho is not a Formosan Chinese, nor even from Fukien, the "homeland" of most of the Formosans.

*   *   *

The trend of these important recent personnel shifts is obviously toward the placing of: (1) strong and completely trusted Central Government men, of proved antidemocratic and anti-Communist records, in all important military commands and particularly in positions facing the occupied areas; and (2) the appointment of men associated with reactionary, antidemocratic internal police organizations to take charge of large cities and new territories after their liberation.

Against this tendency must be placed the facts: (1) that the occupied areas are practically synonymous with the territory now dominated by, and in future to be contested with, the Communists; and (2) that all the important cities of occupied China are threatened by adjacent areas of Communist activity.

*   *   *

The chessmen are being moved into position—for a game that looks far different from the peaceful democratic unification of China described by Chiang.

THE RUSSIAN ROLE

One of the bitter ironies of the history of this era is the fact that the men who were vilified for having allowed "Soviet aggression" to transform China into a Communist state were actually the men who were most anxious to counter Russian influence in China. Yet General Hurley, one of those who led in the vilification, trusted the Soviets' intentions. When he first traveled to Chungking, Hurley flew by way of Moscow and came away convinced that the Soviets would support U.S. policy in China. A second trip to Moscow, after his return to Washington in the spring of 1945, did not change his mind: "Stalin agreed unqualifiedly to America's policy in China as outlined to him during the conversation."* Ambassador Averell Harriman, reporting on this same conversation, was much less sanguine and suggested that unless KMT-CCP relations improved, the Russians might even set up a puppet government in Manchuria and North China.†

It was not, however, Hurley's assessment of Russian intentions which was so inaccurate, for at Yalta the Russians did agree to support the Kuomintang Government. But therein lies a second cruel irony: precisely because the United States was able to gain so much in that much-maligned Yalta agreement, Hurley would be misled in assessing the future of the CCP. Though Service and in fact most of the State Department knew nothing of the Yalta agreements, Hurley had learned of them from Roosevelt when he returned to Washington in March 1945. For Hurley, Yalta would cut the Gordian knot. Despite his repeated assertions that the Chinese Communists were not real Communists at all, Hurley believed that they would follow Moscow's will: "We are convinced that the influence of the Soviet will control the action of the Chinese Communist Party." Believing as he did that the Chinese Communists'

* *Foreign Relations, 1945*, p. 340.
† *Ibid.*, p. 341.

strength had been much exaggerated, Hurley was sure that they would not risk a civil war without Soviet support. "Without the support of the Soviet the Chinese Communist Party will eventually participate as a political party in the National Government."* Moscow, in effect, was expected to accomplish by fiat what Hurley and everyone else had consistently failed to bring about: a KMT–CCP reconciliation on the Kuomintang's terms.

Service knew nothing of Yalta, but he did know a great deal about China. He saw Chiang looking to Russia for a solution to his internal problems with the Communists. Obviously, the Generalissimo was barking up the wrong tree. Service urged that the United States "avoid encouraging or assisting Chiang in these plans," but he could hardly have realized that it was precisely the American Ambassador, Hurley, who was suggesting this course.

The Kuomintang Hopes to Make a Deal with Russia

February 17, 1945
Amerasia Papers, pp. 1345–47

The report is now current that T. V. Soong is soon to make a pilgrimage to Moscow. Similar rumors, concerning Soong and others, have been heard several times since Wallace's visit. But this time there seems to be something in back of it.

From several Kuomintang sources there have recently come suggestions that the settlement of the Communist problem will have to await clarification of its international phases. Chiang's final stiffening in the recent Kuomintang-Communist talks needs more explanation than Chou En-lai's suggestion that he feels he has gotten "face" by the invitation to participate as host at San Francisco. In a conference of high Kuomintang leaders on January 29, Chiang is reported to have made the statement that the Russians were too realistic to back the "wrong horse"—which the Chinese Communists would be after the Kuomintang armies had been strengthened by the supplies brought in by an American landing.

Apparently, therefore, the Central Government actually

* *Ibid.,* pp. 431, 433.

hopes to be able to make some sort of a deal with Russia. On the Chinese side, an understanding is desirable on a number of present or potential problems: the future of Korea, Manchuria and Outer Mongolia; Sinkiang and its minority and border questions; postwar economic relations; and the bringing of the Chinese Communists under the Central Government.

But all these things the Central Government hopes to get. The question is reasonable: What does the Chinese side have to give? The rumor is that T. V. will offer a twenty-year pact similar to the Anglo-Soviet and Franco-Soviet.

It is difficult to see how this offer will be very attractive, under the present circumstances, to the realistic men in Moscow. Still, there may be a number of factors encouraging Chinese hopes. Most high Chinese officials, including T. V., seem convinced that the United States is almost as suspicious and fearful of the U.S.S.R. as they are themselves. They are surer than ever that the Central Government has our definite support (the Ambassador has certainly not discouraged this view). They probably even hope for American good offices in these negotiations with Russia. Finally, they have certainly not missed what they consider the parallel of the French Communist Party moderating its attitude after De Gaulle made his treaty with Russia.

Such hopes of settling the Communist problem by a deal with the U.S.S.R., using American mediation, is the opposite of the good but unpalatable advice given by Wallace: that desirable good relations with Russia depended on first settling China's internal Communist problem.

If the Central Government really hopes to be successful, it is only deluding itself. The Russians in Chungking are being frigid toward the Central Government—and talking freely of their low opinion of it and correspondingly high opinion of Yenan. Furthermore, there is not much exchangeable *quid pro quo:* the Chinese are not likely to make concessions in Sinkiang, Outer Mongolia or Manchuria. Finally, the objective circumstances are not favorable. The Central Government and Chiang are weaker than France and De Gaulle. The Chinese Communists are stronger than the F.F.I.*—and getting stronger rapidly.

* Forces Françaises de l'Intérieur was the secret army which had grown during the German occupation and helped De Gaulle liberate France.

Both Russia and the Chinese Communists can do very well, therefore, by sitting tight and waiting.

This hope of Chiang's and his advisers would seem to be another indication that while Chiang is a very astute operator in his own country, his statesmanship and knowledge of the rest of the world are very limited. It is also a reflection of a common Chinese trait: as sophisticated as the Chinese are, they have a habit, when confronted with an almost hopeless situation, of simply refusing to face it, taking refuge in unrealistic and blind optimism.

The United States will be wise to avoid encouraging or assisting Chiang in these plans.

———————

When Service flew back to Yenan in March, his fears over the imminence of civil war intensified. Especially after talking to people like Ch'en Yi, who was willing to speak quite frankly with Service, it became clear that the CCP was openly preparing for civil war and had little hope of reconciliation with the KMT. One critical battleground for that civil war would certainly be Manchuria. The CCP was certain that the Soviet Union would enter the war against Japan in Manchuria, and it fully expected and planned to infiltrate its forces into Manchuria to take over control in cooperation with the Russians.

During Churchill's visit to Moscow in October 1944, Stalin had agreed to enter the war against Japan in Manchuria. It is possible that the CCP knew of this Russian commitment. On the other hand, they cannot have known about Yalta, for they insisted that "the days of Russian imperialism are over," and that the Soviet Union certainly would not ask for any special rights in Manchuria. Yet Stalin had already, at Yalta, secured U.S. agreement to a lease of the naval base at Port Arthur, the internationalization of Dairen with the "pre-eminent interests of the Soviet Union" guaranteed, and the establishment of joint Soviet-Chinese companies to operate the principal railways in Manchuria. Yalta also provided that the *status quo* would be maintained in Outer Mongolia, while, as Service reported in a separate despatch, the CCP believed that "Outer and Inner Mongolia are parts of China," and given fair treatment and national autonomy "Outer and Inner Mongolia will join together and remain a part of China."* The CCP's ignorance of these clauses in the Yalta agreement which so vitally affected their own country is an indication of the slight extent to which the Soviet Union took the Chinese Communists into their confidence. And this lack of close contact between the Soviet Union and the Chinese Communists spoke ill for Hurley's hopes that the Russians would be able to restrain the CCP from resisting the KMT in a civil war.

Chinese Communist Expectations In Regard to Soviet Participation in Far Eastern War

March 14, 1945
Amerasia Papers, pp. 1405–8

Summary: Although they refuse to permit speculation counting on it, the Chinese Communist leaders seem to expect Soviet participation in Manchuria at a late stage of the war against Japan. They are positive that it will not involve Russian demands for concessions or special rights in Manchuria. The significant result will be Chinese Communist control of that vital area. *End of Summary.*

1. It is very difficult to draw the Chinese Communist leaders into discussion or prediction of the probability of Soviet entry into the war against Japan.

a. They base their reluctance, in the first place, on the basic assertion that China must not expect or rely on foreign assistance. She must, instead, prepare to drive the Japanese from Chinese soil by her own strength and resources. There is absolutely no question in their minds that Manchuria is an integral part of "Chinese soil." One of the oldest and most familiar Communist slogans is: "We must drive to the bank of the Yalu River."

This emphasis on self-reliance is an important part of the Communist Party "line." They insist that effective prosecution of the war demands full mobilization of the people; that this

* Service's "Communist Views in Regard to Mongolia," March 16, 1945, *Foreign Relations, 1945,* p. 284.

requires political indoctrination and the granting of political
rights and economic reforms benefiting the mass of the population; and that the Kuomintang's concentration on the decisive-
ness of outside factors permits it to avoid this vital issue of
mobilizing China's own resources.

Fundamental to this argument is the Communist conception of the war against Japan as a national war of liberation
which must at the same time, in order for its success, be an important and progressive stage in the Chinese revolution. The
primarily conservative Kuomintang fears this "revolutionary"
potentiality of the war—which means democracy and economic
reform as a basis for popular resistance. It has therefore destroyed the United Front, and by refusing to carry out the
measures best calculated to prosecute the war most effectively,
become "defeatist."

By an extension of this logic, the Communist leaders feel
that the permitting of general expectation of easy salvation
through Russian participation will be an impediment to the war
effort and the accomplishment of its underlying revolutionary
objectives.

b. When this theoretical objection has been put aside, the
Communists argue that the Soviet Union has done her full share
in the war already, and that the losses she has suffered in manpower and resources make it unjust to expect or demand further
expenditure in the Far East. Supplemental to this is the statement that, even without active participation, the Russians have
nonetheless contributed to the war by pinning down large Japanese forces in Manchuria.

c. Another line of argument is that the persistent anti-
Soviet attitude of the Chungking Government during the past
several years has certainly not been intended to seek Russian
help or encourage Russian participation. (I intend to amplify
this subject in a separate discussion of Sino-Soviet relations.)

2. Despite these arguments it is apparent, however, that the
Chinese Communist leaders *do expect* that Russia will eventually
enter the Far Eastern war. They insist, for instance, that Russia
must be considered an important Far Eastern power, that she
is uncompromisingly opposed to Japanese Fascism (though
forced by necessity to appease it temporarily to save herself
from the more immediate menace of Germany), and that she will
insist on having a voice in the settlement of the problems result-

ing from the defeat of Japan. They agree that these factors logically require eventual Russian participation in Japan's defeat.

3. As to the probable time of Russian entry, the Communists insist that it cannot be expected for some time yet and probably not until a fairly late stage of the war against Japan. It will take a considerable time *after* the defeat of Germany for Russia to transfer strength and prepare herself in Siberia. (They believe that some Russian forces, especially air and mechanized units, were moved to the European theater.) And just as the Allies had to build up overwhelming forces in England before opening the Second Front, so these Russian forces will have to be strong enough to be sure of success before action is taken. This is particularly true because of the geographical vulnerability of the Maritime Provinces and Siberian lines of communication. A balancing factor will be the speed with which Japanese forces in Manchuria are weakened through general attrition of the Japanese war machine. So far, the Communists think, the drainage from Manchuria to other theaters has not been severe, while some units have been withdrawn, their places are probably being taken by fresh units from the homeland.

In any case, they point out, the Russo-Japanese Neutrality Pact still has a year to run, even if the Russians give notice on April 25, 1945.

4. The form and place of this Soviet participation, such Communist leaders as General Chu Teh suggest, will be direct attack by the Red Army against the Japanese army in northern Manchuria. They suggest particularly northwest Manchuria (perhaps in the vicinity of Lake Nomanhan) as most favorable for Soviet mechanized equipment and offensive tactics. All other suggestions of possible lines of Soviet action are discounted.

a. Passage through Sinkiang to supply and cooperate with Central Government forces they regard as impractical because of the distances involved. Furthermore they are sure that the Russians have no confidence in the effectiveness and disinterested cooperation of the Central Government armies. (By "disinterested" the Communists mean concentration on the defeat of Japan rather than internal political issues.)

b. Attempts to push south through Inner Mongolia and Ninghsia or Suiyuan to contact the Chinese Communists would be impractical because of the very great distances over which there could be nothing but difficult motor transport and because of the exposure to flank attack from the Japanese bases in eastern Inner Mongolia.

c. A drive toward Kalgan to reach Peiping and Tientsin would involve the same problems of transport and distance from bases. Furthermore, joining with the Communist forces in Northeast China and even the cutting off of Manchuria from China would not in themselves achieve any major Russian strategical objective. The Japanese in Manchuria would not be weakened and would still be a threat to eastern Siberia.

5. Communist expectations—or, perhaps, hopes—seem to be about as follows: By the time the Russians are ready to move (say, the late spring of 1946) the situation will be:

a. The Japanese home islands will be under direct American attack.
b. Manchuria will be isolated from Japan by complete American air and naval supremacy.
c. The Communist forces will be greatly strengthened by: (1) continuation of their present rapid growth, and (2) some American supplies and cooperation—probably from the Pacific.
d. Chinese military activity, and possibly an American landing, even though not on a major scale, will hold the Japanese forces in China, cut Japanese north–south communication lines, and thus isolate Manchuria from China.

When the stage has been set, the Red Army will cut off north Manchuria, then advance south. Simultaneously the Communists will commence active infiltration into south Manchuria.

To prepare for this the Communists have expended great energy during the past two years consolidating their base in east Hopei and in extending the area of their guerrilla operations into Jehol and south Liaoning. The "solidity" of this east Hopei base has been tested by the rescue of several American air crews, including a B-29 crew which parachuted near Changli, east of the Peking–Liaoning railway, and was brought from there in safety to Yenan by foot. That the potential significance of these Communist bases on the southwestern fringe of Manchuria is not lost on the Japanese is shown by their present intensive mopping-up campaign, which has been going on in the area for more than three months without conspicuous success.

The Communists also have sent large numbers of political organizers (recruited from natives of the area) into Manchuria and claim a well-established underground and contacts with remnant nuclei of the old "Manchurian volunteers." Communist reticence in discussing the details of these organizations is understandable at the present time. But the Japanese have from time to time announced the rounding up of Communist suspects; anti-Communist measures and propaganda in Manchuria and North China continue unrelenting; and there are stringent restrictions on travel from China into Manchuria. It is interesting that most of the natives of Manchuria now in Chungking seem to believe that Communist organization in Manchuria is fairly extensive.

Possible coordination with this Communist activity from the southwest may come from remnants of old guerrilla forces which are reported to be still existing in the mountains of southeast Manchuria. These units are close to the borders of both Korea and the Maritime Province of Siberia and can probably be supplied from the latter. Any Russian assistance to Korean resistance groups and use of whatever Korean forces the Russians have armed will probably start in the same general area and be related to this activity.

As the fighting in Manchuria develops, therefore, the Red Army will advance southward toward the heart of the country in large-scale frontal attack on the main Japanese army while the Chinese Communists and other affiliated resistance forces will work toward central Manchuria from the southwest and southeast, disrupting communications, creating disturbances, and assisting the Russian main front by tying down as many Japanese forces as possible in the rear.

There is obviously no doubt in the minds of the Communists that the Russians will recognize and cooperate with whatever Chinese forces they meet in Manchuria, i.e., the Communists. This is so taken for granted that it is not worthy of mention.

6. Regarding the possibility of Russian demands of territory or special rights in Manchuria, the Communists are most emphatic. They insist that because "the days of Russian imperialism are over," there will be no such demands. But Russia does want, they believe, a China which will have cordial and friendly

relations with Russia, and which will permit normal use, on a commercial basis and without any infringement of Chinese sovereignty, of Manchurian transport and port facilities. This would mean absence of unreasonable or onerous impediments to trade between the two countries or in transit. Such conditions, the Communists maintain, would be of advantage to both countries.

7. It does not need to be pointed out that such a course of development will leave the Chinese Communists in control of Manchuria. That the Communists are confident of gaining this control by the particular process, described or otherwise, is obvious.

The Communists are fully aware—as is the Kuomintang—of the importance of Manchuria as China's major and only well-developed heavy industrial base. The description of Manchuria as "the Cockpit of Asia" is truer now than when it was used as the title of a book* written twelve years ago on the significance of the original Japanese invasion.

Toward the end of his stay in Yenan, Service made a systematic attempt to assess the nature and extent of contact between the Chinese Communists and the Russians. The result was this precise, factual report which indicated the likelihood of contact between the two Communist parties, but the clear absence of any aid from Moscow and the probable absence of intergovernment relations.

Contact between the Chinese Communists and Moscow

March 23, 1945
Amerasia Papers, pp. 1444–46

Summary: Although it will be denied, channels do exist and there is almost certainly some contact between the Chinese

---

* Percy T. Etherton and H. Hessell Tiltman, *Manchuria, The Cockpit of Asia* (New York: Frederick A. Stokes, 1932).

Communists and Moscow. This is probably through Chinese Communists in Moscow and radio at Yenan. The Chinese Communists have received no Soviet arms.   *End of Summary.*

There is now no travel between the Soviet Union and Yenan. The last Soviet plane to visit Yenan was in November 1942. Planes before that were not oftener than once or twice a year. All came with Chinese Government permission, stopping at Chinese fields in west Kansu and Lanchow, and undergoing thorough search. Their purpose was to serve the small Russian personnel at Yenan, and they were not permitted to carry non-Russian passengers or cargo other than the personal effects of the passengers. When Chou En-lai went to Russia in late 1939 (for medical work on an injured arm) he went at least as far as Lanchow on a Chinese plane. Chinese inspection at Lanchow of the last Russian plane is said to have taken two days. About a ton of medical supplies was taken off and even most of Dr. Orloff's main surgical instruments prevented from coming to Yenan.

The Kuomintang bogey of Soviet military supplies to the Chinese Communists is definitely dead. It is probably impossible for any planes to fly from bases in Outer Mongolia to north Shensi with any useful cargo except the needed gasoline for the return trip. The north Shensi and north Shansi areas have been thoroughly covered by American observers. There are no usable airfields except that at Yenan which could be used by such Soviet planes. Finally, in all the extensive contacts of Americans with the Communist armies, there have been found no Russian arms or equipment.

There are at present three Russians in Yenan.

One of these is a surgeon named Orloff. He says that he is not a member of the regular army but was called up for service about 1938. He was with Soviet forces at Lake Nomanhan and in the Finnish War. In 1942 he was granted three years' leave of absence and was flown to Yenan on the last Russian plane in November 1942. There is no question of his being a *bona fide* surgeon. He has introduced some new Soviet methods and is kept extremely busy doing surgical work in the Central Hospital at Yenan.

The other two are representatives of Tass News Agency. They are generally known by the Chinese names of "Kuo Li" and "Sheng P'ing," and appear about twenty-six and forty, respectively. They have also been here since 1942 and replaced correspondents here before them. They say that they dispatch news only through Chungking and the Chinese censorship. However, they employ Chinese translators and seem to collect a good deal of material. It is difficult to see how such printed material can be sent out except to Chungking through the smuggling channels which the local Communists undoubtedly have. They are stated to have no radio equipment except a receiver. This is confirmed by people who have visited their quarters and by Michael Lindsay, who as radio technical adviser to the Communists knows all local facilities intimately. Whatever the truth of these statements, the Soviet press does not appear to have published news regarding the Chinese Communists which goes beyond that passed by Chungking censors or printed in American publications.

None of these three men seem to be treated as persons of importance. They spoke no Chinese when they came—and still do not speak it well—and lack all the earmarks of "China experts." They do not appear to be on terms of close acquaintance with the chief Communist leaders, nor to be given the "face" shown to Okano, the Japanese Communist. In fact, they are seldom seen except at large social occasions, when they are no more than members of the crowd.

Except for a number of White Russian refugees from cities such as Tientsin, most of whom are treated with extreme suspicion as probably Japanese spies, there are apparently no other Russians in this or the other Communist areas.

More important than the Russians in Yenan may be the Chinese Communists in Moscow. These include the former Chinese representatives to the Comintern, who have been in Russia since the beginning of the war and probably could not return to China if they wanted to. Among them are Li Li-san, at one time leader of the Chinese Communist Party, and a General Chao. These men certainly are in contact with Russian Communist leaders.

Another possible channel of contact is, of course, through the Communist representatives and the Soviet Embassy in Chungking. This contact, however, seems to be limited to avoid arousing Central Government suspicions. I have been told by an official of the Soviet Embassy that they have orders "to stay away from the Chinese Communists in Chungking." The Chungking Communists are nonetheless always invited to anniversary celebrations at the Embassy.

Radio communication between Yenan and Moscow is certainly possible. The Communist newspaper receives its Tass news directly by monitoring Russian broadcasts. Inasmuch as the Yenan transmitter can be heard in San Francisco, it is to be assumed that it can also reach Moscow. There is therefore no reason why this radio traffic cannot be two-way.

The first and to my knowledge only instance of what seems to be public admission of such contact is the recent exchange of messages between the Chinese Communist leaders and Stalin on the recent anniversary of Red Army Day. On March 3, 1945, the Communist news agency published the text of Stalin's reply: "Chairman Mao and General Chu: I thank you sincerely for your warm congratulations on the 27th anniversary of Red Army Day. Stalin." It is possible that these messages were sent through the Chinese Government radio and the Soviet Embassy in Chungking. But the Government radio between Chungking and Yenan is so slow that this does not seem probable.

As long as there can be an exchange of news, it is of course not necessary for there to be much exchange of formal or direct messages. Important Soviet editorials are often reprinted and commented on by the Communist press. These are enough to give at least the Party "line." The same can work in the reverse direction—from Yenan to Moscow.

In spite of all these possibilities for contact, the Chinese Communists consistently deny that they have any "relations" with the Soviet government and complain that they know less than anyone else about such subjects as what the Soviet Union is likely to do. The first part of these statements is probably true—I know of nothing to disprove it. What contact does exist is between the two parties, not governments. I think it likely that such contact exists.

1945 POLICY RECOMMENDATIONS

Though much of Service's reporting in 1945 called into question the premises of Hurley's policy, he was not in the least anxious to provoke an open dispute with the Ambassador. Hurley had already arranged to have John P. Davies transferred out of China, and when Service arrived back in Chungking in mid-January, Hurley bluntly warned him that he would suffer the same fate if he "crossed" the Ambassador. But a combination of events were ultimately to lead Service, together with several other Foreign Service officers, to speak their own minds.

Early in February 1945, Raymond P. Ludden, one of the Foreign Service officers attached to the Dixie Mission, returned from four months and 1,200 miles of travel from Yenan through the Communists' Shansi-Chahar-Hopei base area, almost to the environs of Peking. Here again was direct, firsthand, incontrovertible confirmation of the Communists' strength behind Japanese lines. Service met him in Chungking: "Ludden is a big, blunt, red-faced Irishman. He was a son of the Church, and a man with a rare gift for colorful speech and a great vigor which did not incline him to be cowed by a newcoming fellow Irishman like Hurley. He came back really fired up from this trip."

Both Ludden and Service were assigned to the staff of General Albert C. Wedemeyer (Stilwell's successor): they were in no respect subordinate to Ambassador Hurley or subject to his orders. They were, nonetheless, aware of Hurley's oft-repeated insistence that no one in the Theater (Army or civilian) was to go beyond reporting and venture into policy recommendation. But Wedemeyer was about to return to Washington for consultations. As Ludden and Service discussed the state of the war in China, and the implications of Ludden's findings on his recent trip, they decided that the time had come to "lay some things on the line." Service accompanied Ludden when the latter made an oral report on his trip to Wedemeyer. The general was interested and asked for a memorandum which he might take to Washington. The result was the following joint memorandum urging a policy toward the Chinese Communists similar to Allied policy toward Tito's forces in Yugoslavia.

Military Weakness of Our Far Eastern Policy

February 14, 1945
Tydings, 1980–81

American policy in the Far East can have but one immediate objective: the defeat of Japan in the shortest possible time with the least expenditure of American lives. To the attainment of this objective all other considerations should be subordinate.

The attainment of this objective demands the effective mobilization of China in the war against Japan. Operating as we are in a land theater at the end of a supply line many thousands of miles in length, the human and economic resources of China increase in importance as we draw closer to Japan's inner zone of defense. Denied the effective use of these resources, the attainment of our primary objective will be unnecessarily delayed.

There is ample evidence to show that to the present Kuomintang Government the war against Japan is secondary in importance to its own preservation in power. China's military failure is due in large part to internal political disunity and the Kuomintang's desire to conserve such military force as it has for utilization in the maintenance of its political power. The intention of the Generalissimo to eliminate all political opposition, by force of arms if necessary, has not been abandoned. In the present situation in China, where power or self-preservation depends upon the possession of military force, neither the Kuomintang nor opposition groups are willing to expend their military resources against the Japanese through fear that it will weaken them vis-à-vis other groups. A recent instance is the lack of resistance to the Japanese capture of the southern section of the Hankow–Canton railway. Equally, the Kuomintang is jealously intent on preventing the strengthening of other groups: witness the blockade of the Communists.

The aim of American policy as indicated clearly by official statements in the United States is the establishment of political unity in China as the indispensable preliminary to China's effective military mobilization. The execution of our policy has not contributed to the achievement of this publicly stated aim. On the contrary, it has retarded its achievement. It has had this undesired and undesirable effect because our statements and actions in China have convinced the Kuomintang Government that we will continue to support it and it alone. The Kuomintang Government believes that it will receive an increasing flow of American military and related supplies which, if past experience is any guide, it will commit against the enemy only with great reluctance, if at all.

We cannot hope for any improvement in this situation unless we understand the objectives of the Kuomintang Government and throw our considerable influence upon it in the direction of internal unity. We should be convinced by this time that the effort to solve the Kuomintang-Communist differences by diplomatic means has failed; we should not be deceived by any "face-saving" formula resulting from the discussions because neither side is willing to bear the onus of failure. We should also realize that no Government can survive in China without American support.

There are in China important elements interested in governmental reform by which unity and active prosecution of the war may result. Aside from the Chinese Communists, however, all of these elements are cowed by a widespread secret-police system and lack any firm rallying point. They will remain helpless to do anything constructive as long as statements of our policy indicate that we are champions of the *status quo*.

At present there exists in China a situation closely paralleling that which existed in Yugoslavia prior to Prime Minister Churchill's declaration of support for Marshal Tito. That statement was as follows:

"The sanest and safest course for us to follow is to judge all parties and factions dispassionately by the test of their readiness to fight the Germans and thus lighten the burden of Allied troops. This is not a time for ideological preferences for one side or the other."

A similar public statement issued by the Commander in Chief with regard to China would not mean the withdrawal of recognition or the cessation of military aid to the Central Government; that would be both unnecessary and unwise. It would serve notice, however, of our preparation to make use of all available means to achieve our primary objective. It would supply for all Chinese a firm rallying point which has thus far been lacking. The internal effect in China would be so profound that the Generalissimo would be forced to make concessions of power and permit United Front coalition. The present opposition groups, no longer under the prime necessity of safeguarding themselves, would be won wholeheartedly to our side and we would have in China, for the first time, a united ally.

Whether we like it or not, by our very presence here we have become a force in the internal politics of China, and that force should be used to accomplish our primary mission. In spite of hero-worshiping publicity in the United States, Chiang Kai-shek is not China, and by our present narrow policy of outspokenly supporting his dog-in-the-manger attitude we are needlessly cutting ourselves off from millions of useful allies, many of whom are already organized and in position to engage the enemy. These allies, let it be clear, are not confined to Communist-controlled areas of China, but are to be found everywhere in the country. The Communist movement is merely the most prominent manifestation of a condition which is potentially present throughout China. Other important groups favor the same program as that espoused by the so-called Communists —agrarian reform, civil rights, the establishment of democratic institutions—but the Communists are the only group at present having the organization and strength openly to foster such "revolutionary" ideas.

Our objective is clear, but in China we have been jockeyed into a position from which we have only one approach to the objective. Support of the Generalissimo is desirable insofar as there is concrete evidence that he is willing and able to marshal the full strength of China against Japan. Support of the Generalissimo is but one means to an end; it is not an end in itself, but by present statements of policy we show a tendency to confuse the means with the end. There should be an immediate adjustment of our position in order that flexibility of approach to our primary objective may be restored.

Five days after Ludden and Service had prepared their memorandum for General Wedemeyer, Hurley and Wedemeyer left for Washington. Service had already, as was his custom, provided the Embassy with a copy of the memo, handing it personally to Counselor of Embassy George Atcheson. Then, after Hurley's departure, and knowing that with Hurley in Washington the critical decisions on China policy would soon be made, Atcheson decided that it was time for the professional Foreign Service officers in China to provide their analysis of the situation and their policy recommendations. Atcheson, who was Chargé d'Affaires in Hurley's absence, felt strongly that the Department had not been getting from Hurley a complete and objective view of the situation in China. At his suggestion, then, it was decided to send a telegram from the Embassy's political officers. Though others contributed to the final message and though it went out over Atcheson's name, it was Service who initially drafted the despatch. This fact did not go undetected by Hurley: when he saw the telegram in the State Department, his response (Service was later told) was "I know who drafted that telegram: Service. I'll get that S.O.B. if it's the last thing I do."

The Situation in China

February 28, 1945
Service, pp. 109–12

The situation in China appears to be developing in some ways that are not conducive to effective prosecution of the war, nor to China's future peace and unity.

1. The recent American attempt through diplomatic and persuasive means to assist compromise between the factions in China was a necessary first step in the handling of the problem.

Unity was correctly taken to be the essence not only of the most effective conduct of the war by China but also of the peaceful and speedy emergence of a strong, united and democratic China.

But the cessation of Japanese offensives, the opening of the road into China, the rapid development of our Army plans for rebuilding Chiang's armies, the increase of other assistance such as the W.P.B. [War Production Board], the expectation that the Central Government will share in the making of important decisions at San Francisco, and belief that we are intent upon the definite support and strengthening of the Central Government alone and as the only possible channel for aid to other groups— these circumstances have combined to increase greatly Chiang's feeling of strength and have resulted in unrealistic optimism on his part and lack of willingness to make any compromise.

This attitude is reflected in, among other things, early hopes of a settlement with Russia without settlement of the Communist problems, when nothing was finally offered but an advisory inter-Party committee without any power or place in the Government, and in recent military-political appointments which place strong anti-Communists in the strategic war areas and name to high administrative posts reactionaries such as Admiral Chan Chak (Tai Li subordinate) to be mayor of Canton, and General Ho Kuo-kuang (former commander in chief of gendarmerie) as chairman of Formosa.

2. The Communists for their part have come to the conclusion that we are definitely committed to the support of Chiang alone, and that we will not force Chiang's hand in order to be able to aid or cooperate with them. In what they consider self-protection, they are therefore following the line of action (forecast in statements of Communist leaders last summer if they continued to be excluded from consideration) of actively increasing their forces and aggressively expanding their areas southward, regardless of nominal Kuomintang control, to reach Southeast China. The Department is referred to our 284, February 24, 9 A.M., reporting large movements and conflicts with Central Government forces already taking place. In grasping time by the forelock, the Communists intend to take advantage of the isolation of East China by the Japanese capture of the Canton–Hankow railway, to make themselves as nearly invincible as possible before Chiang's new armies, now in process

of formation in Yunnan, are ready, and to present us the dilemma of accepting or refusing their aid if our forces land anywhere on the China coast. Communists close to the leaders are now talking of the necessity of their seeking Soviet assistance. The party itself is broadcasting demands for Communist and other non-Kuomintang representation at San Francisco, and is actively considering creation of a unified council of their various independent guerrilla governments.

3. The conclusion seems clear that although our intentions have been good and our actions in refusing to deal with or assist any group but the Central Government have been diplomatically correct, if this situation continues and our analysis of it is correct, chaos in China will be inevitable and the probable outbreak of disastrous civil conflict will be accelerated. Even for the present it is obvious that this situation, in which we are precluded from cooperation with the large, aggressive and strategically situated armies and organized population of the Communist areas, as well as the forces such as the Li Chi-shen and Ts'ai T'ing-k'ai group in the Southeast, is unsatisfactory and hampering from a purely military standpoint. As indicated above, the situation is also dangerous to American interests from a long-range point of view.

Unless checked, this situation is apt to develop with increasing acceleration as the tempo of the war in China and the whole Far East is raised, and the inevitable resolution of China's internal conflict becomes more urgent. The time is short and it will be dangerous to allow affairs to drift.

4. If the high military authorities of our government agree that some cooperation with the Communists and other groups who have proved themselves willing and are in position to fight the Japanese is or will be necessary or desirable, we believe that the immediate and paramount consideration of military necessity should be made the basis for a further step in American policy. The presence of General Wedemeyer in Washington as well as General Hurley should be a favorable opportunity for discussion of this matter.

Predicated on the assumption that the military necessity exists, the first step we propose for consideration is that the President inform the Generalissimo in definite terms that military necessity requires that we supply and cooperate with the Communists and other suitable groups who can assist the war against Japan (this would not under present conditions include forces such as the Szechwan warlords who are not in actual position to attack the enemy) and that we are taking direct steps to accomplish this end. We can assure the Generalissimo that we are not contemplating reducing our aid to the Central Government (any aid we give the Communists or other groups must, because of transport difficulties, at first be on a small scale and will probably be less than the natural increase in the flow of supplies into China). We must include in the statement that we will keep the Central Government informed of the extent and types of such aid. We can also tell the Generalissimo that we will be able to use the lever of our supplies and cooperation to limit independent and aggressive action on their part, restricting them to their present areas. And we can point out the advantage of having the Communists helped by us rather than seeking Russian aid or intervention, direct or indirect.

At the time of making this statement to the Generalissimo, he might also be told, if it is considered advisable, that although our effort to persuade the various groups of the desirability of unification has failed and we can no longer delay measures for the most effective prosecution of the war, we consider it obviously desirable that our military assistance to all groups be based on unity and the coordination of military command; that we are prepared to continue to lend our good offices to this end, where feasible and when asked for; and that while we believe that the proposal should come from the Generalissimo, we would be disposed to support: (1) The formation of something in the nature of a supreme war council or war cabinet in which Communists and other groups would have effective representation and some share in responsibility for the formation and execution of joint war plans, and (2) the nominal incorporation of Communist and other selected forces into the Central Government armies under the operational command of American officers designated by the Generalissimo on the advice of General Wedemeyer, on agreement by all parties that these troops would operate only within their present areas or specified extended areas. It should be made clear, however, that our decision to cooperate with any forces able to assist the war will not be delayed by or contingent on the completion of such internal Chinese arrangements.

Such a *modus operandi,* we believe, would bridge the present deadlock in China and serve as a preliminary move toward full solution of the problem of ultimate complete unity. As one result of the recent negotiations, the principal and overriding issues have become clear. The Generalissimo and his Government will not at this time on their own initiative take any forward step which will mean loss of face, prestige or personal power. The Communists will not, without guarantees in which they have confidence, take any forward step which will involve dispersion and eventual elimination of their forces upon which their present strength and future political existence depend. The step we propose taking will exert on both parties the force necessary to break this deadlock, and the *modus operandi* embodied in those two proposals should initiate concrete military and, as an inevitable result, political cooperation, and accordingly provide a foundation for increasing future development toward unity.

These proposals would not exclude the political consultation committee plan which, if adopted, could function alongside the war council and the Government. In fact, it should be expected that the committee would be greatly strengthened.

The statements to Chiang should, of course, be made privately. But the possibility of the logical and much more drastic step, in the event of his refusal to accept it, of a public statement of policy such as that by Churchill in regard to Yugoslavia would be clearly understood.

Even though not made public, however, the fact of our assistance to the Communists and other forces would soon become generally known throughout China. This, we believe, would have profound and desirable political effects in China. There is tremendous internal pressure in China for unity based on a reasonable compromise with the Communists and a chance for the presently liberal groups to express themselves. However, these liberal groups even within the Kuomintang, such as the Sun Fo group, and the minor parties were ignored in the recent negotiations by the KMT but not by the Communists (with whom they present what amounts to a united front) and they are disillusioned and discouraged by what they feel is American commitment to the present reactionary leadership of the Kuomintang. By the steps we propose we would prove that we are not so committed, we would greatly raise the morale and prestige of these liberal groups, and we would exert the strongest possible influence through these internal forces to impel Chiang to put his own house in order and make the concessions necessary to unity.

There is no question that such a policy would be greatly welcomed by the vast majority of the Chinese people (although not by the very small reactionary minority in control of the Kuomintang) and that it would raise American prestige.

The statement has been made to a responsible American by Sun Fo himself that if Chiang were told, not asked, regarding United States aid to Communists and guerrillas, this would do more to make Chiang Kai-shek come to terms with them than any other course of action. The majority of Chinese believe that the settlement of China's internal problem is not so much a matter of mutual concessions as reform of the Kuomintang itself. They also declare, with justification, that American "nonintervention" in China cannot help but be in fact intervention in favor of the present conservative leaders.

Also by such policy, which we consider realistically accepts the facts in China, we could expect to secure the cooperation of all of China's forces in the war, to hold the Communists to our side rather than throw them into the arms of Russia (which is otherwise inevitable if Russia enters the war against Japan), to convince the KMT of the undesirability of its apparent present plans for eventual civil war, and to bring about some unification which, even though not immediately complete, would provide the basis for peaceful future development toward full democracy.

5. This telegram has been drafted with the assistance and agreement of all the political officers of the staff of this Embassy and has been shown to General Wedemeyer's Chief of Staff, General Gross.

BACK TO YENAN

When Service returned to China in January 1945, it was the clearly stated condition of the State Department that he be sent back to Yenan to report from there. He was, however, assigned to Wedemeyer; and Wedemeyer—partly to avoid conflict with Hurley—urged him to delay. On the other hand, Wedemeyer indicated that he did want Service to return to Yenan and even assured Service that he would protect him from any possible opposition from Hurley: " 'Don't worry. You're working for me. You're not working for him.' " By early March, after both Hurley and Wedemeyer had left for Washington, Service had received clear hints from Communist sources in Chungking that the Seventh National Congress of the CCP was about to begin. Accordingly, he made this request for travel orders:

Request for Authority to Visit Yenan

March 4, 1945
Amerasia Papers, pp. 1382–83

1. A National Congress of the Chinese Communist Party is opening at Yenan in the next few days. This is the first such meeting in over ten years. For it, all the important Communist leaders have been assembled at Yenan. The urgency and tension of the present situation in China—in which we cannot but help be concerned—give the meeting special significance.

2. Important decisions may be expected concerning at least the following:

a. Negotiations with the Kuomintang. At present these have broken down and the breach has been accentuated by the Generalissimo's uncompromising March 1 speech. The future Communist line will probably be decided at the conference.

b. Communist military policy. Communist forces are aggressively expanding into South China. The issue of civil war is getting dangerously close. The possibilities of confusion from independent Communist action are obvious—for instance, in fighting for Shanghai.

c. Policy toward the Kuomintang's present plan for inaugurating constitutional government through its authority alone. Minor-party leaders say that they and the Communists will oppose such plans and that revolution will follow.

d. Attitude toward the San Francisco Conference. The Communists have demanded representation there. Will they be content with the demand; or will they give it weight by implementation of present proposals for—

e. A separate government, or semi-government, of their various guerrilla areas. Such action could embarrass the conference and make the China problem more complicated.

f. Policy toward the United States and Russia. Are the Communists, as reported by some sources, now beginning to look to the Soviet Union?

g. China's postwar economic policy and foreign participation.

3. In addition, there should be unprecedented opportunities to learn: Is the Communist Party completely unified? Are there internal policy differences—if so, on what lines? Is new leadership coming to the fore? Do the Communists have any strength in the cities?

4. The Chargé d'Affaires of the Embassy agrees on the need for political intelligence from Yenan at this critical time. He would consider my trip as one of the periodic visits which, General Wedemeyer has stated in response to the State Department's expressed wish for such reporting, would be made by the Political Adviser.

5. I would make it clear to the responsible Communist leaders that my visit is only to listen and observe.

6. Authority is requested to visit Yenan by the next plane and remain there for about two weeks.

Arriving back in Yenan on March 9, Service found the mood and the temper of the times very much changed. The Communist leaders—and especially the younger, second-level men—were far more argumentative and belligerent toward the KMT. Chiang Kai-shek had just, on March 1, made an unusually harsh speech criticizing the CCP. In it, he had revealed a new plan to convene the 1936 National Assembly—a purely Kuomintang body, selected before the United Front of 1937 had had its mildly liberalizing effect on the KMT's anti-Communist policy. To the Communists, Chiang's speech was a clear step backward and they were all the more convinced that the KMT had irrevocably decided on a course leading to civil war. In addition, the Communists were convinced that Hurley was in effect encouraging the KMT on this course.

The Present Communist Attitude toward the Central Government—Preliminary Report

March 11, 1945
Amerasia Papers, pp. 1390–93

Summary: The Communists regard the Generalissimo's March 1 statement as a virtual declaration of war. They have declined to participate in the formerly proposed "Political Advisory Committee" and have demanded one-third representation in the Chinese delegation to San Francisco. They expect this to be refused and will probably then move to create a Federal Council of their "liberated areas." Convening of the Communist Party Congress is being delayed pending clarification of this and other related matters. Meanwhile the Communists are actively increasing their military forces and aggressively expanding their areas of control. *End of Summary.*

Arriving in Yenan on the afternoon of March 9, I have spent most of the time since then in conversations with Ch'en Chia-k'ang (political secretary to Chou En-lai), Ch'en Yi (acting commander of the New Fourth Army), General Yeh Chien-ying (Chief of Staff of the Eighth Route Army), Tung Pi-wu (member of the Central Executive Committee and former Communist representative in Chungking), and Chou En-lai (Communist "Foreign Minister").

It is obvious that the Communists have greatly strength-

ened their attitude. The general atmosphere is defiant determination and expectation of important developments in the near
future. The confidence in Communist strength which has been
noted before is, if anything, even more marked.

The door to compromise has not quite been closed—but
has almost been. There is no expectation that the Central Government will make any compromise in the present situation.
American policy and the attitude of the Ambassador are partially
blamed for this. Chiang is spoken of in the most derogatory
terms and there no longer seems to be a willingness to consider
him as the necessary head of the state.

The Political Bureau of the Communist Party has declined
participation in the "Political Advisory (or, Consultative) Committee" which was proposed at the end of the recent negotiations
in Chungking. Their reasoning and justification are as follows:
Before Chou En-lai made his last trip (in late January) to
Chungking, the Central Government proposed a "Wartime
Political Committee." This was to be a policy-guiding body
under the Executive Yuan and was called by the Kuomintang
a "sort of war cabinet." Actually its powers were vague and it
was not empowered to decide matters in connection with Government reform and the transition to constitutionalism and democracy. Even before Chou reached Chungking, this had been
spurned by the representatives of the minor parties. The Communists immediately took the same action. The Communists
therefore consider the "war cabinet" a dead issue.

The next step was to water down the Communist proposal
for an inter-party conference into a "Political Advisory Committee." This would have no real power, but would at least be
able to consider the broad problems of reform and transition to
constitutionalism. It was this proposal that Chou brought back
to Yenan for a decision as to Communist participation.

Before the Communist reply was sent, the Generalissimo
made his uncompromising and threatening March 1 statement.
In this he failed to mention the "Political Advisory Committee"
and spoke only of the "war cabinet" which the Communists and
minor parties had already refused.

The Communists therefore take the line that Chiang has
taken another step backward, is now not willing even to permit
the Consultative Committee, and is determined to allow con-

stitutionalism only on the basis of action taken by the Kuomintang Party Congress and a National Congress whose members were selected before the war and in which only Kuomintang members will be participants. The Communists regard Chiang's statement that these problems will be "discussed" by the People's Political Council as meaningless because the PPC is 90 percent Kuomintang and in any event has no power. The actual Communist reply has been that in view of Chiang's ignoring of the Consultative Committee in his March 1 statement, they regard the proposal as discarded and consider that no reply by them regarding participation is necessary.

The second matter of immediate and major concern in relations between the parties is representation in the Chinese delegation to San Francisco. The Communists insist that the Ambassador suggested that in order for the Chinese delegation to properly represent all of China, it should have Communist and other non-Kuomintang representation. They are determinedly exploiting this line. They demand one-third Communist and one-third non-Kuomintang representation. Communist delegates would be Chou En-lai, Po Ku and Tung Pi-wu.* If Communist participation is refused, the Communists will probably bring the matter into clearer world attention by setting up a "Federal Council of Democratic Liberal Areas" (the Communist areas, mostly in occupied China) which will be at least a semi-government and will claim to represent at least 100 million people.

The convening of the Communist Party Congress is being delayed to await clarification of this issue. It is expected, however, that it will be called before the end of March. Meanwhile all the important Communist leaders are here in Yenan, and conferences of the main figures are going on continuously.

Communist expansion is freely admitted and justified on the dual grounds of assistance of the war effort and the necessity of "self-protection" against apparent Kuomintang plans to exclude the Communists from the plans for constitutionalism and to eventually liquidate them through civil war. The "self-protection" theme is dominant. Ch'en Yi says that the New

---

* Ultimately, the Kuomintang allowed only Tung Pi-wu to join the delegation.

Fourth Army has now reached a strength of 300,000 regulars, and can easily be expanded to 400,000. Others say: "Give us a year and we will have all of East China from the borders of Manchuria to Hainan." When that has been accomplished, they say, the Communist forces will be at least as strong as those of the Central Government, and it will be the Kuomintang which will be blockaded.

The Communists still express desire for American cooperation and emphasize the need for American participation in postwar economic development of China. But they do not expect such cooperation unless there is a radical change in American policy toward the Central Government. Their statement is interesting [in] that the decision to start expansion into Southeast China was made immediately after General Stilwell's recall, which they interpreted as an American decision to support Chiang and the Central Government only. (My reports of conversations with Mao Tse-tung and Ch'en Yi written late in August 1944 showed that these questions were already under discussion and that the decision would be based on American policy.)

In general, there is nothing to indicate that our recent analysis made in Chungking of the China situation is inaccurate in any important particular. The present tendency is not toward unity but away from it. Conflicts between the Central Government and Communist forces are widespread (the Communists admit fairly heavy losses to their units around Canton but claim these are far more than balanced by growth in the Shanghai area, south Anhwei, Chekiang, Fukien, Hunan and north Kwangtung). Open civil war seems to be expected—without fear by the Communists. They point with satisfaction, for instance, to recent published intentions of T'ang En-po (commander of Central Government forces on the Hunan-Kwangsi-Kweichow border) to "collect the arms from the people" as an indication of the inability of the Central Government to learn lessons from the past or to trust and organize the people, thus playing into the hands of the Communists.

There may be one aspect of Communist southward expansion (in addition to the desire to counter the Central Government before its new armies are ready and to force us into cooperation if we meet Communist armies when we land on the coast) which is not mentioned by the Communists. They seem to expect a strong Japanese effort to consolidate themselves in North China. The most important fighting now going on is a large-scale mopping-up campaign to clear out the Communist positions in east Hopei, south Jehol and south Liaoning. This is apparently intended to establish a *cordon sanitaire* between China and Manchuria and is being conducted with unusual determination and ferocity. The Communists claim that whole areas are being either depopulated or made into fortified areas in which the whole population is concentrated into garrisoned villages—as was done in parts of Manchuria. Large-scale Communist movement southward shows not only a growing determination to control China proper but may also be an effort to get out from under an expected Japanese attempt to crush Communist strength in North China.

The conversation of some of the Communists is more open than ever before in some respects. They say, for instance, that they will have to "seek friends wherever they can find them" (Russia) if they have to fight for their existence. At the same time, they insist that they are Chinese and not bound to Russia. They also suggest a possible parallel between their position and that of the Russian Communist Party after the Revolution in Russia; if the world is against them, they will become an active revolutionary force in all the countries (such as India) which are close to China. These statements do not, however, come from men like Chou and I believe them to be mostly made for effect. There is nothing concrete to indicate that the Communists are concerned with more than their continued existence and freedom to develop in China, which they still believe will be ensured by any genuine democracy and limitation of the present dictatorship.

On March 13, Mao invited Service to a long interview which was in part an attempt to discover what American policy really was, in part an attempt to indicate that the CCP's preferred policy for the postwar years would in no sense threaten the economic or political interests of the United States.

Mao's puzzlement over American policy is quite understandable. In November 1944, Hurley had helped to draft and had endorsed the Communist terms for a coalition government. Then, after his return to Chungking, he reversed himself and became a strong and consistent advocate of Chiang Kai-shek's position. In December the Communists had received two separate overtures from the O.S.S. and the American Army headquarters suggesting concrete plans for direct U.S. aid to the Communist armies. Confused by the many mouths of the American government, Mao and Chou then made their famous attempt to communicate direct with Roosevelt, through a visit by one or both of them to the United States. Hurley, however, discovered this attempt to circumvent him and quickly squelched it.*

The Communists, then, were well aware of the fact that there were divisions within the American government on the subject of our China policy. They knew, furthermore, that Service was likely to be one of those who would support a policy more friendly to the CCP. At the very least, they trusted him to communicate correctly their views. Thus Mao called Service in and explained in the most precise terms why the Chinese Communist Party desired friendly relations with the United States.

The Views of Mao Tse-tung: America and China

No. 10: March 13, 1945
Foreign Relations, 1945, pp. 272–78

Attached is a memorandum of a conversation with Mao Tse-tung. I consider this extensive expression of Chairman Mao's views as of great importance at this critical juncture of China's internal affairs.

Summary: The most important new point brought out in Mao's talk is that Chiang Kai-shek's persistence in pushing through plans for a Kuomintang-monopolized National Congress, without first unifying the country and admitting other parties, will close the door to peaceful compromise. Chiang will

* See Barbara W. Tuchman, "If Mao Had Come to Washington: An Essay in Alternatives," *Foreign Affairs* (October 1972).

have crossed his "Rubicon." The result will be open division of the country. *End of Summary*.

I am as convinced as I was during my talks with Mao last year that American policy is a decisive factor in influencing the actions of the Chinese Communist Party—as well as those of the Kuomintang. Applied to bring about a true coalition government, the Communists will be cooperative. But devoted to support of the Central Government and Chiang, to the exclusion of the Communists, disunity will be stimulated and the consequences will be disastrous.

MEMORANDUM: CONVERSATION WITH MAO TSE-TUNG

Mao commenced by asking a number of questions about my recent trip to the United States. He was interested in American official and public opinion toward the war in the Far East, toward China generally, and toward the Chinese Communists particularly.

He then rather mildly observed that America did not yet have a clear view of the issues involved in China, that it did not yet fully understand the Communists, and that although American policy as recently shown in China was still an enigma, he could not believe that it was fixed and unchangeable. America would eventually realize that support of the Central Government alone was not the best way to fight the war, to speed China's progress toward democracy, or to ensure postwar stability in the Far East. "A few months ago," he said, "we were told that the Kuomintang and the Communists were only this far apart." (Holding his thumb and forefinger about an inch apart.*) "Now it is certainly apparent that we are this far apart." (Extending the thumb and forefinger in as broad a V as possible.)

From this introduction, Mao launched into a long discussion which may be summarized as follows.

Between the people of China and the people of the United States there are strong ties of sympathy, understanding and mutual interest. Both are essentially democratic and individual-

---

* This phrase and digital expression were Hurley's.

istic. Both are by nature peace-loving, nonaggressive and non-imperialistic.

China's greatest postwar need is economic development. She lacks the capitalistic foundation necessary to carry this out alone. Her own living standards are so low that they cannot be further depressed to provide the needed capital.

America and China complement each other economically; they will not compete. China does not have the requirements of a heavy industry of major size. She cannot hope to meet the United States in its highly specialized manufactures. America needs an export market for her heavy industry and these specialized manufactures. She also needs an outlet for capital investment.

China needs to build up light industries to supply her own market and raise the living standards of her own people. Eventually she can supply these goods to other countries in the Far East. To help pay for this foreign trade and investment, she has raw materials and agricultural products.

America is not only the most suitable country to assist this economic development of China, she is also the only country fully able to participate.

For all these reasons there must not and cannot be any conflict, estrangement or misunderstanding between the Chinese people and America.

But the Chinese people are really the rural population, the farmers. Out of China's 450 million, they number at least 360 million. The intellectuals, the civil officials, the merchants, the capitalists are only a thin crust on top. The peasants are China.

A country of China's size and backwardness cannot be made over quickly. China must be predominantly agricultural for a long time to come.

The problems of the Chinese farmers are, therefore, basic to China's future. China cannot industrialize successfully except on the basis of the solution of the agrarian problem, because the farmers must provide the real market for the products of that industrialization.

We have the example of Japan. She was forced to follow imperialism and aggression because she sought to industrialize on the basis of a feudal society. She did not start with the solution of her domestic agrarian problems.

Wallace and other American statesmen and writers (for instance, a recent article by Brooks Atkinson in the *New York Times* on the "Chinese Farmer") show a clear understanding of this fundamental fact about China.

The fundamental demand of the Chinese farmer is freedom from his feudal condition of tenantry and dependence on the landlord-capitalist for credit and purchase of his products. There must be land reform. And democracy. The farmer must have independence and power to protect his own interests.

Neither the farmer nor the Chinese people as a whole are ready for socialism. They will not be ready for a long time to come. It will be necessary to go through a long period of private enterprise, democratically regulated. To talk of immediate socialism is "counterrevolutionary" because it is impractical, and attempts to carry it out would be self-defeating.

The Kuomintang has no contact with the agrarian masses of the population. It is the party of the military and landlord groups who govern through a conservative and unimaginative bureaucracy. It has done nothing, and will no nothing, fundamental to improve the condition of the farmers, to carry out real land reform, or to do away with the still existing remnants of feudalism. It cannot, because to do so would be to attack the basis of power of its main supporting groups.

Afraid of real democracy, the Kuomintang is forced to be fascistic. Thus we have the strange feudal-fascist combination of the present Kuomintang. This is a background and character from which the Kuomintang is unable to divorce itself.

Unwilling to solve the agrarian problem and thus raise the living standards of the farmers as a basis for industrialization, it turns toward the principle of rigidly planned, state-directed and -controlled industrial development. Unable, therefore, to create a solid basis for power at home or for cooperative and amicable relations with Russia and other neighbors, it concentrates on "national defense industry" and engages in the dangerous game of power politics.

The expectation of future conflict, internal and external, is implicit in these policies. If its policies are persisted in, this expectation of the Kuomintang is certain to be realized. Under these policies, which cannot be changed without a revolution within the Party and a whole new leadership, the Kuomintang cannot solve China's basic internal problems, cannot lead the country to full democracy, and cannot be a stabilizing power in the Far East.

The Chinese Communist Party, on the other hand, is *the* party of the Chinese peasant. Its program—reduction of rent and interest, progressive taxation, assistance to production, promotion of cooperatives, institution of democracy from the very bottom—is designed to bring about a democratic solution of the peasant's problems. On this basis, and with its realization of the necessity of free capitalistic enterprise based on the unity, not conflict, of all groups of the people, the Communist Party will be the means of bringing democracy and sound industrialization to China. These are the only possible guarantee of peace and stability.

Just as the Chinese farmer cannot be ignored in China's future, neither can the Communist Party. The Kuomintang is seeking to ignore it. But its guns cannot give it victory. After all, the great majority of the soldiers, as of the people, are peasants. We speak for the people of China because we are for and of the people. And the people know it by our record.

It is to be expected that Chiang will do everything possible to avoid compromise in which he and the groups supporting him will have to yield power and give up their dictatorship. But the road he is taking now leads straight to civil war and the Kuomintang's eventual suicide.

Chiang's refusal to permit any real coalition government and his announced intention of calling the National Congress in November 1945 are the indications of his growing desperation. This Congress will be wholly a Kuomintang creature. Any invitation for a few non-Kuomintang persons to participate will be insignificant and intended only for window dressing. The delegates to this Congress were chosen by the Kuomintang machinery, with only the hollowest pretense of popular elections, at a time (1936) when there was open civil war between the Kuomintang and the Communists. Those delegates cannot pretend to represent the people who have been fighting the Japanese and governing themselves in the liberated areas for the past seven years. They cannot even pretend to represent the people of Chungking-controlled China.

The election of Chiang as President and the legalization of

his government as the "democratic government of China" by this assembly of stooges will be a farce. Such a body is not intended to, and cannot be expected to, do anything else. But the real danger is that this National Congress will be used by Chiang as the means for demanding that the Communists submit to its authority and lay down their arms. Unrepresented, and with the enemy not yet driven from their soil, the Communists and people of the occupied areas will refuse these unreasonable demands. They will then be proclaimed rebels, and the stage for open civil war will be laid.

The danger inherent in this latest tactic of Chiang's—the determination to set up a constitutional government at once on the basis of the Kuomintang alone—must be made clear to liberals in China and to China's most important friend abroad, the United States. This is the reason for our present seemingly violent propaganda campaign against Chiang. This issue is so vital that we have to make as big a noise as possible.

China's liberals, in and out of the Kuomintang, are numerous and increasing. They include the Democratic League and affiliated groups of the Kuomintang, the minor parties, most of the intellectuals, and many of the modern capitalists.

But they cannot overthrow the Party machinery or change the present reactionary leadership of the Kuomintang. They will be powerless to control the new "constitutionalism" planned by Chiang's group. Without the help of American influence, real unity and democracy will have to be won by a long and bitter struggle.

The only hope for a peaceful transition to constitutionalism that will democratically include and represent all the country is a coalition government. Such a coalition government must not wait, for it is also the only way to unify the country now and make effective China's war effort against Japan.

Why does Chiang determine to push through "constitutionalism" now, before the country is regained from the Japanese and the people of the liberated areas given a chance to express themselves? Because he knows that they will not agree. For the occupied countries in Europe, it has been decided that the definite decision of the form of government is to wait until the country has been liberated and the people themselves can decide and choose their own political leadership. This policy is just and we commend the Allied leaders for adopting it. Why is China an exception? Shanghai is bigger than Athens, and occupied China a far larger country than Greece!

America does not realize her influence in China and her ability to shape events there. Chiang Kai-shek is dependent on American help. If he had not had American support, he would have either collapsed before now or been forced to change his policies in order to unify the country and gain popular support. There is no such thing as America not intervening in China! You are here, as China's greatest ally. The fact of your presence is tremendous.

America's intentions have been good. We recognized that when Ambassador Hurley came to Yenan and endorsed our basic five points. He could not have endorsed them unless he knew that President Roosevelt thought likewise.

We don't understand why America's policy seemed to waver after its good start. Surely Chiang's motives and devious maneuvers are clear. His suggestions of "war cabinets" and "inter-Party conferences" did not solve any basic issues, because they had absolutely no power; they were far short of anything like a coalition government. His proposals of "reorganizing the Communist armies" and "placing them under American command" were provocative attempts to create misunderstanding between us (the Communists) and the Americans. We are glad to accept American command, as the British have in Europe. But it must be of all Chinese armies.

Chiang has tried continually to make it appear that the Communists are to blame for the failure of the negotiations. He has pulled a very smart propaganda trick—for foreign consumption—by the promise of immediate "democracy," this year, through a false National Congress. We refuse to believe that Americans are so easily misled.

It is vitally important that America realize that in calling this Congress, Chiang is playing his "last card." It will close the door. Once it has been convened, the die will be cast and compromise impossible. We will fight if we have to, because we will be fighting not only for the democratic rights of the 100 million people in the present liberated areas but for the rest of the masses of China as well.

The National Congress cannot be called while half the

country is cut off or occupied by the enemy and while all parties but the Kuomintang are denied legality. What the situation requires, and the only thing that can save it, is a coalition government. We hope that America will use her influence to help achieve it. Without it, all that America has been working for will be lost.

On March 30, Service received orders to return to Washington "soonest." The Communist leaders, when they heard this, were anxious for one final conference with him, which was held on April 1. They were curious as to the reason for his recall, but he knew nothing himself. All of them were hopeful that perhaps Washington was seriously considering some of the policies recommended in the February 28 memorandum from the Embassy staff. But by this time the Communists clearly did not expect to receive U.S. military aid. One evening sometime before Chu Teh had patted Service on the knee in his jovial, avuncular way and said, "We don't really expect any arms from you. Ultimately, we'll get them from the KMT anyway." What the Communists did want, with civil war now seemingly inevitable, was at least American neutrality. And they gave some preview of their plans for the all-important Seventh Congress, whose proceedings Service would be forced to miss.

Policy to Be Adopted by the Communist Congress— Conversation with Mao Tse-tung and Other Communist Leaders

April 1, 1945
Foreign Relations, 1945, pp. 310–17

Attached is a memorandum of a conversation on this date with a group of Communist leaders: Mao Tse-tung, Chairman of the Central Committee; Chou En-lai, second ranking political leader and functioning "Foreign Minister"; and Chu Teh, commander in chief of the Communist armies. Tung Pi-wu, the Communist member of the Chinese delegation to San Francisco, joined the group near the end of the talk.

General Chou had been informed the evening before of my receipt of orders to return to Chungking. This talk, which lasted for half the afternoon and through supper, was obviously intended to give me an up-to-date statement of the Communist position and the line to be taken at the imminent Communist Party Congress.

Summary: The Communist policy toward the United States is and will remain one of extending cooperation regardless of American action. It must be this because: (1) anything that the Communists can do to assist the American forces will help win the war; and (2) China needs American help after the war. The Communist policy toward the Kuomintang will remain: (1) On one hand, criticism to urge the Kuomintang toward more progressive policies; and (2) the offering of compromise based on the Communist five points leading to a true coalition government and genuine democracy. The decision to establish a "Chinese People's Liberation Union" has been made, but actual formation will not be for several months. This Union will not be a "government" but a consultative body representing the people of the liberated areas (now unrecognized by the Central Government) to discuss common problems, plan joint steps for prosecution of the war, organize resistance in the occupied areas, and stimulate the rest of China to a more active war effort. The Communists will refuse to recognize a National Congress called before the end of the war and they will refuse to accept representation in such a Congress, insisting that the delegates must be freely chosen by all the people. *End of Summary.*

Three points are new and worth notice:
1. The niggardly representation granted the Communists at San Francisco has not changed their decision to create their "union." They are going ahead.
2. The proposed name of the body—"Chinese People's Liberation Union"—has possible significance which the Kuomintang and People of China will not miss. It is not a union of the liberated-area governments, but rather may be interpreted as a union for the liberation of the Chinese people. The implied threat is clear.
3. Mao was vague regarding the date proposed for organizing the union. But Chou's secretary later said privately that

if the Kuomintang persisted in convening its National Congress, the conference setting up the Liberation Union would be held simultaneously.

MEMORANDUM: CONVERSATION WITH COMMUNIST LEADERS

April 1, 1945

I was invited to Mao Tse-tung's residence at 4 P.M. Chou En-lai and Chu Teh were already there. There was about half an hour of general conversation.

All showed interest in the reason for my return to Chungking, particularly whether it might be for return to the United States—which presumably might indicate consultation regarding China. (I had received no indication of the reason for my return.)

Mao repeated previous hopes that American political observation and contact with Yenan would be maintained. He expressed that the developments in China during the coming months would be important and that the Communists hoped for American understanding from on-the-spot contact.

Chou twice made pointed remarks to the effect that it was unfortunate that I could not stay in Yenan another ten days; that I would find the stay worthwhile and interesting. (I took this to be a hint that the Party Congress is to be convened within that time.)

I touched on the military situation. Chu did not consider that the Japanese had yet shown definite signs of intention to take either Sian or Hanchung, but believed that they will eventually take both cities in order to push back American air power and protect their flank and vital communications for the long fight which (the Communists are sure) the Japanese are planning to wage in China.

I recalled that when the Japanese campaign in Honan last year seemed to develop into a threat against Sian, the Communists offered to send troops to join in its defense. There was some looking from one to the other. Finally Chu said that the Communist offer last year had been refused and that the Communists would wait this time to be asked. He did not seem to care to pursue the matter.

Mao then took control of the conversation. He was in exceptionally good spirits—getting out of his chair to act out dramatic embellishments of his talk, and diverging to recall amusing anecdotes. Chou occasionally explained or amplified Mao's points. Chu sat back, silent and smiling.

Mao skimmed over the history of the recent fruitless negotiations with the Kuomintang. He felt that foreigners in general did not yet understand that the Kuomintang-Communist issue was far more than the usual bickering and jockeying between two ordinary political parties. The issues here were basic and vital to China's future.

He proceeded to devote some time to discussion of recent articles in the *Economist* and New York *Herald Tribune,* questioning whether they were typical of the lack of understanding of foreign opinion.

The *Economist* had suggested that Chiang's announcement of the National Congress in November was a clever stroke because it "stole the Communists' thunder," and that the Communists would make a great mistake if they did not join. Mao pointed out that the Communists could not join even if they wished; that it was a strictly one-party assembly whose members were fictitiously elected nine years ago (since when many have become puppets) at a time of open civil war by the Kuomintang against the Communists; that almost two thirds of the people of China (Japanese-occupied and Communist-liberated areas) would not be represented; and that no real democracy could be expected under these conditions from a party which since Chiang's counterrevolution in 1927 had been repressive and antidemocratic. He vigorously insisted that for the Communists to agree to the calling of such a false Congress would be to desert all their principles and betray the people of the liberated areas. It would therefore be a great mistake. (Much of what Mao said in this connection was repetition of his remarks in our conversation of March 13, 1945—see my report No. 10 of that date.*)

The *Herald Tribune* had said that the Communists had "increased their demands" and become "more unreasonable" because of Soviet victories and the attention of Americans in, for

* See pp. 371–78.

instance, the despatch of the Observer Section to Yenan. At great length Mao argued the consistency and unchanging character of Communist policy; how even in the civil-war days the Communists were calling for union on the basis of nationwide resistance against Japan, the granting of democratic rights, and the full mobilization of the people; how the United Front had finally been created in 1936–1937 when these promises were given by the Kuomintang; how the Communists had repeatedly during the war found it necessary to demand the observance of these principles as essential to the unification of the country and successful prosecution of the war. (Interesting confirmation of the validity of this argument can be found by referring to Edgar Snow's *Red Star Over China,* in which he records talks with Mao in 1936. The similarity of Communist objectives then and now is striking.)

As for the effects of Soviet victories and American attention, Mao humorously recalled the civil war when the slogan was "Kill Chiang Kai-shek," the violent recrimination after the New Fourth Army incident (January 1941) when the Communists openly defied the Central Government, and the belligerence created when the Central Government threatened the Border Region with military force in the summer of 1943. All of these, he pointed out, were instances of a much stronger Communist attitude toward Chiang than at present, and all were before Soviet victories and American attention.

Repeating the unchangeableness of Communist objectives, Mao emphasized that the Communists had fought for them when weak, few in numbers and entirely alone, and that they would continue to work toward those objectives regardless of outside influence, for or against.

In one sense, Mao admitted, the Kuomintang's complaints are justified. "Our objectives are unchanged but our voice gets louder as the situation in China becomes more desperate and more urgent, and as more and more of the people see that we are right. Such complaints by the Kuomintang show that it is feeling the pressure. Delay, however, will not help it."

Mao then proposed to give a brief statement of Communist policies toward the United States and toward the Kuomintang, from which it could be seen that they were as consistent and unchanging as the Communist main objectives.

Communist policy toward the United States is, and will remain, to seek friendly American support of democracy in China and cooperation in fighting Japan. But regardless of American action, whether or not they receive a single gun or bullet, the Communists will continue to offer and practice cooperation in any manner possible to them. Anything they can do—such as intelligence, weather reporting and rescue of airmen—the Communists consider an obligation and duty because it helps the Allied war effort and brings closer the defeat of Japan. If Americans land in or enter Communist territory, they will find an army and people thoroughly organized and eager to fight the enemy.

The Communists will continue to seek American friendship and understanding because it will be needed by China in the postwar period of reconstruction. (For amplification of this argument, please refer to Mao's talk on March 13 reported in my despatch No. 10.)

Whether or not America extends cooperation to the Communists is, of course, a matter for only America to decide. But the Communists see only advantages for the United States—in winning the war as rapidly as possible, in helping the cause of unity and democracy in China, in promoting healthy economic development of China through industrialization based on solution of the agrarian problem, and in winning the undying friendship of the overwhelming majority of China's people, the peasants and liberals.

Communist policy toward the Kuomintang will remain on one hand to criticize and try to stimulate progressive reform; and on the other, to offer compromise which can be a basis for real unity, democracy and devotion of the forces of all the country to winning the war. The gist of this compromise is contained in the five points proposed by the Communists and endorsed by Ambassador Hurley. The compromise must mean the termination of the dictatorship of the Kuomintang and Chiang Kai-shek. If Chiang continues as President, he and the military forces must be responsible to a coalition government including all parties. The compromise must include recognition of the Communist armies, as part of the National army, and of the liberated areas as legitimate local governments.

This compromise and the coalition government which must

be its result will of course be temporary. It cannot be perfectly democratic because, with much of the country behind enemy lines or under enemy occupation, it cannot be completely representative. (Mao divided China as follows: Chungking areas 190 million, Japanese areas 160 million, Communist areas 100 million.) It will be the best possible government under the existing circumstances and until it can carry out the transition to full democracy after all of the country has been recovered.

The Communists do not insist on outright and immediate agreement by Chiang to a coalition government. They are willing to discuss the matter and work out details in an inter-Party conference. But such a conference of parties must have authority and be able to make decisions that will control the government and prepare for the transition to constitutionalism.

The crux of the problem is that the Kuomintang will not accept any limitation of its dictatorship and therefore cannot convene a conference that has authority. Chiang has therefore discarded the proposal of an inter-Party conference in favor of his National Congress.

The calling of the National Congress before the end of the war, before the legalization of all parties, and before the election of new delegates by all the people, must be opposed uncompromisingly.

Communist opposition will be to refuse to recognize the Congress or accept its orders. This is the logical course because the people of the liberated areas will not be represented. Then the next move will be up to Chiang. "We will not strike the first blow. We will not fire the first shot."

"But the Congress as now planned will certainly bring civil war. It will be the excuse for Chiang to have the opposition declared rebels. If he is going to continue his bluff, he will (because it is the only means he knows and understands) try to use force. When attacked, we will fight back. We are not afraid of the outcome, because the people are with us. The Japanese haven't been able to wipe out the liberated areas; how can Chiang's conscript, unindoctrinated army of unwilling peasants? Chiang could not whip us during the civil war when we were a hundred times weaker. What chance has he now? We are not worried about Chiang's American arms, because a conscript peasant army will not use them effectively against their brother conscripts fighting for their homes and economic and political democracy. What we are worried about is the cost to China in suffering and loss of life, in destruction of property, in the delay in rebuilding of the country. China needs peace. But she needs democracy more, because it is fundamental to peace. And first she must drive out the Japanese. We think America, too, should be concerned, because her own interests are involved."

I asked what the Communists would do if the Kuomintang asked them to participate in the National Congress by assigning them a number of seats. Chou immediately and emphatically replied that they would refuse. Mao indicated agreement and Chu nodded. Chou amplified as follows: Communist participation in the San Francisco delegation cannot be taken as precedent. Nor can Communist proposals for a coalition government or inter-Party conference. They are arrangements between parties because it is impractical to have the people elect their representatives. But a National Congress to pass a permanent Constitution and set up a fixed form of constitutional government is something entirely different. The membership of the Congress must be elected freely by the people, not bargained for or appointed by political parties.

Mao resumed. At present the liberated areas are not recognized by Chungking. They receive no guidance, help or military supplies, although they are bitterly fighting the enemy in the occupied territory. "They are children without a mother." They face many common problems. They should work and plan together for the most effective prosecution of the war. The Communists are therefore proposing that the various areas send representatives to join in forming a "Chinese People's Liberation Union" (Chung-kuo Jen-min Chieh-Fang Lien-Ho Wei-Yuan-Hui). The purposes of this body will be: to unify the war effort of the people of the liberated areas, discuss common problems, and make joint plans of action for the most effective defeat of the enemy; to stimulate and organize resistance against the Japanese in the occupied areas; and to encourage the people and government in the rest of China to greater efforts in active prosecution of the war.

Mao said with emphasis that this Union would not be a "government" and that "it would be a mistake to consider it one." It will not have the powers or functions of a government, being merely consultative.

Mao avoided being specific regarding the form of organization of the Union, saying that these details could be worked out later. He also cautioned that neither the definite decision to form the Union, nor its exact name, had yet been formally passed by the Communist Party. "But," he said with a slight smile, "they probably will be." (This is not as undemocratic as it sounds. All the delegates to the Party Congress have been assembled in Yenan for some time and important meetings and consultations have been proceeding continuously. It is certain that agreements on all important matters have already been reached. The actual meeting of the Congress, therefore, may be little more than the formal presentation and acceptance of reports, the election of new committees, and the passing of already agreed-upon resolutions.)

To my question of how soon the Union would be formed, Mao replied that it would not be for several months. It would take that long for representatives to arrive from the more distant areas.

I asked how the delegates to form the Union would be selected. Mao suggested tentatively that the People's Political Council of each liberated area would send representatives. He pointed out that these councils were democratically elected by universal suffrage and represented all classes and parties.

To my question whether groups other than those in the liberated and possibly occupied areas would be included, Mao replied that participation would be open to all groups who wished to join. This, of course, would include any groups in Kuomintang China. But he did not see, under present conditions of certain Kuomintang disapproval, how they could participate directly. "Places," he said, "would be saved."

Mao emphasized that all groups in the liberated areas, and if possible in occupied areas, would be represented, and that the Union would have a thoroughly United Front character.

I asked whether the proposal for the Union would be dropped if the Kuomintang agreed to a coalition government. The question was not directly answered. Mao said that "There are coalition governments and coalition governments." If there was an ideal coalition government, it might be assumed that the Union would be unnecessary because the coalition government would take the liberated areas under its wing and do all possible to help the people of China win their liberation.

Epilogue

On April 4, 1945, Jack Service left Yenan for the last time. As he later recalled, "My orders were very vague. They simply said to return to Washington as promptly as possible. There were all sorts of speculation. The Communist leaders hoped that I had been called back for some important consultations or some important meeting on policy. So did I. I was given a special plane. I traveled by myself on an airplane from China as far as Africa. Every time I stopped at a base I was taken to the V.I.P. villa. Every other time I had traveled the rule was 'Mr. Service follows the privates.' This time a lieutenant colonel or a major met the plane with a 'Mr. Service, come this way, please.' Then his sedan would take me off to the V.I.P. cottage. It was a C-54 that took me back to the States. It was on its way back for an overhaul. They had installed a special chair for me, right up behind the pilot's compartment. I sat there like a goddam duck, in a special plane."

When he got back to Washington, Service quickly discovered that all this special treatment did not foretell any favorable hearing for his views on China. On the contrary, he had been recalled at Hurley's insistence, as the Ambassador proceeded to remove from China all the Foreign Service officers who had signed the telegram of February 28. That telegram from the Embassy had received all the attention it deserved in Washington. On March 2 the Acting Secretary of State, Joseph C. Grew, sent it on to President Roosevelt with a memorandum urging that it be considered during the forthcoming visit of Hurley and Wedemeyer. On March 24 (and possibly earlier as well), Hurley saw the President. No record of that meeting or any earlier meeting is available, but the outcome was definitive: the President upheld Hurley.

In an April 2 news conference prior to his departure for Chungking via Moscow, Hurley announced his victory in the policy debate and his continuing blindness to the signs of a widening gulf between the KMT and the CCP. As the *New York Times* headlined its story on the conference: "U.S. BARS ARMS AID TO REDS IN CHINA: HURLEY SAYS OUR UNITY POLICY PRECLUDES FACTIONAL TIES—SEES CLEAVAGE NARROWING."

Ten days later (the day of Roosevelt's death) Service arrived in Washington. His career in China was finished, but his significance for the future of Sino-American relations was not. It was in the course of his consultations in Washington and his briefings of newsmen and private Far Eastern specialists that he met Philip Jaffe and became enmeshed in the F.B.I.'s investigation of the *Amerasia* case, which had, of course, begun well before Service got back to the United States. By late May the F.B.I. was ready to arrest the suspects in the case. Secretary of the Navy James Forrestal, who became involved because one of the suspects was a Navy lieutenant, urged caution at a time when Harry Hopkins was in Moscow in sensitive talks with Stalin, and the San Francisco Conference was proceeding with plans for the formation of the United Nations. Forrestal's diary for May 28 contains the following statement: "I pointed out that the inevitable consequence of such action now would be to greatly embarrass the President in his current conversations with Stalin, because of the anti-Russian play-up the incident would receive out of proportion to its importance."* When the State Department heard that the arrests were to be held up, Grew, on June 2, immediately went to President Truman, who directed the F.B.I. to proceed. On the evening of June 6, Service and the other five suspects were arrested.

As Forrestal had predicted, the arrests caused a considerable stir in Washington and around the world, but the complications were more with the Chinese than with the Russian Communists. The Scripps-Howard papers in particular seized upon the case and put their top Red expert, Frederick Woltman, on it. A banner headline in the June 7 San Francisco *News* proclaimed: "COMMUNISTS HAD ACCESS TO U.S. SECRETS." On the 8th, Woltman continued his assault, and with

* Walter Mills (ed.), *The Forrestal Diaries* (New York: Viking, 1951), p. 65.

scant attention to the facts proceeded to focus on Service's role. Under another banner headline, "REDS CAUSED STILWELL AND CHIANG BREAK," the *News* printed Woltman's second story:

Secret military and police data stolen from State Department and other Government files was [*sic*] used to help turn this country against Generalissimo Chiang Kai-shek and in favor of the Chinese Communists, it was learned today following the arrest of six persons by the FBI on charges of conspiracy to violate the Espionage Act . . .

John Stewart Service, the State Department's principal adviser to our embassy in China. . . . was also openly sympathetic to the cause of the Chinese Communists, it was further learned. Mr. Service, representing the State Department, accompanied a highly secret military strategic commission to Yenan, the Communist area, last year. It was after the commission returned that sharp disagreements arose between Chiang Kai-shek and General Joseph Stilwell, as a result of which the latter was returned to this country.

After the right-wing press, obviously aided by government sources with motives as questionable as their facts, had distorted, inflated and politicized the case, the liberal press began to react. Pointing out that the arrests were made under the Espionage Act only because the government had been unable to pass an Official Secrets Act, editorials in the *New York Post,* the Washington *Post,* and the New York *Herald Tribune,* a broadcast by Walter Winchell, and columns by Drew Pearson, Charlton Kent, Hal O'Flaherty and I. F. Stone all suggested that the arrests were an attempt to stifle opinions critical of State Department orthodoxy as represented by Grew.

Stone gave the case the fullest treatment and also came to the most troubling conclusions. Writing in *P.M. Daily,* he observed on June 8 that "every one of the six arrested has been critical of the dominant State Department attitude as symbolized by Under Secretary Grew. Three of them have books scheduled for publication criticizing the State Department and the Kuomintang." On the 11th he warned of the real dangers inherent in the case:

. . . the effect of the arrests and of the Red scare campaign in the Scripps-Howard, Hearst and Patterson-McCormick papers has been to frighten into silence many of the men in the State Department and other agencies of the Government who are critical of current trends in our Far Eastern policy. . . . [T]he arrests have developed into a Red scare and the Red scare is being used to support a purge and the effect of the purge is to sublimate [substitute?] prejudice for facts in official thinking about China and those prejudices may be paid for in American lives.

Viewing all this from Yenan, the Chinese Communists accepted the interpretation of the American press that the arrests were fundamentally political, and decided that they signaled the end of any American attempts to reach some *modus vivendi* with the CCP. In the words of Stuart Schram's authoritative biography of Mao Tse-tung,

The change in this climate [of good will and cooperation between the CCP and the United States] can be dated very precisely; it begins with the *Amerasia* case in June 1945, when John S. Service was arrested for having given copies of his reports to Philip Jaffe. the editor of this publication. It will be recalled that in late 1944 and early 1945 Service had spent six months in Yenan with the U.S. military mission. Jaffe, who had prepared the unexpurgated translation of Chiang Kai-shek's *China's Destiny,* was no doubt also favorably known in Yenan. The Communist press therefore reacted with extreme violence. A *Liberation Daily* editorial interpreted the arrests as a turning point in American policy toward China. The Communists, said the article, were not hostile to the American people, nor to the American Government, but they were hostile to American imperialists like Hurley and his ilk. The editorial, which was written throughout in a sharp and almost aggressive tone, concluded with a warning that, if the American authorities chose to support the Chinese reactionaries, they would receive from the Chinese people the lesson they deserved.*

From this time forward, with only a brief interlude when Hurley's resignation was followed by the Marshall Mission to China, Chinese Communist propaganda became increasingly hostile to the United States. Mao Tse-tung's own public pronouncements show an unmistakable change. Even after Hurley's

* *Mao Tse-tung* (Baltimore: Penguin Books, 1967), pp. 231–32. For a condensed translation of the *Liberation Daily* editorial, see *Foreign Relations, 1945,* pp. 418–20.

press conference of April 2, Mao's speech "On Coalition Government" to the Seventh Congress of the CCP, could say that "Contrary to the expectations of all foreign and domestic reactionaries, the three great democracies—England, America and Russia—have all along remained united."* By July, however, Mao (if he had not in fact penned the June 25 editorial on the *Amerasia* case) picked up the phrase "Hurley and his ilk" and made it a constant refrain in his criticism of "American imperialist elements." There was no further talk of the United States as one of the "three great democracies." Instead Mao warned of the threat posed by "Hurley and his ilk": "This section of American ruling persons, besides preserving Chiang Kai-shek's dictatorship, also plans to transform China into her colony."†

Thus the United States lost its chance to forge a policy of friendship and cooperation with the Chinese Communists. Instead, we tied ourselves ever more closely to the Kuomintang and earned the enmity of the Chinese Communist Party. When Service reported on the Communists' desire for a united China friendly to the United States, he had warned that "This does not preclude their turning back toward Soviet Russia if they are forced to in order to survive American-supported Kuomintang attack."‡ That, of course, is precisely what happened. In internal policy, civil war produced a parallel radicalization within the CCP. Mao's interview with Guenther Stein, as reported by Service, foretold such a change in its discussion of Yenan's moderate land policies: "The possibility of confiscation cannot be ruled out, because it depends on internal peace. Civil war will probably be followed by outright confiscation—by the masses themselves."§

There is no certainty that the policy of Service and the others would have guaranteed continued friendship between the United States and the CCP. On the contrary, once the Chinese

---

* *Mao Tse-tung chi* (*Collected Works of Mao Tse-tung*), edited by Takeuchi Minoru (Tokyo: Hokubo-sha, 1971), p. 185.
  † *Ibid.*, p. 292.
  ‡ See p. 309.
  § See p. 254.

Communists emerged victorious—either through civil war or through a gradual and peaceful capture of control of a coalition government (for coalition government might have been possible under the Service policy)—their need for American friendship would decrease and the likelihood of discord between the two powers would increase. There would have been, however, far less likelihood of violent conflict. If we had tolerated the Chinese Communists' rise to power, there would have been little need to so threaten China as to draw her into the Korean conflict, or to prop up military dictators in South Vietnam in order to "contain" China.

Why, then, were Service's recommendations rejected?* The best chance for a flexible and realistic policy toward China and Chiang Kai-shek was lost when Stilwell was recalled in October 1944 and Gauss resigned one month later. The reasons for the Stilwell recall are many and complex. It was probably impossible to force a prickly and unwanted American commander down the throat of the Generalissimo—Roosevelt's own candidate for Big Four status. This was doubly true during an election campaign which many commentators predicted would terminate in a close election, which Roosevelt called "the dirtiest in history," and which saw Dewey engaging in some pre–Cold War attacks on Communists in the New Deal. In the fall of 1944, H. H. Kung was in Washington to keep Chiang posted on these realities of American politics, and these factors undoubtedly strengthened the Generalissimo's resolve to resist Stilwell and all that he stood for.

Once Stilwell was out and Hurley emerged as a major influence on America's China policy, the chances for the adoption of Service's flexible policy were considerably diminished. Still, the presentation of the Embassy telegram of February 28 to Roosevelt, for consideration during the course of the Hurley-Wedemeyer visit to Washington, did represent one last chance. There is no doubt that Roosevelt was seriously considering the sort of policy envisaged by that telegram. In March 1945 he

---

* For earlier answers to this question, to which I am heavily indebted, see John Service's own *The Amerasia Papers: Some Problems in the History of US-China Relations,* especially pp. 113–28, and Barbara Tuchman's "If Mao Had Come to Washington: An Essay in Alternatives," *Foreign Affairs* (October 1972).

called in Edgar Snow for an interview. Snow gave this account of one part of the conversation:

By now he recognized the growing strength of the Chinese Communists as the effective government of the guerrilla areas. He was considering giving them direct help against Japan, as a matter of military expediency.

The President asked a few questions about what, concretely, the Eighth Route (Communist) Army could do with our aid in North China. He then said that we were going to land supplies and liaison officers on the North China coast, as we drew closer to Japan. . . .

"I suppose the position is that as long as we recognize Chiang as the sole government we must go on sending all supplies exclusively through him? We can't support two governments in China, can we?" I asked.

"Well, I've been working with two governments there." The President threw his head back decisively. "I intend to go on doing so until we can get them together."*

In talking of supporting "two governments in China," Snow was putting a face on the operation which would not have been necessary had Roosevelt gone through with his plans. If, for example, the United States decided to fly supplies direct to Communist forces from bases soon to be secured in Okinawa, the Administration could accurately have pointed out that the Eighth Route Army was actually the Eighteenth Group Army of the Republic of China, that its commander, Chu Teh, held a commission from the National Government in Chungking, that the Shensi-Kansu-Ninghsia Border Region and the Shansi-Chahar-Hopei Base Area, from which the Communist forces operated, were recognized local governments of the National Government, and that the CCP recognized Chiang Kai-shek as the legitimate head of state in China and even displayed his picture alongside the other members of the Big Four in the caves of Yenan.

During the course of March 1945, however, Roosevelt was dissuaded from following this policy. In part, his decision was undoubtedly influenced by purely military considerations. It

* Edgar Snow, *Journey to the Beginning* (New York: Random House, 1958; Vintage paperback, 1972), pp. 347–48.

should be recalled that the Embassy telegram of February 28 urged the "paramount consideration of military necessity," and made its own recommendation conditional on the agreement of "the high military authorities of our Government . . . that some cooperation with the Communists and other groups who have proved themselves willing and are in a position to fight the Japanese is or will be necessary or desirable . . ."* This deference to the military was even more explicit in Washington. When John Carter Vincent, chief of the State Department's Division of Chinese Affairs, spoke to Wedemeyer on March 12 about the Embassy recommendation to aid the CCP, he told the General that

the question of whether or not such limited material aid could be effectively used against the Japanese to further our prosecution of the war was one which only our military authorities were in a position to decide and that their decision should be based solely on military considerations. If the answer should be in the negative, then there would be no question actually for the State Department to decide.†

Wedemeyer admitted his own ignorance of the Communists' military strength and its usability against Japan, but his general inclination was to discount it. Chief of Staff William D. Leahy, for example, gives this account of one March meeting of our military leaders:

Hurley, Lieutenant General Wedemeyer, and Commodore Miles discussed the Chinese military problems with the Joint Chiefs of Staff on March 27. They all were of the opinion that the rebellion in China could be put down by comparatively small assistance to Chiang's central government.‡

By this time, of course, the issue had already been resolved in Hurley's March 24 meeting with the President. It is symptomatic of the significance of that resolution, however, that the military

---

* For the full text of the telegram, see pp. 358–63.

† *Foreign Relations, 1945*, p. 271.

‡ William D. Leahy, *I Was There* (New York: McGraw-Hill, 1950), p. 337. Miles was the commander of SACO, the U.S. Navy contingent which collaborated with the KMT secret police under the notorious Tai Li.

was now discussing the Chinese Communist problem not in terms of arming the CCP to assist in fighting Japan, but in terms of suppressing the "rebellion in China." For Hurley, however, this approach seemed to come fairly naturally. In fact, he had informed the Generalissimo on February 16 that after the war was over, his U.S.-equipped army would have a walkover if he fought the Communists.* That, surely, was a unique way of persuading Chiang to follow a policy of peaceful unification of China.

In retrospect, it appears quite evident that Wedemeyer and the others were hampered by a conventional American military mentality. They were incapable of appreciating the strength of a supremely unconventional popular guerrilla force like the Chinese Communist armies. Service's reports were constantly stressing the *political* strength of the CCP, the foundation of that political strength in the Communists' social and economic policies, and the intimate relation between that political strength and military strength. Wedemeyer was not convinced. To him, the tons of supplies which the United States was then pouring over the Hump to the KMT armies were unquestionably a more important determinant of military strength. Thus he ignored the reports of Service and others: "I felt better qualified to pass judgments on the employment of military tactics and techniques. Thus, when my political advisers made recommendations of a military nature, I was not influenced particularly by them."† Wedemeyer, then, was not capable of perceiving sufficient military potential in the Chinese Communist armies to make it either necessary or desirable to arm them to fight the Japanese.

The predominant voice of the military and the limitations of that group's conventional wisdom are still not a total explanation of the decision to uphold Hurley. Roosevelt, if no one else, was aware of the political significance of the decision and was firmly committed to the effective unification of China. In the absence of such unification, his dreams of China as a great power were surely a chimera. He was also aware of the fact that the CCP-KMT negotiations had broken down by February, and was

* Charles F. Romanus and Riles Sunderland, *Time Runs Out in CBI* (Washington: Office of the Chief of Military History, 1959), p. 338*n*.

† General Albert C. Wedemeyer, *Wedemeyer Reports!* (New York: Henry Holt, 1958), p. 319.

presumably cognizant of the warning in the Embassy telegram that Chiang's confidence of exclusive and growing U.S. support for his armies was making the Generalissimo quite unwilling to compromise. In continuing to follow Hurley's policy, however, Roosevelt was not abandoning hopes for unity in China. He was merely accepting Hurley's means to that end, which in this case entailed trusting Moscow to pull our fat out of the fire.

Here the governing factor was undoubtedly the euphoria over the agreements reached at Yalta. Roosevelt and his entourage returned quite confident that they had, in Harry Hopkins' words, "won the first great victory of the peace."* And despite the considerable amount of nonsense written about the "sell-out" at Yalta, it is now quite clear that the United States was indeed able to strike an extraordinarily good bargain there. At the cost of nothing more than a few concessions to Soviet influence in Manchuria—concessions which the Russians would have been able to wring out of any Chinese government anyway, following their entry into the war against Japan—we were able to guarantee both Soviet entry into the war against Japan and Soviet adherence to a treaty of friendship and alliance with Chiang Kai-shek.

Once Hurley found out about this last clause, he had his answer to the problem of Chinese unity: the Russians would force the Chinese Communists to accept Chiang's terms. Implicit in this line of reasoning were two key misperceptions. First, it was assumed that the CCP was not strong enough to stand up to the KMT on its own. Here, once again, the logic of the conventional military mind was probably decisive. Second, it was assumed that the CCP, like any other Communist party, was susceptible to the absolute direction of Moscow. There were any number of government experts on Communism who were feeding this line to the President. So Roosevelt accepted Hurley's solution and sent him off to Moscow to make sure that Stalin understood his obligations under the Yalta agreement. When Stalin indicated his willingness to support U.S. (i.e., Hurley's) policy in China, the issue was settled and the flexible policy of realism was dead.

---

* Robert E. Sherwood, *Roosevelt and Hopkins: An Intimate History* (New York: Harper and Brothers, 1948), p. 870.

Roosevelt may not have seen it this way: he may not have regarded his decision in March as final and irrevocable. In fact, in sending Hurley back to Moscow and then Chungking, he may simply have been giving him one last chance. One suspects that in part, Roosevelt was displaying an inevitable tendency to postpone a difficult decision. To adopt the policy recommended in the Embassy telegram would not have meant abandoning Chiang—but it would have dealt a severe blow to his prestige. To take this action so soon after Chiang's elevation to his exalted status as one of the Big Four would have been a difficult step indeed. In March there seemed no need to make such a major shift in U.S. policy. With Chiang promising, most recently in a speech of March 1, to reform and open up his government, with Hurley promising that Chiang was indeed a democrat, with the Japanese offensive now halted and no immediate prospect of KMT collapse, there was no need to act hurriedly.

The problem was, of course, that postponement made it all the more difficult to adopt an alternative policy. Soon all plans for a landing on the China coast, which would undoubtedly have brought us into direct contact with Communist forces, would be dropped. Without the rationale of military expediency, in the war against the Axis, it would have been virtually impossible— in terms of American domestic opinion—to aid both the CCP and the KMT. Our greatest flexibility was during the war. After August the momentum of Hurley's policy was irreversible. By the end of the war, Wedemeyer had an efficient system of American liaison officers operating throughout Chiang's armies. This tied us to the KMT, and it was a natural next step to airlift these armies to the coast so that they, rather than the CCP, could accept the surrender of Japanese troops and assume the mantle of power in Japanese-occupied China. In the end, the United States found itself totally committed to Chiang, and Chiang totally committed to a suicidal policy of civil war. When Hurley retired in a huff in November 1945, President Truman recalled General George C. Marshall from his recent retirement as U.S. Chief of Staff to head the Marshall Mission to China (December 1945–January 1947). But by this time, however, even the prestigious General Marshall could not save us from involvement in a disastrous and embarrassing defeat.

To avoid this fate Roosevelt would have had to recognize

the full logic of Service's position. He would have had to perceive that exclusive support for Chiang so increased the Generalissimo's intransigence that civil war could not be averted, and that in civil war a Communist victory was inevitable. To Service, in the field and on the ground in China, these propositions were unquestionably true. But to Roosevelt, far from the scene and without any certain means to judge the relative validity of conflicting reports from Hurley and his Foreign Service officers, those truths became more questionable. It was particularly difficult to accept the notion of inevitability.

The acceptance of inevitability does not come easily to Americans. We are a "can do" people, and in 1945 we were on the verge of winning a world war on the basis of that principle. The United States was at the height of its power. Our arsenals supplied armies all over the world, and our ships and planes circled the globe. Only the United States would emerge from the war with its industrial and military might not diminished but increased. It was difficult to believe that anything could be inevitable and beyond our ability to manipulate and control— and it was unthinkable that a poorly armed bunch of Asian peasants could march to an "inevitable" victory in China.

The fact that these Asian peasants were Communists only further compounded the problem. How, in Henry Luce's "American Century" could we accept as inevitable a Communist revolution in China? Surely there was something that could be done to prevent such an eventuality. Surely the Foreign Service officers were indulging in typical negative, defeatist reporting. What was needed was a positive, active "can do" policy carried out by a "can do" man. And there could be no more appropriate man for the job than Patrick J. Hurley. It is easy to scoff at Hurley's follies, but it is only fair to recognize that those follies were larger than one man: they belonged to the nation and the age.

Finally, as we assess Roosevelt's decision to reject the recommendations of Service and the others, it is worth remembering that in much of the American press at this time, the Cold War had already begun. Our China policy was very much an issue. On March 15, Representative Walter Judd had made a major speech in Congress which specifically attacked the notion of arming the Communists in China as we had armed Tito in

Yugoslavia. Judd warned of a "concerted propaganda campaign against the Central Government of China and the Generalissimo," and identified three sources for this campaign: the "imperialists of Europe . . . the Communist group in China and the Communists in America . . . [and] persons in our own War and State Departments." When we consider the vilification which was heaped upon the China Service officers in the 1950s, despite the fact that their policy had been rejected, one can only guess what the reaction would have been if their recommendations had been adopted in 1945. Even if that policy had succeeded in bringing about a coalition government, and the Communist victory had been both delayed and peaceful, the China lobby would have argued that we had in effect assisted the Chinese Communists to gain control of China. That accusation would have had a certain amount of truth to it—and such a policy would have been unthinkable to most Americans.

Hindsight, then, can be misleading. In Korea, we got some idea of what it would take to stop Chinese Communist armies, even when they were fighting on foreign soil. In Vietnam, we learned that social and national revolutions are not easily suppressed. With the Sino-Soviet dispute, we learned that the Chinese Communists' ties to Moscow were not unbreakable. Now, after all this, it is possible to say with some certainty that we would have been much better off if the Foreign Service officers' advice had been taken. But without Korea and Vietnam, the correctness of their policy would be far more difficult to demonstrate. Yet there's the rub: had their policy been followed, we probably would never have had those wars to prove that the policy was indeed correct. Such is the tragedy of the policy and the career of John S. Service: only in rejection could there be vindication.

Index

ABOUT THE AUTHOR

JOHN S. SERVICE, the son of American missionaries, was born in Chengtu, China. He was educated at the Shanghai American School and when his family returned to the United States on a furlough, was graduated from the Berkeley High School in California. A graduate of Oberlin College, he returned to China in 1933 and was posted to a clerkship in the American Consulate at Kunming, the extreme southwest of China. He was commissioned as a Foreign Service officer in 1935 and worked in China until his recall in 1945. He is the author of *The Amerasia Papers: Some Problems in the History of US-China Relations*. Until recently, he worked at the Center for Chinese Studies in Berkeley.

ABOUT THE EDITOR

JOSEPH W. ESHERICK received his B.A. from Harvard University, and his Ph.D. in history from the University of California, Berkeley. He is the co-author, with Orville Schell, of *Modern China: The Making of a New Society from 1839 to the Present*. He has traveled extensively in Asia, most recently on a two-year Ford Foundation grant, and now teaches Chinese history at the University of Oregon.